Guatemalan Indians
and the State: 1540 to 1988

Symposia on Latin America Series
Institute of Latin American Studies
University of Texas at Austin

GUATEMALAN INDIANS AND THE STATE: 1540 to 1988

Edited by Carol A. Smith
with the assistance of Marilyn M. Moors

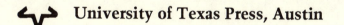 University of Texas Press, Austin

Copyright © 1990 by the University of Texas Press
All rights reserved
Printed in the United States of America

First Edition, 1990

Requests for permission to reproduce material from this work should be sent to:

Permissions
University of Texas Press
P.O. Box 7819
Austin, Texas 78713-7819

♾ The paper used in this publication meets the minimum requirements of American National Standard for Information Sciences—Permanence of Paper for Printed Library Materials, ANSI Z39.48–1984.

Library of Congress Cataloging-in-Publication Data

Guatemalan Indians and the state, 1540 to 1988 / edited by Carol A. Smith
    with the assistance of Marilyn M. Moors.
        p.   cm. — (Symposia on Latin America series)
    Edited papers presented at the March 1988 meetings of the Latin
    American Studies Association.
    Includes bibliographical references (p.).
    ISBN 0-292-72744-5
    1. Indians of Central America—Guatemala— Government relations. 2.
Indians of Central America—Guatemala—History. 3. Indians of Central
America—Guatemala—Social conditions. I. Moors, Marilyn M., 1934–   . II.
Latin American Studies Association. III. Series.
F1465.3.G6G82   1990
972.81' 00497—dc20   90-35620
                                                                    CIP

Contents

Maps

Figure

Tables

Preface

Before and after the sessions of the Latin American Studies Association at which most of the following papers were presented, two other panels treated the present political and economic crisis in Guatemala. While these panels had representatives of most major political groups in Guatemala, they did not include representatives of Guatemala's majority, the Indian population. Nor did anyone on those panels bring up the "Indian question" and how it might be relevant to Guatemala's political and economic problems today. In fact, Guatemala's present crisis was described in terms that would not distinguish it from any other Central American country. But politics in Guatemala has always been different from that of other Central American countries, no less today than in the past, because of the importance of Indians to Guatemalan political and economic life. The papers in this volume represent an effort to deal with this neglected issue, an issue that we believe to be the single most important determinant of Guatemala's distinctive history and social order.

The neglect of Guatemala's cultural specificity by those attempting to analyze national-level political and economic life is not a new phenomenon. It is only especially surprising today, because Indians were the major actors in the most sustained attempt at revolutionary transformation in Guatemala's history (see Arias, chap. 11), the cause of the current political and economic "crisis." Indian political activism in Guatemala is not new either, as the chapters in this volume attest. Yet the cultural amnesia of Guatemala's political leadership through time has conspired to keep the "Indian question" out of broader discussions of political economy. Also at fault is an academic division of labor that assigns culture and Indians to one group of specialists and national political relations to other specialists. This collection does more than juxtapose studies of local culture with analyses of the state and political economy. Each chapter addresses both sets of issues to raise a new set of questions about Guatemala's political culture.

Guatemala has been called the land of eternal tyranny because of the monumentally brutal way in which the state has oppressed Mayan Indians from the conquest in 1524 to the present (Simon 1987). The persistence of Indians—who, in order to retain their distinctive cultural practices, have resisted all attempts by the Guatemalan state to fully proletarianize them—would appear to be directly related to the development of an increasingly oppressive state. Hence the thematic focus of this book: the forces producing and reproducing Guatemala's different cultures, communities, and classes; how these different groups have related to each other and to the state at different points in time; and the way in which these relationships have affected the development of Guatemala's distinctive political economy. We believe that an understanding of these forces and relationships can be gained only by examining the particulars of Guatemalan history.

While the past must inform our interpretations of the present, the present must also inform our interpretations of the past. That is, history must be reinterpreted by each generation, so as to reflect the concerns and understandings that come from the events and social circumstances that impinge on that generation. The events affecting the present generation in Guatemala—the extraordinary level of violence that enveloped the Indians of the western highlands in the 1980s (see Manz 1988; Dunkerley 1988); the continued massive assault on traditional culture, in both religious and secular terms (see Carmack 1988); the movement from a militarized state to a militarized civil society (see Anderson and Simon 1987; Simon 1987); and the major transformations taking place in Guatemala's traditional export-oriented economy (see Williams 1986; Inforpress 1987; Painter 1987)—are so momentous they require us to reconsider Guatemala's history with the aim of finding clues to these particular developments in it. In this sense *Guatemalan Indians and the State* provides a revisionist social history of Guatemala.

Roughly half the chapters in this volume were written by historians, historical geographers, or ethnohistorians (chaps. 2, 3, 5–7), the rest by anthropologists (chaps. 4, 8–12). All are well known in the field of Guatemalan studies and have produced major works on some aspect of Guatemalan social life or history. Yet the particular focus of this book is not the particular specialty of any one of us. The questions we ask here were to a large extent forced upon us by recent events in Guatemalan history that led us to reexamine our materials in a new way.

The collaboration among us has a relatively long history. All of us have contributed articles to the Guatemalan journal *Mesoamérica*, a journal devoted to the interdisciplinary and international exchange of views and information. On this basis, many of us began exchanging papers with one another. In 1985 most of us met for the first time at a round-table on "Rural Guatemala in Historical Perspective" at the November 1985 meetings of Social Science and History. We owe special thanks to Kris Inwood who organized this panel, provided a transcript of the discussion, and suggested the themes for discussion. At that point we decided to organize a double panel on "Guatemalan Indians and the State" at the Latin American Studies Association (LASA) meetings of March 1988.

As a result of this sustained collaboration, the authors in this volume have learned a great deal from one another, anthropologists drawing on the special expertise of historians and vice versa. Thus, unlike previous generations of scholars who honored a "local" (anthropological) and "national" (historical) division of labor on political-economic and cultural questions, we all consider the relations involved at both local and national (sometimes international) levels. And by employing both history and ethnography in our analyses we attempt to show how relations at the local and national level interact with and affect one another.

Marilyn Moors prepared a transcript of the discussions that followed each of the two LASA sessions and sent it to each of the authors along with first drafts of the written papers. Marilyn also acted as a clearinghouse for final drafts, which she distributed to all of us. Most important, Marilyn edited all of the papers with an eye to the thematic focus as well as to wording and style. She also prepared the final drafts in comparable and legible form and compiled the joint bibliography and index of the volume. Without Marilyn's very considerable and able assistance, this volume would never have reached its final form.

Marilyn would like to thank Montgomery College for granting a sabbatical leave that provided the space for this long effort. I would like to thank the University Research Council at Duke University for funds that allowed the final preparation of manuscripts and maps. I would also like to thank Charles Bergquist and the staff at the Center for International Studies at Duke University, who were especially helpful in making the LASA sessions possible. Finally, I wish to indicate my considerable indebtedness to Marilyn Moors for the many different ways in which she assisted the project, adding as much to its intellectual content and coherence as to its final organization as a manuscript.

We dedicate this book to the Mayan Indians of the present with the hope that they not only maintain the symbols of their traditions that enrich the world, but that they find a way to carry the Guatemalan nation out of its present state of oppression and despair.

Carol A. Smith
Antigua, Guatemala
June 1989

Guatemalan Indians
and the State: 1540 to 1988

1. Introduction: Social Relations in Guatemala over Time and Space

Carol A. Smith
Department of Anthropology, Duke University

The following essays constitute the first real social history of Guatemala. This history focuses on the continuously interactive relation between Indian communities and the state, beginning when most Indian communities had definitively lost their sovereignty to the Spanish colonial state (1540), and ending when the modern Guatemalan state penetrates for the first time in history down into the Indian community (1988). The volume is organized chronologically, five chapters in part 1 treating the sixteenth through the nineteenth centuries; five chapters in part 2 treating the twentieth century. The concluding essay (chap. 12) attempts to summarize our findings as they bear on the contemporary situation in Guatemala.

This introductory chapter outlines some of the differences between our approach and that of a preceding generation of scholars with respect to the main topics treated here: Guatemala's multiple cultures, its continuously coercive state, its never-achieved nationhood, its inchoate class relations, and its varied Indian communities. It also describes some of the basic units of analysis assumed in the following chapters—the distinctive features of Guatemala's natural and economic regions; how we have periodized Guatemalan history, and what we mean by state, community, and class.

Culture and Power

The persistence of Guatemala's Indians, descendants of the great Mayan civilizations, persuaded earlier generations of anthropologists and historians to focus on the specificity of Guatemalan cultural patterns. Virtually all previous scholars addressed one or another of the following questions: What are the defining features of modern Indian culture?[1] What elements of Mayan tradition are presently retained?[2] What kind of culture do non-Indian Guatemalans have (Adams 1956b)? How have political and economic changes in Guatemala affected Indian culture?[3]

What are the social units bounding different Indian groups and cultures (Tax 1937)? How can one characterize the social relations existing between Indians and non-Indians?[4] Do the practices and beliefs of modern Indians represent a culture of conquest or a culture of resistance?[5]

These remain important questions, but with the exception of the last (which is almost exclusively a debate among Guatemalan scholars), they neglect the relation of culture to power. Thus, the authors in this volume pose questions about culture in a significantly different way: Under what political and economic conditions did certain postconquest communities retain Indian culture (chaps. 2, 4)? Why is postconquest Mayan culture fragmented by community rather than by class (chaps. 4, 9, 10)? What have been the political and social consequences of the continuous struggle between Mayan Indians and the state (chaps. 3–6, 10, 12)? What explains the uniquely brutal treatment of Indians by the modern Guatemalan state (chaps. 5–8)? How can racism coexist with assimilationism, both official and nonofficial (chap. 7)? Are Mayan Indians only now awakening as a self-conscious "political class" (chaps. 8, 10, 11)? What will be or can be the cultural content of a modern Guatemalan nation (chaps. 11, 12)? In addition, all of us attempt to show how Indians, even as their cultural forms and relations have varied over time and space, have affected as well as been affected by changes in the Guatemalan state and economy.

What is novel about our approach, then, is the way in which it brings a cultural perspective to questions of power (and vice versa) and by doing so helps dispel many of the myths concerning the unchanging nature of Guatemalan Indian communities and their relation to the state. Equally important, our cultural perspective on non-Indian features of Guatemala (e.g., the state, the nation, the oligarchy, and the *ladino* or non-Indian) shows that culture is relevant to more than the behavior of exotic peoples—a point often overlooked, even by anthropologists. It also helps explain certain aspects of national institutions, such as the state and the military in Guatemala, whose actions or features are frequently interpreted in only instrumental ways.

By continuing to concentrate on issues of culture, we focus on that which makes Guatemala a relatively unusual historical case of conquest and colonialism, even within Latin America. In doing so, we are not indulging in antiquarian culturalism or "orientalism," wherein we "explain" Guatemala's uniqueness in terms of its uniqueness.[6] Instead, we attempt to find a pattern of relationships between selected cultural and social elements by examining one human case closely through time, expecting that our findings will add to a general historical understanding of the issues involved: cultural resilience, ethnic relations, class formation, nationalism, state power, and social control in modern nation-states that are part of the Third World. Insofar as the "national question" has defined that which is peculiarly Guatemalan in Guatemala's history, it is the central question addressed in each of the major epochs described here.

Our reexamination of certain political issues of relevance to Guatemala also forces us to reexamine these issues as they reflect upon ourselves, both as scholars and as members of an international elite.[7] A noteworthy point in this regard is that neither international nor scholarly attention has fastened on the current violence in Guatemala to the degree that it has on that of other Latin American countries (e.g., Argentina or Chile). It seems likely that this is so because in Guatemala the great majority of those tortured, disappeared, or killed are not white, middle class, and European in culture (as in Argentina and Chile), but Indian, which is to say, the quintessential "other" in both physical and cultural terms. At the same time, Indians are persecuted by a state regime that draws precisely on white, western, and Christian traditions to sanction its iniquities.[8] These facts, as noted by James Dunkerley (1988:431), suggest a "general need to look again at the [modern] deconstruction of liberal racism . . .," an issue I take up below.

Indians and Non-Indians

Guatemala's present population of some eight million people is considered by most scholars to be about half Indian.[9] Most of Guatemala's Indians are descendants of the Maya, but then, given the very small numbers of Europeans who immigrated to Guatemala (Mörner 1985), so are most of Guatemala's non-Indians. Thus, what has distinguished Indians and non-Indians over time has not been biological heritage, but a changing system of social classification, based on ideologies of race, class, language, and culture, which ideologies have also taken on different meanings over time. Lutz and Lovell (chap. 2) describe the colonial system of social classification, Smith (chap. 4) suggests how that system changed in the nineteenth century, while Adams, Watanabe, Smith, and Arias (chaps. 6, 9, 10, 11) describe variations in the twentieth-century pattern.

The modern system of social classification is complicated by several intersecting sets of divisions, which are not shared by all Guatemalans. On the one hand, there are "Indians," a social category used by social scientists, census officials, and non-Indian Guatemalans—but by very few Indians. Indians recognize themselves as members of specific communities, which usually, but do not always, correspond to the smallest administrative division, the *municipio*.[10] On the other hand, there are "ladinos," a social category used by social scientists, census officials, Indians, and some but not all ladinos. The first three groups define ladinos as those Guatemalans who are not Indian. But people within that residual category often distinguish themselves or one another as significantly different subcategories: redressed Indians, "old" ladinos, whites, or Europeans (Adams 1956b; Pansini 1977).

At no time in Guatemala's history has a color bar prevented people who are phenotypically Indian from being accepted as ladino in Guatemala. But this is not to say that race and color play no role in Guatemalan social identity. Folk theories about heritage are key to understanding the systems of social classification that have variously created Indians, ladinos, Creoles, and whites over time (see chaps. 2, 4, 9). The ascending social categories of black, Indian, ladino, and white are based in an ideology about race that includes beliefs about the genetic make-up of people in these different categories (i.e., that ladinos are *mestizos*) as well as a system of racial ranking. The link between race and class—that Guatemala's elite is mostly white rather than mestizo, whereas ladinos often share the same class position as Indians—reinforces the folk racial hierarchy. For this reason many upper-class Guatemalans prefer to designate themselves as something other than ladino—as Creoles, whites, or Europeans. The ideology of race and class has changed significantly over time (cf. Mörner 1967; Burns 1980; C. Smith 1987a), but not the social ranking of different racial groups. Thus, today most Guatemalans point to cultural differences when distinguishing social groups, but at the same time believe that culture merely embodies race and class.[11]

The fact that many Indians have adopted ladino practices with varying intensity over time (see van den Berghe 1968; Early 1975; Brintnall 1979a) reinforces Guatemalan belief that most ladinos are, ultimately, redressed Indians. Hence the ambiguous social evaluation of people considered ladino. Nonetheless, white liberals in Guatemala's postcolonial state have encouraged Indian assimilation (chaps. 3, 7, 8), hoping in this way to eradicate the cultural divisions they thought prevented the emergence of a modern "civilized" nation. On these grounds many scholars argue that race is no longer an issue in Guatemala. But if we reexamine (or, in Dunkerley's phrase, deconstruct) the way in which beliefs about culture have created a new form of "liberal racism," we can agree with most of Guatemala's Indians that racism remains a problem in Guatemala. Following this line of reasoning to its logical conclusion, we can also see that racism is an issue that affects many North American interpretations of Guatemala.

Scholars have also long debated the degree to which there is a relationship between ancient and modern Mayan culture. According to one major Guatemalan scholar, Severo Martínez Peláez (1971), there have been no Maya in Guatemala since the sixteenth century, only Indians: The Maya were destroyed with the conquest; Indians are a cultural deformation, the residue of Spanish oppression. Others, such as Barbara Tedlock (1982) and Robert Carmack (1979, chap. 6), see considerable retention of "nativistic tradition" among modern Indians, while at the same time acknowledging that Mayan tradition has been reworked in each generation. The cultural authenticity of modern Guatemalan Indians is not really debatable in these terms. Everyone agrees that the conquest and the colonial institutions that followed (i.e., the *encomienda, repartimiento, congregación*, and religious indoctrination, discussed in chap. 2) had a major impact on Mayan culture—as they did on elite Guatemalan culture. At the same time, however, the survivors of the conquest who continued to identify themselves as Indians retained a core of beliefs and traditions that continues to anchor Indian cultural identity in the present (see chaps. 6, 9).

The debate about the retention of Mayan tradition is not really about the nature of Indian cultural identity. It is about the nature of *Guatemalan* cultural identity and social arrangements: what they are and what they should be (see chaps. 11, 12). In this argument, Guatemala remains divided into conquered and conquerors, Indians and ladinos, because its basic institutions continue to be colonial in nature ("feudal" according to some). Without a basic transformation in these colonial institutions, there can be no single Guatemalan national identity. The question at issue, then, is whether or how to reject and transform Guatemala's divisive heritage. This is not simply an intellectual issue, since every political struggle since independence has encountered it as a major political question (see chaps. 4, 7, 8, 12), even if the question was never clearly posed as such.[12]

In most of the debates about social and cultural divisions in Guatemala, the question of *Indian* cultural identity has been the contested issue. Non-Indian intellectuals, who have dominated the discourse, believe that as long as Indians retain their separate identity, Guatemala cannot achieve the status of a modern nation. For them a modern nation implies not only unity, but the eradication of what they believe to be the very symbol of backwardness—a group of people still rooted in the traditions of a colonial past.

For Indians, however, the issue is not identity, but justice. Most Indians wish to retain their distinctive traditions, while taking a position of economic and political equality with others in a modern (i.e., developing) multicultural nation (COCADI 1989). Indian intellectuals now taking a position in the debate point to the problem of non-Indian identity, an identity they assert is purely negative without the existence of an exploited "other" and the reason non-Indians cannot accept the possibility of a modern nation that is multicultural (cf. Cojtí Cuxil 1989). They suggest that non-Indians can more easily accept the depreciated position of Guatemala in the modern world by pointing to and at the same time distancing themselves from what they perceive to be the reason for Guatemala's backwardness, the continuing existence of Indians. Since Indians and non-Indians share few assumptions about culture, identity, or the nature of a desirable Guatemalan nation, it is not surprising that Guatemala remains culturally divided. As the following essays show, each attempt by the modern Guatemalan state to eradicate cultural divisions in order to create a unified nation has been either brutal or half-hearted, such that the attempt has merely recreated the division between Indians and non-Indians in stronger form.

Guatemala's Natural and Economic Regions

Within the small compass of its 42,000 square miles, Guatemala can be divided into three basic natural areas (see map 1). The largest natural region, nearly half the national territory, includes the entire lowland area of the north, which drains into the Atlantic Ocean. This area includes the Petén, the Caribbean littoral near Lake Izabál, and a strip running through northern Huehuetenango to Alta Verapaz, now known as the Franja Transversal del Norte. This vast tropical frontier has historically supported a very low population density and has been exploited mainly for forest products and by slash-and-burn agriculture; at present, however, the area has increasing numbers of subsistence farmers together with cattle ranchers and considerable mineral potential—a situation in which conflict is virtually guaranteed. The population of the northern lowlands remains sparse though extremely diverse, including recent Indian and ladino settlers, as well as black populations, from the earlier Black Caribs to more recent Jamaican migrants.

The highlands, approximately one-third of the area of the country, have always held more than half of Guatemala's rural population. The highlands consist of rugged mountain ranges in the middle of the country, framed on both sides by a piedmont and delimited on the southern side by thirty-three volcanic peaks, many still active. The several mountain ranges are dissected by deep canyons and gorges, making travel and transport in the area relatively difficult. The population is widely dispersed over the landscape, relatively few highland people living in towns or even small villages (see Hunt and Nash 1967). Most highland people have access to some of their own land on which they grow corn and beans as well as a wide variety of other food crops. The nature of economic and social adaptations varies so widely in the highlands, however, that care must be taken to specify the time and area before characterizing it. Most scholars distinguish the *occidente*—the higher western highlands, the Mayan Indian heartland—from the flatter, dryer *oriente*—or eastern highlands, whose population is presently mostly ladino.

The third natural region, the Pacific lowlands, divides into two portions with corresponding differences in land use. The higher *boca costa*, whose rich soils are constantly replenished by volcanic ash, is taken up by large coffee plantations; the lower Pacific littoral has sugar and cotton plantations as well as large cattle ranches. The permanent population of this area is primarily non-Indian, though Indians make up the bulk of the seasonal labor force. Before major plantations were introduced into this zone in the latter part of the nineteenth century, the population was relatively sparse and agricultural exploitation of the area was erratic and limited. Today, this zone holds nearly one-third of Guatemala's population.

Guatemala's natural areas have been integrated into different economic regions as new market connections between areas were forged in response to major shifts in the national economy.[13] Lutz and Lovell describe both highland and lowland core areas in the colonial period, as defined by economic importance (see map 5, chap. 2). Most of the western highlands was economically peripheral, even though the relatively dense population of the area provided the Crown with most of its revenue in the form of tributes. Little changed with independence except that the core area shrank to a small region surrounding the national capital, now moved thirty miles east of its original location. Only with the introduction of coffee in the latter half of the nineteenth century did most of the southern lowlands become a core economic zone (see chap. 5). The economic operation of the coffee *fincas* (plantations) cannot be considered apart from their connections to the adjacent western highlands, which provided their labor supply and most items of domestic consumption. Thus, one could argue that the entire western portion of Guatemala, delimited by Mexico on the west and by Guatemala City on the east, was the core economic zone of Guatemala from 1870 through 1950 (C. Smith 1978).

After World War II, economic growth in Guatemala brought about the development of new agricultural exports on the south coast, much improved transportation, industry in the national capital, and greater reliance on imported goods for both business and domestic consumption. In response, Guatemala City grew rapidly and presently holds some 20 percent of Guatemala's population, dwarfing all other cities by a multiplier of 15 to 20. Thus, the national capital must once again be seen as the "core" zone of Guatemala (C. Smith 1985), with the western

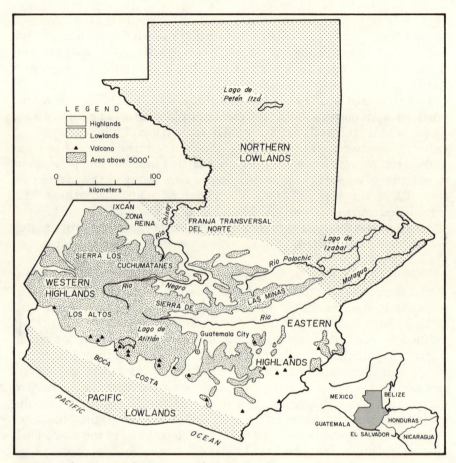

Map 1. The Natural Regions of Guatemala

highlands relatively peripheral to the national economy.[14] (Map 2 shows the modern economic regions and roads of Guatemala as of about 1970, based on economic activity and land use.)

Apart from the national capital, the only real metropolis in Central America, Guatemala remains largely rural. The only important provincial towns are departmental capitals, none of which exceeds 100,000 in population. (The only formal administrative divisions in Guatemala are departments and municipios; department boundaries cut across the basic natural divisions of Guatemala and have no real political functions except administrative, whereas municipios are the locus of local power relations as well as of the Indian community.)[15] The most important commercial centers are located in the highlands, including the national capital, Guatemala City, situated in a mountain valley that divides the

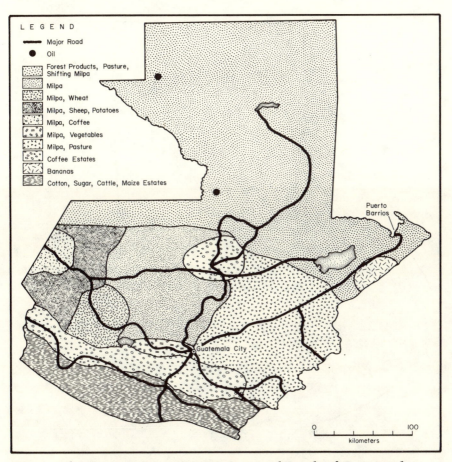

Map 2. The Current Economic Regions and Roads of Guatemala

eastern from the western highlands. The lowland areas north and south
are even more rural than the highlands, though the northern area holds
Guatemala's major port (Puerto Barrios) and several important commercial towns have developed on the south coast in this century. (Map 3
shows the major cities and administrative districts in modern Guatemala.)

Different economic regions have been involved in Guatemala's successive attempts at rebellion and revolution in the postindependence
period. The Indian revolt that opened the independence period included
most of the municipios in the department of Totonicapán, the only
Indian area that was little involved in the 1980s attempt at revolution
(chap. 12). The nineteenth-century rebellion that brought a guerrilla
leader to power in the 1840s (chaps. 3, 4) was centered in the Mita district

Map 3. The Major Towns and Departments of Guatemala

of eastern Guatemala, an area then as now mainly populated by ladinos. The small guerrilla movement of the 1960s (chap. 12) was also located in eastern Guatemala, in the relatively remote northern departments of Izabál and Zacapa. The most recent insurgency of the late 1970s and 1980s (chaps. 11, 12) involved most of the (Indian) western highlands, including the boca costa. While the armed insurgents themselves were mainly located in the more isolated areas north and south of the densely populated highlands, support was widespread throughout the rural area. Map 4, which locates the main insurgent areas in these four different periods, suggests that popular resistance in Guatemala has been based mainly in partially commercialized smallholder ("peasant") areas, as Wolf (1966) suggested was typical of twentieth-century insurgencies. Yet, as the authors who examine these particular outbreaks of violence

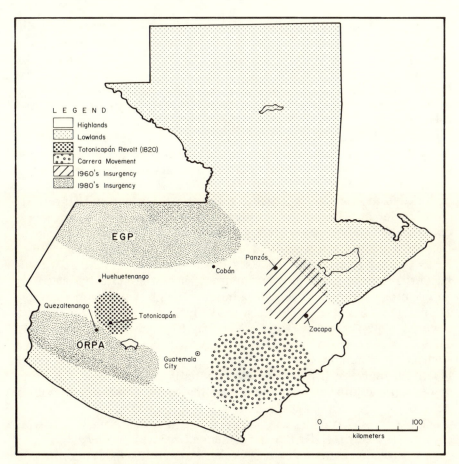

Map 4. The Insurgent Regions of Guatemala over Time

argue (chaps. 4, 11, 12), this is too facile a reading of political life in Guatemala. Ethnicity has also played a role in all of Guatemala's major rebellions. More important, state response to particular forms of struggle has shaped where and when open conflict would take place (see especially chaps. 5–8, 10, 12).

Theoretical Issues: The State

Throughout this work, we have focused attention on relations between Indian communities and the Guatemalan state, rather than on other political groups in society, such as classes. We do this in the conviction that we can locate the main political dialectic in Guatemala in the relations of power and culture embedded in the two institutions of community and state. The persuasiveness of this argument depends on the particular meanings we give to the terms *state*, *community*, and *class*, theoretical as well as definitional issues treated in this and the following two sections. I should note that, while the theoretical framework presented here was developed after rather than before the following essays were written, it is an attempt to model the social relations described in the historical narrative.

Neither of the two classic ways of treating the state in the social science literature, liberal or Marxist, allows one to describe the state as an autonomous actor in social relations or to assume the existence of a special dialectic between the state and those governed by the state, as we do here. Both standard approaches reduce the state (and state interests) to other elements in society—either to society as a whole (liberal theory) or to the dominant classes (Marxist theory)—calling upon the concept of the state mainly to describe a certain functional arena for action. Recently both liberals and Marxists have criticized the standard formulations, pointing out times and places where the state has been an autonomous actor, and suggesting how one might better understand it as such (e.g., Skocpol 1979; Carnoy 1984; Evans, Rueschemeyer, and Skocpol 1985; Mann 1986; Migdal 1988).[16] Since few of these new theories of the state are especially illuminating about Third World states such as Guatemala, we have not explicitly used them in our particular historical analyses. (My concluding chapter is the exception.) I outline some of the arguments they make here mainly because they provide a defense for the kind of approach we take in this book.

Let us assume that the state is a set of institutions and personnel who administer a territorially demarcated area over which they attempt to monopolize the use of force (the Weberian definition). Where in this definition can we locate the source of state autonomy? According to Michael Mann (1986), the locus of state autonomy resides in the distinctive way in which state power is organized. Power relations exist everywhere and take many forms—ideological, economic, and coercive. The state can never fully monopolize power, nor are the means of state power unique. In other words, the state wields ideological, economic, and coercive power, just like the various institutions of civil society with which it often competes for power (e.g., religious and military groups, the dominant classes, local communities). What is peculiar to the state, as opposed to these other social institutions, is the way it organizes power through territorial administration. Because state power (in multiple forms) is channeled through a spatially centralized, concentrated, hierarchical organization over specified areas, it has the potential to delimit and diffuse other forms of power, often thereby using other forms of power for its own purposes.

This peculiarity of state power gives the state a particular interest vis-à-vis other institutions in society: an interest in controlling a bounded territory through its territorial forms of administration. This interest is two-sided: on the one hand the state must maintain itself domestically, by controlling and incorporating the population it seeks to govern by means of its administrative system; and on the other hand, the state must maintain itself with respect to competing territorial entities—that is, other states or forms of territorial organization. As long as a state exists in an arena of competing states, it must necessarily defend and maintain its administrative structures—or lose them to a stronger power (cf. Skocpol 1979). A state formed through conquest, such as Guatemala's, exists only to the extent that it creates a territorial administration, with its own centers of power, and incorporates the conquered populace into them—defeating or incorporating other contenders for power over the area, such as the preconquest Indian communities and kingdoms of Guatemala.

To maintain its administrative structures, a state must also have some capacity to compete with or co-opt other groups in civil society in order to regulate social relationships, to extract resources, and to use those resources in determined ways (Migdal 1988:4). Because Guatemala's Indian communities have always attempted to regulate themselves and have usually resisted state extraction of their resources, the relationship between Indian communities and the Guatemalan state has typically been antagonistic. Other groups in Guatemala have also resisted state power (e.g., the church, the oligarchy). But because these groups have been more useful in helping the state meet its own basic organizational goals, their relationship to the state has been more symbiotic than oppositional. The Guatemalan state in turn has assisted these other groups in achieving their ends—as long as these ends complemented rather than conflicted with the organizational goals of the state. Because Indian communities have retained relative autonomy vis-à-vis the state from the colonial period up to the present, they are the most developed and independent element in Guatemala's civil society.[17]

Depending on the kinds of relationships established with various groups in civil society, states may be more or less powerful along several dimensions. Michael Mann (1986) identifies two dimensions of state power: one is despotic power, or the degree to which the state may undertake a range of actions without routine, institutionalized negotiations with various groups in civil society; the other dimension is infrastructural power, the state's ability to actually penetrate civil society and centrally coordinate the activities of civil society through its own infrastructure. According to Mann, state infrastructural power has grown exponentially through history, as societies have become more complex and as the burden of social regulation is increasingly turned over to a state; but, he argues, the exercise of despotic power has varied widely over space and time, existing in states that are infrastructurally weak as well as strong. I will separate a third dimension of power from Mann's list, that of hegemonic power: the ability of the state to tame the institutions of civil society through its manipulation of national political ideology.[18] Modern nation-states typically exercise little despotic power, not because of their great infrastructural power, but because they have penetrated the institutions of civil society ideologically.

Traditional agrarian states, such as those in Latin America up into the twentieth century, have sometimes held despotic power, but rarely have held broad infrastructural or hegemonic power. Their infrastructural power is limited by the fact that they have neither the organizational nor financial capacity to create local-level institutions for governance. For this they rely on preexisting institutions (community forms of control or local elites)—which are always potential competitors to state power. Guatemala's colonial state brought along one of its own preexisting civil institutions, the missionary church, to staff the lower levels of its territorial administration in the Indian areas (van Oss 1986). This allowed a tiny state bureaucracy to control the conquered Indians rather quickly, but at the same time precluded a different kind of state maneuver: separating out a group of local indigenous elites who would work in the interests of the state rather than of the community. Thus, by establishing a simple, "cheap," and ideologically powerful system of administration, the state also helped create relatively homogeneous or corporate Indian communities that would be extremely resistant to state manipulation without the legitimating influence of the church (cf. Wasserstrom 1983).

The colonial state also used Spanish settlers and their Creole descendants to manage other state functions (Wortman 1982). What later became the lowest level of state administration (the municipios) were first given as *encomiendas* (gifts of Indians) to local settlers to administer. It appears that in their haste to organize an entirely exotic society along simple administrative lines, the colonial state organized encomiendas around preexisting territorial units (Lovell and Swezey 1989; Kramer 1989), a factor that helped Indians maintain their identity during their most difficult period, when as many as 80 percent of them died (see Lovell 1985). Most encomiendas were taken over by the state within several generations, at which point the real territorial authority of the colonial state was established.

By using these various mechanisms, the colonial state was extraordinarily successful in using limited resources to quickly establish an administrative presence over an unruly conquered population.[19]   But there was a price: the colonial state had to share power with the church and the Creole elite. Using the terms developed above, the colonial state bargained away its despotic powers, always having to negotiate with the church over laws affecting Indians and with local elites over the division of revenues. Perhaps more important in the long run of history, the local administrative units, known as *pueblos de Indios* in the colonial period and as municipios after independence, could take advantage of the colonial state's weak control over them by developing institutions through which they could continue to resist state control. Since the Indian elite was eliminated rather than co-opted, Indian communities did not contain groups with different interests vis-à-vis the state.

A curious feature of the colonial state is that, while it was weak in terms of infrastructural and despotic power, it was hegemonically strong in the Indian areas—at least in comparison to the postcolonial state. If we examine the institutions of the corporate Indian community during the colonial period—the Catholic mission, the *caja de comunidad* (community treasury), the *cofradia* (a religious sodality), and the *cabildo* (town council)—they were "brokerage" rather than "barrier" mechanisms, established as such by the church to *mediate* between community and state (MacLeod 1973; Collins 1980). As long as the missionary church helped administer these institutions, Indians basically accepted both church and state as legitimate forces over them; and, under these circumstances, community autonomy was acceptable to the state. But when and where church power and legitimacy vis-à-vis Indian communities waned and the state attempted direct intervention in Indian communities, mainly to increase its revenues (see chaps. 3 and 4), what were once "brokerage" institutions welded together to become "barrier" institutions, the means by which the corporate Indian community could express its opposition to the state.[20]

Several other elements in the administrative form of the colonial state allowed Indian communities to develop an increasing capacity to resist state intrusion in their affairs (see chap. 2). The colonial bureaucracy—small and distant from the imperial command center in Spain and concentrated in a single administrative center in Guatemala—created a very simple administrative hierarchy: the colonial administrative seat (Guatemala City), a handful of provincial centers (first *corregidores*, later *departamentos*) from which the state sent emissaries into the conquered territory—a sea of undifferentiated pueblos de Indios (now municipios). This simple territorial organization exists today.[21] Had the colonial or postcolonial states been able to concentrate the widely dispersed Indians into towns (pueblos), or had they created a differentiated hierarchy of Indian towns, this system might have worked better than it did to penetrate and reorganize Indian institutions. But despite continuous attempts by the state (and church) at *congregación* (concentrating Indians into towns), most Indians remained widely scattered over their lands (where they remain to this day), recognizing mainly the boundaries and institutions of the noncentralized Indian community.

The Guatemalan state that formed in the postcolonial period lost both legitimacy and control over the native population as the interests of different members of the secular and religious elite diverged—which significantly weakened the infrastructural power of the state (see chaps. 3, 4). Thus, Guatemala suffered more than elite wars for state power in the nineteenth century, a phenomenon common to Latin America; it also suffered a mass popular uprising (see chaps. 3, 4), which changed the nature of state rule (chaps. 5, 6) as well as the class/race divisions (chap. 4) institutionalized in the colonial period. From this time forward, the despotic power of the state over Indian communities increased vastly, even as the state ceded power to (and thus had to negotiate with) the locally dominant class, the Creole elite. But as Mann points out, despotic power is intrinsically limited in range. A despotic state can wipe out an intransigent Indian community, but it cannot control a large group of communities who deny its legitimate control over them. The actions of a despotic state, in fact, often strengthen the mechanisms of resistance held in civil society (see also Migdal 1988) and thus rarely achieve hegemonic control.

By the end of the nineteenth century, Guatemala had developed a relatively strong state apparatus (i.e., a much deeper and broader infrastructure) by which it could collect information and impose its will (see McCreery, chap. 5). The coercive mechanisms of this state provided the Indian labor force for the new plantation elite (chaps. 4–6). But even with its greater powers of coercion, the state could not substitute its own infrastructure for that existing in Indian communities. It had to operate through new brokerage institutions within those communities, and also had to contend with the resistance provided by the old corporate mechanisms of those communities (see Carmack, chap. 6). Because this "stronger" state had lost all legitimacy within Indian communities, it was even weaker than the colonial state with respect to imposing its own institutions on the local communities. Thus, while certain colonial institutions did penetrate into Indian life (e.g., the cabildo, the cofradia, the Catholic church), if only to be reorganized and reinterpreted by the Indian community, there are no analogous "plantation" institutions within Indian communities: only the signs of state coercion.

The coercive state tradition was briefly broken in 1944–1954, when real popular elections were held, once again affecting class and ethnic structures in Guatemala (chaps. 7, 8), but was reimposed when popular agitation threatened to get out of hand. Guatemala's present militarized state, which has been termed a "permanent counterinsurgency state" (Anderson and Simon 1987), is yet another coercive response to popular resistance, reflecting the state's inability to control the Indian population by other than violent means (see chaps. 11, 12). Both types of modern state, democratic and military, have imposed certain institutions on the Indian community: the reform period required elected officials to replace community elders; the military state now imposes a paramilitary civil-patrol system on them. But neither of these attempts by the state to "penetrate and centrally coordinate the activities of civil society through its own infrastructure" has been entirely successful. When it has not simply rejected these institutions out of hand, the corporate Indian community has reformulated them along its own lines, making them work for the community rather than for the state. The cultural distinctiveness of Indian communities itself remains a visible repudiation of state attempts to create a national hegemonic culture. The fact that all such efforts to assimilate or incorporate Indians into the nation in the postcolonial period have been forced rather than urged on them, has led to further loss of state legitimacy in Indian communities.

The postcolonial states in other Central American countries (except for Costa Rica) have followed a similar pattern—the development of greater coercive power together with the loss of popular legitimacy. For this we must credit the rise and expansion of export-oriented agriculture, which created a small and politically powerful coffee oligarchy, and the U.S. role in supporting that oligarchy against popular pressures (cf. Williams 1986). But the unusual strength, independence, and intransigence of Guatemala's current military state remain unaccounted for in this analysis, such that we must attempt to identify internal factors for it. As we look over the long sweep of postcolonial history, it becomes obvious that the Guatemalan state has always had to struggle against recalcitrant Indian communities in order to carry out any of the basic mandates of a modern capitalist nation. Despite their incredibly meager political and economic resources, Guatemalan Indians have provided a powerful block of opposition to all attempts to draw them into national life on any terms other than their own, their terms being those of continued political and economic autonomy. To break down their considerable resistance, state rather than simple economic coercion has always been necessary. Thus, virtually all of the scholars in this volume find it more helpful to analyze political life in Guatemala as constituted by a struggle between Indians and the state rather than between peasants and landlords or workers and capitalists. To this extent we bring a perspective on Guatemalan history different from that previously depicted.

Theoretical Issues: The Corporate Community

When we talk of "the Indian community" here, we refer to an incredibly diverse set of places. We can say in general that Indian communities are concentrated in the western highlands and tend to correspond to particular administrative units (municipios). But while some communities consist of fewer than five thousand Indians with no ladinos in their midst (Santiago Chimaltenango, chap. 9), others have as many as eighty thousand Indians, together with one or two thousand ladinos who are *not* part of the "community" (Totonicapán, chap. 10). Some communities are nucleated, with people living in small villages, and relatively traditional, like Santiago Chimaltenango. Others are widely dispersed, with people living in family groups spread over the landscape, mostly on family-held land, and relatively nontraditional, like Totonicapán. There is, however, no clear relationship between size, wealth, presence of ladinos, occupation, and degree of "tradition."

Guatemalan Indians speak some twenty different Mayan languages, and each community tends to have a different dialect (as well as other distinctive customs) that sets it apart from other communities. Some communities are rich, some are poor, some are dependent on local land for income, others migrate to the lowland plantations for income, and yet others consist mainly of artisans and traders. This diversity is not a recent phenomenon—a result of different degrees of acculturation—but a long-standing phenomenon, a result of differences in pre-Hispanic heritage, or various and changing economic options, and of historical experience (chap. 2).

Cultural diversity is also a strongly held value by Indians who retain a sense of community, possibly because Indian identity is rooted in the community (rather than in a general sense of "Indian-ness"), possibly because it is and has been a protection against state control. Guatemala's state personnel (almost entirely ladino throughout history) know very little about "real" Indian life in the countryside; their lack of knowledge translates into a certain lack of control—at least with respect to exercising hegemonic power. What might be an attractive state agenda in one area is almost certainly unattractive in another, so the Guatemalan state has rarely been able to persuade Indians to follow any general state policy. Thus, out of diversity comes unity: what Indian communities generally share is their tradition of acting as corporate units in political struggles with the state—despite the fact that they may have different economic and political reasons for those struggles.

While the Guatemalan state has almost always acted against all Indians as a class, Indians have rarely acted as a self-conscious class (i.e., a united political group), more often reacting to their oppression as separate communities. At the same time, economic conditions in the western highlands, from the turn of the century to the present, have created the conditions for class differentiation among Indians, even among Indians from the same community (see chap. 6). Why, under these conditions, does a sense of community identity remain strong among most highland Indians, suppressing the expression of class interests within communities and preventing class unity between Indians and non-Indians (chaps. 9, 10)?

Many students of Guatemala have attempted to explain this contradiction by assuming the continued existence of "the closed, corporate, peasant community," a concept introduced by Eric Wolf in 1957 (see, e.g., Reina 1966; Nash 1967; Stavenhagen 1975; Warren 1978). Wolf introduced the concept to explain the nature of peasant communities in seventeenth-century Mexico when large *haciendas* were encroaching upon Indian lands and labor. As Wolf described it, such an entity evolved throughout Mesoamerica (and Central Java) so as to guarantee "a measure of communal jurisdiction over land" and in order to "restrict membership, maintain a religious system, enforce mechanisms which ensure the redistribution or destruction of surplus wealth, and uphold barriers against the entry of goods and ideas produced outside the community." The closed corporate community is viewed not so much as "an offspring of conquest" but as the product of "the dualization of society into a dominant entrepreneurial sector and a dominated sector of native peasants." Although the configuration has experienced "great changes since the time it was first constituted," Wolf (1959:214–215) contends that "its essential features are still visible." He thus considers "the present-day Indian community as a direct descendent of the reconstructed community" that emerged mainly in the seventeenth century from a synthesis of Spanish and Maya culture.

The conditions Wolf thought brought the closed corporate community into being hardly obtain in modern Guatemala; nor are they especially persuasive for seventeenth-century Guatemala, when there was relatively little hacienda expansion (see chap. 2). Moreover, as Wolf has recently noted (1986), the concept was not designed to deal with peasants drawn into wage relationships with capitalist enterprises, as many Guatemalan Indians have been since the late nineteenth century. But there are other and more serious problems with the concept of the closed corporate community for Guatemala. First, it assumes that certain social customs that imply closure—such as restricting marriage partners to those within the community—reflect or reinforce political and economic tendencies toward closure. But, while it is still possible to talk of Indian communities as being closed with respect to choice of marriage partners, it has never been possible to talk of them as closed to economic changes (see especially chaps. 2, 5, 11), nor even to political changes (chaps. 6, 8, 11—as long as those political changes did not threaten the unity of Indians vis-à-vis the state. The point here is that social, economic, and political relations in Indian communities exist in a dynamic tension rather than in an unchanging determinate relationship.

Second, the concept tends to reify colonial institutions within Indian communities, without giving due consideration to the transformation of those institutions through history. The colonial cargo system, for example, operated as a way of selecting political leaders in Indian communities up until very recently, but the way in which the system operated within the community and its political meaning to the community have changed enormously over time (see chaps. 9, 11; see also Wasserstrom 1983). Other colonial institutions (e.g., the maintenance of a community chest) are long dead, having little relevance in the present. And yet other precolonial institutions remain (a large number of religious beliefs and the maintenance, whether formal or informal, of the prestige and local power of community elders), sometimes uneasily, sometimes comfortably with new religious and political groupings (see Arias, chap. 11). For these reasons, we find it much more useful to look at the ways in which community institutions have reconstituted themselves historically in relation to changing historical circumstances. Community relations remain strong, often corporate, not because of the dead weight of the past, but because of the continuing importance of community relations to an oppressed people ruled by an extremely repressive state.

Finally, the notion of the closed corporate community is one that makes struggle over land appear to be the primary, if not singular, goal of the Indian community. Yet we find that strong Indian communities have existed, whether or not threatened by the seizure of their land. This is not to deny that Guatemalan Indians frequently have had to struggle against incursions on their land—from the eighteenth century to the present (Melville and Melville 1971), as most of the following chapters document. And land remains more than an important economic resource to most Indians: without a territorial claim in a community of one's ancestors and the means to secure part of one's own food supply, a Guatemalan Indian has great difficulty in retaining his or her identity as an Indian (see Watanabe, chap. 9). Thus, struggles for community land (which in Guatemala have been mainly struggles with the state rather than with expanding haciendas), help explain the persistence of Indian identity with a particular piece of land or community. But it cannot explain the unity of Indian communities whose economic base is mainly artisanal or commercial (Tedlock 1982), or why Indian communities divided over territorial claims (or other economic interests) still exist as political communities (chap. 9), or why communities with few vestiges of colonial institutions remain corporate in a political sense (chap. 10). In sum, all of the authors in this volume have discovered *corporate* Indian communities (i.e., communities with a relatively unified political agenda) to be important political entities in each period of Guatemalan history; but none of us has found Wolf's concept of "closed, corporate community" adequate to explain their existence.

Thus, Lutz and Lovell (chap. 2) find some corporate communities forming and disintegrating at different points in the colonial period, usually in response to outside political pressure; McCreery and Carmack (chaps. 5 and 6) document how some of those communities were reconstituted in the plantation period—after a period of considerable openness, according to Smith (chap. 4). Adams and Handy (chaps. 7 and 8) describe significant economic and political changes in those communities during the reform period, together with a persistence of strong local identity. And Watanabe, Smith, and Arias (chaps. 9–11) portray various new as well as traditional elements constituting the modern corporate community in the previolence period. But in every period, however much the political form of the corporate Indian community may have changed, Indian identity has been based in the community as the community struggled with a coercive state to retain as much political and economic autonomy as possible.

Looking at the wreckage of modern Guatemala, brought on by a weak but despotic state that attempted to eradicate the bases for the autonomous Indian community once and for all, we have also been forced to reexamine the meaning and value of community to Guatemala's modern Indians. The "enduring yet ineffable meaning" of community to Indians (chap. 9) blocked the possibility of a unified Indian struggle against the state. Thus, we find that unified community interests can suppress (or mystify) the expression of internal class differences, while splitting what would otherwise be common class interests; we also find that community identification can complicate and exacerbate the larger ethnic divisions between Indians, ladinos, and whites that continue to plague Guatemala, and can fuel racist beliefs on all sides (chaps. 10–12). Yet communities, whether real or imagined, are also the vehicles through which classes become active agents of struggle (Thompson 1963) and national identities are forged (B. Anderson 1980). How Guatemalans define their communities has been and will be the most significant determinant of Guatemala's political future.

Theoretical Issues: Class Relations

Given the existence of the corporate Indian community throughout

Guatemala's postconquest history, how can we discuss the general class position of Indians at different points in time? Are Guatemala's modern Indians mostly a peasantry, a semiproletariat, or a petite bourgeoisie ("penny capitalists")? And out of what did they become such? Do most Indians and ladinos share the same or a similar class position? We have no simple answer to these questions because class relations cannot be considered apart from other relations equally salient: those of ethnicity, those of community, and those created by the dialectic between community and state. At the same time we agree with other students of Guatemala that we cannot interpret the meaning of these other relations without considering them in a class context. Where we differ from most other students of Guatemala on this point is in our insistence that Indians and ladinos have not been imprisoned in an unchanging class relationship with each other from the colonial period to the present. The most stable element in Guatemala's class relations is the state's role in defining and manipulating them, and this has caused continuous change. It is useful, therefore, to describe class relationships and positions within particular "political" rather than economic epochs.

We identify four major political periods: colonial (1540–1800), independence (1800–1870), the early plantation period (1870-1944), and the modern period (1944–present). Significant economic changes accompanied the political transformations that mark this particular periodization (see, especially, chaps. 3, 5, 8). But most of the authors in this volume believe that only two of these breaks signal a transformation in the mode of production: 1540, when a colonial economy was firmly established; and 1944, when capitalism, *tout court*, was fully realized by the abolition of forced labor. We see the periods preceding 1944 as neither fully capitalist (as posited by V. Solórzano 1977), feudal (the position taken by Martínez Peláez, 1971), nor "colonial," that is, an economy in which colonial institutions and class relations remained dominant (as argued by Stavenhagen 1975). Instead, we describe a localized and changing mixture, beginning mainly as a state-directed tribute economy combined with elements of merchant capitalism, which increasingly becomes a state-directed, coercive form of capitalism mixed with petty commodity production.[22]

The challenge here is to document changes in both local and export-oriented economies, changes based in local relations of production as much as in world economic conditions. Lutz and Lovell (chap. 2) describe different kinds (and levels) of colonial exploitation and then assess how each kind of exploitation created different sorts of rural communities, Indian and non-Indian. Woodward (chap. 3) and Smith (chap. 4) depict an economy that is basically artisanal, in that small farmers and craftsmen are economically dominated by a small merchant class (see also Wortman 1982; C. Smith 1984a). The class-ethnic situation in the early nineteenth century is extremely complex, regionally varied, and possibly more fluid than at any other point in Guatemalan history. McCreery (chap. 5) and Carmack (chap. 6) discuss the most dramatic, speedy, and significant economic transformation in Guatemala's history—the establishment of a full-scale plantation economy—which nonetheless was unable to create "real" as opposed to "formal" capitalist relations of production.[23]   Unlike most who have depicted that period in Guatemalan history (C. L. Jones 1940; Mosk 1955; Torres-Rivas 1971; V. Solórzano 1977), they make clear that the form of the coffee-export economy institutionalized in the late nineteenth century was not dictated by the desires and needs of the world economy or even of Guatemala's Liberal elites. The form it took was dictated by the social relations established between coffee entrepreneurs and workers, both groups holding various interests and powers, all of which affected the eventual nature of Guatemala's coffee economy. The authors who treat the modern period (chaps. 7–12) continue to show a variety of groups, political interests, and economic adjustments, as they are influenced by class, regional position, and ethnicity. The revolt of 1944, which ushered in a new political era, was closely followed by legislation that ended the forced labor laws (chap. 8). From this point forward, one can argue that capitalist relations of production became dominant in Guatemala's economy, even though capitalist relations do not penetrate into Indian communities or dramatically change the artisanal basis of the domestic economy (chap. 10). One might also argue, especially in light of the very short period in which Guatemala enjoyed a nontyrannical state together with real capitalist relations of production, that civil society in Guatemala has been too weak to support a fully developed form of capitalism—in which the state retreats to the role of mediating rather than generating particular economic interests (see chap. 12).

Having established that Guatemala's economy has features that differentiate it from simple "feudal" or "capitalist" economies, how have we defined actual social classes at different points in Guatemalan history? What, for example, has been and is now the class position of Indians? Most North American scholars have considered them peasants in every historical epoch, whereas most Guatemalan scholars have considered them peasants in the past but semiproletarians in the present. Since the answer one gives to this question hinges on the definition one has of "class," it is useful to briefly review the main positions in the literature and the assumptions on which they are based. With this information at hand, the reader will better be able to take his or her own position on the class position of Indians, a question on which the authors have not reached full agreement.

North Americans routinely put all Indians in the class position of peasants. Robert Redfield (1956a) and Sol Tax (1953) began this tradition, but North Americans continue to consider Indians to be peasants without embarrassment to the present day (Warren 1978; Handy 1984; Hawkins 1984; Woodward 1985a) though with a certain amount of self-acknowledged confusion. Since North Americans had little concept of a social formation in which there are *class relations*, they meant by class the position individuals held in relation to particular economic and political resources. In the case of Guatemala, the people of concern (mostly Indians) were rural, they almost all farmed small plots of land, they exercised virtually no state-level political power, and their social relations took place mostly within single communities that appeared relatively homogeneous. (About 75 percent of the people in western Guatemala fit this definition; most of these people also consider themselves Indians.) Even as they debated which of these characteristics was the most essential for defining a peasantry (see Shanin 1971), North American scholars have used one or another of them to define peasants. Since Guatemalan Indians seemed to have most of these characteristics, no one doubted that they were peasants.

Twenty years ago Eric Wolf pointed out that the defining characteristic of peasants was the relationship they held to nonpeasants—that is, peasants were rural cultivators who produced a fund of rent for economic superiors (Wolf 1966:10). This *relational* definition of peasants, which advanced theoretical discussion considerably, has become the accepted definition for peasants in North American scholarship. Yet scholars continue to describe Guatemalan Indians as peasants even though most Indians fit this definition poorly if at all. As several of the following studies show (see especially chap. 10), a good many Indians cannot be considered rural, less than half can be considered cultivators in occupational terms (most farm, but they obtain the bulk of their incomes from other work), virtually none produce a fund of rent in any traditional sense (or in any of the ways discussed by Wolf), and this has been true for the entire postcolonial period (C. Smith 1984b).

Unlike North Americans, Guatemalan scholars define class on a national rather than localized basis, and thus their arguments center on the nature of the social formation in question. Most Guatemalan scholars agree that Guatemala is a dependent or "colonial" social formation, a form of peripheral capitalism, which provides the analytic foundation for their class analyses (see, e.g., Guzmán Böckler and Herbert 1970; Flores Alvarado 1971; Martínez Peláez 1971; Torres-Rivas 1981). Indians are considered the most exploited group within this formation, their exploitation explained in terms of dependency theory:

surplus value is transferred from Indians through non-Indians (ladinos) to international capitalists through unequal exchange and mechanisms of monopoly control. Much of the Guatemalan analysis of exploitation is abstract, if not doctrinaire, and there exists little documentation of the precise mechanisms at work and how they affect local class structure.

Flores Alvarado (1971) and Torres-Rivas (1981), who emphasize production over exchange, are more explicit than others. They argue that Indians constitute the bulk of the seasonal workforce on plantations and on these grounds replace the class category of peasant with that of semi-proletariat. They note that Indians require wage income in order to subsist on their tiny plots of land, and they suggest that Indians exist basically as reserve labor for the coffee, cotton, and sugar plantations that dominate the national economy of Guatemala. They still consider Indians a single class (a rural proletariat or semiproletariat), but they point out that non-Indians also belong to that class. For them the major political question is not the class position of Guatemalan Indians, but whether Guatemalan Indians recognize (or can come to recognize) that they share the same class position with others who are not Indians.[24]

Since the issues involved in defining particular classes are extremely complex and politically loaded (as indicated by the debates described above), it is unrealistic to believe that the authors of this volume will fully agree, much less have the final word on them. Not every author, for example, takes my position that only colonial Indians can be considered peasants (in that they paid tribute to economic and political superiors), and postcolonial Indians are better understood as smallholders, artisans, petty commodity producers, or semiproletarians (in that they had no direct economic relations with economic superiors). But we all take a similar position with respect to certain basic aspects of class *relations* in Guatemala, namely:

(1) There was little or no "class" difference between Indians and ladinos until the plantation period; only Indians were subject to tribute, but both Indians and ladinos were mostly self-employed, producing small surpluses for trade, rather than tenants on large estates.[25] (2) With the development of coffee plantations, many Indians were reduced to the position of a "semi" or seasonal proletariat, while ladinos became either tenant farmers in eastern Guatemala or a full-fledged proletariat on the plantations; while most urban production remained artisanal, most "managerial" or "middle" positions in production (both rural and urban) were monopolized by ladinos. (3) The coffee oligarchy, only some of whom existed as important families in the colonial period, was mostly "white" and "capitalist" (rather than seigniorial) in their economic intentions if not their means. (4) A major element in the maintenance of Indian cultural identity has been Indian resistance to full proletariani-

zation and to capitalist relations of production within the community. And (5) in this respect, Indians feel little class identity with ladinos.

These aspects of class in Guatemala complicate political relations enormously. For one thing, class relations in Guatemala have almost always been mediated by the state, rather than existing as stark relations between oppressed and oppressor. In addition, relations of exploitation have varied widely by region, and in each region class relations have been mediated by culture (ethnicity) and community in different ways. Finally, the perduring reality of relatively class-homogeneous Indian communities has masked the real nature of class exploitation in Guatemala, as has the division between Indians and ladinos, who are in different class relations in different regions of the country. Thus, the authors in this volume basically believe that class, ethnic, community, and state relations in Guatemala have always and everywhere vastly complicated each other so that no general or singular analysis will do.

In summary, it is worth noting that, while we have not reached a consensus about every theoretical issue concerning Guatemala, we have reached a consensus about the critical scholarly issues in Guatemala today. In the aftermath of Guatemala's most horrendous period of political struggle, we all agree that serious scholarship in Guatemala must address questions about the cultural as well as the political-economic relations between Indians and the Guatemalan state as these relations have developed over time and varied over space.

Notes

1. Anthropologists of the 1940s and 1950s (e.g., Tax 1942, 1952; Redfield 1956b), anxious to provide a cultural rather than racial definition of Guatemala's Indians, attempted to define Guatemala's Indians on the basis of certain cultural traits (language, dress, religion), following the approach to culture typical of the era (see Warren 1978, for a critique of the approach as applied to Guatemala). They described a continuum of people, more or less Indian or ladino, regardless of what the persons involved considered themselves to be (cf. Adams 1956a). A later generation (e.g., Colby and van den Berghe 1969; Pansini 1977), influenced by Barth (1969), took the position that ethnic identities were not primordial—and thus there were no objective criteria such as language, dress, or religion by which identity could be established. For them, identity was established by relationships and boundaries between groups in which the elements defining the groups could change with time and circumstances. The key phenomenon for these anthropologists was "passing," that is, that over time Indians could and did become non-Indians or ladinos (cf. van den Berghe 1968). At roughly the same time, those influenced by a Marxist perspective (cf. Stavenhagen 1975; W. Smith 1977) argued that Indian culture was maintained by the power structure to facilitate "superexploitation." In all of these lines of reasoning, the persistence

of Indian culture into the twentieth century resulted from the fact of Guatemala's backwardness and marginality to the political and economic currents of the modern world, a view with which the authors in this volume take issue.   X

2. The early students of surviving Mayan tradition (e.g., La Farge and Byers 1931; Oakes 1951) were eclipsed by the functionalists who dominated early anthropology in Guatemala (see note 1). Augmented by the kind of ethnohistoric expertise brought to the field by Robert Carmack (1973, 1979, 1981), such studies are presently experiencing a strong revival (see, e.g., Tedlock 1982; Hill and Monaghan 1987).

3. With very few exceptions (see note 2), studies of cultural change among Guatemalan Indians have assumed that national or world-level institutions have transformed Indian communities, without considering the way in which these institutions have been affected by local culture and social patterns (cf. La Farge 1940; Adams 1957; Nash 1967; Stavenhagen 1975; W. Smith 1977; Warren 1978). Recent historical work (e.g., McCreery 1976, 1986; Lutz 1982; C. Smith 1984a; Handy 1984; Lovell 1985; Pinto Soria 1986) is only now beginning to revise that picture.

4. Scholars have variously described relations between Indians and non-Indians in Guatemala as relatively benign cultural separatism (Tax 1942; Redfield 1956b), race relations (cf. Siegel 1941; Gillin 1945, 1948, Brintnall 1979a), caste relations (Tumin 1952), cultural pluralism (Colby and van den Berghe 1969), and culturally disguised class relations (Martínez Peláez 1971; Stavenhagen 1975; W. Smith 1975). At various times debates have raged over the characterization issue (race, caste, class), based on the fact that members of the oppressed majority (Indians) could "choose" to become members of the oppressing group (ladinos), and had been able to do so virtually since the conquest. The child of mixed biological heritage, moreover, was not automatically assigned to the group of lowest social prestige—as is the situation with blacks in the United States. These two phenomena meant to North American anthropologists that one could not consider Indians in Guatemala a "castelike" group, and that to talk about racism in Guatemala was to impose a North American view of differences on a very distinct situation. Those who have contested this view have either chosen to talk in broadly "national" class terms (e.g., Stavenhagen 1975) or to discuss the difficulty of passing at the local level (e.g., Brintnall 1979a). Only now are scholars of Guatemala attempting to deal with ideology and practice at both local and national levels and their interacting effects.

5. These have been the terms of a recent debate about Indian culture within Guatemala (cf. Gúzman Böckler and Herbert 1970; Martínez Peláez 1971; Solórzano Foppa 1982; Rosada 1987; Cojtí Cuxil 1988), where local scholars address the "Indian question" as it bears on issues of class, revolution, cultural authenticity, and national identity. North Americans have played little role in this Guatemalan debate, which is surprising given the centrality of this issue for scholars in other parts of Indian Latin America (for Mexico, see González Casanova 1965; Warman 1981; Wasserstrom 1983; Farriss 1984; for Peru, see Stern 1982; Mallon 1983; Spalding 1984; G. Smith 1989). For a discussion of the Guatemalan debate in relation to these others, see C. Smith (1987c).

6. This charge, originally made against anthropologists and historians who

dealt with "oriental" cultures (Said 1978) could easily be leveled against much Guatemalan ethnography, early and late. But since 1970, marked by Richard Adams's national-level treatment of Guatemalan culture and institutions (1970), the more characteristic failing of Guatemalan history and ethnography has been that of emphasizing world-system economic forces and ignoring local-level and culturally distinctive social relations in Guatemala (C. Smith 1984a).

7. Until recently, North American scholars who worked in Guatemala have been notably nonreflexive about their contradictory role as scholars from the imperial centers that have added to the oppressive social conditions in the country they have studied (C. Smith 1987c), even as they have adopted Latin American critiques, such as dependency theory, of their homelands and their scholarship (see Cardoso 1977). Current events in Guatemala, more than "postmodern critiques" of anthropology (e.g., Marcus and Fischer 1986), have done much to change that (see, e.g., C. Smith and Boyer 1987; Carmack 1988).

8. This wording is taken from Dunkerley (1988:431), whose controlled outrage about the willful ignorance of the West about the situation in Guatemala is refreshing, if unique.

9. Virtually all modern sources estimate the current Indian population of Guatemala as 50 percent or more (e.g., Carmack et al. 1982), though the 1980 census identifies only 41.9 percent of the population as Indian, down from 53.6 in 1950, and 64.7 percent in 1880 when the first official national census was taken. While it was common for earlier students to attribute the changes in population to "passing" (cf. van den Berghe 1968), John Early (1975) has shown by careful reconstruction of birth and marriage statistics that much of the change can be attributed to changing census definitions of Indians.

10. Sol Tax (1937) was the first to insist that the municipio was the appropriate unit for studying Indian communities rather than language areas. Most have assumed this was so because this unit was imposed upon Indians by the Spanish administration (cf. C. Smith 1984b). Recent historical work on municipios has complicated the picture, since some have found units other than municipios (parcialidades) to have been the key social groupings before congregación (see Hill and Monaghan 1987), while others suggest that what are now municipios existed as communities even before the conquest (see Lovell and Swezey 1989). Few, however, dispute that municipios bound the relevant community in most parts of western Guatemala (see, e.g., Collins 1980; Piel 1989). Since Tax, most anthropologists have accepted the municipio as the relevant cultural unit (e.g., Wagley 1941; Reina 1957; A. Moore 1967; Nash 1967; Madigan 1976; Falla 1978a; Warren 1978; Brintnall 1979b; Watanabe 1984). Unfortunately, this has led anthropologists to concentrate on small or nucleated municipios, which do not represent the communities of most Indians.

11. For interesting discussions of the widespread Western belief that culture embodies race and class (heritage, broadly defined), see Szwed (1975) and Stolcke (1984).

12. One example of this willful ignorance of Indians by Guatemala's political elite can be taken from the 1880s, when the Liberal state was attempting the most momentous political-economic transformation ever experienced in Guatemala, the creation of a coffee-export economy. In a four-year run of a newsletter

of the period devoted to the ensuing changes (*El Progreso*) only one article directly addressed the "Indian question" as a factor in those changes. Yet the main underlying issue in the discussions was how Indians would be drawn into the new economy (Steven Palmer, personal communication). One sees the same pattern of deliberate ignorance combined with fear (cf. Adams, chap. 6) in Guatemala's present newspapers.

13. The following discussion of regions in Guatemala distinguishes natural regions, based mainly on altitude (the most significant natural limitation on land use in Guatemala), and economic regions, based on human use and transformation of the landscape (see C. Smith 1978 for a fuller discussion of the difference). Most regionalizations of Guatemala have mixed natural, economic, administrative, and cultural criteria, following local usage. The distinctions made here do not assume that which is socially determined to be natural, thus highlighting the economic, political, and cultural transformations of landscape and spatial relations through history.

14. Until very recently the bulk of Guatemala's plantation labor force has come from the western highlands. Today, however, much of the labor comes from local settlements and cities, from El Salvador, and from eastern Guatemala. Thus, one can no longer see the western highlands as a key economic zone in modern Guatemala, a phenomenon that has allowed the military to wreak havoc in the area in the 1980s with relatively little lowering of plantation production.

15. Guatemala is currently divided into twenty-two departments, each with an administrative center through which state bureaucrats, appointed by the state and almost invariably ladinos, oversee local politics. Municipios are smaller administrative units, whose political representatives are members of the local community and are selected in a variety of ways depending on the ethnic composition of the community (see Silvert 1954; Kitchen 1955). There are 325 municipios in Guatemala, approximately 150 of them mostly Indian; most of these are located in the western highlands of the country.

16. According to most of the cited authorities, liberal social scientists mean by the state the institutions of territorial governance and control; they assume that various interest groups compete for control over those institutions, that the state itself has no particular interest, and that one can treat only particular state regimes when talking about state interests. Marxists, in contrast, assume that the interests of the state are those of the dominant classes, be they capitalist or noncapitalist; they too assume that the state has no interest independent of the classes directing it.

17. Migdal (1988) argues that a similar dynamic exists in much of the Third World where, he suggests, one typically finds "strong" societies and "weak" states. The argument he develops is that the mid-level organizations of social control in civil society (e.g., legal systems, religion or ideology, education), usually being colonial importations, are often state impositions rather than independent forms of organization, and thus do not moderate or legitimate state control at the local level. Under these circumstances, state power is basically coercive rather than hegemonic, which leads to the kind of dialectic we describe here between local-level resistance and greater state coercion. Where we differ from Migdal is in locating much of the explanation for the phenomenon in the

history of internal social relations rather than in the pressure of external political forces.

18. This notion, originally developed by Gramsci (1971), helps explain why certain states that are relatively weak in terms of infrastructural power (such as colonial Guatemala or prerevolutionary China) can maintain power without continuous or strenuous use of coercion. Interesting treatments of the way states can manipulate cultural belief and nationalist myths to gain greater hegemonic control in society can be found in Fox (n.d.).

19. We consider this point to have been reached in the 1540s, some twenty years after the conquest, because a state administrative system had by then replaced raw military power (see MacLeod 1973; Woodward 1985a; Kramer 1989).

20. Collins (1980) describes this process in one Guatemalan community, Jacaltenango. A fuller description of the process can be found for neighboring Chiapas (part of colonial Guatemala) in Wasserstrom (1983).

21. See note 15.

22. None of the authors in this volume attempts a full theorization of mode of production or relations of production in Guatemala. Most of us emphasize historical and political variations in both capitalist and noncapitalist production relations, an approach usefully captured in theoretical terms by Michael Burawoy (1985).

23. The distinction between formal and real subsumption of labor in capitalism was made by Marx (1976b, Appendix), who shows the limits to capitalist development in economies where labor power is not yet a commodity—that is, where workers are coerced rather than voluntary.

24. Guzmán Böckler and Herbert (1970) provide more explicit detail about the mechanisms of internal exploitation than others. They pay special attention to the unequal distribution of land and the great disparity between Indian and ladino per capita ownership of land. There is no question that ladinos do monopolize the most productive resources in Guatemala, land being only one of these resources. But class relations are determined by more than people's relations to things, such as productive resources; they are determined by people's social relations to each other. The question, then, is what role does land, for example, play in mediating relations between social groups. In the case of western Guatemala, where there is little in the way of landlord-tenant relations, the relation is at best indirect.

25. A few large sheep estates existed in the sixteenth and early seventeenth centuries (Lovell 1985), but they required few workers. The indigo boom in the eighteenth century established large estates mostly in what is now El Salvador (MacLeod 1973) and those parts of eastern Guatemala where Indian culture was mostly eradicated. In general, however, estate production in Guatemala was quite limited until the late nineteenth century (Pinto Soria 1981), and always occurred in fairly small regions of the country (MacLeod 1983a).

Part 1:
Historical Formation

2. Core and Periphery in Colonial Guatemala

Christopher H. Lutz
Centro de Investigaciones Regionales de Mesoamérica
Antigua, Guatemala
W. George Lovell
Department of Geography, Queen's University at Kingston, Canada

Almost twenty years have elapsed since Murdo MacLeod (1973) published his landmark work on Spanish Central America. MacLeod's labor, as the late Charles Gibson (1974) was quick to recognize, produced an "intelligible framework" against which all subsequent studies of land and life in colonial Guatemala henceforth could be measured. MacLeod, however, was not only diligent enough to hack a trail through the historiographic unknown; he also has been honest enough to admit that what he mapped out as an early pioneer must inevitably be refined, modified, and altered by later settlers of the same scholarly terrain (MacLeod 1983a:189–190). Anyone who has contemplated the insightful maxim of Engels—that nothing is eternal but eternally changing—would likely consider MacLeod's acknowledgment a matter of common sense, but the academy tends still to be populated by many who prefer the world of knowledge to be tidy and fixed, not blurred, fragmented, and subject always to continuous reassessment.

Our intent in this chapter is to take one element of MacLeod's framework and develop it in the light of some research issues that have emerged since the time he first formulated his ideas about the nature of the colonial experience in Central America. We focus attention on the divide between, in MacLeod's schema, a ladino "east" and an Indian "west" in Spanish Guatemala. Our discussion casts the cleavage observed and explained by MacLeod, the scars of which persist and bleed to this day, in terms of the historical evolution of a developed core and an underdeveloped periphery. We examine, first, the resource base of Guatemala as perceived by imperial Spain, defining the territorial extent of a colonial core and a colonial periphery. Our chapter then sketches, for core and periphery, patterns of landholding and settlement, after which we outline salient conditions in both regions of economic and social life. We lean heavily for our portrayal on long-standing interest on the part of Lutz (1982) in the city and environs of Santiago, today

Antigua, and on the part of Lovell (1985) in the Cuchumatán highlands. While Carol Smith, foremost of all, has already contributed much to the formulation of core-periphery relationships in Guatemala, what concerns us most is to give such representations concrete, colonial-period origins (C. Smith 1978, 1987b).

The Resource Base

Spaniards appraised the resource base of Guatemala in accordance with certain needs and desires dictated by their culture. Theirs was a multi-purpose enterprise, one in which spiritual, political, and economic motives figured to varying degree. They looked at Guatemala through very different eyes than did its autochthonous inhabitants, and set to work immediately. Very soon after Spanish hegemony was established, the cultural landscape began to change dramatically, the process of transformation set in motion by inadvertent as well as planned courses of action.

The mark of imperial Spain, to summarize MacLeod, was traced differentially as follows. Being entrepreneurs, lay Spaniards were drawn to areas where environmental conditions or natural endowments would maximize material enrichment. They also preferred, as much as possible, to settle and live in parts that resembled, more than were dissimilar to, their places of origin. For these reasons, early on, colonial Guatemala began to assume a very different appearance to the north and west of Santiago, where opportunities to generate wealth were slight, than it did to the south and east of the capital city, where greater potential existed for Crown and private gain (MacLeod 1973:308, 1983a:193–95).[1]

The divide MacLeod identifies is not entirely one that separates "highland" from "lowland." Such a distinction, while neat and convenient, would in fact be misleading. If we think, cardinally, of all the lands lying south and east of Santiago as forming the "core" and all those lying north and west as forming the "periphery," this binary geography fits our present state of knowledge reasonably well. It does so because such a conceptualization enables us not only to accommodate MacLeod's dichotomy but to elaborate upon it by identifying highland and lowland regions within both the core and the periphery (see map 5). Thus defined, the core includes the colonial capital and its surrounding jurisdiction (the Corregimiento del Valle, largely coterminous with the present-day Departments of Sacatepéquez, Chimaltenango, and Guatemala) as well as the eastern highlands (present-day Jalapa and Chiquimula), the eastern lowlands (El Progreso and Zacapa), and the southern lowlands all along the Pacific coast from Soconusco (in present-day Mexico) to

Map 5. Core and Periphery in Colonial Guatemala

Sonsonate (in present-day El Salvador). The periphery incorporates a vast expanse that stretches from the Sierra de los Cuchumatanes (in present-day Huehuetenango and El Quiché) past the Sierra de Chamá (in present-day Alta Verapaz) to the Sierra de Santa Cruz (in present-day Izabal) as well as the northern lowlands drained by the Río Ixcán, the Río Xaclbal, the Río Chixoy, and the upper tributaries of the Río de la Pasión.

The resource base of the core attracted the attention of Spaniards much more than did the resource base of the periphery. Consequently, Spanish colonists settled first in and around the Valleys of Almolonga and Panchoy, where wheat could be grown and cattle raised: white bread and red meat, to the conqueror, were infinitely more palatable than Indian corn and the strange fowl we know today as turkeys. Thereafter, with their African slaves, Spaniards spread south and east into lower-lying *tierra templada* and *tierra caliente*, lands where the climate ranged from warm to hot, where soils were generally fertile, and where, most important of all, cash crops such as cacao, cochineal, indigo, sugarcane (primarily for the preparation of cane liquor or *aguardiente*), and tobacco could be cultivated (MacLeod 1983a:193–203; Zamora Acosta 1985:295–301). A sustained Spanish presence, together with accelerated rates of native depopulation, saw in these parts the emergence of ladino Guatemala, a region inhabited predominantly by people of mixed Maya, Spanish, and African descent. Limited commercial options in the periphery, by contrast, meant always that Spaniards there were few in number: Indians, even at the nadir of the demographic collapse brought about by sicknesses introduced unknowingly by Europeans and Africans, never constituted a minority of the population (Lovell and Swezey 1982; Zamora Acosta 1983; Newson 1986:3–7). They and their ways survived the biological and cultural onslaught of conquest to produce, especially in the far north and west, an Indian Guatemala that endures today.

Landholding and Settlement

The lure of warmer, lower altitudes in the highland core guided Spanish rationale for founding there a capital city from which to govern. Santiago en Almolonga was founded in 1527, but was destroyed by mud slides that swept down the slopes of Agua volcano in 1541, resulting in a search for another site for the capital city. The new capital, known as Santiago de Guatemala, was established a little north of the former one (today Ciudad Vieja) in the Valley of Panchoy (Markman 1966:11; Lutz 1982:39–41, 55–61). Since the distance between sites chosen for the capital was not great, landholding patterns changed very little as a result of the move. From the late 1520s Spanish *vecinos* (Spanish residents) received grants of land in Almolonga, Panchoy, and neighboring valleys, land on which they settled their Indian slaves. These slaves were instructed on how to grow wheat and to tend cattle, and were expected also to provide residents of the capital with corn, fruits, and vegetables, in addition to furnishing Spanish households with fodder for their horses and firewood for their kitchens.

After Indian slavery was abolished, around 1550, an expanding Spanish population then moved north and east of Santiago into other parts of the highland core. In these parts, around Comalapa, Chimaltenango, Sumpango, and Amatitlán, more wheat farms were established and, on temperate land, sugar *ingenios* (farms) and *trapiches* (mills). These estates certainly encroached on Indian holdings but, with the native population in precipitous decline throughout the sixteenth century, a decreasing amount of land was necessary to support dwindling Amerindian numbers (Lutz 1981, n.d.a).

Occupation by the conqueror of fertile terrain in the highland core, however, does not mean that the landscape literally became one of Spanish settlement. Most landowners actually lived in Santiago and arranged for other Spaniards and *castas*—people of mixed Maya, European, and African descent—to administer their estates. Creole families tended to own rural properties but were not the dominant elite in colonial Guatemala. Land was cheap and the returns from working it were relatively modest. Stephen Webre (1980, 1981) has shown that economic power in Guatemala, by the late sixteenth century, came to be held by peninsular Spanish newcomers, colonists who arrived with ample capital and with well-placed connections. Their ranks, Webre demonstrates, were replenished by other peninsular arrivals throughout the seventeenth and eighteenth centuries.[2]

While most elite Spaniards lived in Santiago, several towns in the highland core began by the late sixteenth century to be settled by castas, free blacks, and nonelite Spaniards. These people were employed in trading activities that supplied the capital, but also engaged in the transport of commodities between the highland core and the lowland core, which lay farther south and east. When the Indian population of the highland core, after a century or more of decline, began finally to stabilize and then to grow, with population recovery came increased pressure on land resources. The end result, especially in some communities close to Santiago, was Indian landlessness and loss of Indian identity, or ladinoization. We can only surmise that this process shifted eastward toward the end of the eighteenth century with the decision to relocate the colonial capital, following a series of disastrous earthquakes, on the present site of Guatemala City (Zilbermann de Luján 1987; Lutz n.d.a:25–27, n.d.b).

Contemporaneous with the process of settling beyond the immediate vicinity of Santiago was a gradual occupation, by Spaniards and their African slaves as well as by free castas, of the lowland core, a region that today includes the *boca costa*, or Pacific piedmont, the Pacific coastal plain, and the Oriente. As in the highland core, on suitable parts of these lands Spaniards established *haciendas* (estates), ingenios, and trapiches. More chronic Indian depopulation throughout the lowland core, however, left even more land available for Spanish exploitation. The use of it, consequently, tended to be more extensive than intensive. Cattle *estancias* (ranches) were set up, but in many parts the animals reverted to a feral state and roamed wild. Far more Indian communities in the lowland core than in the highland core, in spite of Crown prohibitions, came to have growing numbers of poor Spanish and casta populations.

These people worked on nearby estates, hunted cattle for hides and tallow, engaged in the manufacture and sale of clandestine liquor and, most persistently of all, sought to seize control of Indian cacao production (MacLeod 1973, 1983a:193–203; Lutz n.d.b).[3]

Cacao is an interesting case. So long as Indians survived, most of the groves that grew it remained in their hands. But Spaniards, whether as *encomenderos* or traders, were the recipients and handlers of the harvested crop, and the large profits to be had from the sale of cacao accrued to them, not to Indian producers.[4] In spite of Indian migration from highland to lowland areas in order to bring in the harvest, cacao production declined as local Indian communities in the Oriente and along the Pacific coast thinned out or, in some cases, disappeared altogether (MacLeod 1985:58, 1973:87).[5]

Unlike cacao, which depended heavily on year-round Indian labor and which was most often grown on Indian land, the other major export crop of the colonial period—indigo—was cultivated, harvested, and processed for export on Spanish holdings known as *obrajes de tinte añil*. Indians (actually prohibited by law from being compelled to work in obrajes), African slaves, and castas produced this valuable and much-sought dye. Unlike other crops, *xiquilite*, the grass from which indigo comes, could be conveniently grown in conjunction with the raising of cattle (MacLeod 1973:380–381). Labor demands being less, indigo in the seventeenth century replaced cacao as the preeminent export earner for entrepreneurial Spaniards. While these two cash crops did much to gear the resource base of the lowland core to the booms and busts of an export economy, it is important also to observe that huge expanses south and east of Santiago were worked less ambitiously, producing grains, cattle and other livestock, tobacco, and sugarcane for local consumption. These activities did not make many people rich, but they made possible effective Spanish and casta settlement of sizable areas of the lowland core (MacLeod 1973:191–192; Lutz n.d.b, n.d.c).[6]

Landholding and settlement patterns in the periphery differed quite markedly from those that prevailed in the core. To portray the periphery as devoid of entrepreneurial potential would not be accurate. Scattered throughout the highland zone, around Quezaltenango, Totonicapán, and Huehuetenango, were pockets of fertile land where wheat grew well and cattle thrived, two conditions always conducive to the arousal and maintenance of Spanish interest (Veblen 1975; Lovell 1983b). More important, though, than these admittedly modest ventures in mixed farming was the emergence, in the seventeenth century, of commercial ranching, especially the raising of sheep, mules, horses, and cattle on the lush upland meadows of the Cuchumatán *páramo* (high plateau) above Chiantla and Aguacatán. Here were amassed, by shrewd and careful purchase, properties that by the eighteenth century comprised some of the most sizable haciendas in all Central America (Lovell 1985:118–139).

What is crucial to realize, however, is that Spanish acquisition of land in the periphery was not attained at the expense of chronic dispossession of native communities. Indians who lived near Spanish towns obviously lost out. So also did those whose lands bordered on the large Cuchumatán ranches, although it must be recognized that these operations came into being on alpine pastures never fully utilized as part of the aboriginal economy. Native communities in the highland periphery simply did not have to contend with the intensity of Spanish pressure that was exerted on land in the colonial core, primarily because of a relative lack of exploitative options. Furthermore, Indians along the northern edge of the highland periphery had the additional advantage of occupying and farming, if only on a temporary basis, the sparsely settled terrain of the lowland periphery. This practice was not without risk, for in these remote parts lived unsubdued, hostile tribes like the Lacandón and Chol Manché. We know almost nothing about what went on in the lowland periphery, save that it constituted a zone of refuge, an open frontier whose dense rain forests lay well beyond the reach of Spanish control, and that highland groups (the Ixil, the Kanjobal, the Kekchí) would periodically migrate to fish, hunt, gather, and farm there. The land base of native communities in the highland periphery, in theory protected by a legal system Indians quickly learned to engage, was thus left reasonably intact, even if certain Old World animals, plants, fruits, and vegetables altered the complexion of what was grown and now grazed on Maya fields (Crosby 1972; Borah 1983:40–43; Lovell 1985:128–129).[7]

Much more tampered with in the periphery, but in the end with mixed results, were indigenous patterns of settlement. The domestic arrangements in place when the Spaniards arrived, with populations considerably more dispersed than nucleated, suited neither lay demands for efficient provision of tribute nor the church's concern with speedy conversion to Christianity. By the mid-sixteenth century the ambitious task of resettling scattered groups in more accessible locales was well under way, led in the highland periphery (as in the highland core) by friars of the Dominican, Franciscan, and Mercedarian orders. More so than their secular counterparts to the south and east, members of the regular clergy charged with the evangelizing mission of *congregación* (forced native resettlement) found their work beset constantly with problems (Lovell and Swezey 1990). Judged purely on the evidence of the number of towns and villages founded—some three hundred throughout Guatemala by 1600—congregación left a lasting imprint on the landscape (van Oss 1986:31–32). But all over the highland periphery, centripetal motion propelled either by missionary zeal or fiscal urge ran counter to sensible centrifugal tendencies on the part of Indians. For various reasons—to flee from an outbreak of disease, to escape the demands of officialdom, or to cultivate ancestral land—Indians resisted the nucleation imposed on them by steady repopulation of distant places they or their predecessors were moved from. Again, the hand of the conqueror left its mark, but not always in the manner envisioned by imperial design (Lovell 1983a).[8]

Conditions of Economic Life

The economy of the highland core in the early sixteenth century was based almost exclusively on the exploitation of native labor, which was furnished by Indian slaves or provided under terms spelled out in specific grants of *encomienda* as *servicio personal* (personal service).[9] Much of this changed after 1550, when Alonso López de Cerrato abolished both Indian slavery, concentrated in and around Santiago, and servicio personal, much more widespread throughout the Audiencia jurisdiction over which he presided (Lovell, Lutz, and Swezey 1984). Indians who lived in barrios within the capital or in pueblos within the core henceforth paid tribute in cash and foodstuffs, and were taken on by Spaniards under the favorable hiring arrangements, for the latter, of *repartimiento* and *servicio ordinario* (normal labor service) (Sherman 1979:92; Lutz n.d.a).[10]

While encomiendas of certain Indian pueblos within the core remained in private hands, more and more were taken over by the Crown. This was especially true of cacao-rich pueblos, over which the Crown ultimately wrested control from once-powerful encomenderos. We discern, by the late sixteenth century, a situation wherein the Crown exercised its authority to a greater extent over core encomiendas, allowing those of the periphery, valued at much less, to remain in the possession of individuals (see Sherman 1979).[11] The cacao boom, however, was by this time long past its peak.

Tribute was paid to individual Spaniards and the Spanish Crown by all married adults, both women and men, and by widows, widowers, and single persons over sixteen and less than fifty-six years of age. These categories remained unchanged, with the exception of minor adjustments, until the 1750s, when women were declared exempt from tribute payment (Lutz 1982:191; see also Cook and Borah 1971–1979:1, 275–276). Tribute by itself might not have been overly burdensome to many communities, but under Spanish rule Indians had to meet a number of other fiscal obligations, some legal, several others decidedly less so. One exaction peculiar to the core, levied on Indians who lived around

Santiago on lands owned by Spaniards, was the *terrazgo*, a system whereby rents were paid on house plots and adjacent *milpas* (Lutz 1982:102–105). In addition, all Indian communities, both in the core and in the periphery, had to fulfill fiscal and labor obligations to the church (MacLeod 1973:314–315; van Oss 1986:85–89).

While most Spanish bureaucrats aspired to enrich themselves at the expense of their Indian subjects, this goal was not always easy to attain, more so if an administrative charge was located in the highland core, where the watchful eyes of higher, more concerned authorities might prevail (Sherman 1979:197–198). More serious abuses of office tended to occur in the lowland core, where various government representatives, such as *alcaldes mayores* and *jueces de milpa*, sought to procure, by whatever means necessary, a share in the cacao trade (MacLeod 1973:76, 210, 240).[12]

When Spanish officials in the lowland core were not extracting payments and bribes from their Indian subjects, they devised other ways to make money. One was simply to overlook, for a suitable fee, consistent violation of the laws governing Indian labor, such as the illegal use of Indians in obrajes de tinte añil. Similarly, *jueces repartidores* in the highland core, charged with administering the labor repartimiento, could ignore (again for a price) the illegal hiring-out of Indians by a Spanish farmer (*labrador*). These recurrent abuses, at the same time as they enriched corrupt Spaniards, simply made life even more difficult for subordinate Indians (MacLeod 1973:186–189, 209, 295, 313; Luján Muñoz 1988:61–66).

The system of labor repartimiento in the highland core, even without abuses of office, placed a tremendous burden on Indian communities. From the mid-sixteenth century on, Indians here toiled under the demands of repartimiento. They were set to work at various tasks: they farmed, tended flocks and herds of animals, hauled loads, helped build houses, baked bread, or cleaned streets in the capital city. The topic is in need of detailed, systematic analysis, but evidence indicates that Indian communities had to provide up to one-quarter of their male tributary population at any given time to work for a token wage of three to five *reales* per laborer each week. The amount paid inched upward during the course of the colonial period, but was seldom a sum commensurate with the value of labor expended. In the highland core, repartimiento obligations were in force up to forty-nine weeks each year, the only periods free of the duty being Holy Week, the days around Christmas, and the time during which celebration of a town saint occurred. This meant, effectively, that able-bodied male tributaries were required to work away from their communities as much as twelve weeks each year. Practically nothing is known about the use of repartimiento labor in the lowland core, except for its use in lead mining in Chiquimula (MacLeod 1973:261; Sherman 1979:191–207; Lutz 1982:339,356).[13]

Agricultural labor in the lowland core appears to have involved more the use of cash advances, including mild varieties of debt peonage, than outright coercion. Such a strategy encouraged Indians from both the core and the periphery to abandon their communities, and tributary obligations, in order to work on Spanish-owned estates. These migrations served only to promote further ladinoization among an already diminished indigenous population (MacLeod 1983:193–194, 1985).

We still know relatively little about Indian systems of production and exchange, with the notable exception of cacao (see MacLeod 1973:76–83).[14] Indians appear to have operated with relative freedom when they dealt in inexpensive items such as corn, vegetables, and firewood. When they traded in more desirable or expensive items, say cacao or cotton cloth, Indians soon ran into trouble, including even outright theft of their merchandise. In Santiago, Spanish authorities attempted from time to time to protect Indian merchants who arrived in the capital from shakedowns and forced sales at the hands of African and casta *regatones* (middlemen) who ventured out from the city to meet incoming traders. These regatones, however, were quite often in the employ of Spanish *patrones* (bosses). For the Indians, the only practical precaution against this plunder was to travel in groups and to hope that a show of numbers might dissuade potential thugs and robbers from mounting an attack. The safest course of action, if not the most profitable, was to trade in inexpensive products with low resale value (Lutz 1982:338).

The few Spaniards who sought wealth and prosperity in the periphery did so by concentrating their energies on two main activities, mining and ranching. The extraction of silver at Chiantla, while never as profitable as the operations set up around Tegucigalpa, yielded incomes not to be scoffed at, both for private individuals who, in the early sixteenth century, first organized mining and for the local clergy who enjoyed the proceeds later on (Lovell 1985:106, 213). Silver from Chiantla was used to decorate church altars throughout Guatemala. Livestock ranching, again focused on Chiantla, where annual fairs featuring prize heads of cattle, sheep, and horses attracted buyers from all over New Spain, brought handsome returns for the handful of families who dominated the enterprise, and must also have generated, in the form of taxes, tangible returns for the Crown. Repartimiento drafts from nearby Indian communities supplied the mines and ranches with necessary labor, but there is evidence also that the tending of livestock for Spanish hacendados carried with it the risk of debt peonage (Lovell 1985:106–107, 121–126).

If mining and ranching, for the most part, were carried out within the boundaries of colonial law, most certainly not was the practice of forced sale or acquisition known as the *reparto de efectos*.[15] By this means government officials and even parish priests would require Indians to purchase from them goods they could not afford or had no obvious need of. A related abuse was to distribute loads of raw cotton and demand that it be worked, without pay, into thread and cloth. The finished item was later sold at market, with profits accruing to the distributor, not the producer (Lovell 1985:108–111).[16] Involvement with reparto de efectos was certainly not restricted to Spaniards who presided over native charges in the periphery, but available evidence suggests that distance from responsible bureaucracy in the capital meant a higher incidence of the practice north and west of Santiago than in the highland or lowland core.

The above features aside, most Indians in the periphery dealt indirectly with Spaniards as participants in a tribute economy. Twice each year native communities were required to furnish, either for encomenderos or the Crown, stipulated amounts of locally and regionally available products. These were then auctioned off, with cash benefits passed on to the appropriate recipient. Indian tribute in Guatemala always amounted to a significant portion of total Crown revenue.[17] Only after demands for tribute had been met could energies be marshaled toward the mundane but vital chores of Maya peasant life, especially the cultivation of corn, upon which all family and group survival ultimately depended.

Conditions of Social Life

The social life of any collective is difficult to depict without invoking case particulars that depart significantly from, and in the end undermine, general patterns and processes. Indian communities in Guatemala are no exception. We find it hard to imagine, for instance, that what Adriaan van Oss (1986:75) calls the "hermetic" Indian community was ever commonplace in colonial Guatemala, least of all in the core zone. This does not mean, however, that Indian communities in the core were obliterated by Spanish intrusion. We perceive, above all else, marked spatial variation in how the impact of colonial rule was felt. Certain factors helped determine the preservation or decay of core communities. These include: (1) the survival, after the disastrous epidemics and demographic collapse of the sixteenth century, of a viable population base, which ensured that a community could maintain itself and eventually recover; (2) the extent of Spanish encroachment onto community land; (3) the ability to maintain control of sufficient terrazgo-free agricultural lands to support community numbers; (4) the capacity to obtain new lands, which often pitted one community against a rival, adjoining one; (5) the size of Spanish and casta populations living either within an Indian community or close by; and (6) the option of exploiting local craft skills or a raw material base, which would lessen dependence on earning a living outside the community. Another key variable, of course, was altitude, especially the influence it exerted on whether or not land could produce crops sought by Spaniards and ladinos. In core communities where most or all of the above conditions were favorable, Indians could adapt and survive, despite often overbearing pressures. Where, say, half or more of these conditions did not apply, Indian communities withered and even disintegrated. Some specificity, some detail, is clearly in order.

The Indian barrios of Santiago, with small surviving populations by the late sixteenth century, changed radically in the face of shortages of agricultural land, excessive labor and fiscal demands, and incursions into their living space by castas. Nearby, San Lucas Cabrera limped through the seventeenth century only to breathe its last gasp and die, as an Indian community, in the eighteenth. Other core communities, including the Milpa of San Lorenzo Monroy, were farther away from the city and managed to maintain a viable population base. But San Lorenzo was affected by Spanish pressure on its land and by the burden of terrazgo payments, which jointly contributed to its gradual ladinoization by the late colonial period (see Lutz 1981).[18]

By contrast, San Lorenzo's neighbor to the west, San Antonio Aguas Calientes, a community situated on the northern shore of Lake Quinizilapa, survived remarkably well. When, about 1550, Indian slaves belonging to Juan de Chaves were emancipated, their former patrón, before departing for Spain, bequeathed to them the lands upon which San Antonio stood. This good fortune, among other things, meant no terrazgos had to be paid. San Antonio thus grew in size and shaped for itself a strong Cakchiquel identity, which lingers still (Lutz 1981; Annis 1987:28).

San Miguel Dueñas, on the southern shores of Lake Quinizilapa, had quite a different experience. Dueñas lies at a lower altitude than San Lorenzo. Around it, sugarcane can be grown. Spaniards encroached, settled African slaves, and exacted terrazgos from surviving Indians. The slave contingent became a nucleus of free mulattoes who, in the course of time, came to be considered ladinos. Rich lands, the Dueñas experience indicates, were both a blessing and a curse, the former if they could be retained, the latter if they prompted an interest on the part of the Spaniards that led, ultimately, to the ladinoization of Indian inhabitants (Lutz 1981; Annis 1987:24).

Indian communities in the lowland core, in aggregate, did not fare nearly as well as their counterparts in the highlands. Disease here, early on, took a heavy native toll. Later, seventeenth-century epidemics of more tropical than temperate Old World origin ravaged the survivors of the first waves of pestilence. These communities, furthermore, occupied lands on which cash crops could be grown. Already weakened by disease, they suffered even more with Spanish and ladino takeover of their lands (MacLeod 1973:229; Lovell and Swezey 1982; Newson 1985:27–34, 1986). With land acquisition came piecemeal settlement of the countryside, Spanish and casta residence within Indian communities, and also the founding of exclusive Spanish-casta population centers such as La Gomera and Villa de la Concepción de las Mesas (Luján Muñoz 1976). The intensity or degree of miscegenation varied from place to place, but the trend overall was the irreversible creation, in embryo, of the ladino in Guatemala. Indians who survived in these parts often had no recourse but to rent properties from newcomers who had usurped the native estate (Pinto Soria 1980:43).

Any evaluation of the nature of Maya social life must inevitably address Eric Wolf's celebrated model of the closed corporate peasant community. What perhaps needs to be stressed about this formulation, something that current debate on the subject tends to overlook, is that Wolf envisioned peasant communities in Mesoamerica as forming a cultural continuum toward only one end of which lie closed and corporate properties. His model, it seems to us, allows for situations in which communities can be less closed, less corporate. In the Guatemalan context, we might best regard Indian communities as social units regulated by systemic triggers that cause "closure" under pressure but permit "opening" in its absence. Thus perceived, Indian communities (in the periphery as well as in the core) varied internally along an "open-closed" continuum, their character at any given time dependent on the interplay of the variables identified earlier.

If we apply Wolf's model to the periphery, in theory we might expect communities there to be generally more "open" than "closed," chiefly because they were subjected to less external pressure than core communities. The available evidence is scant and inconclusive. Several studies exist that focus on how Maya communities have changed over time, but only two that we are aware of chart social evolution especially in terms of Wolf's vocabulary—the doctoral dissertation by Anne Collins (1980) on Jacaltenango and the recent collaboration of Robert Hill and John Monaghan (1987) on Sacapulas.[19]   Collins, by a meticulous sifting of materials housed in local as well as national archives, finds in the colonial experience of Jacaltenango the formation of a closed corporate community along the lines advanced by Wolf. Hers, to the best of our knowledge, is the first explicit attempt to test Wolf's hypothesis by innovative, ethnohistoric reconstruction. Hill and Monaghan, who were unable to work with local sources but who mine national ones most thoroughly, produce a rich ethnohistory that allows Sacapulas to be looked at, somewhat ironically, either as support for Wolf's model or as a case study that contradicts it. By demonstrating that Sacapulas was made up of several distinct social groups the Spaniards called *parciali-dades*, Hill and Monaghan illuminate a social heterogeneity brought about by indiscriminate congregación that runs counter to Wolf's construct. But, looked at carefully, parcialidades exhibit individually the very characteristics Wolf considers typical of closed corporate bonding. The colonial experience of Sacapulas, with parcialidades holding land and paying tribute as discrete Indian parts of a Spanish-conceived whole, may not be representative, but it is instructive (Hill and Monaghan 1987:43–62).[20] Among other things, what happened in and around Sacapulas enables us to view Indians, as Nancy Farriss (1983) insists we must, not as helpless puppets who marched to the beat of the conqueror's drum, but as flesh and blood actors who challenged authority, made a stand, and controlled their lives as best they could.

Revisionist depictions, by Farriss and others, have created Indians as subjects, not objects, as players who shaped their social situation as much as they were conditioned by it. While, historiographically, we acknowledge the importance of this development, it would serve little purpose, indeed would be counterproductive, if every Mesoamerican community were thus portrayed. Conquest was a variable experience, but it operated in Guatemala, whether in the core or in the periphery, always to ensure that Indians remained beholden and subservient to Spaniards. Ladinos, in time, came to replace Spaniards as the bane of Maya existence. If some elements of Wolf's model stand in need of reformulation, at least one does not. Conquest society was made up essentially of two social classes, the "dominant" and the "dominated," the conqueror and the conquered (Wolf 1957:8). In Guatemala, the latter never mounted a serious challenge in three hundred years to the rule and authority of the former, as occurred elsewhere (Martínez Peláez 1973; Taylor 1979; McFarlane 1982). In understanding how colonial subordination was first imposed and later maintained, we would be most remiss to underestimate the role of terror, the function of fear (Taussig 1987).

Efforts and Outcomes

Attempts by the Spanish Crown to create throughout its American dominion a "republic" of Spaniards that would exist harmoniously alongside a "republic" of Indians is widely acknowledged to have failed. In Guatemala, the "politics of segregation" that inspired the concept of "the two republics" had little to do, according to Magnus Mörner (1967:150–151), with making the "strong Indian character" of what we observe as the periphery and the "quite clear division" that existed between it and the core. Rather, asserts Mörner, "more likely it is due, historically considered, to a relative lack of economic stimuli" for outside penetration of the periphery and what he terms a "self-conscious attitude" on the part of the Indians who lived there. Nonetheless, Mörner concedes that "segregationist legislation served the Indians as a legal resource through which to strengthen their resistance against the intruders." He concludes, however, that "Indian aversion" was "more effective than the letter of the law in driving out undesirable intruders," even if "segregationist legislation" conformed to and served to reinforce a "spontaneous attitude." While we agree with Mörner that segregation, even to the north and west of Santiago, failed miserably as a protective policy, one could argue that parts of the periphery, at least in appearance, resembled what the Spaniards had in mind when they spoke of a "republic of Indians." By contrast, the more urbanized and proletarian-ized parts of the highland core, and virtually all the lowland core, suffered a near complete cultural transformation. In many instances, disease and miscegenation heralded the total destruction of Indian communities and the birth of a ladino society. In other instances, even close to Santiago and at higher altitudes in the Oriente, Indian communities held out, sometimes against shattering odds, up to independence and beyond.[21] The validity of general propositions notwithstanding— the Indian "west" and ladino "east" of Murdo MacLeod, the closed corporate peasant community of Eric Wolf, the notion of a colonial core and a colonial periphery suggested here—we must always when studying Guatemala be prepared to live with legitimate exceptions, no matter how much they cut against the grain of accepted or preferred designations.

How decisive a role, overall, did Spanish colonial policy actually play in the survival, decay, or destruction of Guatemalan Indian societies? While acknowledging the intent of enlightened legislation like the New Laws, and the commendable efforts of people like Bartolomé de Las Casas, Alonso López de Cerrato, García de Valverde, or Juan de Ramírez, we would contend that the conscious vision of imperial Spain amounted to very little.[22] Economic marginality in the Spanish scheme of empire, along with the unforeseen variable of Old World sickness and crucial ecological factors such as altitude, climate, and soil fertility, shaped the colonial experience in Guatemala more profoundly than did social blueprints like "the two republics." We must never forget, warns Carlos Fuentes (1985:33), to distinguish in Latin America between the "real country" and the "legal country." Under Spanish rule, the Maya of

Guatemala inhabited the former not the latter terrain, as they still do today, only under different terms of conquest.

Notes

1. For an appraisal of the cultural values and material preferences of the early Spanish settlers in the New World, see Foster (1960) and Sanchiz Ochoa (1976).
2. On the late-eighteenth-century elite, see Gustavo Palma Murga (1986:241–308). Jorge Luján Muñoz (1988:88–89), in agreement with MacLeod (1973:217–221), suggests a possible Spanish move to the land (wheat raising) in response to the seventeenth-century depression.
3. For a case study of Indian depopulation, increasing land availability, and extensive land use in central Mexico, especially cattle raising, see Lesley Byrd Simpson (1952).
4. The encomienda was a system of taxation by which means individual Spaniards or the Royal Treasury received tribute in goods and services from designated Indian communities. *Encomenderos*, recipients of encomiendas, traded them and made deals related to their worth as if they were capital investments. While theoretically the encomienda had nothing to do with land or landholding—it was designed to function as a fiscal not a territorial element of empire—in the realm of actual practice, encomiendas soon became place realities as much as tax realities. People lived in them, raised families in them, grew crops and tended animals in them, made salt and wove cotton cloth in them, and moved back and forth from highland to lowland ones in order to meet Spanish demands for cacao. Encomiendas, then, became real places, not just pensions or rewards scribbled on pieces of parchment (Lovell and Swezey 1990).
5. On cacao production and society in Soconusco, see Janine Gasco (1987).
6. For a more detailed discussion of cash crops in El Salvador from pre-Hispanic to modern times, see William R. Fowler, Jr. (1987:139–167). On tobacco cultivation in eastern Guatemala during the late colonial period, see Lawrence H. Feldman (1985:81).
7. Studies that depict life and economy in the lowland periphery include Jan de Vos (1980), Grant D. Jones (1983), and Nicole Percheron (n.d.).
8. For an example of population movement in the highland core, see Barbara E. Jones-Borg (1986:133, 139–140). For an example of Maya population movement in colonial Yucatan, see Nancy M. Farriss (1978).
9. See note 4.
10. Repartimiento in Guatemala took two forms: it was most of all a draft of forced native labor; in addition, the repartimiento (or reparto) de efectos was a mechanism of forced sale and compulsory acceptance of certain goods or commodities (see Lovell 1985:179).
11. Our knowledge of the encomienda in early colonial Guatemala, especially the pre-1548 history of the institution, has been considerably enhanced by the work of Wendy J. Kramer (1990).
12. Rich, unused, but badly damaged material on the abuses of *jueces de milpa* may be found in the Archivo General de Indias (AGI): Contaduría 971A and 971B. Useful material on this office can also be found in Manuel Rubio

Sánchez (1982).

13. Both the Archivo General de Indias and the Archivo General de Centroamérica (AGCA) contain extensive documentation, especially on seventeenth- and eighteenth-century repartimiento. A recent study that discusses repartimiento in the highland core is Pinto Soria (1987:33–37).

14. In late-sixteenth-century Sonconusco and Zapotitlán, Spaniards pushed the surviving Indians into a near "mono-crop" export economy, necessitating the importation of basic foodstuffs (maize and beans) and cotton clothing (MacLeod 1973:76; Feldman 1985:84–87).

15. See note 10.

16. Examples of this practice also appear in investigations into the conduct of *jueces de milpas* (AGI, Contaduría 971A and 971B). For examples of widespread use of the *reparto de efectos* and other abuses by *alcades mayores* in numerous highland and lowland jurisdictions in the 1760s, see *Boletín del Archivo General del Gobierno* (1937:274–329).

17. According to Miles Wortman (1982:145), tribute represented more than 80 percent of revenues collected by the Audiencia of Guatemala during the first half of the eighteenth century. See also Juan Carlos Solórzano (1985:99).

18. Sheldon Annis (1987:24) doubts the importance of San Lorenzo's lack of a land base as a cause of its ladinoization, pointing out that loss of land began in the late nineteenth and early twentieth centuries with the spread of coffee cultivation. But, study of colonial land tenure patterns in this region may show that Indian loss of land in the Panchoy and Almolonga valleys was well under way before 1800. For preliminary indications of this trend, see Lutz (n.d.a:25–27).

19. Studies that examine aspects of Indian social evolution during colonial times, but that are not predominantly concerned with how Wolf's model does or does not apply, include Robert M. Carmack (1979, 1981), Shelton H. Davis (1970), John Hawkins (1984), Douglas Madigan (1976), Sandra L. Orellana (1984), Karl Sapper (1985), and John M. Watanabe (1984). We would also call attention to the myriad publications of the Mission Française du Chixoy published in four volumes of the *Cahiers de la R.C.P. 500* (Centre National de la Recherche Scientifique, Institut d'Ethnologie, Paris) under the title "Rabinal et la vallée moyenne du río Chixoy. Baja Verapaz-Guatemala." The articles in these volumes by Nicole Percheron and Michel Bertrand are especially useful. A fine diachronic study of one community, viewed and explained in a regional context, is that by Jean Piel (1989).

20. The supremacy of the parcialidad over pueblo at Sacapulas is also discussed in Carmack (1973:37–39, 206–209), Lovell (1985:81, 85, 200–204, and 1988), and Lovell and Swezey (1990).

21. The dissertation (in progress) of Michael Fry, a graduate student in history at Tulane University, will help fill in gaps in our knowledge of Indian survival in eastern Guatemala. Fry's dissertation focuses on the Mataquesquintla area of Jalapa from 1750 to 1850. Currently see Fry's (1980) master's thesis.

22. On López de Cerrato, see Sherman (1979:129–152 passim); on Lic. García de Valverde, see AGI:Guatemala 10; on Bishop Juan de Ramirez, see Sherman (1968) and Mario Humberto Ruz (1984). On Las Casas and the New Laws, see, among an already vast literature that the celebrations of 1992 will surely augment, MacLeod (1970).

3. Changes in the Nineteenth-Century Guatemalan State and Its Indian Policies

Ralph Lee Woodward, Jr.
Department of History, Tulane University

The emergence of a Guatemalan national state became clear following the Liberal Reforma of 1871, but it was to some degree an evolutionary process that had begun a century or more earlier. In fact, the principal issues that divided and shattered the former Kingdom of Guatemala in the nineteenth century were largely products of changes that occurred throughout the Spanish empire in the closing decades of the colonial period. The Bourbon monarchs of eighteenth-century Spain sought, through a series of administrative, military, economic, and ecclesiastical reforms, to reverse the decline that the seventeenth century had brought to Spanish prestige and power. While historians have collectively dubbed these the "Bourbon Reforms," rather than a unified policy program they were a series of often unrelated decisions stretching from about 1714 to the end of the century. Taken collectively, however, the Bourbon policies laid the foundations for the development of the liberal-capitalist state that would eventually be associated with the Liberal party in Guatemala from 1871 to 1944.

Much of the administrative reform concentrated on centralizing the Spanish imperial system, essentially creating a more modern, ministerial structure at the top and clarifying lines of command with the colonies. It included, after the model development in Bourbon France, appointment of intendants in the colonies with broad powers over financial and military affairs. Although no intendant was appointed for Guatemala itself, appointment of intendants in 1786 for Chiapas, Honduras, Nicaragua, and El Salvador contributed to the rising separatism of those provinces and thus contributed to the definition of the modern state of Guatemala along its present territorial lines (Fiehrer 1977:96–365). If this unintentionally contributed to the fragmentation of Central America, other administrative and military reforms were designed to strengthen the authority of the central government in Guatemala City, while the ecclesiastical reforms began to check the traditional power of the clergy, beginning the official anticlericalism that would characterize Liberal policy in Guatemala throughout the nineteenth century. The most fundamental of the reforms, however, were commercial and economic revisions that sought to expand Spanish trade and government revenues through rapid expansion of agricultural and mineral exports, beginning a transition from feudal agrarian traditions to export-oriented capitalist development, a trend that has continued to the present day (Wortman 1982:127–156).

In Guatemala most of the population was engaged in subsistence agriculture, either on village common lands or on Creole-owned haciendas. Surplus production went to the towns and cities, which were few. The capital, Santiago, was the only major city. There the principal activity was the ecclesiastical and political administration of the kingdom, including supervision of the commerce of the whole area from Chiapas to Costa Rica. Cattle raising was an important activity among rural Creoles who imitated the life-style their forefathers had brought from southern Spain in the sixteenth century. Small, ladino-owned farms produced wheat and other staples, but most food came from the Indian communities. Indeed, Indian productivity of subsistence goods was the key to life and survival. Capitalist enclaves, although of significance since the sixteenth century, were a minor part of the total socioeconomic picture (MacLeod 1973:348–373; Woodward 1985a:25–60).

The Bourbon Reforms

The Spanish Bourbon response to the industrial revolution in northern Europe stimulated a notable shift to agroexport production in many parts of the empire. Reduction of taxes on commerce, freer trade, increased incentives to production, expansion of African slavery, encouragement of new technology, improved roads and navigational aids, more liberal credit and capital accumulation laws, easier acquisition of land for agriculture, and authorization of new commercial organizations all promoted capitalist growth and a trend away from subsistence agriculture toward plantation production for export. Central America was not the most conspicuous of the areas that underwent this change, but it was definitely within the pattern throughout the century. Not until the outbreak of wars arising from the French Revolution was that growth trend arrested in Guatemala, leading to a serious depression during the quarter-century preceding independence (Meneray 1975; Woodward 1985a:61–91).

Although much of the agroexport expansion was in El Salvador, Guatemala was closely involved in both shifting production patterns and merchant financing of the indigo exports. Central America was drawn more closely into the north Atlantic economic system, which provided exchange for expanding imports of foreign merchandise by Guatemalan Creoles. Inevitably, the benefits were not uniformly distributed among the population. The expansion of exports caused changes in land utilization and began a process of ladino encroachment on traditional Indian lands. The land and labor demands of indigo and other export commodities put pressures on Indian communities in the more densely populated areas (Browning 1971:111–138). Moreover, the demand for capital placed more emphasis on money transactions, moving the economy away from the barter that had characterized much of the domestic trade. Increased trade, legal as well as contraband, put new demands on road and port development, and the Guatemalan government had to pay greater attention to its inadequate transportation infrastructure (Woodward 1966:35–41, 60–64). The increased production, overseas trade, and what later would be called "modernization" of Central America added a burden on the lower classes whose labor was exploited without commensurate compensation to extract the agricultural and mineral commodities as well as to work on roads and other public works. Together with the conversion of some land from subsistence to export use, this inevitably began a trend toward reduced food supplies that would eventually lead to malnutrition or dependence on foreign food imports, a problem that reached awesome portions in some parts of the isthmus by the twentieth century (Woodward 1985c:117–120).

A further factor of notable importance in the evolution of the Guatemalan political structure was the growth of *ayutamientos* (municipal government) in the late colonial period. The ayutamiento had long been the stronghold of the Creole elite in the capital, but provincial ayutamientos now strengthened regional identifications. After years of inactivity, several municipal corporations began to function after 1800. By 1810, not including Indian municipalities, there were ayuntamientos functioning in Guatemala City, San Salvador, San Miguel, Ciudad Real, Comayagua, León, Granada, Nueva Segovia, Cartago, Sonsonate, Tegucigalpa, San Vicente, Rivas, Quezaltenango, and Santa Ana. Except for the capital, however, only the pueblo of Quezaltenango was within the present-day boundaries of Guatemala, suggesting the importance of this development in the emerging nationalism of the Central American provinces. The number of functioning ayuntamientos expanded rapidly following the assembling of the Cortes of Cádiz in 1810, providing an opportunity for substantial local political expression at the close of the colonial period, much of which was directed in a separatist spirit against the dominance of Guatemala City (Herrarte 1963:104; Rodríguez 1978:92–112).

At the same time, paradoxically, another effect of the economic expansion of the eighteenth century was to increase economic interdependence among the provinces. Intercolonial trade had been discouraged for most of the colonial period in defense of the commercial monopolies of Seville, Mexico, and Lima. Yet the Bourbons gradually revised this policy to allow Central Americans wider trading possibilities both within and beyond the kingdom. Moreover, the rise of contraband along the Caribbean coast increased opportunities for trade among the Central Americans. Within the kingdom, there was greater movement of merchants, intellectuals, bureaucrats, and clergy than formerly. Guatemala City was, of course, the metropolis for all these people. A significant number of aggressive peninsular immigrants, many from northern Spain, came to Guatemala at this time, marrying into established Creole families and playing major roles in the commercial growth that was occurring. These immigrants were vital to the capitalist transition that was occurring (Cardoso and Pérez Brignoli 1977:87–110).

The economic changes wrought by the Bourbon Reforms inevitably caused reactions among those who did not share the gains or who were threatened by the changes. Among the elites, the emerging capitalist structure was at the root of the Liberal parties that would dominate much of the nineteenth and twentieth centuries in Central America. Those who doubted the methods or wisdom of the changes and who clung to more traditional, neo-feudal ideas, formed the core of the Conservative parties, and their strength in Guatemala was concentrated in the merchant guild (consulado), which the Crown chartered in 1793. These two political factions would struggle bitterly in the nineteenth century before the eventual triumph of the Liberals after 1860. The growing demand for land and labor to produce the export crops strained the relationship among Creoles, ladinos, and Indians, inevitably creating doubts over the wisdom of the capitalist policies and contributing to rising tensions among the lower classes (Woodward 1965:544–566, 1966; Pinto Soria 1983).

The Cádiz Constitution of 1812

The Napoleonic wars and the subsequent struggle for Spanish American independence imposed new tensions and strains on the Guatemalan state as the nineteenth century opened. The powerful influence of liberalism was present both in the French-imposed Spanish government of Joseph Bonaparte and in the resistance government at Cádiz that won the loyalty of most of the American dominions, including Guatemala, as colonial representation for the first time gave Central American Creoles a direct voice and vote in the Spanish government and in the writing of the influential Constitution of 1812. Characteristically, while the

Creoles had argued that the Indians should be counted as a basis for colonial representation in the Cortes, they were careful to ensure that only Creoles were selected as representatives (Rodríguez 1978:79–80). Indians received considerable attention at Cádiz, as Rodríguez (1978:84) has reported:

> The Cádiz deputies were in complete agreement that the Indian was the forgotten American who had always lived in miserable conditions and that something had to be done for him. The acknowledgment of the Indian's plight was not new in Spanish history. Throughout the colonial period, Spanish officials had written much protective legislation concerning the Indian. It was undoubtedly implemented on occasion; but it was frequently ignored because of pressure from vested interests overseas. Americans at Cádiz chose to emphasize the victimization of the Indian in their controversy with Spaniards over the American Question. The abuses of the *corregidores* and the *repartimiento* sales of worthless goods to the Indians came in for much comment. In the heated arguments, Spaniards who had lived in the New World charged the American Creoles of abusing the Indians wantonly. On occasions, these local elites had preferred compulsory work levies to the payment of regular wages. Regardless of the charges and accusations of blame, speakers on both sides agreed that reform was long overdue.

The Cádiz legislators debated questions of Indian land and labor, and enacted a number of provisions ostensibly both to protect the Indian and to ensure his equality with other subjects. Indians welcomed the abolition of the hated tribute, but the realization they would now have to pay other taxes, the same as other subjects, in Guatemala caused considerable resentment and was a factor in the rising Indian restlessness at the time of independence. Other legislation provided for distribution of public land to the Indians and for means to help them develop its production, but it also recognized their right to sell their land to others. The Cádiz reforms appeared humanitarian in tone, but were in fact later used as a means of transferring Indian and public lands to agrarian entrepreneurs for plantation development (Rodríguez 1978:84–86).

The Cádiz Constitution, which became the model for most of the constitutions that would be adopted after independence, inaugurated several important changes in the Guatemalan state. Especially important in terms of the relationship between the state and the population were the provisions providing for election of town councils, a provincial deputation that was the first step toward a legislative assembly, limited freedom of the press, and colonial representation in the Spanish Cortes. The holding of elections throughout the kingdom beginning in 1810 began a process of open political participation and debate at both the municipal and national levels that suddenly made politics a major part of Central American life, at least among the propertied classes. Revocation of these reforms upon the restoration of Fernando VII following Napoleon's defeat in 1814 brought an abrupt reversal in this trend in Guatemala, with the strong-armed Captain General José de Bustamante restoring authoritarian rule. Yet the Spanish Revolution of 1820 restored the constitution and ushered in an active political dialogue in the Central American capital that would lead directly to independence and the turmoils that followed in the breakup of the old kingdom (Rodríguez 1978; Schmit 1978). The political reforms brought by the constitution provided political definition and substance for the Creole liberals who had already begun to articulate economic and social grievances.

Heated dialogue between liberals and moderates in the public press preceded the establishment of independence. Pedro Molina, a physician of illegitimate parentage and without close ties to the principal families, but representing the Creole intelligentsia for the first time openly challenged the traditional institutions and the continuation of Spanish rule. Answering him was José Cecilio del Valle, who had come to the capital from a Honduran ranching family for an education and stayed to become one of the colony's leading intellectuals and attorneys, widely respected by the Creole elite. He had risen in position and importance during the Bustamante years as a loyal servant of that government, and he now cautiously counseled moderation regarding independence. Leading Creole families, headed by the Aycinena clan, supported Molina's rabble-rousers, for they had suffered considerable damage under the Bustamante regime's strict enforcement of tax and contraband regulations, while they were at the same time uneasy with the return to power of the Spanish Liberals. José del Valle, on the other hand, had the support of the colonial government and other peninsular residents, the opponents of free trade, and traditionally conservative Creoles (Woodward 1985b:471–477).

Independence

The new importance of local government became apparent as Agustín de Iturbide's plan for independence of the viceroyalty of New Spain spread southward in 1821. The ayuntamientos in each town reacted independently to events in Mexico. In Chiapas, the ayuntamientos of Comitán, Ciudad Real, and Tuxtla each declared separately for the plan in late

August and early September and joined independent Mexico. In Guatemala the acting Captain General, Gabino Gaínza, agreed on September 14 to the Diputación Provincial's request for a general meeting of the representatives of the principal institutions. In a stormy session the next day, Creole and peninsular leaders debated the issues while a crowd outside clamored for independence. In the end, most of the delegates voted for independence. Virtually nothing else changed. The Spanish bureaucracy, headed by Gaínza, remained. The Guatemalan patricians were left in control of the government and the economy. Having escaped from the Spanish Liberal regime, the Creole elite no longer needed its alliance with Molina and the more radical Liberals; the Conservative party was born.

The decision taken in Guatemala City in favor of independence was meant to apply to the entire kingdom, but the idea of local participation was now so powerful that each municipality voted separately as news traveled southward. All accepted independence from Spain, but there were variations in their approaches to the future, so that as the national period opened Central America was politically fragmented and caught up in a wave of regional and local acts of separation. While Conservatives across Central America generally endorsed annexation to Mexico, Liberals called for an independent republican federation. Because they controlled the apparatus of government in Guatemala and most of the other states, the Conservatives succeeded in thwarting Liberal efforts to resist annexation, with the assistance of a Mexican army, but the dispute led to war between San Salvador and Guatemala and inaugurated the period of violence that would characterize the first half-century of Central American independence (Woodward 1985b:474–476).

Guatemalan adhesion to Mexico, however, was short-lived as the empire collapsed with the Plan de Casa Mata in 1823. Mexican Liberals then established a republic. With news of Iturbide's abdication, the Central American provinces responded enthusiastically to a call for a Central American constituent congress, which, under the presidency of the Liberal Salvadoran priest Matías Delgado, on July 1, 1823, declared the former kingdom a free and independent republic, under the name of the "United Provinces of the Center of America." Mexican recognition came almost immediately as the Congress set to work drafting a republican constitution. The document they created in 1824 reflected Liberal attitudes on government, and their resentment against the Conservative patrician clique in Guatemala City that had initially gained the ascendancy. They were quick to remove class privileges, abolishing all titles of distinction, royalty, or nobility, including even the use of "don." The same decree included a prohibition of the use of any ecclesiastical titles except "padre," and changed the terminology used to describe the principal institutions of government (Marure 1895:11–12; Menéndez 1956, 1:20, 126).[1] While Liberals generally had the upper hand in this government, the congress included important moderate and conservative representation. The final document was a compromise that blended elements of the Spanish Constitution of 1812 with the United States Constitution of 1789, but it was widely recognized as a pro-Liberal constitution. Consistent with Liberal egalitarian thought, it recognized the legal equality of all citizens, guaranteeing their "liberty, equality, security, and property." It also outlawed slavery and provided for an extensive list of guaranteed individual liberties, while preserving Roman Catholicism as the religion of the state "to the exclusion of the public exercise of any other." It recognized no special protective status of the Indian. The central feature of this constitution, which would have considerable impact on the federation's trajectory, was its unicameral legislature with relatively weak executive and judicial branches. While most of the federal power resided with the legislature, the constitution also provided for five autonomous state governments and legislatures, similarly structured (Gallardo 1958, 2:103–138). This constitution established the basis for a federation government that paid too little attention to the political tradition of the country and provided inadequate authority or revenue to the central government (Flemion 1973).

The constitution itself, however, was not the principal cause of the failure of the federation. This republican effort suffered from the beginning from serious personal, factional, and territorial rivalries that no government was able to contain. Yet the structure of both state and federal governments contributed to a wide gap between expectations and achievement in the first decades of independence. The Hispanic tradition of strong executive leadership could not be so easily discarded, and the constitutional provision of a strong legislature created serious conflicts between the two branches of government. Moreover, continued economic difficulties and inadequate provision for revenues for either state or federal government contributed to the failure of the country to develop the infrastructure and services in support of a more prosperous nation, which the Liberals had promised (R. Smith 1963). But the bloody civil war from 1826 to 1829 left the country weak and divided. Liberal victory in that struggle behind the leadership of the Honduran General Francisco Morazán resulted in the imprisonment and exile of prominent conservative leaders and clergy, setting the stage for the Liberals to launch their economic and political reforms. José Francisco Barrundia came to typify most especially the liberal radicals that led the Liberal effort in the 1820s and 1830s to transform the former Spanish colony into a progressive, modern state. He pressed this forward under the administration of Dr. Mariano Gálvez, Governor of Guatemala from 1831 to 1837.

Liberals and Conservatives

Gálvez presided over the enthusiastic and reforming efforts of the Liberals to modernize Guatemala. In concert with Morazán's federal government, they began by destroying the remaining institutional structure of the Hispanic period. They abolished the consulado and other colonial institutions. They expelled the religious orders, the archbishop, and other prominent clergy in an outburst of anticlericalism that assaulted the traditional prestige and privilege of the clergy. Between 1829 and 1831 the Guatemalan government censored ecclesiastical correspondence, seized church funds, and confiscated the property of the religious orders. In 1832 Gálvez stopped collection of the tithe, ended many religious holidays, confiscated more church property, decreed the right of the clergy to write their wills as they pleased, and legitimized the inheritance of parents' property by children of the clergy. Later the Guatemalan legislature authorized civil marriage, legalized divorce, and removed education from church supervision. Behind the leadership of Barrundia, the legislature sought to replace the Spanish institutional and legal framework with more modern instruments modeled especially after North American and French paradigms. The climax of this trend came in 1836 when Guatemala adopted the *System of Penal Law* written by Edward Livingston for Louisiana, but rejected by the Louisiana legislature in 1826 as too great a departure from the Roman legal tradition in that state (Rodríguez 1955:3–32; Arriola 1961:195–243; Lyons 1974).

The Liberal reforms theoretically favored Indians by granting them equality before the law and access to more land and opportunity. In practice, however, most Indians had neither the resources nor education to take advantage of the opportunity. Liberalism simply exposed them to greater exploitation. At the heart of the liberal state was a desire for rapid economic growth through expansion of agroexports. Thus, the process begun under the Bourbon Reforms was again pushed forward and contributed to growing resistance from the indigenous peoples, especially in El Salvador and Guatemala.

The federation period thus witnessed the first wave of the liberal reformism that would come to dominate Guatemala after 1871. It envisioned a strong state that would assist private capital in developing the agricultural resources of the land. The civil disorder and turmoil of the first two decades of national independence and the failure of the federal government to establish its preeminence over provincial governments, in actuality, left a legacy of weak government, with a theoretically strong legislature that in times of crisis turned over most of its power to the chief executive. The rural uprisings beginning in 1837 would ultimately bring a crisis between legislature and executive that would bring down the Gálvez government in 1838 and usher in three decades during which the state was dominated by the conservative elite of Guatemala City. The story of this major uprising that brought Rafael Carrera to power has been detailed elsewhere (Tobar Cruz 1959; Beltranena Sinibaldi 1971; Woodward 1971; Ingersoll 1972). It was a powerful popular reaction against the Liberal reforms that resulted in the final collapse of the Central American federation and in the domination of Guatemala by the caudillo Carrera for most of the period from 1839 to his death in 1865.

While Carrera's government justly has been given credit for defending Indian interests during the mid-nineteenth century, it should be understood at the outset that the principal beneficiaries of Carrera's revolt of 1837 were the aristocratic, conservative elite of Guatemala City. Mariano Gálvez's decree of July 26, 1838, allowed those exiled in 1829 to return to Guatemala, and many had taken positions of responsibility in both the private and public sectors even before Carrera's April 1839 victory. Juan José Aycinena led their coalescence as a political force. Like Aycinena, many were clergymen. Others headed important merchant or planter families. Discredited after their defeat by Morazán in 1829, by 1839 they had been accepted back into the social and economic life of the state, and they joined Liberal members of the old elite, such as José Francisco Barrundia, Manuel Arrivillaga, and Miguel García Granados in directing the government. This class had suffered much since the beginning of the nineteenth century, but they were still the most durable element of the Guatemalan upper class. Their economic interests were best represented through their *fuero*, the consulado, restored in August 1839. In addition, positions in the hierarchy of the Guatemalan church and in the *cabildo* of Guatemala City allowed them to consolidate their power in the most powerful institutions in the state, especially following the downfall of Gálvez and during the rise of Carrera to military power (Woodward 1966:xvi–xvii).

The Conservative State

Under Carrera, who controlled the state almost constantly from 1839 until 1865, strong executive authority was clearly reestablished. The central government was remarkably small, consisting primarily of ministers of Government (*Gobernación*), Foreign Relations and Ecclesiastical Affairs, Finance and War, with a few functionaries to assist them in their tasks. Since the same individual often exercised more than one of these ministerial posts at the same time, there were normally only two or three ministers in the government. They each had a tiny staff, and even the revenue department employed only a few dozen officials in all. The judicial branch consisted of an attorney general and a few judges. The army was the principal government expense after debt service, consuming from a third to half of the annual budget, but it was not large by modern standards. The governing of the country was primarily carried out by the corregidores, one in each department, appointed by the president. These were usually, although not always, military men, and they had broad powers of police, finance, and general administration over their jurisdictions, serving as justices of the peace and as judges. They worked closely with the municipal governments and the various private corporations, such as the church or the consulado, which operated in their departments, and with the landowners of the region who looked to the corregidores to enforce the laws that protected them. The legislature met annually, but exercised little real authority, serving primarily as a forum for legitimizing the will of the caudillo and for formulating laws to implement his policies. A small executive council, the name and composition of which changed periodically, served to advise the president on a more regular basis. In essence, much of the centralization that had characterized the Liberal reforms was eliminated, and there was a real turning back toward the more feudal, Hapsburg tradition of decentralized government, with strong authority resting in the Captain General (a title Carrera also bore, in addition to President) and in the local political chieftains (corregidores).

Presiding over the state during much of the turbulence of the early 1840s was Mariano Rivera Paz, a skillful politician from Cobán who was important in managing the delicate relationship between Carrera and the Guatemala City elite. Rivera Paz set the conservative tone for the new government in his first annual report to the Constituent Assembly on May 31, 1839, as he reviewed the past and offered a program for the future. He recalled that the passions of the first years of independence had been "the exaltation of everything new and the wish to destroy everything that existed." The Liberals, he said, had "proscribed moderation and prudence under the hateful names of 'servile' and 'retrograde,'" so that "honorable and peaceful men had fled from public affairs, persecuted by the revolutionary furor that led the country into the misery and disorganization in which it is found." But now, he declared, society, "by its instinct for preservation is trying to reorganize itself." He reviewed the "misguided" liberal programs and the violations of rights, suggesting both the emotionalism that surrounded the issues and the involvement of the rural masses in this dialogue:

There was neither personal security, nor respect for property, nor liberty, nor justice. The decrees on divorce and civil marriage produced a great scandal, for they clashed with our customs and created misunderstandings. The honorable peasant whose conscience had already been tortured in a thousand ways, now found insecure the honor of his daughters, even in the confines of his poor hut, and felt the peace of his family, the last refuge for the downtrodden, disappear. Trying violently to establish codes projected for Louisiana, the result was the immediate and sudden suspension of the administration of justice, scandalous immunity for criminals, resulting in fear and alarm, which the absence of justice and magistrates in a community would naturally produce.

He reminded the assembly how fiscal mismanagement, unpopular tax policies, and forced labor and military service all had contributed to a will to resist among the people and sparked Carrera's Revolution of Mita and the War of la Montaña. He charged the Liberals with repeatedly thwarting the popular will in Guatemala. It was Carrera who had in the end restored peace and, as the country resumed its commerce and normal life, "inaugurated a sincere conciliation." Morazán had destroyed Guatemala's armed forces, incorporating them into the federal army or disbanding them. In Rivera's view, Carrera, in alliance with Francisco Ferrera in Honduras, had become the savior of the state and the republic.

With the federal pact broken, Rivera Paz now charged the assembly with rebuilding Guatemala on a foundation of peace and prosperity. The restoration of the power and prestige of the Roman Catholic clergy, which would be a salient feature of the Carrera years, was made clear from the start as he demanded from the legislators "a great patriotic and constant effort," beginning with satisfying "the religious needs and desires of our people. . . . There is no example either in antiquity or in modern times, of a people without religion," he declared as he urged the assembly to decree "solemnly that the Government of the State professes and respects the Catholic religion." Restoration of the church to its former position was the first priority in the effort to return to the security and tranquility of the Hispanic era, as he urged the assembly also to restore, "insofar as possible, the form that the laws of Spain established for political government." He emphasized the point: "If we have not been able to establish new laws, while we give ourselves an adequate constitution, what can we do but look to the old ways to pursue the peace and security that it gave us?"

He advocated the same for the judicial system, tax structure, and municipal government, as well as restoration of the consulado to promote development of agriculture and commerce along traditional lines. And he noted that public education, referring to the church's earlier educational system, was now in total disarray, especially outside the capital, and had to be reestablished. He repeated a constant conservative charge that "the desire to bring our countries advances and improvements by enacting the legislation of enlightened nations, without being prepared to receive them, has produced nothing more than trouble and evil, missing the desired objectives. Our liberalism must be limited to giving our people a general education and improving their habits." The educational system existing before independence, he argued, despite its defects, provided a basis for development, rather than great but impracticable projects. Above all, he emphasized, it was necessary to provide primary instruction in the small towns, for while the Liberal legislation had called for establishing a more sophisticated system by force, "we have seen even the few primary schools that we had before independence disappear" (Rivera Paz 1839). Carrera also sent a message to the assembly, calling on it to replace the Liberal legislation with "a system that will conform to our customs and especially to the religious principles that we profess" (Carrera 1839a).

Thus, the Guatemalan state turned away from the liberalism that had dominated the country since independence in 1821 toward a revival of the social and political security of the Spanish colonial system. This reversal, in large part made possible by the popular uprising supported by large numbers of poor, rural Indians and ladinos, would have a profound effect on many of them and would contribute to the survival of distinct Indian cultures in Guatemala, although such Indian communities were fast being absorbed by rapid expansion of agroexport capitalism in other regions of Latin America.

Under the guns of Carrera and directed by the patrician landholding, commercial, and ecclesiastical elites of the capital, the assembly moved expeditiously, beginning with the restoration of the religious orders and an invitation to the exiled Archbishop Ramón Casáus to return to Guatemala (Asamblea Constituyente 1839a).[2] In congratulating the assembly on these acts Carrera reaffirmed the revolution's commitment to a theocratic state:

Our oppressors in the excess of their desperation insult us from afar, calling us barbarians, savages, fanatics, and serviles. What irritates their furor is that after having exhausted their efforts to extend the demoralization and impiety, the people, with their liberty restored, are proving that all the efforts to corrupt them produced nothing more than to strengthen in our hearts our love of the holy religion that we inherited from our fathers. To sustain

them we armed ourselves and have triumphed, overcoming a
thousand obstacles. Now that the designs of our old oppressors are
exposed, we shall know how to die before once more seeing our
religion insulted and our temples profaned and robbed. Firm in our
resolution, and united by the same sentiments, we shall be invin-
cible. (Carrera 1839b)

The process of returning the church's property also began (*Actas de la
Asamblea* 1[5] October 19, 1839:24). During the remainder of 1839 the
conservative consolidation and restoration of Hispanic institutions and
customs continued (*El Tiempo*, July–December 1839). In August the
assembly reestablished the national mint and the merchant guild (*El
Tiempo* 1[24] August 15, 1839:95; Woodward 1966, xvi–xvii, 55–127
passim).[3] Later it revived the office of corregidor, restored education to
church supervision, established a national bank, and revived the *re-
sidencia* examination for all public officials in the state (*El Tiempo* 1[39]
October 11, 1839:153–154; 1[45] November 3, 1839:178–179; and 1[48]
November 14, 1839:189; Pineda de Mont 1869–1872, 1:504–511).

The legislators closed their first session with more decrees designed to
restore the Hispanic tradition. They reduced taxes on foodstuffs in
another response to popular demand (AGCA, B, leg. 214, exp. 4941, fol.
607; *Gaceta oficial* 1[44] June 10, 1842:191), and reestablished the former
alcoholic beverage controls (*El Tiempo* 1[57] December 11, 1839:225–226).
They abolished the hated head tax altogether (Pineda de Mont 1869–1872,
2:263), but restored the tithe tax and enforced its collection (*Gaceta
extraordinaria*, August 14, 1841:1). They decreed a new "Declaration of
the Rights of the State and Its Inhabitants," which, although it maintained in print many civil liberties, clearly turned the direction of the
state toward authoritarianism (*El Tiempo* 1[60] December 21,
1839:225–226). Roman Catholicism once more became the official
religion and regained its *fuero* and *cabildo eclesiástico* (*El Tiempo* 1[146]
November 26, 1840:582; Montúfar 1878–1887, 3:381–382). The session
adjourned, having definitively terminated the Liberal revolution.[4]

Government under Carrera was characterized by decentralized control, in contrast to the Liberal dictatorships that followed. While
Carrera's word was law, the actual machinery of the government was
quite small. Carrera had only two ministers at the beginning of his
regime, and although these were eventually expanded to four, there were
only three throughout most of his rule. Government offices and agencies
were few, with quasi-public corporations following patterns developed
under Spanish rule, carrying out most of the functions later associated
with government. Thus, the church maintained the schools, hospitals,
and other charitable institutions; the consulado supervised construction

and maintenance of highways, bridges, and port facilities, and with the *Sociedad Económica de Amigos del País* promoted production and economic diversification; autonomous municipal corporations, both in the capital and in the departments, performed most governmental functions relating to police, public order, and maintenance of local streets, plazas, and markets, although the central government sometimes took an interest in such things; and the bar and medical associations (*colegio de abogados* and *protomedicato*) performed services relating to their professions in addition to protecting their own interests, such as codification of laws and supervision of pharmacies. There was a Supreme Court (successor to the colonial audiencia) appointed by and dependent upon the executive, and a few other government tribunals, but much justice was still in the preserve of the privileged corporations (consulado, church, university, the military, etc.), appeals from these fueros, except for the *cabildo eclesiástico*, heard by the Supreme Court justices. The major surviving innovation resulting from the Liberal reforms at the beginning of independence and from the Cádiz experience was the annual convening of an elected assembly for a month or two to enact legislation and to endorse the actions of the caudillo. But it was clearly subservient to the caudillo and less important in practice than the Council of State, composed of the caudillo and leading officials, which established policy and made government decisions on a regular basis. Carrera also appointed a Council of War on occasion to advise him on military matters, but the army, except in wartime, was relatively small and clearly subservient to the caudillo. Its officers and even its ragged troops occupied an especially privileged status in Guatemalan life, however, a position they often abused (Woodward 1983:5–6).

Especially after 1855 Carrera spent much of his time away from the capital, at his country *fincas*, in the health spas of Amatitlán, Escuintla, or making periodic *visitas* through the state. He kept a firm hand on the reins of government, but because of these long absences his ministers and the Council of State, made up of the clique of conservative and often talented patricians (many of whom were indeed related to the extended family of the Marquis de Aycinena), played the major role in actually governing the state.[5]

Authority in the countryside rested most heavily with the landowners and with the political bosses, or corregidores, in each department.[6] Also appointed by the caudillo, loyalty to whom was their primary responsibility, these local governors wielded enormous power over their mini-kingdoms. Records of these corregidores in the archives of the Ministry of the Interior (Gobernación) reflect their powerful position with respect to the Indian communities in their jurisdiction and their direct relationship to the caudillo.[7]

Carrera's Indian Policies

The new government's attitude toward the Indians was consistent with its return to the Hispanic traditions. On August 16, 1839, the Constituent Assembly, recognizing that Indians were a majority of the state's population and that it was in the public interest not only "to protect this numerous class of the society, but also to develop and improve its customs and civilization," decreed a code for dealing with this class. Noting that the Liberal program had mistreated and exploited Indians under a system that operated under the pretext of their equality, the committee reporting the bill said that the system of the colonial era was really better. That system "compelled them to work, to provide public service on certain projects and to pay taxes; but it also gave them protection against the influential and the powerful in their land claims." It provided for their care and welfare and for their self-respect, the committee added. The Liberals had abolished all that, and the Indians had consequently lost their respect for law and order. The new code clearly reversed Gálvez's idea of incorporating the Indians into western civilization. It even called for restoration of the office of Indian interpreter and instructed departmental officials to have the decree translated into indigenous languages. Gálvez's program had aimed at assimilating the Indians within a conceptual framework of egalitarianism. The conservatives claimed this meant exploitation, with the danger of rebellion and violence. Instead, they offered paternalism and protection (Asamblea Constituyente 1839b; El Tiempo 1[27], August 30, 1839:106).

This approach did not, of course, confer either autonomy or equality on the Indians. As Mario Rodríguez has pointed out, the Indians, in effect, received for their support of the overthrow of the Liberals "a return to their status of second-class citizens" (Rodríguez 1955:30). But the Conservatives challenged the Liberals' attempt to enact general laws as if the state's inhabitants "were equal in customs, civilization, and circumstances." The Indians, Conservatives argued, were in fact culturally, economically, and politically in different circumstances and therefore the laws should recognize those differences. While enlightenment of the Indians by Western standards might be a desirable goal, it would take a long time. In the meantime, the Indians and whites should be treated separately, with laws that differentiated and did not attempt to suggest equality where it did not exist. In theory, at least, the Conservative approach offered the Indians protection from excessive exploitation and thereby permitted their cultural survival.[8]

The larger historical question of whether Indians in Guatemala in fact benefited from the restoration of their "second-class citizenship" has been dealt with elsewhere, especially by Keith Miceli, who suggests that

Carrera's pro-Indian policy did indeed protect the Indians from further encroachment on their land and labor during the 1840s, but that after 1850 that protection began to lessen as Carrera became more clearly attached to the Guatemalan elite (Naylor 1967:626–629, 634; Miceli 1974; Woodward 1979; C. Smith 1984a:200–202). Julio Castellanos's fine work on coffee in nineteenth-century Guatemala corroborates that interpretation, but from the evidence he presents on encroachment on Indian land and labor for agro-exports it is clear that the Indians were not seriously threatened during the Carrera era. Carrera himself often acted in defense of Indian lands and interests. Immediately after Carrera's death in 1865, first under the administration of General Vicente Cerna and even more following the Liberal Revolution of 1871 a major assault on Indian land and labor took place (Castellanos Cambranes 1985:40–264 passim).

It is undoubtedly true that the cochineal boom in central Guatemala, beginning under liberal initiatives in the 1820s but reaching its peak during the conservative years, took some land out of subsistence production and encroached on Indian holdings in the vicinity of Antigua and Amatitlán, but it had little effect in the populous Indian districts of Los Altos. It would eventually be coffee production that established the dominant *finquero* (plantation) class and threatened both the subsistence and the cultural survival of the Indians (Woodward 1966:41–51; Castellanos Cambranes 1985:53–55, 81–119).

The accelerated demand for Indian land and labor that the coffee plantation economy stimulated can be said to have begun, as Castellanos Cambranes suggests, in the 1850s. Nevertheless, its impact was minor until after 1865, not only because the amount of coffee production remained relatively small until then, but also because the Conservative policy also encouraged production of coffee by Indian communities, as opposed to the emphasis on individually owned plantations that Liberal policy favored.

We can see in the Verapaz an example of the conservative focus on community lands for coffee production and at the same time get some idea of how this became a first step toward later transfer of such lands to private control. Areas formerly producing cochineal were among the first into coffee production, but new areas in the Verapaz and Los Altos also became important, often involving persons not represented in the conservative faction that controlled the government. Many of these coffee producers, especially in Los Altos, eventually became associated with the Liberal opposition to the Guatemalan elite. Community lands were used for production of coffee to a great extent and often began the process of conversion of these lands to private holdings. This was especially promoted in the Verapaz, a relatively underdeveloped area until the rise of coffee cultivation. The Dominican Order had dominated it in the colonial period, and had allowed the continuance of much community ownership. The municipality of Cobán, encouraged by the departmental corregidor, made special efforts to promote planting of coffee and sugar on communal lands beginning in 1859. On May 30 of that year the Carrera government approved a plan for the Cobán municipality to loan from its funds up to 500 pesos (worth U.S. $500) at 6 percent annual interest for terms of up to five years, per single individual for the protection and development of agriculture. With collateral of real property, double that amount could be borrowed. It also authorized, as it had done elsewhere, the municipality of Cobán, or any other municipality in the Verapaz, to rent its community lands for coffee cultivation at the rate of 1 real per cuerda per year. Rentals not paid for two years could be repossessed by the government, and the corregidor was designated to enforce these rules. By providing both land and capital for development, the Verapaz government claimed that it was opening the way for "the poor classes" to become coffee planters (Gaceta de Guatemala 11[30], June 4, 1859:1–2). By the end of October seven coffee planters had received municipal funds under this arrangement, and by June of 1860 it had stimulated considerable coffee cultivation, with the result that the Verapaz became one of the leading producing regions within a few years (Gaceta de Guatemala 11[66], November 16, 1859:1; 12[11], June 14, 1860:1). By March 1, 1862, there were thirty-nine coffee fincas in Cobán, with thirty-two more in nearby San Pedro Carchá and four in San Miguel Tucurú. The corregidor reported that nearly seventy thousand coffee plants were now producing in the department, with two million more in various stages of being established (Gaceta de Guatemala 13[33], April 13, 1862:2; El Noticioso 1[10], December 28, 1861:2–3). Juan José de Aycinena noted remarkable growth of coffee culture in the Verapaz by 1865, and urged the government to encourage even more use of community lands. Completion of a new road to Salamá, he pointed out, would soon allow easier marketing of Verapaz coffee (Aycinena to Ministro de Gobernación, Guatemala, April 17, 1866, AGCA, B, leg. 18604). At the same time, there is evidence in the archives of the Ministry of Gobernación that the administration of the renting of community lands of the department was open to abuses and corruption. Accusations against the political commissioner in Carchá, Miguel Molina, in 1866 for mismanagement of community funds derived from coffee production suggested that abuses of this system could and probably did occur. In time, but principally after 1865, these community "rentals" were by various means transferred to private ownership (Juan E. Valdés, Corregidor del Verapaz, to Ministro de Gobernación, Salamá, April 28, 1866, AGCA, B, leg. 28604).

Conclusion

It has not been the intention of this chapter to detail actual Indian
conditions under the Conservatives, but simply to indicate the significant change in direction that government policy took beginning in 1839.
Carrera's alliance with Indian and ladino peasants in the reactionary
uprising of 1837 checked the liberal trend toward agro-export organization of land and labor that had begun with the Bourbon Reforms of the
eighteenth century. While Carrera, as Miceli and others have pointed
out, frequently and personally intervened to defend Indian lands and
rights, the conservative elite in Guatemala City itself rejected the
egalitarian policy of the liberals that had, and would later, lead to
exploitation of Indian land and labor. Although running directly contrary to general world trends in the nineteenth century, the conservative
policy of protecting and segregating the Indian communities, as Bradford
Burns has suggested in his *Poverty of Progress* (1986), offered an alternative mode of development that put greater emphasis on subsistence than
exports and on the stability of traditional community social organization in preference to the economic nationalism that nineteenth-century
liberal capitalism emphasized so strongly in Latin America.

Notes

1. *Audiencias*, for example, became *cortes territoriales*, and *ayuntamientos*
became *municipalidades*.

2. A petition with more than eight hundred signatures had been presented
to the assembly on June 11 requesting this. *Actas de la Asamblea* 1(2) August 27,
1839:10, and (5) October 19, 1839:21–22; *El Tiempo*, June 21–July 15, 1839;
Pineda de Mont 1869–1872, 1:242–243, 273.

3. Regarding problems of currency, see Pavón (1840).

4. See *El Tiempo* 1(56) December 7, 1839:221–222, for a review of the
assembly's accomplishments.

5. Among the most important of these conservatives during the Carrera era
were Luis and José Batres, Manuel Francisco Pavón, Juan Matheu, Mariano and
Pedro Aycinena, José Nájera, Manuel Echeverría, José Milla, Andrés Andreu, and
Manuel Cerezo. Among the more extreme conservatives, mostly clerics, were
Antonio de Larrazábal y Arrivillaga, José María de Castilla, Francisco de Paula
García Peláez, Bernardo Piñol y Aycinena, Basilio Zeceña, Jorge Viteri y Ungo,
Javier and José María de Urruela, José Mariano González, Marcelo Molina,
Marcial Zebadúa, Joaquín Durán, Manuel Joaquín Dardón, José Luna, José
Farfán, and Antonio José de Irisarri. In the 1840s, a number of prominent liberals
also served under Carrera's leadership, notably Miguel de Larreinaga, Miguel
García Granados, Alejandro Marure, Felipe Molina, José Mariano Vidaurre, and
José Antonio Larrave. A few of these liberals continued to hold seats in the
Assembly later, but no longer gained appointive offices. For a careful look at the

leading members of the Aycinena clan, see Chandler (1988 and 1989).

6. The situation paralleled rather closely that described by Wolf and Hansen (1967).

7. These records for the mid-nineteenth century in the AGCA are for the most part unclassified, although they are generally organized chronologically in *legajos*. They are, however, available to researchers and are presently being cataloged by the AGCA staff. See Woodward (1983).

8. See the quotation from *El Café*, September 8, 1839, in Rodríguez (1955:30) for an example of this line of Conservative thinking. Rodríguez also provides a fine example of the Liberal criticism of the Conservative policy toward the Indian in a quotation from *El Popular* (Quezaltenango), December 4, 1839.

4. Origins of the National Question in Guatemala: A Hypothesis

Carol A. Smith
Department of Anthropology, Duke University

The working population of Guatemala today divides about equally into two culturally distinct groups. One group, termed *Indians* in both popular and scholarly discourse, are people who retain a considerable amount of Mayan tradition, including the use of Mayan languages. The others, known as *ladinos*, are popularly assumed to be descendants of Spanish/ Indian liaisons (i.e., to be mestizos) but are in fact mostly Mayans in biological heritage who have assimilated national language and culture. Most Guatemalan scholars believe that those people who have maintained their distinctiveness as a culture (or nation) are those who have been unable to resist the superexploitation of "colonial relations of production" (argued most persuasively by Severo Martínez 1971). Most North American scholars believe that those who have retained Mayan culture are those who have developed special social mechanisms to protect themselves against the superexploitation of colonial relations of production (see, e.g., Tax 1952; Wolf 1957). Almost everyone believes that the key period in which Indians and ladinos were created as opposed cultural/political groups was the colonial period, when the Spanish Crown and clergy separated and protected native populations as a special class who could be self-sufficient while paying tribute and supporting the nonproductive Spanish settlers; most also believe that the persistence of the cultural division between Indians and ladinos today is a political anachronism.

In this essay I wish to challenge both versions of the conventional wisdom to suggest that class differences emerged between Guatemalan Indians and ladinos in the *postcolonial* period and that this class difference was reinforced by a linear reading of Guatemala's political history, which "blamed" culture rather than real political relations for the continued existence of two separate and unequal groups. The point of my argument is not to deny that Guatemala's colonial legacy played a role in the creation of Indians and ladinos. It is, rather, to suggest that Guatemalan Indians and ladinos do not share a similar class position in the present about which they are mystified. Even today Indians and ladinos mostly belong to two distinct classes. They were created and maintained as such in the modern, not the premodern, era.

The conventional wisdom about the perduring difference between Indians and ladinos in Guatemala rests upon known and agreed-upon historical facts. Indians and ladinos were significant social categories throughout Central America in the colonial period. Today, however, they are significant only in Guatemala; elsewhere there are basically only whites and mestizos or, in the case of postrevolutionary Nicaragua, mestizos.[2] The colonial social category "ladino" disappeared in the rest of Central America in the nineteenth century as Indians were assimilated into national culture. It would appear to follow that colonial relations of production remain only in Guatemala. What this "naturalized" linear history ignores, however, is that social meanings are not historically constant. What ladino means today in Guatemala (and the group of people to which it refers) is quite different from what it meant in earlier periods. Why Indians and ladinos remain important social categories in contemporary Guatemala can best be explained by *changes* rather than *continuity* in Guatemalan history—that is, by the way in which certain political contests between Guatemala's Indians and its other groups were temporarily won or lost.

As evidence for these arguments I will examine three points in Guatemala's nineteenth-century history, during which ethnic identities and relations were quite different from what they are today and during which efforts at incorporating Guatemala's various populations into the nation (in both political and economic terms) took very different forms. In 1821, at the beginning of the period I examine, Guatemala was not a separate state; its economy was undeveloped rather than underdeveloped; and its main social division was between whites and nonwhites rather than between Indians and ladinos. At the end of the period, 1944, Guatemala had a fully developed coercive state; it was well into the pattern of capitalist underdevelopment common to the Third World; and its main social division was between Indians and ladinos rather than between whites and nonwhites. The events that took place in that period were critical for creating the class and ethnic divisions that shape Guatemalan politics today. Thus, I will argue, we can understand the present position of ladinos and Indians in Guatemala only by understanding the special political history of modern Guatemala.

The Colonial Background

Because power was highly centralized within colonial Guatemala, the province of Guatemala—administrative center of a political unit that stretched from southern Mexico to Costa Rica—attracted and held more Spanish bureaucrats and their elite descendants than did other provinces of the isthmus. At the same time, Guatemala had a denser surviving Indian population than other provinces, and Indian communities rather than individual Indian workers provided the main source of wealth in the colony (Solórzano 1986). These two factors contributed to the special character of social relations in colonial Guatemala. Because the colonial apparatus was located in Guatemala, state mechanisms for protecting Indian communities and extracting revenue from them for the Crown were more effective than they were in outlying provinces; and because there were few mines or major exports that the state could tax in Guatemala, the state had to extract revenue directly from Indian communities (MacLeod 1973).

State protection of Indian communities had a two-sided character. On the one hand, no one but the church or Crown had easy access to Indian labor or products in Guatemala. But on the other hand, the church and Crown directly exploited Indians in Guatemala rather than acting as mediators between them and Spanish settlers. This kept most Guatemalan Indians more isolated from non-Indian settlers than Indians in other parts of the New World. It also prevented the rise of a powerful landed oligarchy in the province, holding power independent of the state.[3] Thus, it established the central contradiction in Guatemala, that between Indian communities and the state rather than between peasants and landowners or workers and capitalists.

These special conditions, together with the spatial separation of Indians and non-Indians (the former mostly rural, the latter mostly urban) saved Guatemalan Indians from the fate of many Indians in the rest of the colony—that is, the wholesale destruction of their communities and separate social identities (Newson 1986, 1987). These conditions did not, however, maintain Indian culture in a pristine form. Indians retained some of their rituals and their separate languages, mainly through the active intervention of the church, which could better maintain its exclusive access to Indian souls and resources through these means (van Oss 1986). But in most other respects, Indians were as highly assimilated in Guatemala as elsewhere. Elements of culture that today distinguish Indians from non-Indians—their religious practices, dress, and community forms of political rule—are not surviving pre-Hispanic forms but a fusion of native and Spanish traditions (Martínez Peláez 1971). What maintained Indians as Indians in the colonial period, in short, was that Indians were wards of the state and payers of tribute.[4]

By the end of the colonial period, Indian communities remained strong only in western Guatemala and southwestern El Salvador. Elsewhere, slave running, forced migration, expropriation, miscegenation, and the like, created other social categories, known throughout Central America as *castas*, some of whom were known as ladinos (MacLeod 1973; Lutz 1985, 1988). The castas were not necessarily mestizos or people of mixed descent—though people of mixed descent were usually known as one or another of the castas. The term *ladino* was applied specifically to Indians who had lost ties to their particular communities through a variety of processes (MacLeod 1983a).[5] Members of the castas (including ladinos) were neither owners of resources nor subject to regular payment of tribute. Most of them farmed unclaimed land (mainly in eastern Guatemala), worked as artisans and petty merchants in the towns and cities, or became personal retainers of one sort or another for the Spanish ruling class (which included the clergy). While legally distinct from Indians, ladinos did not belong to a different economic class, nor was their social status higher than Indians in the colonial period (MacLeod 1973).[6]

The two dominant classes in the colony (peninsulares and Creoles) were more divided by privilege and interest than were the two lower orders. Peninsulares were people of Spanish descent, born in Spain, who held positions in the system of imperial governance and thus ruled the colony. And Creoles were people of mostly Spanish descent, born in the Americas, who lacked positions in the imperial system but who held local power through a variety of mechanisms (Woodward 1985a). United mainly by race, racial ideology, and their shared rights to Indian labor, Creoles and peninsulares were divided by the fact that the latter held ultimate authority in the colony. Guatemalan Creoles, unlike their counterparts in other parts of the New World, rarely held positions of power that were not granted to them by the state (Wortman 1982). The growing divorce of power between peninsulares and Creoles ultimately undermined the Spanish colonial system. The collision did not begin in Central America, because of the especially dependent position of Central American Creoles. But Central American Creoles were sufficiently resentful of their weak political position to jump at the opportunity provided by others' demands for independence.

The gradual disappearance of Indian communities throughout the Spanish empire and the development of the new and anomalous social category of castas also played a role in the disintegration of the colonial system. Without Indians, the system simply did not function properly. Yet the disenfranchised castas, who had fewer rights than Indians, were not the leading social actors in the independence movements. The white Creoles led these movements with the aim of taking power rather than of transforming its unequal distribution. Five Central American states eventually emerged from the independence movements, but insofar as they lacked a popular base these movements were simply anticolonial rather than "nationalist" in character. In fact, Benedict Anderson (1980:50) suggests that the drive for independence throughout Latin America was spurred more by fear of popular mobilization against elite privilege than by anger at colonial restrictions on elite privilege.[7]

Surprisingly, Guatemala was the most nationally integrated Central American state in the early nineteenth century, though later it was to become the most divided. What made Guatemala's situation different was the way in which Guatemala's aspirations to become an isthmian power created the conditions that would exacerbate ethnic divisions. When it still seemed plausible that Guatemala might rule the entire isthmus, elite Liberals overcame Conservative inertia to make a brief attempt to incorporate Indians and other members of the "lower orders" as equal citizens in what would be a Central American nation. The attempt, unique in Central America, was brief, quickly reversed, and never again attempted until 1944. What was accomplished in this period was less important than the reaction it provoked.

Imposed Integration: Guatemala's Early Liberal Period

Literate (white) Guatemalans in the early nineteenth century identified strongly with European civilization. For many, the end of colonial rule opened the possibility for universalizing European values in America: "Latin Americans believed Europe to be the focal point of history, regarding their own histories as extensions of European history.... The question was not whether to Europeanize but how" (Burns 1980:45, 46). Liberal ideas spread widely throughout Central America, but only in Guatemala did Liberals succeed in quashing internal conflicts to legislate sweeping reforms of a Liberal (and nationalist) character in the early nineteenth century. Progressive Guatemalans, wanting to both "enlighten" and "whiten" their nation, attempted a vast overhaul of national institutions in imitation of Western models. They also attempted to encourage European migration in order to improve the local racial stock.[8] While Guatemalan progressives blamed Spanish colonialism for Guatemala's backwardness, they had no program for development other than a dependent, imitative one. As they saw it, development required all of Guatemala to become as Europeanized (and, they hoped, as white) as the Creole elite.

Most Guatemalan Liberals assumed that the most significant obstacle to developing Guatemala was the existence and special status of Indians. To achieve liberal aims, therefore, Indians had to be actively integrated into the Guatemalan nation as equal citizens rather than as special wards of the church and state. The assumption was that Indians could become "useful farmers" if the feudal barriers standing in their way were removed. And at that point in time, it should be emphasized, the development model was the United States, whose growth was thought to be rooted in its small property–holding system and free-market economy, both based in equal citizenship. The propellant to this whole utopian vision of freedom was a dream of economic growth that would place Guatemala among the leading nations of the world (see Braiterman 1986).

Guatemala had never been an especially wealthy colony and its major export product of the late colonial period, indigo, was suffering a severe slump at the time of independence. Indigo was produced by forced or wage labor on moderately large estates. Because of protections given to the Indians, labor for indigo production was supplied mainly by the various castas, including ladinos. Those Indians pulled into indigo production became ladinos because they lost touch with their Indian communities. Thus, at the end of the colonial period the native peoples of the indigo-growing areas (in eastern Guatemala) were mostly ladinos (MacLeod 1983a). The most promising export of the early independence period was cochineal, a dyestuff extracted from insects. The production and processing of cochineal was controlled almost entirely by small-holders, both Indians and castas, located mainly in central Guatemala. Cochineal required no large-scale organization of production; indeed, it may have been uniquely resistant to large-scale production systems (Macleod 1983a:200). The dominance of cochineal production in the early independence period (as opposed to indigo or coffee, which had very different production possibilities) is probably relevant to the way in which the Guatemalan elite envisioned how they would develop in the 1820s and 1830s.

Guatemala's first constitution,[9] written in 1824, established the equality of all Guatemalan citizens and eradicated the protections given by the Crown to special groups such as Indian communities and the church. At the same stroke it put Indians and ladinos (which had become the general term of reference to members of the castas) in the same legal as well as class position. It took nearly a decade for the constitution to have any effect because of uncertainties over the Central American Union, fiscal problems, divisions among the elites, and strong church resistance. The implementation period was 1831 to 1838, under the presidency of Mariano Gálvez. Gálvez's reform program, which was rapidly if unevenly implemented, had five major planks: to restrict the power of the Catholic church and to create a secular state; to institute a new and more viable taxing system; to rationalize property-holding by eradicating most communal forms of tenure; to encourage European migration by offering colonists favorable terms in the acquisition of land; and to break down Indian insularity by using educational and political means to draw them into the Guatemalan nation.

Gálvez had little success in implementing any of these programs. By its end, his administration had collected few of the many taxes it had imposed on rural cultivators or artisans, it had surveyed and titled less than half of the national territory (mostly the unpopulated part), and it had attracted virtually no permanent white settlers. Indians remained relatively autonomous and culturally distinct. Only the Catholic church had been effectively disempowered, something that happened throughout Latin America in this period. Popular reaction to Gálvez's anticlerical legislation was mixed. Most people were indifferent to the confiscation of church property and were delighted by the end of the church tithe; they were less happy about putting the state rather than the church in control of education, marriage, and divorce. There is little evidence, however, that the popular revolt that eventually toppled Gálvez was motivated by religious concerns (Ingersoll 1972:78).

The Gálvez attempt to undermine Indian culture through educational reform and various forced assimilation programs also had relatively little direct impact (Braiterman 1986). But Indians began to associate cultural assimilation programs with much more dangerous attacks on their political rights, while Guatemala's white elite, who embodied the Guatemalan state at that point, came to see Indian cultural backwardness as the source of the political rebellions brought on by the final and most "progressive" part of the Liberal program.

What brought resistance to a head and created the conditions for a broad rebellion that included both Indians and non-Indians was Gálvez's attempt to create modern judicial forms in the rural areas through the Livingston Codes.[10] While this reorganization of the judicial system was meant to make all citizens equal before the law, in practice it meant curtailment of the political autonomy already enjoyed in rural communities. Based on legal interpretation of statutes rather than old traditions, the Livingston Codes required a literate population. Yet few people in rural communities, whether Indian or non-Indian, were likely to become literate under the limited and fumbling educational programs of the period, especially after Gálvez had closed church schools pursuant to his anticlerical policies. The effect of the Codes, then, was to make such people more rather than less prey to those who would represent them. And those who would represent them, now representatives of the secular state, had even fewer interests in common with rural smallholders than had the clergy. Thus, for people in rural communities, the Livingston Codes, usually introduced to them as a tax on their community chest and a forced-labor jail-building project, were anathema. In their view, this new legal system would make rural communities much more vulnerable to all the threatening legislation of the period—which the relatively autonomous rural communities, whether Indian or ladino, had rather successfully resisted to this point. Not surprisingly, as Gálvez attempted to impose the Livingston Codes in 1837, revolts occurred throughout rural Guatemala.

The Gálvez period was clearly a "progressive" period in Guatemalan history and has been enshrined as such in Guatemalan histories. But it provoked the most unified political reaction among Guatemala's masses, Indians and ladinos alike, yet seen in Guatemalan history. The "reaction" was once attributed to church machinations (to which the lower orders were assumed more vulnerable than others). A revisionist trend, mostly among North American students of Guatemala (Woodward 1971; Ingersoll 1972; Miceli 1974; Burns 1980; but see also Solórzano 1987) now attributes the reaction to well-grounded fears of capitalist incursion on precapitalist forms of property. Attention to the details of the reaction, however, suggests that the rebels were much more concerned about losing their political autonomy than their property. As long as their community institutions were intact, people in them seemed capable of staving off attacks on their property. The greatest threat to the community was the "nationalist" program of the Gálvez period, the attempt to create equal, free, individual citizens within a homogeneous nation. Because the nationalism of this period was an imposition of elite culture on the masses and because it had no respect for local cultural forms, it provoked a popular, cultural reaction.

Precapitalist Divisions: The Carrera Period

Rafael Carrera, who came to be known as "the protector of the people," was born a casta (of indeterminate origin) in Guatemala City,[11] held jobs variously as a servant, an irregular member of the army, and a pig merchant, before settling as a small farmer in the Mita district of eastern Guatemala, where he came to lead the popular resistance against the Gálvez reforms at the tender age of twenty-two. Nineteenth-century sources provide more information about Carrera himself (down to guesses about the percentage of African and Indian "blood" in his veins) than about the people he led in the uprising; they tell us even less about the particular issues galvanizing the masses. What the sources do make clear is that between 1837 and 1839 Carrera led a popular uprising in eastern Guatemala that included as supporters both ladinos and Indians. Carrera also had the strong support of the local clergy, though the church elite (mostly white and resident in the capital) were less enthusiastic about him (Ingersoll 1972:79).

The ostensible cause of the popular uprising in eastern Guatemala was a cholera epidemic together with the actions taken by the government to contain it. But as a major chronicler of the period points out, the rallying cry of the time was not just "the government is poisoning our waters," it also included "so that they can steal our land" (Ingersoll 1972:46). Ingersoll convincingly argues that the underlying causes of the 1837 revolt were the economic and political threats to rural communities discussed above. We find further evidence for this view in the demands made by the rebels in June 1837, namely: (1) abolition of the Livingston Codes; (2) abolition of the head tax; (3) the return of the Archbishop, the religious orders, and political exiles; and (4) protection of civilian life and property together with respect for Carrera's orders as law under pain of death to violators (Woodward 1971:56). Later that year the rebels added two additional demands: (5) repeal of the civil marriage and divorce laws; and (6) termination of the English colonization contracts (Braiterman 1986:64).

Given the concern with church issues in several of these demands, one might assume, as many Guatemalan historians have, that Carrera and his followers were simply conservative supporters of the church. But Carrera's relation to the church was not simple. He did not support the reinstatement of the church tithe, he did not want clergy to hold office, and he did not return the church property confiscated by the earlier Liberal governments. Ingersoll's interpretation of Carrera's church position (1972:77–113) is probably the most reasonable: Carrera supported the local clergy who had usually acted in the interests of the masses, but he did not support the power of the church hierarchy, which was every bit as exploitative of the masses (whether Indian or ladino) as were others of the white Creole elite.

Though Carrera rose to power on the basis of leading the 1837–1839 popular revolt in eastern Guatemala, most of whose active followers appear to have been non-Indians, it is important to see his movement in the context of several major popular revolts of the period that involved Indians.[12] Between 1811 and 1831 there had been almost continuous revolt by Indian villagers in the western highlands, mainly over issues of tribute (Martínez Peláez 1973). From that time on, government control over the area was extremely shaky in that many communities refused to pay tribute, others refused admittance to government officials doing land surveys or censuses, and yet others hounded unpopular priests or officials from office (Ingersoll 1972:45–76). While Carrera did not appeal to the Indian communities of the western highlands until after his first national victory (in 1839), he appears to have had their support (as well as Indian support in eastern Guatemala) from the beginning (see chaps. 3, 5). It would be entirely wrong, therefore, to see Carrera's movement as one representing ladinos; it represented the interests of both Indians and ladinos as they existed in that period.

Because of Carrera's overwhelming popular support (as well as continued divisions among the Creole elite, each faction of which tried to woo Carrera to their cause), he was able to enforce most of his demands by 1840, even though he did not take formal power until 1844. In response to his demands, Guatemala's 1839 constitution reflects a changed attitude toward Guatemala's Indians:

> Although nature has given all men equal rights, their condition in society is not the same. . . . To establish and maintain social equilibrium, the laws must protect the weak against the strong . . . Thus, the Indian being in this [weak] group, the laws must protect them and better their education, to avoid their being defrauded of what belongs to them in common or as individuals, and so that they will not be molested in the usages and customs learned from their ancestors. (Quoted in Ingersoll 1972:260)

With this justification, the National Assembly decreed a return to the colonial Laws of the Indies concerning the Indians, which established a permanent commission for their protection and development. It also recreated the office of Indian Interpreter, provided for the special handling of Indian cases in the court system, and reestablished the traditional offices of the Indian villagers. A further law in 1841 provided for separate municipal elections for Indian and non-Indian officials (Ingersoll 1972:274).

To a student of Guatemala's modern period, the most striking aspect of the documents that describe Carrera and his regime is their failure to make clear distinctions between Indians and people who are now known as ladinos. Carrera himself was a mestizo, but many contemporary sources refer to him as "the Indian." Carrera's first supporters came from the Mita district in eastern Guatemala, a district that is now almost entirely ladino, but which was described as mainly Indian in the nineteenth century.[13] Few communities in the area, whether Indian or not, held the protected status of Indian communities common to the western highlands. Yet the literature of the nineteenth century suggests that Guatemalan Creoles considered the entire population of the Mita district to be effectively "Indian." European descriptions of the Carrera rebellion describe it as an "Indian" rebellion (Ingersoll 1972:160–203). Gálvez himself warned that Guatemala faced in the Mita district a "race war." The conclusion one must reach is that Guatemalans did not then distinguish among Indians and ladinos the way they do today. Both Indians and ladinos belonged to the lower orders; both groups were distinguished from Creoles by non-European culture, nonwhite blood, and position in the national division of labor. As far as the white Creole elite was concerned, there was little difference between the two. Surviving records do not tell us what Indians and ladinos thought of each other; but it is clear that in the nineteenth century, Indians and ladinos could unite behind a common political cause.

Most interpreters of the Carrera epoch, such as Hazel Ingersoll, see the period as reactionary rather than progressive. Yet most accounts, including Ingersoll's, acknowledge that the increasing political autonomy of rural communities of that period was coupled with increasing rural involvement in commodity production, as the cochineal boom spread its effects throughout the country. Guatemala did not sink into self-sufficiency and economic decline during the Carrera years, as predicted by the Liberals, but actually experienced sufficient financial prosperity that the government and army could expand without imposing additional taxes or labor levies on rural communities. One of the unintended results of the Carrera years, in fact, was that Indians who retained freedom of movement and trade from the Liberal reform era became more fully integrated into the national economy than ever before. While they continued to maintain tradition (language, dress, religion, and the like), they did not do so as marginalized "precapitalist" remnants. They did so as the mainstay and primary producers of Guatemala's growing market economy.[14] Land litigation was fierce during the Carrera period, but the legal procedures gave no undue advantages to foreign settlers or to the Creole elite. Carrera's "modern" nationalist sentiments can also be seen in his legislation against foreign imports, and his suspicion of external capitalists.

Populist governments are often thought to thrive on ethnic divisions. But the most unusual feature of the Carrera period is the degree to which ethnic division seemed muted. The main social division was that between the white Creole elite and the nonwhite masses. Carrera's movement and programs, in fact, promoted class rather than ethnic or racial unity, an extremely radical phenomenon for the era. But inasmuch as Carrera did not confiscate elite property or prevent white Creoles from holding government office, he did not institutionalize a revolutionary state; nor did he develop a coherent populist ideology. He merely used popular support and coercive methods to keep the Creole elite from taking economic as well as political control over Guatemala's nonwhite population for some thirty years.

The strength of popular discontent with Gálvez's "universal citizenship" program proves that an imported nationalist ideology could not build an integrated nation. At the same time, the Liberal conquest of Guatemala six years after Carrera's death suggests that neither can class-unified populist nations be built on precapitalist relations of production—at least in a capitalist era. The actions of the powerful Liberal state that *did* establish capitalism in Guatemala suggest further that, where appropriate, the goal of nationalist integration could easily be sacrificed to the goal of capitalist growth. Indians and ladinos were not opposed to one another in the Carrera interlude. But they became opposed groups in the following era because Carrera's success showed that Guatemala's masses could not be dispossessed as long as they remained politically unified. In building a stronger state apparatus and fomenting capitalist development in Guatemala, the new Liberals found it both possible and useful to divide the masses.

Redrawing the National Divisions: The New Liberal Era

Liberalism had changed in the forty years since Gálvez, less infused by the smallholder, democratic vision inspired by the North American revolution, more "practical" about major development goals. Latin American historians associate the philosophy of the time, still borrowed from Europe, with Comte: positivism, progressivism, social Darwinism (Burns 1980:35–50). It was the heyday of expansive capital investment in Latin America. Justo Rufino Barrios, who was to implement the new Liberal program in Guatemala, was not a philosopher but a major landowner, member of the white Creole elite, and man of action. He saw in coffee, already a major crop in Costa Rica and El Salvador, a golden opportunity for economic expansion in Guatemala. And Barrios was determined to take advantage of that opportunity.

Coffee was indeed a good investment for the planter class. It constituted 50 percent of Guatemalan exports when the Liberals took office; by 1876 the quantity exported had almost doubled and by 1884 quintupled (Mosk 1955). Between 1870 and 1900 the volume of Guatemala's international trade increased twentyfold. A fair number of Europeans, especially Germans, migrated to Guatemala, bringing with them skills, small amounts of capital, and their highly valued culture. Wealthy planters built opera houses, schools, and parks, transforming Guatemala City into a pseudo-European capital. Balancing those accomplishments were "a return to monoculture, declining food production for local consumption, rising foreign debt, forced labor, debt peonage, the growth of latifundia, and the greater impoverishment of the majority" (Burns 1980:106). Given these high costs of creating a coffee economy, how was it accomplished so smoothly and quickly? The answer cannot be reduced to the development of new relations of production, but changes in the general economic climate were highly significant.

One of the main differences between the two Liberal periods in Guatemala was the presence of foreign investors whose goals paralleled those of the Creole elite. Europeans knew the coffee market and what was needed to build a coffee economy: French and U.S. investors built (and owned) the necessary railroads and ports; British and German merchants set up (and controlled) the marketing channels; and German planters experimented with (and demonstrated) the most efficient and profitable ways to grow coffee. Between 1871 and 1883 the Guatemalan state sold nearly 100,000 acres of land that it had designated unclaimed, mostly to those with connections to the government, for coffee production (Handy 1984:65–69). Because of the speed with which land was acquired and the means by which it was acquired (personal connections to the new ruling clique), Guatemala was to develop a large-estate rather than small-estate coffee economy—and to have one of the smallest but most powerful coffee oligarchies in Central America (Williams 1986).

Coffee requires more labor in the harvesting season than it does at other times. But harvesting can be done on small farms by family labor (Costa Rica), on large farms by a settled permanent labor force (El Salvador), or by recruiting seasonal labor from smallholders who have no other connection to the coffee economy. Guatemala followed the third course, in part because of its large estates and in part because the development of coffee plantations did not simultaneously dispossess many smallholders (Cardoso 1975). The Barrios state experimented with many different ways of acquiring coffee labor (McCreery 1976), but within fifteen years had worked out a system that was to dominate Guatemala's economic and political relations thenceforth (Cardoso 1975; Cambranes 1985). The several different means of obtaining labor cobbled together through force of necessity soon took on the appearance of a natural symbiotic system between white planters, ladino plantation agents, and Indian seasonal workers. Coercive apparatuses were basic to the functioning of the coffee labor system until 1945.

One means of acquiring labor was state levy on Indian villages, a system that resurrected the colonial forced-labor tradition: "In 1876, Barrios ordered . . . Indian villages . . . to give the number of hands to the [white] farmers that the latter asked for" (Handy 1984:67). Another means was debt: "By the 1920s virtually all of the men in many [Indian] villages were weighted with a sizable, ever increasing debt to an estate owner" (ibid.:67). Still this was not enough. Hence a process of acquiring Indian land in the highlands began, reaching a high point in 1877 with the passage of a new agrarian law that abolished all forms of communal property. Some highland Indians were completely dispossessed and became permanent workers on the lowland plantations (and ladinos) in the process. Most others held on to some land but were required to work seasonally on plantations in order to buy the food they could no longer produce sufficiently for themselves.

The entire process whereby Indians were coerced into becoming the plantation labor force in the Barrios era has been well documented by historians who emphasize the violence of the process (Cardoso 1975; McCreery 1976, 1986; Cambranes 1985; Williams 1986). Indians resisted, rebelled, and went to court. But no major sustained uprisings occurred in this period or afterward (see chap. 5). Given the immediately preceding history of Guatemala, when a popular movement took state power with Indian support, one has to wonder why Indian resistance was so weak. I suggest that it was weak because the Barrios state, taking power in an ethnic context in which different positions among the nonwhite masses were not yet clearly defined, created a special social existence and class position for ladinos in the coffee region, thus dividing popular interests.

The historians of Guatemala, in noting that Indians were the primary target of state coercion in the Barrios era, have assumed that such targeting was natural.[15] But was it natural that the equally despised ladinos became the agents of Indian oppression in the coffee region rather than equal targets for plantation labor needs? It was, I would argue, not. Only when ladinos became a special class of plantation and state agents did they command a significantly higher social status than Indians in the social judgment of the time. This is not to argue that Indians could just as easily have taken on this new role. Ladinos (who at this point in time were presumed to have some white blood) filled the newly created class positions because, as "partial" whites, they did not challenge the traditional ideology of race hierarchy in taking the mediating role as agents between plantation owners and workers. Racial hierarchies, partially reinforced by class, continue to exist throughout the New World. What is notable about the phenomenon in Guatemala is that the emergence of agrarian capitalism, which eradicated distinctions between Indians and non-Indians in the coffee zones of the rest of Central America, created divisions between Indians and non-Indians in the coffee zones of Guatemala that did not exist in the precoffee era.

Why was Guatemala different? The answer lies in the preexisting distribution and separation of the different ethnic groups in Guatemala, together with the fact that the creation of coffee plantations did not simultaneously dispossess Indians of their land. As noted earlier, the corporate Indian villages of the colonial era were located mainly in the western highlands of Guatemala. During the colonial period non-Indians could not reside in these communities unless they represented either the church or the Crown. In other parts of Guatemala—the towns, the southern lowlands, and the eastern highlands—Indians and ladinos were not so spatially segregated and the economic difference between Indians and ladinos was insignificant (MacLeod 1983; Lutz 1988). When ladinos began to move into the western highlands, they did so as special agents of the state and coffee economy—that is, as a different class.

With the creation of coffee plantations in the southern piedmont of western Guatemala, large numbers of people (Indians and ladinos) migrated to the West, mainly from the relatively impoverished areas of eastern Guatemala.[16] Some of those who migrated to western Guatemala became the permanent labor force on the plantations. Others were hired by the plantations as agents, to find seasonal (Indian) labor in the corporate communities of the western highlands. Yet others, no longer restricted by colonial law, simply moved into Indian communities, not to become smallholders like the Indians, but to become the main instruments of the debt peonage system—as merchants, liquor sellers, labor contractors, and, for the first time, landlords (Davis 1970). Ladinos also became agents of the state, working in the interests of the coffee oligarchy, in the western highlands. Thus, state militias, which under Carrera were almost entirely Indian (Ingersoll 1972:273), became "under Barrios . . . almost exclusively . . . ladino" (Handy 1984:71). And ladinos increasingly took control of local politics in the Indian areas, as the literate secretaries, if not the actual mayors, of Indian municipios. These people became what people in the western highlands mean by the term *ladino* today.

The term *ladino*, which meant "Spanish-speaking Indian" during the colonial period, had come to refer to castas (people of mixed biological descent) by the time of independence.[17] The casta system, which labeled mestizos by the precise nature of their racial descent, had become unworkable after several centuries of biological mixing, because it was no longer possible to trace peoples' actual genealogy. The terms *casta*, *mestizo*, and *ladino* had all come to mean anyone who was not culturally Indian, regardless of specific descent, blurring the many racial classifications used in the colonial era. By the Barrios era *ladino* had become the term most commonly used to refer to this very mixed group of people. But by the early twentieth century, the term *ladino* had disappeared in the rest of Central America (to be replaced by mestizo) and ladino had come to mean something new in Guatemala: oppressor in the western highlands of Guatemala, and homeless (and therefore permanent) worker in the cities and lowlands. For with the coffee economy, the class positions of Indians and ladinos began to diverge. Only in the eastern highlands, distant from the coffee economy, did ladinos share the same class position as Indians, that of small subsistence farmers (Adams 1956b).

Two examples will suffice to illustrate the process whereby Indians and ladinos became separate and opposed classes in the western highlands. According to Colby and van den Berghe (1969), the Ixil area of the western highlands (three municipios in the department of El Quiché, not untypical of the remoter areas of the highlands) was isolated from ladinos until the late nineteenth century. An 1803 document reported no ladinos in the area. When an early pioneer arrived in 1887, there were no ladinos "except for the priest and a handful of mestizos *who lived like Indians*" (ibid.:69, emphasis mine). In the 1893 census there were 98 ladinos out of a total population of about 12,500. The first settlers were state-appointed municipal officials and labor contractors. "Their labor-contracting activities expanded into money-lending which, combined with the sale of cane alcohol, and the spread of clandestine distilling, gradually reduced more and more Indians to a state of perpetual indebtedness" (ibid.:72–73). Before this time, the Ixil were self-sufficient in food and engaged in a lively trade in pigs and cattle for export; by 1925 the Ixil were importing corn and beans. By the turn of the century the Ixil area (whose total population was about 12,500) exported some 8,000–10,000 workers per year (no doubt, some individuals more than once). In 1904 political power in the largest municipio was in the hands of two "ladinoized principales" and a ladino secretary. By 1924, dual governments (Indian and ladino) were established, with effective power in the hands of ladinos (ibid.:75–76).

Robert Carmack (1979) has documented the way in which ladinos came to live in and exert control over another large Indian municipio in the department of Totonicapán, which prior to the Barrios reforms had had little contact with non-Indians. The first ladino settlers arrived in the early 1870s as merchants and labor contractors. In 1874 the most fertile land of this municipio was taken out of Indian hands and put into those of ladinos by the actions of the state-appointed provincial governor, who rationalized this move as one that would enhance the area's productivity. A major revolt ensued in which neighboring municipios, also predominantly Indian, participated. But the revolt was brutally suppressed with the assistance of the recently immigrant ladinos armed by the departmental governor. Afterward, local governance of the rebellious municipios fell into the hands of one of Barrios's cronies, Teodoro Cienfuegos, who had become one of the major landlords of the region. Appointed as provincial governor in 1885, Cienfuegos assisted further ladino settlement in the smaller communities of the area. These ladino settlers became the exclusive bearers of arms and the informal agents of the increasingly coercive state. Cienfuegos appointed the new settlers to many local offices in the area and through these and more violent means kept potentially rebellious Indians under tight control. Similar events took place throughout the Indian highlands in the last quarter of the nineteenth century (Davis 1970; King 1974).

Yet even as Indians lost some critical aspects of their economic and political autonomy in this period, they held onto others, most particularly their small parcels of highland land as well as certain symbols of community that defined them as distinct from (and united against) the ladinos among them (see C. Smith 1984a, 1987a). That is, while partially proletarianized, Indians retained much more personal autonomy from white rule than did ladinos, who were granted the power to exploit Indians but only through the agency of white power. Those who were to become the modern ladinos (whether they were "redressed" Indians or old members of the castas) were those who lacked the economic bases for remaining politically independent of white Creole power. Those who were to remain Indians, on the other hand, were those who actively resisted (and had the economic or communal means to resist) becoming completely dependent upon white Creole power.

In a word, plantations created proletarians, semiproletarians, and agents of the proletarianization process. The proletarians and agents were to become ladinos; the semiproletarians were to remain Indians. As this process occurred, Guatemala's rural population, which was mostly "Indian" in the social judgment of the Carrera period, became one-third ladino by 1950. Virtually all the "Indian" villages of eastern Guatemala, remote from the plantation labor dragnet, became ladino. Virtually all of the permanent residents of the plantation lowlands were ladinos, either migrants from former casta areas or "redressed" Indians who had lost land in their villages. At the same time, those municipios continuously tapped for seasonal labor became "an indigestible, culturally hostile core of corporate Indian communities" (McCreery 1976:152), even as their local autonomy was eroded, their corporate mechanisms weakened, and their very territories invaded by people who identified themselves as non-Indians, or ladinos. Essentially, Indians, who had been coerced into semiproletarian status, resisted the status of full proletarian.

The plantation heyday closed in 1944 with an urban revolt that had little connection to economic conditions in the western coffee region. At that time, virtually all Indians were required to carry passbooks that recorded the days worked in fulfillment of enforced labor contracts to either plantations or the state. In the western highlands ladinos were in political control of most Indian villages as the traditional systems of Indian governance were placed under their jurisdiction. In addition, ladinos monopolized wholesaling, transport, and labor contracting in the Indian towns, made up the skilled labor force on the plantations and in the cities, and also dominated the national bureaucratic apparatus as teachers, lawyers, accountants, technicians, and the middle ranks of the army. Many ladinos owned small businesses, a few owned large firms.

At the national level, as opposed to the western highlands, the class distinctions between Indians and ladinos were not so clearly marked. In eastern Guatemala, many ladinos remained smallholders, like the Indians of the area; notably, most Indians in this region, culturally distinct in the early nineteenth century, could not be distinguished from ladinos by the mid-twentieth century (Adams 1956b). In the southern plantation area, both Indians and ladinos were plantation workers, though Indians as opposed to ladinos were coerced rather than voluntary workers, and members of the two groups usually held different job positions on the plantation (Pansini 1977). In the western highlands, however, where most Indians maintained their permanent residence, ladinos did not share the class position of Indians, having become agents of labor (and of the oppressive state) rather than laborers themselves. Under these circumstances, Indians came to identify ladinos with both state and class oppression.

Ladinos themselves differentiated into distinct classes within Guatemala, some staffing the bureaucracy of the expanded state, others coming to own various firms as well as farms employing Indians or other ladinos, while yet others became workers or remained rural smallholders. But class difference could not become as salient as ethnic difference because of the particular way in which class and ethnicity were intertwined: that is, because Indian and ladino smallholders (i.e., those in similar class positions) were spatially separated; because class differentiation among Indians remained extremely limited such that the agents of Indian oppression were mainly ladinos; because even oppressed ladinos could claim a higher social position than Indians; and because the real owners and rulers of Guatemala, the white Creole elite, became increasingly invisible as a distinct ladino class became their agents. Thus, the coffee economy reorganized the regional and class patterning of ethnicity in Guatemala, disguising the interests that Indians and many ladinos might still have held in common, and created the internal divisions within Guatemala that still wrack the present. Whereas the primary political division in the nineteenth century was between the white elite and the nonwhite masses (both Indian and ladino), the primary political division in the twentieth century came to be that between Indians and ladinos. The white/nonwhite division did not disappear; it simply became less apparent.

Meanwhile state power under the new Liberals had expanded and centralized, such that all political decisions and appointments were made at the national level. Three powerful despots ruled Guatemala for forty-seven of the seventy-three years between 1871 and 1944, assisted at the state level by Guatemala's small white coffee oligarchy and at the local level by a new ladino "class." A professional army had been developed, stronger than any in Central America. Wealth was highly concentrated and many Indians were in desperate economic circumstances. Yet rural political protest was limited, social life seemed stable, Indians appeared and were portrayed as passive sheep. Guatemala was divided into two hostile camps, but this division strengthened rather than weakened the state.

Conclusion

Though no Central American state achieved national unity before World War II, Guatemala remains unique in still having a markedly divided nonwhite population, that is, in having an "Indian problem." The origin of this problem can be found in the nineteenth century, and is both internal to Guatemala and external to it. The internal problem was the spatial segregation of Indian and ladino smallholders together with the class division between Indians and ladinos in the western highlands. These divisions allowed Guatemala's Creole elite, threatened by the political unity of Indians and ladinos in the Carrera period, to retain economic power and to regain political control. Ladinos were willing agents of Creole power, not only because some of them benefited from the exploitation of Indians but because all of them benefited from being treated as non-Indians. Ladinos did not have to share power with the Creole elite to be privileged—even as smallholders in eastern Guatemala, or as a full-fledged proletariat in the cities. For even as capitalist relations of production expanded, they were limited by the fact that Indians bore the brunt of absolute rather than relative exploitation.[18]

The reinforcement of ethnic divisions by class divisions in the western highlands thus rested on a paradox. As capitalist relations of production expanded to create a new class position for some ladinos, it maintained noncapitalist relations of production between Indians and ladinos. Indians, the coerced labor force, could not be fully proletarianized as long as they remained coerced (which differentiated them as a class from virtually all ladinos); while ladinos, the voluntary (i.e., fully proletarianized) labor force, were to take on certain noncapitalist class roles vis-à-vis Indians which in the colonial period were exercised by state agents rather than by an independent class—that is, the roles of landlord, merchant, and labor recruiter. Essentially, then, Guatemala's capitalist state created two noncapitalist classes in western Guatemala: that of coerced labor (Indian) and that of labor-coercer (ladino). These noncapitalist relations of production were stronger in 1944 than they were in 1844, which accounts for their modern-day entrenchment. The class reinforcement of ethnic divisions was accompanied by a new and virulent form of racism in Guatemala, much more powerful than that of the colonial period, in that it continued to bar ladinos from full exercise of power in Guatemala even as it granted them the power to more fully oppress Indians.

The external factor that helped create Guatemala's class-reinforced ethnic division was the world order of the late nineteenth century. In that period the elites of peripheral states had far more to gain from pursuing capitalist development (even though it be incomplete and dependent capitalist development), than from building states legitimated by popular support. Certainly in Guatemala's case, the coercive state that came into being under Barrios rewarded its Creole elites much more highly than the populist state under Carrera. The Barrios state, moreover, was stronger, wealthier, and more stable than any other state in nineteenth-century Central America, even though it was based on a polarized ethnic situation. And though coercive, the Barrios state was not incapable of building its own kind of legitimating myths (of racial difference), which were wholeheartedly endorsed by all but the Indians of Guatemala. Obviously, we cannot see the social relations and nationalist myths required to build this state as being "functional" for Guatemala in the long run. But we can see from the Guatemalan case that successful state-building does not require either the myth or the reality of national unity as some social theorists have maintained (e.g., Tilly 1975; Nairn 1977; Gellner 1983; A. Smith 1983).

Guatemala's second Liberal state built on the social possibilities given to it by its colonial heritage as well as the opportunities provided to it by the world coffee market in the latter third of the nineteenth century. Yet it is clear that it was not preordained that the division between Indians and ladinos, which today plagues any attempt to build other than a coercive state in Guatemala, was an inevitable outcome of building a coffee export economy on the social relations bequeathed by Spanish colonialism. Coffee export economies were built in the four other Central American countries (which also held Indians, castas, and white Creole elites in the colonial period) in the same period examined here. Yet none of them emerged from the experience with a marked social division between Indians and ladinos. Instead Indians were gradually eliminated as a social category, assimilated to the numerically dominant mestizos, even as white Creoles continued to hold power. The marked social divisions between Indians and ladinos in Guatemala can thus only be explained by Guatemala's distinct economic and political history.

At the same time, the contrasting examples of other Central American states, few of which display a greater degree of national (or cultural) unity than Guatemala, indicate that the problem of ethnic division among the lower classes is not what prevents nation-building in Central America— or other parts of Latin America. The intrinsic division in Central America is that between locals, whether assumed to be pure or mixed, and nonlocals, those whose power and identity rest upon ties outside of the national territory. Those ties, based in race or culture as the embodiment of race, are also ties to imperialism, whether of the Spanish or post-Spanish variety. And because the division between the whites and nonwhites (which is also the division between locals and nonlocals) is reflected in class and cultural differences as well as assumed race differences, the division is not easily mystified by myths of national unity. Only as nonwhites take more than symbolic positions of political and economic power in Central America (as they have in postrevolutionary Mexico and Nicaragua)—or only as nonwhites have been essentially eliminated as a social category (as they have been in Costa Rica) is it possible to develop unifying myths of national identity.

Seen in this light, the division of Guatemala's masses into Indians and ladinos is not the impediment to national unity that it appears. Guatemala under Carrera, which had distinct groups of Indians and non-Indians, was more nationally unified than any Central American country (other than postrevolutionary Nicaragua) has been heretofore. The Carrera period, moreover, opened up quite a different alternative to nation- and state-building in Guatemala than that which occurred under Barrios. It is true that following through on that alternative would have fully disempowered the white colonizers of the New World who, in the long run, were disempowered nowhere in the nineteenth century. It is also true that the nineteenth century saw few anti-imperialist movements as radical as that which occurred in Guatemala under Carrera. But a few such movements did exist. The fact that these exceptions remain a silent space in general Western (and Latin American) thought helps "naturalize" the belief that economic development and nation-building cannot take place in a context of cultural plurality and that colonized people are forever doomed to failed development and coercive states—except possibly with Western intervention.

Notes

1. I have learned more about the differences between history and anthropology from writing this essay than from any other scholarly endeavor. My friends who are historians (e.g., Steve Palmer, Howie Machtinger, Robert Carmack, Ralph Lee Woodward, Chris Lutz, Robert Williams, and David McCreery) all asked for more evidence, clarification of detail, and a strong narrative line uncomplicated by comparative flourishes. They strongly suggested that I present this essay as a hypothesis rather than proven historical fact, given my dependence on rather weak secondary materials. My friends who are anthropologists (Brackette Williams, Katherine Verdery, Les Field, Charlie Hale, Richard Fox) asked for theoretical clarification and comparative relevance, uncluttered

by complicating details. I am sure this compromise will satisfy neither group, though I am grateful for the considerable assistance received from both.

2. Ladinos do exist as a social category in southern Mexico where class and political relations among Indians, "mestizos," and whites have been similar to those in Guatemala (cf. Wasserstrom 1983), though the timing of the political conflicts creating the categories has been slightly different. A white Creole elite group still exists in modern (postrevolutionary) Nicaragua, but its social and political supremacy has been challenged by the Sandinista revolution of 1979; there are also small Indian groups in Nicaragua, but they are politically important only because of the way they have been manipulated by foreign powers (see C. Smith, Boyer, and Diskin 1988).

3. In the latter part of the colonial period, Guatemala did have a few major aristocratic families associated with indigo production and trade. But even these individuals owed their position to state protection through the merchant Consulado, a state-directed monopoly on export trade (Woodward 1966). Apart from these few families, most members of the Creole elite in Guatemala, apart from the very powerful church, did not have major economic enterprises that afforded them independence from the state as did Creoles in other Spanish colonies, such as Mexico or Peru (Wortman 1982).

4. It is probably more appropriate to talk in terms of social orders or "estates" in the colonial period than of social classes, given that free labor and capitalist relations of production were so little developed in colonial Guatemala. My point here, however, is to suggest some of the similarities between the Indian/ladino division in the colonial and modern periods as a contrast to that which existed in the nineteenth century, when cultural differences were not reinforced by class or economic differences.

5. Few Indians, at least in the western highlands, appear to have chosen to become ladinos voluntarily in the colonial period because it meant separation from the main form of property not monopolized by the white elites, the lands held by corporate Indian communities. Lutz and Lovell (chap. 2) describe the different circumstances that led Indians to become ladinos in the colonial period.

6. MacLeod (1973) observes that castas were as fully depreciated as Indians, if not more so, and that the Crown was quite concerned during the entire colonial period to draw them into "useful" work, by which they meant work in enterprises owned or controlled by whites. Because of their anomalous position, castas were known for unruly, antisocial behavior and were considered the "criminal element" in colonial society.

7. Anderson, however, considers the Creole revolts of the nineteenth century to have been true "nationalist" movements, in the sense that they were inspired by attempts to distinguish "American" culture from Hispanic culture. It is nonetheless notable that the American culture aspired to was pan–Latin American, that is, the culture of the white Creoles; since Creoles in each country were concerned above all to distinguish themselves from the lower orders in their countries, they clung to external sources of identity (whether European or North American) and did not develop any sense of local cultural identity. A sense of local or national culture among Latin American elites, in the sense of being rooted in particular traditions and histories (and thus necessarily involving the

masses) is still largely absent in much of Latin America.

8. Mariano Gálvez (1831–1838) was the first Guatemalan to pursue the strategy of attempting to lure European immigrants to Guatemala (Braiterman 1986), but in this he was only following a general trend in nineteenth-century Latin America (Mörner 1985). According to Mörner, Guatemala was less successful than most Latin American countries in this strategy. But the attempt continued throughout the nineteenth and twentieth centuries. Rufino Barrios (1873–1885) even tried to bribe white workers to come to Guatemala with offers of high wages (McCreery 1976), with notable lack of success, thinking that white workers would be much more productive than native workers. It may not be necessary to point out the racist assumptions in these strategies.

9. The constitution of 1824 was that of the Central American Federal Republic, which included Guatemala, El Salvador, Honduras, Nicaragua, and Costa Rica.

10. Observers of the time believed that an outbreak of cholera, which priests described as divine retribution against attacks on the church, was the main factor behind the rebellion. Ingersoll (1972) carefully undermines this view and argues that the main factor was the Liberal attempt to privately title land. Yet if we are to take the rebels' own voice into account, their main concern seemed to be the Livingston Code and the head tax—as well as some (but far from all) attacks on religion (see Woodward 1971:56).

11. During the entire period that Carrera was in power, there was considerable concern about his racial background. His family historian concluded that he was 72 percent Spanish, 17.5 percent African, and 10.5 percent Indian (Ingersoll 1972:105). He was often called "the Indian" because he "looked like one." It was widely rumored that he was adopted and that his antecedents were of either higher or lower racial status than his family background indicated, depending on whether the rumor originated with someone who admired or despised him.

12. Carrera did not actually take formal power until 1844, abdicated in the face of new uprisings in eastern Guatemala among his former followers (the Lucíos) in 1848, and then took power "for life" again in 1851. Upon taking power for a second time, with the strong backing of the Indians from western Guatemala, Carrera put down the Lucíos revolt, even though that revolt was in his home territory and led by his original (mestizo) followers who were disappointed in the rewards they received for supporting Carrera earlier (Ingersoll 1972:285-331).

13. The Mita district was later broken into three departments. The population in two of these (Jutiapa and Santa Rosa) is now more than 90 percent ladino, and in one of them (Jalapa) it is two-thirds ladino. As described by Ingersoll, the Mita district was an area of farmers, merchants and, weavers that had been relatively prosperous in the colonial period, but had been in decline since the beginning of the nineteenth century. On the basis of local sources, it was predominantly Indian at the time of the revolt (Ingersoll 1972:47–49). According to Lutz (1988), the region at the time of independence (thirty-five years before the revolt) may have been about one-third ladino or casta, two-thirds Indian.

14. My evidence for the increasing commercialization of Indians during the Carrera period is mostly indirect, though Carmack (1979) provides evidence

supporting the view. I would like to thank David McCreery for seeking such evidence for me in the archives. McCreery did not find information that would either support or refute my hypothesis here.

15. Handy, for example, observes that considerable changes had occurred in race/ethnic relations between the 1840s and 1870s. In his view, the "division between white and ladino had been eroded" (1984:72) and, in consequence, ladinos identified themselves more closely with white Creole interests. The problem with this interpretation is that there is little evidence that ladinos held any more real power in the 1870s (except the power to exploit Indians) than they did in the 1840s. Thus, I argue that rather than the difference between ladinos and whites having been eroded, the difference between ladinos and Indians had been exacerbated. Ladinos did indeed identify themselves more closely with white Creole interests, but white Creoles then (as now) did not identify themselves more closely with ladinos.

16. Population growth rates in the plantation area between 1893 and 1921 were about twice those of Guatemala as a whole; in a period that saw the doubling of Guatemala's total population, eastern Guatemala's population remained relatively stable, indicating a high rate of migration out of the area (C. Smith 1978). Accompanying these population movements were changes in the ethnic composition of the population in different regions. According to my calculations based on official censuses, the western region of Guatemala (which includes the south coast plantation area but excludes the Vera Paz area north of Guatemala City) was 90 percent Indian in 1880, 79 percent in 1893, 82 percent in 1921, and 76 percent in 1950. Ethnic change in eastern Guatemala is variable, depending on the early composition of the population. Jutiapa, El Progreso, and Santa Rosa, for example, are nearly one-fourth Indian in the 1964 census; Jalapa and Chiquimula change less, from over half Indian in 1893 (66 percent in the case of Chiquimula) to some 15 percent less in 1964. Zacapa was 41 percent Indian in 1893, 19 percent in 1950, and 11 percent in 1964.

17. According to Lutz (1982:433–434) the term *ladino* meant Spanish-speaking Indian throughout the sixteenth and seventeenth centuries. By the eighteenth century, some people meant by the term *mestizo* persons of Hispanic culture. In the census of 1778 it was explained that the term *ladino* included all those of mixed race "because it was impossible to know the true origins of all such people." By the nineteenth century the system of nomenclature distinguishing different casta groups was clearly in flux. Thus, an English traveler, Henry Dunn, observed in 1829 that "the offspring of Negroes and Indians, are included under the term Mulattoes, by which they are generally known; sometimes, however, they are called Mestizoes or Ladinos" (Parker 1970:114). While currently the Guatemalan state and many Guatemalan people use the term *ladino* to mean anyone who is not culturally Indian, most people of European descent reject the term for themselves because it still carries the association of mixed (and thus inferior) descent.

18. By these terms I mean that a significant portion of the surpluses produced by Indian labor is expropriated by capital essentially through the use of force, whereas the surpluses produced by (most) ladino labor is expropriated by capital through the economic mechanism of a wage that pays less than the value produced by that labor.

5. State Power, Indigenous Communities, and Land in Nineteenth-Century Guatemala, 1820–1920

David McCreery

Department of History, Georgia State University

The most evident characteristic of nineteenth-century Guatemalan politics was the dramatic increase in the power of the state. This was an outcome of the policies of the Liberal regimes of the 1820s and 1830s and of the coffee-fueled neo-Liberal Reforma after 1871. And it came at the expense of the political and economic autonomy of the rural population, especially that of the indigenous communities of the western highlands and the Alta Verapaz. Remembering that in nineteenth-century Guatemala, as today, land was the chief source of wealth and power for the elite and of subsistence for the rural poor, this chapter will focus on state intervention in the ownership and use of rural property. It questions two widely held perceptions about these years. One involves the way in which and the extent to which export agriculture, and particularly coffee after 1860, invaded and engrossed Indian lands. The other concerns what indigenous communities did when faced with such encroachment. The chapter traces government land policies, examines the efforts of successive regimes to enforce these, and considers how the population in the countryside reacted to new demands and pressures.

Perhaps no aspect of the history of Guatemala in the century after independence is more misunderstood than the fate of the lands of the Indian communities. The general consensus has it that "small holdings and *ejidos* (communal lands) were nationalized [or] outlawed," or, specifically, "[i]n 1877, President Justo Rufino Barrios abolished communal ownership of land" (Jonas and Tobis 1974; Grieshaber 1979).[1] This understanding results in part from taking word for fact: the law passed by the Liberal regime in August 1836, for example, announced that "all ejidos will be converted to private property" (Pineda de Mont 1869–1872, III:679), and the 1877 decree mentioned above provided that "when an individual asks for land from . . . ejidos or other community property . . . it will be measured and put up for public auction" (Mendez Montenegro 1960:136). More broadly, it reflects our general ignorance of Guatemalan rural history, a history still to be investigated and written. In the absence of adequate studies, the tendency is to reason by analogy, often faulty, with the histories of neighboring or apparently similar countries or to take law for reality, something few would be so rash as to do for present day Guatemala. While it is undoubtedly true that the nineteenth century witnessed a "massive assault on Indian lands" (McCreery 1976:457), the process was both more complex and more subtle than is generally recognized.

A second and related idea is that the rural indigenous population reacted violently to Liberal policies and the impact of the market economy: "Throughout the late 19th and early 20th centuries, highland villages rose in revolt against Liberal demands on the their labor and land" (Handy 1984:72).[2] Such a description, however, more accurately characterizes the conflicts of the 1830s and 1840s (Woodward 1971)—though land disputes were only one among many causes for these *tumultos* (riots)—than it does that of the turn of the century. If there were occasional and quite spectacular "rebellions"[3] against some of the specific results of Reforma policies (AGCA MG, leg. 28595, ex. 39, 51; McCreery 1988), what is most notable about the second half of the century is precisely the decline in violent opposition to the state. The contrary argument (i.e., that violent resistance was the common response) might appear to be rooted in common sense: the state and the planters, in a harshly exploitative and grotesquely one-sided relationship, took from the indigenous population their land and labor, factors the Indians themselves needed for survival. Logically, the Indians resisted, with violence when necessary, as they had in the past. Too, such an interpretation satisfies the need of many historians and social scientists to see peasants and indigenous populations as positive actors, not simply passive victims, of their own history. The problem for Guatemala is that it cannot be sustained empirically. Indeed, all evidence suggests few and a declining number of Indian tumultos after mid-century. An interpretation of the nineteenth century focused on uprisings would require, as the evidence will make clear, a low regard for the abilities of the indigenous population to accurately assess its reality.

Late Colonial Land and Social Relations

To understand how the land situation in Guatemala developed after independence, it is necessary to begin by looking at the last years of the colony. In most areas of what is presently the republic, and particularly in the western highlands where the indigenous communities concentrated, *latifundia* hardly existed. A few haciendas (e.g., Chancol in Huehuetenango or Chuacorral and Argueta north of Lake Atitlán) survived uneasily in an Indian-dominated highlands, and Creole and ladino cattle ranches had begun to move into lands abandoned by the extinguished towns on the south coast. Hardscrabble farms dotted the Oriente.[4] But the characteristic feature of the colonial period was the failure of the elites to penetrate the countryside as landowners or producers (Cortes y Larraz 1958:5, 115). The profits of the colony, such as they were, were to be had in commerce and office holding or, after mid-eighteenth century, in the indigo fields of El Salvador, not in the *altiplano* or the decayed cacao groves of the coast. Thus, much land remained in the possession and use of the indigenous communities. Colonial law in Guatemala recognized the right of each Spanish or Indian, but not ladino,[5] municipio to an ejido (community lands) of one square league.[6] For various reasons some towns never actually obtained this, though most in fact claimed and used much more (AGCA A3.30 2578 37864). Within the community itself, land was held in every imaginable combination of use tenure and private property; *costumbre* (custom) ruled. With a greatly reduced rural population—probably not until the end of the colonial period or even the mid-nineteenth century did populations begin to approximate preconquest levels—and much open space, conflict over land, if more or less traditional between some neighboring communities, was rarely a serious problem for the colonial state.

By the end of the colonial period, the term "ejido" had lost its original meaning of village common land. It now applied more broadly to all of the lands a village possessed or claimed or of which it made use. These might include: (1) the *astillero*, strictly community land available to all for wood and water, for the temporary pasture of animals, or, in some cases, for rent in small plots for cultivation by the poorer members of the community; (2) land purchased by and for the community, or by the central state for the community, either from private individuals or from public lands. In the late colonial period this often took the form of *composición*, payment to regularize long-term but technically illegal possession (AGCA A1.23, leg. 4570, exp. 39326; de Solano 1977:114); (3) land owned or possessed by individuals, families, or *parcialidades* (residential clan groups) of the village (Hill and Monaghan 1987); (4) tracts claimed or used since "time immemorial" by the village or residents of the village without, at least from the perspective of the state, any legal basis. These latter the state commonly referred to as *excedientes* or *excesos* (i.e., excess land over the community's legal ejido), and they technically continued to be state land, called *realenga* in the colonial period and *terreno baldío* after 1821. There were also large tracts of state-owned land that remained unoccupied or only occasionally hosted a transient flock of sheep or a roving woodcutter. Both the colonial and the national state after 1821 recognized rights of de facto possession but, largely for fiscal reasons, sought to induce communities to title the land they used.

All *vecinos* (legal residents)[7] of the village generally had access to community lands for subsistence agriculture and stock raising. Most practiced shifting *milpa* (corn and beans) farming. Land surveyors (*agrimensores*), when they measured ejidos, commonly reported crossing large areas of *guatales*, the *monte* or second growth on fallow milpa land. Two sets of circumstances, however, might impede free access to and movement across community lands. Local power figures, whether hereditary or self-made *caciques*, Crown-appointed *gobernadores*, or elders (*principales*), and often in collusion with ladino officials or the local priest, sometimes conspired to gain control over tracts of community land, whether as legally titled private property or simply in de facto possession (AGCA 1855:leg. 28568, exp. 248; leg. 28619, exp. 254). In addition, well-off (by village standards), or particularly well-organized or large families or clans, might seek to establish preferential rights to certain areas. These residential groupings not uncommonly solidified into identifiable *cantones* or *aldeas* (hamlets), and reinforced their claims with ancestor crosses as well as surveys, composición, and title documents. Eventually they might seek independent municipio status (Hill and Monaghan 1987:chap.9).

Outsiders who attempted to gain access to community land usually found this difficult. Under Spanish rule and for most of the nineteenth century prior to 1877, villages could sell land to those from outside the community only with the specific permission of the state (Pineda de Mont 1869–1872:658, 663). The government, dependent for much of this period on revenue from Indian tribute, generally resisted the alienation of community resources, and before 1821 laws forbade, or discouraged, non-Indians from settling in the towns. The Indians shunned the few that managed to establish themselves there, treating them as a separate *parcialidad de ladinos* and specifically excluding them from participation in community land ownership (AGCA-ST Huehuetenango 1901:paq. 21, exp.10). Only for the most pressing need would a village consider selling land to someone not a native of the town. Within the community, of course, individual property of various sorts existed, parallel to and often intermixed with community-owned tracts. Such parcels, whether held as state-sanctioned private property or as a fixed possession in the peculiar tenure system of the community (AGCA, "tierras" 6033 53213), had existed at least from the immediate postconquest years. In general, though, and apart from clan claims, individual private property in land made little sense in a regimen of shifting cultivation.

When ladinos did penetrate village lands prior to 1877, it was usually through the institution of *censo enfiteusis*, a form of long-term rent available, at the discretion of the municipality, to vecinos and outsiders alike (Pineda de Mont 1869–1872:66). Towns typically entered into such agreements to raise money to meet tax demands, to fight an epidemic or other natural disaster, or to fund schools and public works. The annual rent for vecinos was usually 2 percent of the estimated value of the land; noncommunity members might be charged 3 percent. Contracts typically ran nine years and could be, and commonly were, renewed. Renters might sublet or sell their *dominio útil* (use rights) over the land, as well as any improvements or plantings they had made.[8] Over time individuals tended, and, indeed, some actively sought, to confuse dominio útil with legal ownership and to attempt to treat the land as private property. But the law was clear, and where the municipio detected and contested this usurpation, the state supported it (AGCA-ST Chimaltenango 1858:paq. 3, exp. 6).

Social Relations before Coffee

The first decades of independence brought a cascade of new land laws notable both for their ineffectualness and for the hostility they engendered. Intent on modernizing their country to conform to the ideas of Bourbon political economy and imported English liberalism, and to meet such specific criticisms of Guatemala's problems as those raised in the famous *Apuntamientos* of 1810 (Garcia Laguardia 1971:appendix), the leaders of the new state, and particularly the Liberals who dominated government policy from independence until 1839, passed law after law meant to convert ejidos and terrenos baldíos into private property and "family farms": "the small number of property owners is one of the causes of our backwardness" (Pineda de Mont 1869–1872:658). To stimulate the productive use of land, they substituted a land tax, the *contribución territorial*, for the *diezmo* or tithe (AGCA B.78.24 714 15935; AEG "Libro de la contribución territorial, 1833–1839") and auctioned off to private individuals the properties of the church's regular orders (Holleran 1949:58–59).

Fundamental reform of an institution as deeply rooted in custom as land would have been difficult under the most favorable of circumstances; to undertake it in the midst of the civil wars that wracked Guatemala from the 1820s to the 1840s was suicidal. It is perhaps the best example of the first-generation Liberals' inability to reconcile largely utopian theory with reality, and it accomplished the unlikely feat of bringing many of the large landowners together with the indigenous population in opposition to the state. War, pestilence, and banditry stalked Guatemala in the 1830s, making a mockery of the Liberals' dreams of enlightenment and progress.[9] The stagnation of exports and the effects of the fighting curtailed state resources, while the demands of war drained off what little income was to be had. The state was strong enough to generate opposition but not to put its policies into effect; it could irritate and injure but it could neither protect nor control, especially in the countryside. A flurry of reactionary laws at the end of the 1830s could not save these Liberals, and in 1839 a peasant revolt lead by Rafael Carrera swept them from power (Ingersoll 1972). Harried by intrigue and revolts, foreign wars and disease, the Conservatives who succeeded to power were no more able than had been the Liberals to enforce their writ in the rural areas. They simply made less effort to do so.

In a well-known chapter published some forty years ago, Oliver La Farge (1940) suggested that the years from the late 1830s through the 1860s were something of a golden age in the Guatemalan highlands for community autonomy and freedom from outside intervention. Recent research tends to bear this out. A fragile and beleagured state issued laws and decrees but could visit little effective attention on a rural population that resisted paying taxes and for whose land and labor the ladino elites had little use. The Conservatives revived the Laws of the Indies but, in fact, more neglected than protected the Indians. The church, weakened by disputes with the state and by declining revenues, lost much of its hold on the village populations. Enlightenment reforms, economic decline, and social chaos combined to strip the community *cofradías* (religious brotherhoods) of many of their resources and properties, prompting a marked decline in church and state interest in these institutions (AEG, "Cartas" February 8, 1855, #0042, correspondence of cura of Jacaltenango, March 16, 1857). This situation freed up both the *cabildo* (town government) and the cofradías to become more genuinely indigenous political and religious vehicles. The communities, abandoned by the church and the central government and harassed but not overwhelmed by disease and war, were left for a generation largely to themselves to bring to full fruition the institutions of corporate organization associated with the "closed corporate peasant community" and "traditional" society.[10]

It is instructive, if not particularly edifying, to discover that the Indians of the altiplano used a good measure of their unaccustomed liberty to fight among themselves over land. Whereas the Spanish colonial regime had been able to enforce a minimum of order, if not justice, in the countryside, with the near collapse of the central state the villages laid into each other with enthusiasm and ferocity. Repeatedly the government sent surveyors to attempt to bring an end to these conflicts by drawing acceptable boundaries. They met with little success. The bewildered head of an 1850s survey commission reported,

for example, that just in the area immediately north of Lake Atitlán
(AGCA MG:leg. 28569, exp. 33):

> SOLOLA had *pleitos* (disputes) with Totonicapán, hacienda "Ar-
> gueta," Santo Tomás Chichicastenango, and Concepción Chiric-
> hiapa.
> SANTO TOMAS CHICHICASTENAGO was in conflict with
> Sololá, Tecpán Guatemala, Chiché, and Totonicapán.
> CHICHE fought with the hacienda "Tululche" and the town of
> Chinique.
> ZACUALPA disputed boundaries with Canillá and haciendas
> "Tululche" and "Chuacorral."
> SANTA CATARINA IXTAHUACAN fought, apparently, all of its
> neighbors, including Zunil, Cantel, and Santa Clara la Laguna.

Every hand was turned, seemingly quite literally, against its neighbor,
as well as against any representative of the national government foolish
enough to intervene. Prior to mid-century few of these disputes could
have been motivated by genuine economic need. Communities such as
Zunil or Santiago Atitlán or San Antonio Palopo, located along main
travel routes or sited on poor land, probably developed land shortages
even before the end of the colonial period (AGCA-ST Quezaltenango
1833:paq. 2, exp. 15; AGCA-ST Sololá, 1896:paq. 9, exp. 5; Madigan
1976:73). But, generally, war, epidemics, and natural disasters limited
the population growth;[11] one estimate is of a general annual rate of no
more than 1 percent for these years (Woodward 1983). Except for a few
haciendas dating back to the colony, outsiders rarely involved themselves as claimants in these conflicts. While some of the disputes
between the towns focused on small parcels of particularly good quality
land (AGCA "tierras" 6022 52101), much of the terrain over which the
villages fought was so cold, rocky, and without water it could have been,
in the absence of critical shortages, of little economic interest to anyone.
Other motives for land disputes included efforts to control areas and
sites linked to the ancestors and to traditional religious practices and to
control land in order to dominate populations that might be made to pay
service to the municipio and to the church in the *cabecera* (chief town).
Struggle over land was also a useful mechanism to help construct and
reinforce community solidarity (Van Young 1984). If Spanish colonial
policy did not explicitly set one community against another, it sought,
in the interest of control and exploitation, to isolate one village from
another and to destroy any basis of identification across indigenous
society not strictly supervised by the church and the state.[12]
It will not do, of course, to carry this sort of functionalism too far, for

the inhabitants of the municipalities fought among themselves with an enthusiasm almost equal to that with which they battled their neighbors. While it is of little use to attempt class analyses of nineteenth-century indigenous society (Wolf 1982:chap. 3), there were rich individuals and families, and there were conflicts, and commonly these focused on land. Some disputes pitted the general population of *maceguales* (commoners) against their economic or hereditary betters, and others involved conflicting claims by families or parcialidades. The most common disputes, however, were simply boundary squabbles between neighbors of more or less equal situation (AGCA "tierras" 6022 52101). Aldeas, too, fell out among themselves, as well as with the cabecera.

One example, that of Santa Catarina Ixtahuacán, will do to illustrate these points.[13] For more than forty years violence wracked the community, dominating both internal politics and relations with neighbors and the state. One of the most densely populated municipalities of the central highlands and set on generally poor quality land, Santa Catarina began to suffer scarcity even before the end of the colonial period. In response, the inhabitants moved in two directions. They encroached on the lands of neighboring towns, including Santa Clara la Laguna, Cantel, Zunil, Santa María de Jesús, and San Miguel Totonicapán and resisted violently any efforts to return them to their former boundaries. The *catarinecos* also squatted on vacant lands of the adjacent *boca costa* (piedmont), whether state terrenos baldíos or the ejidos of towns that had died out in the seventeenth and eighteenth centuries. Here they again ran into problems with their neighbors. Zunil, for example, responding to similar land shortages, resettled in the same period several extinguished towns and erected aldeas on state land. The claims of these overlapped with those of Santa Catarina, prompting decades of conflict. Hard working, serious—Santa Catarina was one of the few municipalities able to enforce a ban on alcohol sales—and notoriously ferocious, Santa Catarina terrorized its neighbors and intimidated most of the state's representatives who sought to intervene. Even the priest existed on bare sufferance.

The central regime's lack of control over the countryside is perhaps nowhere more evident than in its inability to bring to an end the decades of conflict during which Santa Catarina tore itself apart. The problems stemmed from differential population growth within the municipality. Though technically only an aldea, the community of Nahualá by 1840 had more inhabitants than did the cabecera. Nahualá and its satellite communities also supplied the bulk of the population which had settled in the lowland areas colonized by the municipio. Thus, by mid-century Santa Catarina proper increasingly found itself surrounded and outnumbered by a population that, for its part, more and more resented and resisted being forced to give time and taxes for the support of government and religion in the cabecera. Characteristically, the catarinecos reacted forcefully, attacking and attempting to drive dissidents from the community.

Not only could state authorities not bring this situation under control, they commonly had little or no idea what was going on. This ineffectualness reached a peak of comic horror in an extended correspondence regarding a head in the possession of government officials. Apparently it had been cut off an individual to punish him for something and as an object lesson to someone, but to whom it had belonged, who had cut it off, and why, no one could discover! When the central government was not otherwise occupied elsewhere defending itself from one or another band of rebels and bandits that plagued the countryside in these years, it sent troops to pacify Santa Catarina. But these were expensive to maintain in the field and seem to have done little beyond conspire to smuggle in alcohol. Ladino officials ordered to investigate the situation found endless reasons to avoid exposing themselves to the dangers of Santa Catarina, knew little of what was going on, and cheerfully contradicted themselves from one letter to the next.

While the villages thus occupied themselves, Guatemala's export economy began to shift from cochineal to coffee. A series of disastrous cochineal harvests in the 1850s, the specter of aniline dyes wiping out the markets for natural dyestuffs, and Costa Rica's success with coffee drew the attention of Guatemalan planters to the new crop (Solís 1979:chaps. 48, 49). As an export staple, cochineal had always been limited by the precarious nature of the production process and by inadequate transportation facilities, and, as a consequence, it failed to rise above the level of artisan handicraft production or to expand much beyond the areas immediately around Antigua and Amatitlán.[14] Much of Guatemala proved to have ideal soils and climate for coffee, however, and production spread quickly to embrace wide areas of the countryside, from the Alta Verapaz to San Marcos on the Mexican border, previously largely untouched by export production. The result was the most fundamental change in the nation's economic, social, and political structures since the conquest.

Social Relations after Coffee

Coffee provided both the motivation and the wherewithal for the state to assert control over rural Guatemala, as this comparison of budgets from 1870 and 1890 shows (Solís 1979:1089–1091; *Memoria del Ministerio de Gobernación–1891*:63).

Budgets	Gobernación (Government)	Guerra (War)
1870	$113,736	$67,323
1890	$303,167	$307,832

Coffee also prompted the accumulation and investment of unprecedented amounts of local and foreign money capital and credit, the contracting and temporary migration of large numbers of workers, and the construction of modern transport and communications facilities. By 1871 coffee amounted to half, by value, of the country's exports (Solís 1979:911), but planters were certain it had not yet begun to approach its full potential. Increasingly, their dissatisfaction focused on the state.

Central to this dissatisfaction was the inability or the unwillingness of the Conservatives to mobilize or to allow individuals to mobilize the production factors necessary to expand coffee production at the rate and to the extent that the planters deemed possible and desirable. Thousands of acres of state land sat practically useless for want of communications and labor and because inadequate surveys made it impossible to obtain clear title. Promising coffee land existed in the ejidos of a few indigenous communities that had survived on the south coast or that Indians from highland municipalities had resettled. Several of these had or sought to control very extensive areas: San Antonio Suchitepequez at one point claimed some seven hundred square leagues, and San Martín Sacatepequez claimed more than one thousand *caballerías* (caballería = 112 acres) in the Costa Cuca (the piedmont of the department of Quezaltenango), already singled out in the 1860s as a prime coffee area (AGCA-ST, Suchitepequez 1812:paq. 3, exp. 2; AGCA-ST, Quezaltenango 1815:paq. 1, exp.15). Pioneer coffee planters solicited land from the coast communities in censo enfiteusis. But most towns resisted, pointing out that permanent crops such as coffee were at odds with the nature of communal ownership and of shifting subsistence agriculture; when pressed, riots threatened or broke out (AGCA, MG, leg. 28593, exp. 130). Existing laws supported such community resistance, and the state generally enforced these. The Conservative regimes of Rafael Carrera (1839–1865) and, especially, Vicente Cerna (1865–1871) took steps to promote coffee (Clegern 1979),[15] but failed to carry forward such schemes as single-mindedly as the planters wished.

It is hardly suprising that many of coffee growers supported the Liberal Revolution of 1871. General Justo Rufino Barrios, himself a coffee planter from the San Marcos/Mexico border, seized control of the state and within a decade turned the country, with considerable assistance from market demand and foreign capital, into a major coffee producer. His Liberal Reforma built and encouraged private investors to build roads, railroads, ports, telegraphs, and other infrastructural improvements; the state founded an agricultural bank and encouraged the capitalization of private banks and the expansion of merchant banking. State policy swept aside obstacles to the use of land and labor for coffee and other commercial production. Exports boomed (McCreery 1983b).

Although a revised general land code did not appear until 1894 (Mendez Montenegro 1960:234–238), the Liberal regime began almost immediately to issue decrees and new regulations meant to make land more readily and cheaply available for commercial agriculture. Among these was an 1873 provision that facilitated the sale of the lands of the Costa Cuca for coffee. Declared baldíos, in spite of various communities' claims, this land was to be sold at fixed prices rather than the generally more lucrative but awkward and time-consuming auction procedures specified for the alienation of state land under existing laws (Mendez Montenegro 1960:123–164). Other decrees opened public lands in the Alta Verapaz, Izabal, and Zacapa for cattle, rubber, chicle, wood cutting, and similar activities (Mendez Montenegro 1960:150–158). Potentially most revolutionary of all was Decree 170 (Mendez Montenegro 1960:133–141). Issued in January 1877, this ended censo enfiteusis. In the interest of development and the presumed superior efficiency of private property, the law gave tenants who held parcels in censo a short time in which to buy these. The selling price was to be calculated by capitalizing the rent, but whereas, for outsiders, for example, the communities had calculated this rent as 3 percent of the estimated value of the land, under Decree 170 for purchase purposes the rent was taken to be 6 percent of the land's worth, effectively cutting the price in half! And the income from these sales went to the central government, not to the communities. Land that renters did not wish to buy or that had not been rented could, under article 13 of the decree, be denounced and purchased by anyone.

The Liberals did not "abolish" or "outlaw" community property. While an 1881 law in neighboring El Salvador declared "[t]he ejido system in El Salvador is abolished" (Browning 1971:208), in Guatemala ejidos maintained a de facto and a de jure existence. The *ley agraria* of 1894 repeated the guarantees of the 1820s and 1830s land laws, which recognized the rights of legally constituted communities to ejidos (Mendez Montenegro 1960:234–238).[16] Claims to excesos received recognition as well. The Liberal Reforma in Guatemala maintained community lands in part because indigenous villages produced most of the country's food; in the late nineteenth century capitalist production of food for the domestic market could not compete with peasant production, even had investors been willing to divert funds from the more profitable fields of coffee and import-export trade. Preserving the ejidos also reinforced the communities' role as suppliers and reproducers of seasonal labor for the coffee estates (McCreery 1983a, 1986). Where a town lacked adequate resources, the state might intervene to help it acquire more land (Mendez Montenegro 1960:260). The actual situation of given villages at any point in time varied widely, depending upon the specific outcome of several centuries of internal and external struggles.

If the Liberals did not end community lands, they did privilege private property. Specifically, they encouraged, and usually wrote into titles issued to villages, the conversion of ejidos and titled excesos into individual plots (AGCA-ST, Huehuetenango 1889:paq. 11, exp. 10). Any such transformation from community to private property, however, required a series of positive acts by the individual and/or the local authorities. Unlike El Salvador, Guatemala proclaimed no blanket decree. Instead, actual or would-be possessors had to apply individually to the state for title and carry forward complicated and expensive procedures more or less in cooperation with the municipality. Many did.[17] But in areas where the cultural values of community land ownership and use persisted and where no internal conflicts or outside speculators seeking land forced a change, the regime of community and clan property might remain in effect.[18]

The nature of coffee production in Guatemala dictated that, whatever the law, its expansion did not immediately threaten the survival of most communities. For towns of the boca costa (e.g., Pochuta, Samayac, San Franscisco Zapotitlán, or Coatepeque), of course, coffee hit the local economy and society as a tidal wave, engrossing land and converting local inhabitants into colonos (resident workers) or day laborers on the fincas (coffee plantations).[19] But by the 1870s and 1880s these were a very small proportion of Guatemala's towns and of its rural population. At the other pole were those towns wholly contained in the highlands (e.g., much of central Quiché and the high valleys of the Cuchumatán mountains). Coffee growers initially had no use for or interest in the cold community lands of these villages. Only gradually did the mechanisms of labor recruiting for coffee prompt planters and their agents to invade highland ejidos, seeking control over land as a means to control workers and creating the infamous fincas de mozos, farms that produced workers (McCreery 1988; T. Adams n.d.). Even these intrusions resulted not so much in the villages' actually losing land as in finding the conditions under which they had access to the land changed.

The largest number of Indian communities fell somewhere between those with all or none of their lands in the coffee piedmont. Many had ejidos in the highlands but supplemented these with seasonal corn production on hot country land. Villages that actually bordered the coffee lowlands—for example, Santiago Atitlán or San Pedro Sacatepequez (San Marcos)—claimed the right to cultivate land there as part of the excesos of their community ejidos or simply on the basis of traditional use rights (Madigan 1976:chap. 5; Orellana 1976:chap. 8). Others (e.g., Momostenango, Zunil, or Rabinal) sent inhabitants to found new aldeas on the coast or north of Uspantán and Nebaj in the "Zona Reina" (AGCA-ST Quezaltenango 1851:paq. 4, exp. 5; 1878:paq. 9, exp. 17; AGCA-ST Quiché 1906:paq. 22, exp. 8; Carmack 1979:247–253). The overall effect of the expansion of coffee was to reduce and constrain the access of these highland Indians to piedmont and coast lands but not, in most cases, to cut it off abruptly or entirely. Individuals and communities responded, too, to the new laws and the new competition for land by titling tracts on the coast or by renting, for money or labor, hot country land. In other cases they simply continued to "squat," buttressed by tradition and need, on land that might technically be terrenos baldíos or private property but over which the legal owners were unable or unwilling to assert their rights. The coffee revolution upset the established subsistence equilibrium of towns dependent on part-time cultivation in the lowlands, but it did not immediately threaten the survival of these towns or the economic and social heart of the comun, the "lands of the ancestors" most closely surrounding the village. Only with the rapid increases in population after 1900 would their plight become evident.

The immediately damaging effects of coffee's demands for cheap land and, especially, cheap labor were, nevertheless, substantial and readily apparent to the indigenous population. How did they react? Contrary to popular imagination, tumultos or revolts were rare after the mid-1870s and their number tended to decline, even as coffee production continued to increase. Violent outbursts did occur, but never on the scale or with the success of the 1830s and 1840s. And of those that did happen and can be linked to coffee, most actually took place in the 1860s before the Liberals took power, or in the early and mid-1870s, before the new regime consolidated its control. Many of these "revolts," when examined, prove, in fact, to have little or no socioeconomic content or to be outright fabrications growing out of local feuds or ladino paranoia. The records of the appeals court at Quezaltenango do reveal a burst of violence in 1898, but most of these resulted not from coffee but from Estrada Cabrera's seizure of power in that year. Perhaps, it might be argued, under the Liberals restive Indians were simply shot out of hand rather than brought to trial; an examination of the records of Gobernación (Ministry of the Interior),[20] however, while it reveals scattered additional examples of conflicts brought on by the invasion of coffee and the summary repression these provoked, just as it shows other instances of conflict for the years before 1871, suggests nothing that significantly alters the shape of the curve below.

Cases

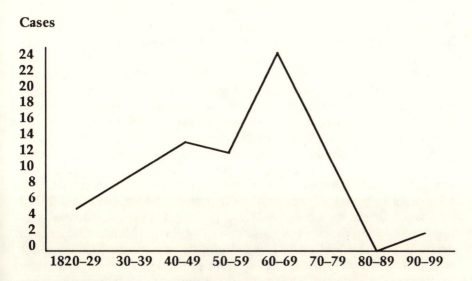

Figure 1. "Rebellions"—Juzgados de Primera Instancia, 1820–1900[21]

An independent measure of the extent to which violence decreased was the fate of the land surveyors who criss-crossed the countryside measuring grants, sales, and ejidos. Before the 1870s they commonly worked in peril of their lives. Routinely, surveyors asked for, and occasionally a pernurious and preoccupied state provided them, an escort of soldiers. Without this, a number had occasion to flee for their lives when their measurements went against local demands and expectations. Less fortunate ones were imprisoned by municipal officials, manhandled, or even killed by enraged mobs (AGCA, MG 1859:leg. 28578, exp. 133; 1865:leg. 28598, exp. 52). In contrast, by the 1890s even when the villagers felt aggrieved they generally contained their anger and turned instead to petitions to *tata presidente* or to the courts. More and more, in the words of the inhabitants of Santa Eulalia, they "went before the law" rather than take up arms (Davis 1970).

The muted nature of the conflicts that accompanied the spread of coffee after 1871 was the result of several factors. The pressure for land was dispersed over a wide area and for an extended period of time. Few communities faced an immediately identifiable "life or death" situation, and none saw it as an issue around which they could unite with other towns. If a community lost its coast lands, the inhabitants still had the ejidos around the village. But, as pointed out above, few towns actually lost access to all of their hot country lands, at least not all at once. More commonly, the villages exchanged vague or traditional claims to a quite extensive area for clear, at least temporarily, title to lesser amounts. For those not yet suffering severe population pressures and land shortages—and few were before the end of the century—this may not have seemed, or indeed have been, a bad bargain. Santiago Atitlán, for example, lost the use of much land between the town and Patulul but titled one hundred caballerías of ejidos, and many individuals and family groups from the town acquired tracts on the piedmont and lower coast (AGCA-ST, Sololá 1811:paq. 1, exp. 5; 1894:paq. 2, exp. 7). Atitecos, forced out by the creation of the municipio of Chicacao, received in compensation twice as much state land nearby, as did the vecinos of Santa Catarina Ixtahuacán made to leave Parraché (AGCA-ST, Sololá 1895:paq. 7, exp. 7). If ladinos and ladino towns, usually led by local militia members (AGCA-ST, Sololá 1889:paq. 4, exp. 10; McCreery 1988), received the lion's share of the new lands to the north opened up in the 1880s and 1890s, indigenous communities were not shut out.[22]   Overall, the fate of a community depended on a village's location and population, and the resulting demands for land and/or labor made upon that particular town, and on how quickly local leaders came to understand the changing situation and to effectively play by the new rules.[23] Broad generalities are of little help. However, in all but the most severe cases, the effects of the coffee revolution were subtle and incremental and extremely difficult for the indigenous communities to mobilize, or to remain mobilized, against.

Too, the Liberal regime sought as much as possible to minimize violence in the countryside. The goal of national leaders and their planter allies was to enrich themselves, which, in a happy coincidence, they equated with national development. It was not simply to harass Indians. Violence discouraged needed foreign and domestic investment, led to distruction of equipment, plantings, and infrastructure, and interrupted the labor supply, as the experience of the 1830s and 1840s clearly demonstrated. In this context, it should be remembered that, prior to the 1930s, labor not land was the scarce production factor in Guatemalan export agriculture.

For their part, the indigenous population quickly learned that if violence broke out, the balance of power had turned decisively against them. The days when a community such as Santa Catarina Ixtahuacán could hold the state at bay for decades were past. The Liberals created the modern, centralized state in Guatemala and tied it together with a network of telegraph lines that, by the end of the 1880s, penetrated all corners of the country. *Comandantes locales* (local military chiefs) and *comisionados políticos* (state political agents in the local communities) kept tabs on anything "unusual" in their jurisdiction and reported it up the hierarchy to the president; telegraph operators worked late into the night sending reports on local conditions and receiving official orders, circulars, and labor requisitions.[24]

The new regime began professionalization of the military, creating an officers' training school in 1873 and arming the regulars and the militia with modern repeating rifles (McClintock 1985:chap. 1). Even masses of Indians armed only with rocks, sticks, and colonial-era shotguns were no match for this. The Liberals put in place and organized the means for the central state to project itself into the interior as had never before been possible.

A brief look at one of the better known tumultos of the last decades of the century, the outbreak of violence at San Juan Ixcoy in 1898 (McCreery 1988), confirms the new preponderance of state power. Conflict over land arose in the early 1890s between San Juan and members of the ladino militia of Soloma to the north and that of Chiantla to the south. These groups presented the government with claims to hundreds of caballerías, which they labeled terrenos baldíos but which San Juan regarded as traditional community property. In an effort to stave off such claims, San Juan put in its own for 250 caballerías. To pay for measuring and titling this land, the principales of San Juan sold labor from the community to the coffee finca Buenos Aires. But violence broke out between the towns and threatened the agrimensor, who fled the area, bringing the measurement process to a halt. When finca agents demanded promised labor, the Indians, who linked the labor sale to the titling process, refused to go. Finally, apparently goaded by the *habilitadores* (plantation labor agents), the sanjuaneros on the evening of July 17, 1898, set fire to the cabildo where a hapless group of labor agents slept and cut them down as they attempted to flee. Hoping to eliminate dangerous witnesses, the Indians then spread out through the village to kill the rest of the ladinos living there. One managed to escape to Soloma. Early the next morning the militia of Soloma and, evidently alerted by telegraph, that of Chiantla rode into town, killing unknown numbers of Indians and sending some sixty to Huehuetenango for trial. There could hardly be a more graphic demonstration of the state's capacity for repression.[25]

If the indigenous population less and less commonly rose up in revolt, it did resist. To escape labor demands, individuals and groups fled to other towns and fincas, into the wilderness, or across the borders to Belize and Mexico (McCreery 1983a, 1986). Towns went to court over land disputes and courted the personalist intervention of the officials and the president. Above all, the communities manifested a constant and well-founded suspicion of and consistent, if usually nonviolent but certainly not passive, opposition to ladino and state schemes. Liberal rule, as does that of any state, rested ultimately on the proven ability of government agents to deliver effective violence to communities and individuals in response to unacceptable resistance to the mandates of the state and the classes whose interests that state served. But the regime and, particularly, the planters had no wish to make uninterrupted war on a population whose labor was vital to their prosperity. The result, therefore, was compromise, though, admittedly, a compromise heavily weighted in favor of finqueros. Violence by no means disappeared from the countryside. Above all, it permeated the labor recruiting in the villages and labor relations on the fincas. What had largely disappeared was the tumulto as an effective form of resistance by the indigenous community to the state. The primeval Indian, fire and machete in hand, remained a vivid ladino nightmare, though one, at least until very recently, with less and less basis in fact.

Conclusion

This chapter has argued several points. The social, economic, and, particularly, the land situation within and between communities, and between communities and ladinos in nineteenth-century Guatemala was much more complex than is usually understood. This complexity increased after mid-century under the impact of growing demands for land and labor to service the export economy. There existed vast differences in wealth and security within and between the communities, the result of geography, differential rates of population growth and ecological degradation, family and clan claims, and the accidents of history. Coffee exacerbated these. The uneven development of capitalism in the industrial centers and, as a result, the ebb and flow of the world capitalist system meant that various regions of Guatemala found themselves drawn into the coffee economy at different times and under different conditions.[26] The interaction of these differing circumstances with the peculiar situation and conditions of each community had the result that the process of incorporation, while exhibiting broad similarities, was specific to each case. To discover and examine the regional and local variants of this process of primitive accumulation remains an important object of the rural history of Guatemala.[27]

The efforts of the Liberal state after 1871 to organize the exploitation of land and labor for export production were more sophisticated, more subtle, and more suited to Guatemala's situation than is usually credited. In contrast to the direct assault on village lands characteristic of El Salvador after 1881, which provoked a half-century of uprisings, Guatemala's Reforma Liberals undertook what might best be described as a flank attack on the resources of the indigenous communities. They did this for several reasons. There was some fear, at least early on, of a repeat of the successful peasant-based reaction of the 1830s. Liberal ideology held that the Indian was lazy, dirty, and drunken, but it also portrayed him as sly, vicious, brutal, and prone to violence. The revolt of the Remicheros (Rubio 1935:166ff) in the Oriente and a succession of minor risings in the highlands in the 1870s and 1880s linked to the folk memory of Serapio Cruz[28] suggest that fear of a highland-wide tumulto was not entirely misplaced, at least until the state reorganized and reequipped the army and consolidated its control. The highland towns also reproduced cheap labor and sustained it in the off season and produced most of the country's food and many necessary handicrafts (e.g., woolen cloth). Most of all, of course, the coffee planters in the majority of cases did not need core community lands for productive purposes and only slowly and indirectly penetrated them as a by-product of labor recruiting. The initial impact of Liberal land policy and coffee was, thus, to cut away at peripheral community lands while reinforcing control over the core ejido.

Far from increasing with the effects of coffee, overt violence, with the exception of that associated with labor recruiting and control, declined in all areas and at all levels of Guatemalan rural society during the course of the nineteenth century. Rural banditry almost disappeared.[29] More to the point, violence between communities and between communities and the state over land, a staple of rural life in the first half of the century, dropped off dramatically after 1871. Liberal land laws and state efforts to enforce these touched off no widespread revolts as occurred in El Salvador and Nicaragua in this period. If one wishes to argue that the state is by definition institutionalized violence, and class violence at that, augmented state power may be equated with increased violence, but the very effectiveness of the state meant that this violence remained increasingly imminent rather than manifest. Coffee devastated the indigenous population and communities, but their reaction was muted by the growing power of the state and was, therefore, transmuted or channeled into new vehicles, vehicles probably more effective for indigenous purposes than the old tumultos and certainly less likely to bring down the soldiers on the community.

Notes

1. See also Julio C. Cambranes (1985) for a more subtle vision of land loss still fundamentally in agreement with the argument cited.

2. For a more developed argument of the rebelliousness of the indigenous population, see Carmack (1979:264–269, 1985).

3. William Taylor (1979:114), writing about colonial Mexico but in terms equally applicable to late-nineteenth-century highland Guatemala, defines

"rebellions" as "localized mass attacks, generally limited to restoring a customary order. . . . [S]pontaneous, short-lived outbursts by members of a single community in reaction to threats from outside. . . ."

4. Alcabala lists for the last years of the colony give a good indication of the distribution of rural property: AGCA, A3.5 1155 20488 (Quezaltenango), 352 7308 (Huehuetenango and Totonicapán), 352 7309 (Sololá), 352 7314 (Verapaz), and 352 7320 (Chiquimula), among others.

5. On the ladino/mestizo "agrarian block," see Martínez Peláez (1971:366–417) and Pinto Soria (1980:36, note 39); for an example of a ladino settlement—Zaragosa—struggling with a land shortage see AGCA-Sección de Tierras (AGCA-ST), Chimaltenango, paquete (paq.)1/expediente (exp.) 17 (1830), paq. 2/exp. 7 (1840), and paq. 20/exp. 8 (1900).

6. Measurements changed over the three hundred years of the colony, but one square league ("*a sitio de ganado mayor*") equaled approximately 38 3/8 "new" caballerías (as opposed to 36 "old" caballerías); a "new" caballería contained slightly less than 112 acres.

7. By definition this excluded all ladinos illegally living in *pueblos de indios*.

8. For examples of censo and the sale of dominio útil around Antigua during the cochineal boom, see the records of notaries José María Llerena, 1830–1844 and José María Cáceres, 1847–1877, AGCA.

9. See, for examples, the violence cataloged in the AGCA card file under "Asaltos en cuadrilla," box 2-28.

10. For a review of the literature on the "closed corporate community," see Frank Cancian (1967); an extended recent critique of the concept can be found in Robert Wasserstrom (1983).

11. One of the worst was the locust epidemic that swept up the west coast from the south in 1801 and lasted until 1806 (AGCA, A1.2.5 2835 25289); locusts remained a problem for Guatemalan food and export agriculture until at least the 1940s (*El Imparcial*, August 16, 1943).

12. On the transition from indigenous population to "Indians" in Guatemala see Martínez Peláez (1971:chap. 5); more broadly, see Steve Stern (1982).

13. The following paragraphs are based on a wide range of material, including: AGCA-ST, Sololá, paq. 2/exp.5 (1853) and paq. 6/exp. 2 (1860); AGCA, MG leg. 28586 exp. 200, leg. 28600 exp. 184, 185, and 186, and leg. 28610 exp. 351, and AEG, "Cartas," January 2, 1854, #001.

14. See AGCA, MG, leg. 28536, exp. 145 for a description of cochineal production in Sacatepequez.

15. The Conservatives drew up and approved but apparently never published a new land law: AGCA, MG, leg. 28623, exp. 159 (1870).

16. For an example of the earlier laws, see Pineda de Mont (1869–1872:658).

17. Compare the experiences of the two neighboring towns of Comalapa (AGCA-ST, Chimaltenango, paq. 8/10 [1889]) and Poaquil (AGCA-ST, Chimaltenango, paq.9/exp. 2 [1892]). For reasons not yet clear, there was a burst of *lotificación* (the conversion of community holdings into lots of private property) in highland towns in the early 1890s, but this still involved only a small percentage of the indigenous communities.

18. A common subterfuge meant to satisfy Liberal laws was for a *principal* or

principales to title community land in their name(s): AGCA-ST, Quiché, paq. 7/ exp. 7 (1893). For some of the problems to which this might lead, see Shelton Davis (1970:chap. 4).

19. See, for example, the memories of this experience in Pochuta: Instituto Indigenista de Guatemala, "monografía," # 264 Pochuta.

20. There exists a card file index in the AGCA of some use for Gobernación for the years from the 1830s to 1900. Many of the cards in the index inaccurately reflect the contents of the *expedientes*, however, and in some cases *legajos* have been reorganized and/or renumbered, rendering the index useless for these materials.

21. These figures come from the indices to *Juzgado de Primera Instancia, criminal*, available in the AGCA. Included in this count are many cases labeled "tumulto," "rebelión," "sedición," and anything that indicated resistance to authority. Each of these was checked for all of the western departments, the south coast, the Verapaz, and the chief departments of the Oriente; for several departments (e.g., Chiquimula or Escuintla) indices are not available or began only after the period treated here. In many cases there was no evident political content to the disturbance but these were, nevertheless, included in the count, as it often was unclear from the documents exactly what was happening. Similar indices are available, and were checked, for the appeals courts.

22. For dozens of titles in the Barillas (Huehuetenango) area, see AGCA-ST, Huehuetenango, paqs. 14–30, and for Uspantán, see AGCA-ST, Quiché, paqs. 5–29.

23. It is a mistake to think that the indigenous population of nineteenth-century Guatemala lost land chiefly because they did not understand the new laws or their implications. They disagreed with Liberal views on the nature and proper use of land, but their reluctance to enter into titling procedures stemmed more from problems of the costs involved, distrust of ladino officials and courts, and the often shaky basis of their own claims than from ignorance.

24. For a list of telegraph offices and the dates they were established, see *Memoria del Ministerio de Fomento* (1924:251–253).

25. Carmack (1979:264–269) describes a similar revolt arising out of land conflicts in the 1870s at Momostenango. He notes that "[Justo Rufino] Barrios reacted quickly and with force," visiting a "horroroso castigo" (terrible punishment) (p. 267) on the town.

26. The uneven development of capitalism at the center meant that the export sector drew in different areas of Guatemala at different times and under different conditions. See Carol Smith (1984a).

27. The best introduction to primitive accumulation remains Karl Marx, *Capital*, vol. 1, pt. 8: "So-Called Primitive Accumulation."

28. These erupted as late as the mid-1880s (AEG, "Cartas," May 20, 1886, #343).

29. Compare travelers' accounts from the 1830s and 1840s, for example, Robert G. Dunlop (1847) or John L. Stephens (1841), with those of the 1880s and 1890s, such as William T. Brigham (1887) or Anne C. M. Maudsley (1979 [reprint]).

6. State and Community in Nineteenth-Century Guatemala: The Momostenango Case

Robert M. Carmack

Department of Anthropology, State University of New York, Albany

The general focus of this inquiry, which draws heavily on a particular case study (Santiago Momostenango), is the nature of the relationship between the state and native communities of Guatemala in the nineteenth century and the ways it changed during the period. I am particularly concerned with determining the extent to which Guatemalan Indian communities have been creatures of the state, or, conversely, local organizations with some degree of autonomy—communities developed by the native peoples to defend their interests against external political domination. Two related issues deal with the developing capitalist (coffee) economy's impact on the communities, especially in terms of its causing internal stratification; and the nature and function of native culture in maintaining integrated Indian communities.

The questions raised here are of very broad theoretical interest, since they have direct bearing on the historical processes by which the modern world was created. Much theoretical discussion has taken place on these questions, especially within the framework of the Marxist and Weberian (pluralist) positions. These theoretical positions share concern for certain issues that must be given special attention in historical studies like that of Momostenango. These issues are: the nature of social class divisions and their relations to power, particularly between landowner and peasant classes in "early modern" societies; the nature of the state, as the expression of the dominant class (Marxist) or a bureaucratic system of repressive authority (Weberian); and the sources and nature of conflict, either between classes or with the state itself. The next two sections of this chapter delineate how such issues are expressed in this specific Guatemalan case. The concluding section discusses their implications for these two theoretical positions.

The Specific Case of Santiago Momostenango

A general outline of relations between the state and Indian communities in nineteenth-century Guatemala has already been worked out (see especially Woodward 1971, 1976; McCreery 1976, 1983a, 1986; Burns 1980, 1986; Handy 1984; C. Smith 1984a; Cambranes 1985; and the other studies in this book). Against the backdrop of these more generalized reconstructions of relations between the state and the Indian communities of nineteenth-century Guatemala, I present my empirical findings relative to the specific case of Santiago Momostenango. Though far from complete, I believe it to be one of the best-documented community studies for the period in question, and it has the added advantage of being part of a larger study that includes an analysis of the preceding pre-Hispanic and colonial historical periods, as well as the succeeding contemporary situation.[1]

Pre-Hispanically, Chwatz'ak (Momostenango) was a province of the Quiché state, and formed a community only in a broad, political-economic sense. Officials representing the ruling lineages of Utatlán administered state affairs from at least three small centers (the largest was Chwatz'ak), assisted by military leaders who resided in wards surrounding the centers. Almost the entire population of the province, some seven to ten thousand persons, was made up of tribute-paying commoners organized into patrilineages and residing in the rural zones. Momostecans paid maize and other food products as tribute, as well as gold and lime, apparently mined in the local area under the direction of the Quiché rulers. The Quiché state's authority system linked up directly with the leadership of the local patrilineal structure, but its legitimacy was weak such that rebellion and conflict were continuous.

The colonial Momostenango pueblo formed a community largely created by the *caciques* (descendants of the pre-Hispanic Quiché ruling class), and it corresponded closely in territory and social composition to the pre-Hispanic province. The patrilineal structure of the rural Indians remained intact, though at the wider community level cacique authority was gradually eroded and increasingly shared by the Spanish priests and commoner Indian *principales* (elders). The Spanish king and Audiencia officials in Guatemala were generally accepted much as Momostecans had accepted the rulers of Utatlán, and tribute obligations in goods and services may not have greatly exceeded those of pre-Hispanic times. State and community relations changed during the eighteenth century, however, with the growth of small Creole haciendas along the margins of Momostenango's territory and the tightening of regional and local political control as a result of the Bourbon reforms. This interference in community life, attributed by the Indians to the Creoles rather than to the Spanish government per se, was countered by massive and violent rebellions led by small groups of commercially oriented Indians. They joined in the regional, nativistic Atanasio Tzul movement (which tried to establish a Quiché "king"), and so were involved indirectly in the colony's independence movement (Contreras 1951).

The postindependence Gálvez government had little success in applying its liberal republican programs to the Momostenango community. The rebel Indian leaders from the independence period remained in power, and rejected all attempts to impose land reform, elections, or "contributions." They used guerrilla warfare to fend off regional troops, and in the end won concessions that allowed them to continue conducting community affairs according to their own customs. The Liberal government essentially established a parallel political order among the resident Creoles (for the most part ranchers considered to be Spanish), but its influence on the indigenous order appears to have been largely symbolic: with respect to the Indians, political-economic control (allegiance to the state, tributary obligations) above the community level scarcely existed.

The Liberal government gradually paternalized its relations with the Momostenango Indians, and made some headway in subordinating the community to its authority and economic needs. But the critical breakthrough came with Carrera and the conservative program he supported. There is no indication that the Momostecan Indians participated in the revolt that brought Carrera to power, but we know that they approved of the new programs he instituted, and quickly personalized their relations with him. Already in 1841 they were appealing directly to Carrera as "Lord General, Chief of State," and eight years later, when he was forced to flee to Mexico, the Momostecan Indians organized a rebel army that played a major role in the regional conflict that helped him return to power.

The Carrera regime did not dismantle the dual (Creole-Indian) political system of Momostenango, but continued to work through the Creole officials established by the prior Liberal regime. The highly paternalistic programs administered by the Creoles (in collaboration with resident ladinos), plus the channel of direct appeal to Carrera, made it possible for the state to rule again over the Indians and begin to appropriate taxes and fees from them. Nevertheless, the Indians as a whole resented the privileged position of the Creoles, and on more than one occasion showed that their opposition to local Creoles and ladinos was greater than their support for Carrera. An 1850 communique from Carrera's corregidor of Totonicapán to the Momostecan Indians reveals just how far the regime had to go in its paternalism in order to control the Indians in their struggle against Carrera's Creole officials.

The Señor General of Guatemala when he sent me to the *corregimiento* assured me that the people of Momostenango would respect authority, but if they did not, the rebels would be punished; and the Señor General Carrera told me that if they did not keep the order and obey the corregimiento he would send me a strong division of troops with cannons . . . I love the town of Momostenango very much, and all the government and the justices love Momostecans as children . . . The Excellent Señor General Carrera . . . invites you to listen to reason and work in accord with the corregimiento in order to remove any pretext or motive for punishment, so that it cannot be said in the other towns of the Republic that Momostenango is bad and does not know the laws. (AGCA, Gobernación, Totonicapán, 1850)

Such entreaties were necessary because the Indians were threatening to kill all the Creoles and ladinos of the community. There is abundant evidence in the documents that relations between the Indians and Creoles remained extremely hostile and tense throughout the Carrera period. Tensions within the Indian sector were great too, and they appear to have increased right up to the end of the Carrera regime. This is illustrated by a murder that took place in Momostenango in 1864 (AGCA, Ramo Judicial, Totonicapán, leg. 20, 1864).

One night in May 1864 the Indians Diego and Antonia Paza, husband and wife, were hacked to death by machetes in one of the rural cantons of Momostenango. Elaborate judicial proceedings were launched to solve the case, involving the *corregidor, juez de primera instancia, juez preventivo,* and *cirujano* (regional legal officials), along with the *alcalde municipal* (local mayor). Yet, the only conviction obtained was of an old woman for perjury, as she tried to protect her son, alleged to be involved in the killings. The testimony taken makes it clear, however, that the killers were all from the Paza patriclan (*parcialidad*), and that they executed rather than murdered Diego and Antonia. The couple had been accused of stealing the sheep of clan members, and of practicing witchcraft (*itzibal* in Quiché) against other clansmen—some of whom had died—in order to appropriate their lands. Apparently the whole affair was well understood in the canton, and the local Indian officials (*alcalde auxiliar, cofrades, principales*) acquiesced to it. Therefore, despite the efforts of municipal officials to find witnesses, no one would testify against the executioners, and the case did not prosper.

The details that came out as a result of the judicial proceedings shed light on the nature of social forces operating in the community at the close of the Carrera period. For example, the continuing strength of the traditional rural patriclans and cantons is notable. We know from studies of contemporary Quiché Indians that to practice witchcraft against clansmen is an egregious crime, and calls for execution or expulsion. It is clear that customary native law was operating in this case, and that it was respected by the entire Indian sector of the community, from clan members, to neighbors, to auxilliary officials.

It is noteworthy, too, that all the municipal and regional officials were Creoles and ladinos (most of them Creoles, but that distinction is not made in the document). The juez preventivo introduced into the case the old Spanish paternalistic laws relative to the Indians: he argued that the Indians had to receive special treatment because they were ignorant, had not been taught the Gospel, did not know the seriousness of their wrongs, treated women merely as slaves, and so on. Nevertheless, the ladino officials acted as a unified political order, an order that appears to have been largely different from and opposed to the Indian political order. Perhaps the ladinos did not apply their authority with as much force as during earlier periods, but their pressure was clearly felt and resented by the Indian majority.

It surely is significant that the murdered couple was accused of trying to take over clan lands. Farm and pasturage land was obviously in short supply. People still farmed and raised sheep, but most of the clan members involved in the incident, plus other canton inhabitants, worked at some kind of commercial activity: weaving, or selling cloth, pitch, lime, or other goods outside Momostenango. Subsistence-oriented farming and pasturing continued to be important, but perhaps it was not an adequate means of economic provision at this time and place.

If there were already tensions between the state and the Momostecan Indian community under Carrera, they were to be dramatically intensified under the Liberal Barrios regime. I have documented in prior publications Momostenango's loss of a significant portion of its agricultural lands through state appropriation and adjudication of land disputes with other communities (Carmack 1972). The Momostecan Indians were hit hard too with labor obligations on the coffee plantations, always backed by force, though increasingly debt peonage was used to fulfill the obligations. The political order staffed by ladinos, greatly strengthened and rejuvenated by liberal ideology, began to apply authority with a force far stronger than that of the previous Liberal or Carrera regimes.

Such powerful political-economic pressures brought to bear on Momostenango incited the Indians to all-out rebellion. Led by rural chiefs, they launched guerrilla warfare against the local liberal officials and militias. They soon joined with a national-based conservative rebel movement, through the mediation of a local Creole caudillo by the name of Julian Rubio (alias "Ramon Carrera"). The Momostecan Indians were defeated along with the national Conservative rebels by the military forces of the Liberal government, which were far superior. At Momostenango several rebel leaders were executed, the houses of suspected sympathizers were burned and their property seized, and many people were removed from the zones of major conflict. An uneasy peace slowly settled over Momostenango, not only because of the decisive military defeat of the rebels but also because the Liberal government, beginning with Barrios himself, began to make concessions to the Indians of the community.

As important as the Barrios period was for developments in Momostenango, the post-Barrios years were perhaps even more important with respect to long-term effects. This was the time when local ladinos, descendants of influential Creole families of the past, were able to establish and consolidate personal ties with the highest national leaders on the one hand, and with the Indians at the local community level on the other. Patronage at the national level was gained through bold military support for the winners of the struggles for national power at times of succession (especially when Reina Barrios and then Estrada Cabrera took power). With derivative power from the highest levels these local ladino caudillos were able to subject the Indians to their rule.

The political order set up in Momostenango by these ladinos was backed with brute military force. From the end of the century on, they could draw upon the full force of arms from the military wing of the state, as well as the various police agencies, to back them in both their personal and national political agendas. What made the system so effective, far more than the one established by Barrios, was the way these caudillos co-opted local Indian leaders. The mechanisms that they worked out would have provoked the highest admiration of conservatives from Carrera's time. The militia, almost exclusively ladino under Barrios, became the primary vehicle in this process. Indians were given not only a place in it, but also the opportunity to prove themselves and even become officers. The traditional native social divisions were respected, as with the equestrian squadron of caciques (the caciques had been allowed to have horses in the colonial period) and the artillery squadron of San Bartolo (Bartoleños had used cannons in support of Carrera's return to power from Mexico); and the Indians' traditional religion was "rationalized" in such a way that it provided ritual support for all things military (e.g., native priest-shamans, chuchkajaw, were assigned to Indian militia divisions and even to bases in Guatemala City).

This highly paternalistic political order was in place by the end of the nineteenth century, and may be illustrated by a dramatic killing that shook Momostenango in 1899 (AGCA, Ramo Judicial, Totonicapán, leg. 83B, 1899). At about 2 a.m. in February of that year, the Indian Timoteo Ajanel attended the wake of his sister, at the house of his in-laws, the Lajpops. A certain teniente (lieutenant) Fermín, also an Indian, led a patrol of militiamen into the house where he embraced Timoteo and then plunged a knife into his heart. Fermín and his soldiers left, but Fermín was taken into custody a few hours later when complaints against him were made to the alcalde by the deceased's father, Juan Ajanel. The ladino alcalde, acting as justice of peace, had the body examined by an *empirico*, took testimony from the many witnesses, and remitted the case and the prisoner to the Court of First Instance in Totonicapán. The father of the deceased employed the services of a highly skilled and educated ladino lawyer (Licenciado Carranza), while Teniente Fermín's defense was made by an educated Momostecan Indian, Manuel Guzmán. Court proceedings lasted eight months in Totonicapán, and resulted in a guilty decision for Teniente Fermín in 1899. He was sentenced to ten years in prison, and his appeal to a higher court was rejected. In 1901, however, President Estrada Cabrera issued him a pardon, and he was freed from prison in 1904.

The social conditions revealed by the case were very different from those prevailing in the 1864 murders cited above. (No claim is made, however, that either case was perfectly representative of its respective period.) Most of the Indians involved lived close to the town center, and were active participants in the militia organization. (Besides Teniente Fermín and his patrol members, it appears that the deceased, as well as the Lajpops and Guzmán, were militiamen.) The major actors were all significantly "ladinoized": they spoke Spanish, were engaged in commercial activities, had some familiarity with the legal system, and depended on bilateral and friendship ties more than patriclan relations. The way the crime was committed—in a public setting and using a knife—is in sharp contrast with the 1864 killings. Unfortunately, we never learn from the court record what the motive might have been for the killing, but it clearly was not a clan or canton issue. Based on other cases from those years, likely motives would be jealousy over women, competition for military rank, insults against one's dignity; all motives for which the ladinos were constantly fighting one another.

As in 1864, the political order revealed in this case was still one dominated by ladinos. But it had changed in important ways. The law being applied by the authorities no longer legally distinguished between Indians and ladinos. In fact, the Indian defender of the accused presented an elegant argument to the effect that "moral" considerations were not relevant, only legal ones, as befitted "modern legislation." Obviously, too, the authorities could carry out their duties relative to the Indians much more effectively than in the Carrera years. In part this was because the Indians participated more fully in the same system, some of them, in fact, directly as officials of the political order (illustrated in this case by the Indian militia head and the legal defender). The pardon given by

Estrada Cabrera must not be confused with the pardons given to Momostecans by Carrera. As we know from other records, in Teniente Fermín's case the pardon came at the request and through the influence of the local ladino rulers, not directly from the president, thus preserving the Indians' integration in the political system at the local rather than national level.

The political order illustrated by the 1899 murder persisted without radical change until the fall of Ubico in 1944. It permitted both the state and the local ladinos to exploit egregiously the Indians' labor and resources, without being seriously challenged by the Indians. It certainly was not the case that the Indians passively accepted their lot, nor did they wish to maintain their condition unaltered. The political and military forces, combined with internal divisions created by the highly paternalistic system of status inequality, were too great to overcome. Not surprisingly, the system also exercised a heavy constraint on the Momostecan ladinos: despite their desire to become capitalists and to modernize the town, they never were much more than petty *finqueros* and the community continued to be known as "a large Indian town."

Momostenango, then, was not much modernized or capitalized by the Barrios political economy or subsequent "liberal" developments. The town center, while modern in some ways, did not grow significantly in population size. As noted, only a few ladinos became commercial farmers or retail merchants; most were rather poor town artisans. A handful of privileged Indians were specialized, long-distance merchants, an occupation they were able to pursue mainly as a reward for exceptional military performance. The overwhelming majority of Indians, however, remained tied to the land. They provided for their subsistence mostly by weaving blankets, raising and carding wool, and *milpa* (corn and beans) farming. Many (perhaps 70 percent) of these Indians participated in the local and regional markets, and thus were somewhat "commercialized." A small percentage of them (perhaps five to ten percent) fell into chronic debt and migrated annually to labor on the plantations; they were weakly "proletarianized."

Internally, then, class divisions were still incipiently developed at Momostenango, while the status division between ladinos and Indians remained pronounced. One result of the strong status but weak class structures appears to have been, paradoxically, a community less divided into two communities, one ladino and one Indian, than in the past. The reason, of course, was because the ladinos had so thoroughly coopted the Indians. The state had finally achieved tight control over the Momostecan Indians, but it had done so to an important extent by abandoning liberal principles and applying conservative ones.

Comparison and Analysis: Momostenango, the General Historical Reconstruction, and Other Case Studies

Obviously, one community study cannot provide a reliable guide to the nature of changing relations between the state and Indian communities in Guatemala as a whole. The Momostenango case needs to be situated within the general reconstruction of nineteenth-century Guatemalan history that has been summarized in the preceding chapters, and compared with studies of other nineteenth-century Indian communities: namely, Santa Cruz del Quiché (Carmack 1981), San Antonio Ilotenango (Falla 1971, 1978a), San Juan Ostuncalco (Ebel 1969), Santiago Atitlán (Madigan 1976), the Verapaces (King 1974; Cabarrús 1979), and the piedmont communities of El Salvador (Kincaid 1987). These studies differ widely in thesis, content, and documentation, but each provides some reconstruction of changes in nineteenth-century Indian community social life and, therefore, invites comparison with the Momostenango case. Comparisons of this kind should give us a more accurate view of community-state processes, variations from region to region, and significant factors that might help explain the nature of these processes.

For purposes of comparison with the Momostenango case, it will be useful to return to the three clusters of questions and issues summarized at the beginning of this essay as being particularly relevant to an understanding of Guatemalan state and community relations. The first cluster has to do with the nature of state and community relations, particularly the extent to which the communities have been creations of the state as opposed to relatively autonomous historical entities. The Momostenango case is particularly clear on this issue, apparently more so than for many other communities identified as Indian in Guatemala.

The Momostecan Indians played a major role in the early years of the conquest in preserving their community identity, boundaries, and social institutions; the perpetuation of this nativistic "corporate estate" has involved them in an active and long-term process of social construction. Momostecan Indians of the nineteenth century appear to have been the creators of their community far more than would be suggested by more general historical accounts. Effective leadership emerged against every external power that threatened the preservation of their social world, and Indian leaders did not hesitate to organize violent rebellious action when the threats were especially serious. It is not an exaggeration to claim that they wrested major concessions from the Liberal regimes, both early and late in the century, relative to the attempts by those regimes to modernize the community. Even the Carrera state, with its mild reform programs, found it difficult to dominate the Momostecan community, and reluctantly had to yield on many points. All of this is not to claim, of course, that Momostenango was truly autonomous or did not change under the influence of the state. Obviously the community was subject to state power and did change as a result of state policies; nevertheless, it has been too little realized that much of the change took place on the Indians' terms.

It is true that the state's power to dominate Indian communities greatly increased during the nineteenth century. The Carrera regime, for example, exerted more control over Momostenango than did the Gálvez government, precisely because it paternalized relations with the Indians to a far greater extent. The ladino political order that Carrera established was the foundation upon which the Barrios liberals erected a still more powerful political structure. The construction by the state of a political order in Momostenango, however, involved a dialectical process: the power of community opposition to the state also increased during the century. This can be determined from a comparison of the petty merchant native leaders who organized the rebellions against Spanish and later liberal authority in the early part of the century, with the relatively sophisticated native militia chiefs at the end of the century. Although the later Indian leaders were more powerful, they also were more compromised by the local ladino establishment. Thus, the dialectic of power in the community probably diminished rather than increased the revolutionary potential of the community through time, a trend that has continued down to the present day.

Momostenango does not seem exceptional with respect to state/community relationship when compared with the other cases mentioned above. All of the studies stress the active role played by the Indians in achieving relatively acceptable accommodations with the state during the first half of the nineteenth century.

In central Quiché (Santa Cruz and San Antonio Ilotenango), the Indians struggled to maintain control over community affairs, including the old ethnic political boundaries, and were surprisingly successful in doing so. Led by nativistic leaders, they rebelled in opposition to the reimposition of tributes near the close of the colonial period, and again when the Liberals tried to "reform" lands in the 1830s. At Ilotenango the Indians fought pitched battles against Liberal officials and neighboring communities over reforms that diminished their land holdings. In the process they were able to construct a political order of civil-religious officials, principales, and priest-shamans that promoted the traditional community social life they had created and came to accept during the colonial period.

The Indians of Santiago Atitlán are said to have retained considerable autonomy relative to the Republican society, and continued to live according to native community patterns relatively free from outside interference. Ostuncalco Indians were able to forge a municipal political structure that externally defended their community interests against those of the resident ladinos, and internally promoted traditional community institutions. The Verapaz Indians moved away from ladino centers after independence where, presumably, in their dispersed communities they avoided the most serious effects of either Liberal or Conservative programs.

In El Salvador the indigo plantations of the late colonial period broke down many of the native community structures. Nevertheless, led by native leaders at places like Santiago Nonualco, some of the communities rebelled against Spanish tributes, and in the 1830s against the excesses of plantation owners. Through such actions, a few communities in the western and central piedmont survived with their internal cohesion intact.

These case studies reveal the same serious erosion of community autonomy, as a result of the Liberal regimes of the late nineteenth century, that has been documented for Momostenango. As at Momostenango, this loss of political control vis-à-vis the state did not take place without violent opposition on the part of the Indian communities. Nevertheless, by the end of the century the Indians had been placed under tighter state control than perhaps any previous period in their history.

The consequences of the Barrios reforms in Santa Cruz del Quiché are not well known. Nevertheless, it is clear that the Liberal programs fractionated the native community, one important cleavage dividing traditional Indians from those co-opted into militia service. We know that these Indian militiamen engaged in "civil war" against one rebellious native faction (from Lemoa), powerful evidence that community cohesion had been seriously undermined. In Ilotenango, the traditional native political order lost much of its legitimacy, in part because of the forced settlement of land disputes with other communities, and in part because the local leaders became clients for the Liberal authorities (such as in labor recruitment). The community was internally divided, and "witchcraft" began to replace the more integrated traditional means of maintaining political order.

In Santiago Atitlán, the Indians were forced by the Liberals to register their lands. In the process they lost some of the most productive (piedmont) holdings, and many fell into debt peonage to the ladino-owned plantations. Obviously this represented a serious erosion of community autonomy, though the specific details of the process have not been studied. The Liberal reforms also radically transformed the Ostuncalco community. The Indians lost lands to the ladinos, especially their piedmont holdings; they also became increasingly subject to labor obligations on the plantations and saw their traditional political system subordinated to that of the ladino-dominated municipal government. This erosion of community autonomy united the Indians against the ladinos, as they employed legal and eventually violent means to counter their losses. The effects of coffee plantations were felt by Indians earlier in the Verapaces as a result of the advanced commercial activity of the Germans in the area. The Liberal regimes facilitated the appropriation of Indian land and then labor, even setting up special courts to oversee the recruitment of laborers for the German plantations. The Indian communities violently resisted the loss of their political autonomy and economic resources. Led by native "prophets," they repeatedly rose in rebellion from the 1860s on into the next century.

Late-nineteenth-century liberal reforms in El Salvador were even more destructive of Indian community autonomy than in Guatemala. Most communities lost large portions of their lands, and, now faced with a more united and powerful state, many of them were destroyed as corporate units. Nevertheless, the Indians did not give up without a fight, and between 1872 and the end of the century some of them rose in rebellion. In the western piedmont area, a few of the communities retained enough political organization to provide a native identity around which they would later coalesce in a much more violent rebellion, culminating in the *matanza* (slaughter) of 1932.

A second cluster of issues has to do with the stratification of Indian communities: their internal social divisions and the relationship of these to wider regional and national stratification. Such issues, as has long been recognized by students of nineteenth-century Guatemala, are intimately tied to the progressive establishment of capitalism in the form of coffee plantations, and the appropriation of land and labor from within the Indian communities.

Momostenango would appear to fit the reconstructed general pattern reasonably well, particularly late in the century when it lost many of its productive lands and became an important reserve of forced plantation labor. It is worth noting, however, that already by the end of the colonial period a small mercantile native class had differentiated itself from the masses of weaver-cultivators. These native merchants traded widely throughout the highlands and beyond, and maintained relationships with similar commercialized Indians from neighboring communities. They were capable of integrating the Momostenango community as a whole in opposition to the state, and of establishing political alliances with other similarly stratified communities. At this time too (the beginning of the nineteenth century) there were substantial numbers of Creoles and ladinos resident in Momostenango. The economic position of Creoles and ladinos was different from that of the Indians and from each other (the Creoles were commercial farmers, the ladinos artisans or peons), but ethnic status (Indian vs. ladino) rather than economic class dominated relations between the two groups.

Social stratification changed very little in Momostenango during the Gálvez and Carrera periods. Certainly no evidence supports the notion that the division between Indians and ladinos was blurred or softened; relations were hostile and conceptualized within the conquest-derived premise of inequality. Except for periods of major political conflict, relations within the Indian community were governed largely by status rather than class, especially within and between the principales, patri-clans, and rural cantons.

It does not appear that radical changes occurred in Momostenango relative to Indian/ladino relations during the Barrios Liberal period. The ladinos were able to take derivative (mostly military) power from the state to enforce their status domination of the Indians, and they con-structed complex paternalistic mechanisms to facilitate that domina-tion. The evidence is clear, however, that the Indians and ladinos continued to view each other in hostile and unequal terms, and this included the upwardly mobile Indian military chiefs who were potential leaders of the Indian community as a whole.

The general observation about the Barrios reform period—that ladinos and Indians were stratified in economic class terms—fits Momoste-nango in the sense that many resident ladinos did the labor contracting, while Indians provided the labor for the plantations. Yet, the Indians were not strongly proletarianized, nor were the ladinos significantly capitalized. Since the Indians remained mostly tied to the land, they interacted with ladinos mainly through status-mediated political rela-tions (e.g., priest-shamans associated with military units) rather than class relations. This helps explain the above-mentioned diminishing revolutionary potential of the community.

Our comparative cases provide relatively little information on strati-fication within other Indian communities of nineteenth-century Guate-mala, or the development of class divisions as a consequence of external forces emanating from the emerging capitalist economy. In general terms the other cases all point to the same predominance of ladino/Indian status relations over economic class divisions as found in Momostenango during the first half of the nineteenth century. In the cases of Santa Cruz del Quiché, Ostuncalco, and Nonualco (El Salvador), a status distinction between "nobles" and "commoners" continued to be important in legitimating leadership roles, as was also the case in Momostenango.

These cases point to some proletarianization of the Indians during the latter quarter of the century after export coffee production began to flourish. As with Momostenango, however, class development in these communities remained incipient, and the Indians continued to be strongly united along ethnic lines in opposition to the increasingly powerful ladinos. Perhaps the Verapaz Indians were the most proletarianized within Guatemala; indeed, the appropriation of land and labor appears to have been more repressive there than in most other areas of Guatemala. We are told that by the end of the century the Verapaz Indians were left without economic alternatives other than plantation labor, and became defined more as "lower class" workers than as Indians.

El Salvador provides the greatest contrast with Momostenango. There it seems the majority of Indians were strongly proletarianized and in consequence ceased to be defined socially as Indians. Apparently, the less proletarianized Indians were those who organized politically against the capitalist encroachments into their communities, and eventually paid dearly for this with their lives.

A third cluster of issues focuses on culture, especially that of the Indians who resided in the communities. Has Indian identity essentially been defined in opposition to another ethnic unit (Spaniards, Creoles, ladinos), or has it been genuinely nativistic, a traditional thread linked through time with pre-Hispanic social forms? Does content, in fact, whether nativistic or otherwise, really matter?

These are the issues about which some of the most striking differences of interpretation have surfaced relative to Guatemalan Indian communities. The general interpretation has been to see cultural patterns in Indian communities as reactions against hegemonic state forms—largely dialectical constructions, whose content has been externally determined. In the light of the Momostenango case, however, this view would seem to depreciate the agency of Indians and to make external forces overly significant elements in the construction of native culture. In this regard, an important response to the question of whether it matters that a culture is nativistic, is to ask, matter to whom? In communities like Momostenango it has mattered very much to Indians, and, as this is so, it should matter to us as interpreters of a more dynamic history in which agency and culture must be important considerations.

All this is not to deny, of course, that dialectical cultural processes were at work in Momostenango, especially with respect to developments under the supervision of native merchant and later militia leaders of the nineteenth century. But throughout the century an extensive, positive, nativistic cultural construction was also at work. It was promoted by the great rural Indian majority and its traditional leaders, and its agenda had to be championed by the merchant and militia leaders in order for them to win communitywide support. The cultural ideals were highly complex and substantive, and their integrated structure exercised powerful transformative influence on new ideas being introduced from the outside or generated from within. This nativistic "cultural reality" was probably understood by all those who resided in Momostenango during the nineteenth century, ladino and Indian, and major program concessions had to be made to it by both Liberals and Conservatives.

Some of the cultural forms that appear in Momostenango during the nineteenth century represent remarkable constructions of forms from the deep past. We get a glimpse of these in the 1864 execution of the Indian couple according to ancient clan law. As the record of the judicial process reveals, state, local-ladino, and other outside powers were largely irrelevant to this important episode in Momostenango community life. And this was only the tip of the iceberg as far as native culture was concerned—a tiny part of a complex web that included native calendrical and astronomical calculations, priestly and shamanistic rituals, patriarchal authority systems, marriage alliances between lineages, witchcraft, elaborate dance, and myth cycles. No one really familiar with these cultural forms would interpret them as mere dialectical reflections of Spanish or ladino culture, and in our historical studies somehow we must find the way to include them.

This is not an argument for the romantic notion of a surviving, pristine Indian culture in Momostenango or other Guatemalan communities, unaffected by the political-economic forces of the nineteenth century. Culture reconstruction by the Indians was a continuous, ongoing process, but the Indians were active agents and they drew heavily from a traditional heritage that reached all the way back to pre-Hispanic social formations. Unquestionably, important cultural changes were taking place as a consequence of the political and economic forces introduced by Barrios and his liberal successors. Nevertheless, I find little evidence in Momostenango of major cultural transformation—say, the emergence of proletarian ideas among the Indian masses or of overt ideological expressions by the native militia leadership. At a deeper, less transparent, level the cultural expressions that defined the persisting Indian/ladino status division were taking on a more ominous violent orientation, as illustrated by the murder in 1899 of one Indian militiaman by another. The kind of subtle cultural reconstruction taking place at the end of the nineteenth century was part of wider political and economic processes that were creating conditions that eventually would lead to the shattering political crises suffered by Guatemala in the second half of the twentieth century.

The story of nativistic cultural construction found in the comparative case studies is similar to that of Momostenango. This is particularly evident for the central Quiché area, where traditional cultural patterns almost identical to those recorded in the *Popol Vuh* survived all the way into the twentieth century when they were observed by ethnographers. The process by which such preservation occurred is suggested by the Indians' almost constant struggle to maintain their old political boundaries against the state's determination to reform them. At both Santa Cruz del Quiché and Ilotenango, "Christo-pagan" colonial patterns were carried over to the nineteenth century, replete with civil-religious hierarchies, clan and lineage organizations based on patrilineal descent and "bifurcate-merging" kinship terminologies, and ritual specialists versed in the 260-day divinatory calendar. It is clear that native patterns *did* matter in the cultural construction process taking place, and were themselves, along with economic and political questions, a fundamental issue in the Indians' struggle against outside powers. As at Momostenango, in late-century Santa Cruz the Liberals appear to have promoted the association of native culture with the emerging militia organization. An Indian militia unit in 1885 chanted a "war hymn" that mentioned the ancient Quiché deities, to the burning of copal incense and the beating of log drums.

The question of culture is little dealt with in the studies of Santiago Atitlán or Ostuncalco, though the authors suggest that the highly nativistic patterns developed by the Indians during the colonial period were carried forward throughout the century with minor changes. Thus, we are told that at Atitlán cultural patterns had some Spanish elements, but the structures were basically native. With the help of nativistic movements late in the nineteenth century, these syncretistic patterns survived into the present century when ethnographers were able to describe them (Mendelson 1967). At Ostuncalco the Indians continued to recognize "shamans and prayermakers" as their foremost leaders, and to legitimate their authority through the ceremonial drinking of atole and offering of palm leaves. Presumably these patterns continued to be constructed by the Indians throughout the century, though a certain amount of acculturation toward ladinolike patterns ("ladinoization") took place late in the century due to pressures from local ladino authorities and work on the plantations.

The Verapaz Indians apparently carried over somewhat more acculturated native cultures into the nineteenth century, due to their relative isolation and benign treatment by the Dominican missionaries during the colonial period. Subsequently they became culturally even less Indian as a result of influence from the coffee plantations in the area. Nevertheless, ethnographic studies (Cabarrús 1979) from the end of the last century and beginning of this one demonstrate that strong nativistic cultural processes were at work in nineteenth-century Verapaz.

Though nativistic patterns were less developed in the communities of El Salvador than in Guatemala, they provided the basis for a movement to free the Indians of ladino control in the Nonualco region early in the century. We are told that the rebels attempted to reconstruct "lapsed" economic and political native structures. By the end of the century, nativistic patterns in the few communities that still claimed Indian identity had become quite thin (cofradias and caciques are mentioned). Proletarian ideas from within and radical political ideas from without easily overshadowed the weak native cultures in the development of a remarkable revolutionary movement during the early part of the twentieth century.

Conclusions: A Theoretical Discussion

Let us conclude by returning to the theoretical positions mentioned at the beginning of this study. What light is cast on the Guatemalan case when the above empirical data relative to Momostenango and other communities are viewed through these theoretical prisms?

Marxist theory insists on the importance of changing class relations as the capitalist mode of production becomes established in countries like nineteenth-century Guatemala. Particularly crucial are transformations in the relationship between the lords and peasants of precapitalist societies. The changes are measured by such factors as the relative strength of the peasant communities, including the extent to which they maintain control over their lands; the degree to which the lords exercise traditional economic and political control over the peasants; the frequency and scope of conflict between peasants and the lords and/or state. The theory suggests that development toward a more modern social formation occurs when: (1) peasant communities are broken down and their lands appropriated; (2) the lords lose control over the peasants at the same time that rural entrepreneurs gain influence; and (3) peasant uprisings are squashed by the state.

There can be little doubt that the capitalist mode of production became increasingly important in nineteenth-century Guatemalan society, and that its influence penetrated more deeply through time into Indian communities such as Momostenango. Nevertheless, its significance in comparison with precapitalist modes of production was quite limited until the development of the coffee plantations after 1871. This can be shown by an examination of the relations between the Carrera state and the Indian communities, which took on the characteristics of the precapitalist societies that some Marxist writers (Godelier 1978; Bloch 1983) see as being transitional for the development of capitalist social formations. The Indian communities retained considerable autonomy relative to the Carrera state, except for politically obligated "tributes" in the form of labor and military support. As often occurs in such precapitalist societies, the communities recognized their dependence on the ruler himself for their very existence, and imbued his person with a degree of sacredness.

The application of the Marxist model of precapitalist society to the Carrera period in Guatemala cannot be pushed too far, however. As noted above, the Momostecan's loyalty to Carrera fell far short of being divine worship. More generally, capitalist developments remained very limited through the Carrera period. That is to say, the Indian communities continued to be strong and relatively autonomous. Local (Creole) lords lost power over the communities during the period, but this was the result of political centralization (the Indians' loyalty to Carrera) rather than the emergence of local entrepreneurs. Rural rebellion was widespread during the early decades of the century, but it was never effectively controlled by the state. Rather, the communities were appeased and allowed to settle back into their traditional relationship with the state.

A better case can be made that the Barrios-established social formation of late-nineteenth-century Guatemala represented the beginnings of capitalist development and transition to modern society. In this period one finds the emergence of a well-defined bourgeois class (plantation owners, both foreign and Guatemalan); the forced labor of the Indians who provided labor power for the capitalist enterprises (coffee plantations); and the reorganization of the state as a political instrument of the bourgeois class, promoting the production and marketing of coffee in every possible way. Despite these familiar capitalist features, a democratic society was not established in Guatemala, for reasons that will now be made clear.

The Barrios and subsequent Liberal "reforms" weakened the Indian communities, but did not destroy them. As we saw in the Momostenango case, significant portions of community lands were lost, but not enough to separate completely the majority of Indians from their means of subsistence. Only in El Salvador did that occur, and it precipitated a radical movement that could be put down only through extremely violent state repression. In most Indian communities of Guatemala, only a minority was significantly proletarianized, while the majority remained tied to the land and maintained community cohesion.

The traditional ladino landlords were transformed by the plantation system, and in some regions (especially the Pacific piedmont, Verapaces, and Salvadoran coffee zones) were profoundly commercialized. In most of the highlands, however, their class orientation was not radically altered. They were able to use the Liberal system to increase power over the Indian communities, as generally they settled for a more profitable exploitation of the Indians' surplus rather than capitalist venture. These local ladino notables, therefore, were part of the process by which the survival of the Indian communities was made possible.

The Liberal reforms brought in their wake very serious Indian rebellions, as indicated above for Momostenango, Santa Cruz del Quiché, the Verapaces, El Salvador, and, additionally, Huehuetenango (McCreery 1988). These revolts are a clear indication that the Indians considered their traditional way of life to be in serious jeopardy. The state dealt with these rebellions in a manner unprecedented since the conquest for its strength of arms and brutality. The repressive measures taken must have sent a clear message to the Indians about the altered (bourgeois) interests of the state, how the Indians stood relative to those interests (as workers), and the extent to which force would be applied against anyone opposing this new social reality. As the Salvadoran case shows, only major rebellious movements—with intercommunity linkages and ties to urban powerholders—would have any chance of opposing the ruling class, and even then the risks would be very great.

A pluralist model is also applicable to cases such as Guatemala where revolutionary breakthroughs have not occurred. Guatemala underwent considerable economic and political development during the nineteenth century, but the process involved "bureaucratic reforms" from above rather than revolutions from below. In addition, Guatemala remained rigidly stratified and politically dominated by authoritarian regimes.

The social trajectory of nineteenth-century Guatemala, one of development from "above" rather than from "below," is particularly evident with respect to the two Liberal periods, early and late in the nineteenth century. The conservative Carrera regime gained power with support from below, and promoted programs that favored the interests of the rural sector (Miceli 1974). Administration under Carrera was highly patrimonial, though the Momostenango case reveals that the Carrera state through time took on some bureaucratic characteristics. Increased state control of the (Creole) landlord class and the Indians' labor power were other tendencies of the Carrera regime, even though state controls were never very strong. It is evident that the rural communities could rise up in revolt (and did so in some instances), but the capitalist and political pressures on the Indians were generally too weak to touch off such violent reactions. It should be noted, too, that the Carrera regime was under considerably less pressure from outside states than were the Liberal regimes early in the century and after 1871 (Woodward 1976:92–148). The British and Americans were preoccupied with the issue of carving out an isthmian route between the oceans, while the other Central American states were conservative and weak relative to the Carrera government.

It is with the Barrios and subsequent Liberal regimes that nineteenth-century Guatemala took on many of the characteristics that can be considered "development from above." The Liberals created the most powerful state ever seen in Guatemala up to that time, and in the positivist ideology of the period attempted to expand and bureaucratize its agencies. While by ideal Weberian standards the Liberal state's administrative organs retained many patrimonial features, the bureaucratic transformation of political, judicial, military, communications, educational, and economic functions is impressive. The consequences of an expanding "legal" authority were a grossly ranked and racist society favoring the rich elite over the poor masses, and a highly coercive state. The structural parallels between late-nineteenth-century Guatemala and prefascist Prussia and Japan are clear, as Baloyra (1983) has pointed out, and these structures laid the foundation for a type of political system (called "reactionary despotism" by Baloyra) that prevails to this day in Guatemala.

A pluralist model requires us to examine the changing relations between the state and landlords, as well as between the state and rural cultivators. The Liberal state in Guatemala used military organization to gain control over the landlords. In the Indian highlands, local ladinos were successfully co-opted into militia service and made subordinate to the state. The picture is less clear in other areas, especially the piedmont and the Verapaz coffee zones, where many of the landlords were foreigners (Cambranes 1985). The Momostenango case shows how important military domination, controlled by the ladinos, was for the state's ability to subject the Indians to forced labor. Repressive labor in Guatemala took a form somewhat intermediate between the serfdom in Prussia and the exploited peasant communities in Japan (B. Moore 1966:433). Most important, in Guatemala as in early modern Prussia and Japan, the system of state military control of local lords and rural workers effectively blocked the organization of serious revolt, and thus eliminated any possibility of revolutionary change. In consequence, this kind of state control resulted in societies that retained considerable undigested "traditional" structure, leading to internal contradictions that eventually became sources of social crisis.

It is important to note, finally, that the Liberal states of late-nineteenth-century Guatemala came under strong pressures from outside states. Barrios, reminiscent of nineteenth-century Prussian leaders, attempted to unite the Central American countries, at least in part to present a more powerful front to the British, German, American, and Mexican states. After Barrios, the Liberal regimes of other Central American states were themselves more powerful than ever before, and a constant threat to the Guatemalan regimes. And, of course, by the end of the century U.S. power began to be felt much more strongly, a trend that was to be greatly augmented with the development of the U.S. banana monopoly. Unquestionably, the authoritarian regime and racist society that developed in late-nineteenth-century Guatemala were partly the product of these international pressures, just as they were during the same period in Prussia and Japan. The specific processes by which these pressures were translated into programs that promoted state domination of landlords and Indians in Guatemala have not been elucidated by the Momostenango or other cases summarized above, and that remains an important task for future research.

Note

1. I have already published summaries of developments in Momostenango during the nineteenth century (Carmack 1979, 1983, 1988), and here I will only review some of the main points pertaining to the issues of state and Indian community relations. The larger, but unfinished, study from which this is taken is based on documents deposited in archives in Guatemala (including those in the local municipio of Momostenango), Spain, and elsewhere, in addition to more than two years of fieldwork in the community (Carmack n.d.b).

Part 2:
Twentieth-Century Struggles

7. Ethnic Images and Strategies in 1944

Richard N. Adams
Institute of Latin American Studies, University of Texas

Guatemala in 1944 was on the verge of a great transition that was to last over the next several decades. Since independence the country had experienced a long, if irregular, era of Liberal expansion, marked most clearly by the adoption of coffee cultivation and Guatemala's conversion into a country dedicated to the export of that crop. While historians may disagree on periodization, it is not misleading to see the general society as evolving under a nineteenth-century Liberal economic framework that continued up through World War II. The period from 1944 to 1954 (the "Revolution") was an era of significant reform and challenge to that framework, but it ultimately terminated in failure and the country relapsed into the Liberal pattern.

The relation of the Indian population to the state during the rule of Jorge Ubico was ambiguous. The perspective taken by the official representatives of the Liberal Progressives was that the Indian population had been exploited and made miserable, mostly by their being subjected to the *habilitación* (debt peonage) system. Since the passage of the draconian labor laws of the Liberal reform era of the 1870s, Guatemalan *políticos* had not shown the slightest interest in the Indian population as anything more than a source of labor. Indians were not regarded as warranting political attention from the government. Their political invisibility assured their virtual enslavement to the coffee farmers requiring labor for the production of their export crops. By the 1920s, however, habilitación could not keep up with the demand for labor, expanded by growing coffee markets in the United States and Europe. Indians had also learned to use the system to generate the most income for the smallest amount of work. So political attention was again focused on Indian labor.

Ubico continued the habilitación laws until 1936 when he abolished debt peonage and replaced it with vagrancy laws, which declared that every Indian who was not the titled owner of a certain amount of agricultural land was a vagrant and was required to work a certain number of days a year on the fincas, usually the coffee farms. Indians carried passbooks in which their work record was kept, and if labor was needed, those whose records were not current could be rounded up for work. Ubico's official party newspaper, *El Liberal Progresista*, periodically ran editorials lauding the abolition of debt peonage as a humane and progressive act, but the new laws actually guaranteed that more Indian labor would be available for export agriculture.

Ubico also undertook to expand the road system of the country, instituting a road tax that could be paid off (two quetzales) or worked off (two weeks). By and large, the ladinos paid and the Indians worked. Ubico took great pleasure in heading up a motorcycle caravan of officials to visit isolated Indian communities. He would, on these occasions and when Indians visited him at the national palace in Guatemala City, grant specific requests from Indian leaders. For example, the Indians of Panajachel documented why the intensive labor on their small cash crop plots should exempt them from the forced labor laws, and Ubico granted their request (Tax 1953).

Ubico was considered a good administrator and honest enough to virtually eliminate graft from government activities, but he followed in the tradition of antecedent Guatemalan dictators by tyrannizing the political opposition and subjecting everyone to various personal whims. In short, Ubico nationalized control of the Indian labor force, removing it from the control of the farmers and habilitadores, but guaranteeing the labor necessary for coffee cultivation and harvesting. He continued the kind of personalistic relationship with certain Indian leaders that had characterized earlier dictators, but expanded his contacts through his lightning trips to Indian communities. He strongly favored the expansion of U.S. capital and U.S. priorities. His rule ultimately collapsed under the wave of external and internal changes that buffeted Guatemala during World War II (Handy 1984:100).

When Ubico resigned on June 30, 1944, he was replaced in a quick power play by one of his generals, Federico Ponce Vaídes. Elections were then scheduled for December, with the new president scheduled to take office in March 1945. The popular candidate was Juan José Arévalo, a self-exiled philosophy professor from the University of Tucumán, Argentina. Ponce, considered Ubico's close associate, ordered congress to appoint him president and threatened to cancel the elections. He soon found himself the target of demonstrations and strikes, and was ousted in a bloody battle in October 1944 by young army officers (Handy 1984:105). In an effort to gain popular votes in the countryside, he had previously passed the word that he would, if elected, divide among the Indians the extensive German-owned coffee farmlands that had been confiscated by the Guatemalan government during World War II. As it became increasingly clear that his chance of winning the election was slight, he apparently sent further word that should the Indians want "their lands," they should take some action.[2] Whether this was the necessary and sufficient condition is not currently clear, but the reaction in the countryside was growing unrest.

This chapter draws on materials from the principal Guatemala City newspapers of the period and concerns the state of ethnic relations at the very beginning of the decade of the reform era, 1944–1954. We will examine how events concerning the indigenous population were represented in the newspapers *El Imparcial, La Hora, El Liberador,* and *Nuestro Diario* during the period of August through December 1944, together with other news reports that appeared early in 1945.

The materials reviewed here fall into two general groups: news articles and editorials. The news articles do not have identifiable authors, but they are universally ladinos, presumably from urban backgrounds. In most cases it is clear that they have few antecedents in indigenous affairs. The editorials come in general from intellectuals, some of whom had been writing in the *indigenista* genre since the 1930s. Indigenismo was a humanitarian perspective about Indians that emerged late in the nineteenth century, more remarkably in Mexico, but also in Guatemala and elsewhere in Latin America. It was specifically a mestizo ideology that presented Indians as having been long exploited but of intrinsic individual worth, in need of education and of being raised to their proper place in civilization. These authors were urban ladinos and some, such as Luis Cardoza y Aragón and Jorge Schlesinger, later became well known for political polemics and essays. What is clear is that both news articles and editorials reflect an exclusively ladino perspective; there were no Indians writing for the newspapers (or, for that matter, for anything else), and their absence is itself an important statement. The only editorial that reflects a rather more Indian than indigenista view is that of Cardoza y Aragón.

In the development of this literature, however, the year 1944 was critical. It marked the end of the Ubico reign and the beginning of a search for democratic process, which Guatemala has yet to find. While seen by many as the end of the dictatorship and the beginning of the reform era, hindsight suggests that it was the beginning not only of the eventual transition to the military state, but was also the start of the emergence of an Indian ethnicity of nation-state scope.

Indian and Ladino Behavior in the News

In an essay entitled, "A Sea of Indians: Ethnic Conflict and the Guatemalan Revolution 1944–1952," Jim Handy (1989) cites a rash of

Indian uprisings that took place in 1944. Newspapers reported threats of Indian attack on those seen blocking Indian access to the lands promised by Ponce, and thereby openly expressing the ladino fear of violent Indian uprisings. In September 1944 there was a large demonstration by *campesinos* in the neighborhood of La Aurora on the outskirts of Guatemala City. This was followed in October by uprisings in the towns of Patzicía and San Andrés Itzapa in the Department of Chimaltenango, and alleged uprisings in San Juan Ostuncalco and Chichicastenango.

It is interesting to catch the flavor of these incidents as they appeared in the Guatemalan newspapers of 1944. An editorial in *Nuestro Diario* referred to a September 15th demonstration, "with country people from various areas near the capital; and then, with threatening intentions some hundreds of country people from the same region concentrated in the fields of La Aurora . . ." (Valle, *Nuestro Diario*, October 25, 1944). The author notes that it is sad that "these peaceful inhabitants will be contaminated with the poison of a misguided politics with criminal aspects, taking them from their fields of work and forming them into a shock force ready to serve the malicious interests of a political party that is in conflict with—better said, in war to the death against—popular opinion." He refers to the "terrorist regime of Ponce" that promised country people lands in Chimaltenango, El Quiché, and other areas. This was the cause of the "spontaneous reaction among those people who felt themselves defrauded at the instigation of the very people who persisted in deceiving them, with the result now so evident."

On November 8th, under headlines announcing, "Indian Uprising Suppressed in Ostuncalco," *El Imparcial* reported that on October 22, 1944, an uprising in Ostuncalco had been promoted by the town's mayor, Carlos Marroquin Barrios, and the secretary, Martín Castillo Reconos, both "undesirable elements because of their affiliation with the Liberal party . . ." It continued,

> The residents realized the danger they were in when one of them was speaking casually with the local commandant. A number of Indians armed with clubs and machetes approached in a menacing attitude intending to attack them. Disarmed before they could attack, the Indians said they were acting under the instigation of the very same commandant. Later all of the outskirts of the town were discovered to be full of armed Indians, awaiting the agreed upon signal, the ringing of a bell.

Perhaps the strangest report came from Quezaltenango, announcing a large uprising in Chichicastenango:

The Department of Quiché is living with the anxiety inherited from the recent Liberal Progressive regime, now translated into a latent threat of Indians stirred up against ladinos.

We have received letters from the departmental capital complaining of the threat of the aborigines who have been trying to rise up to exterminate the ladinos or whites, in conformance with a plan provided by the propagandistas of General Ponce's Liberal Party during the recent election campaign, interrupted on the 20th of the current month.

During the night of the 23rd—says our informant—we lived through tense hours here in the departmental capital, because the arrival in a warlike manner of people from Quezaltenango was announced, and at the same time the news was circulated that 4000 Indians of Chichicastenango had risen up against the ladinos of that town. In the midst of this affliction we were further disturbed by the passivity of the authorities of whom we had requested arms for self defense.

In Chichicastenango—reported another informant from the capital of El Quiché—a captain named Jesús Ramirez was trying to convince the Indians to revolt, and was telling them that the new government—that of the revolution—would not give them "their lands." "Their lands" referred to the land formerly owned by the enemies of Guatemala (the Germans), the bone of contention used by the Liberals for *poncista* propaganda and against the independent parties of Guatemala.

We took note of this accusation from El Quiché because, in view of what happened in Patzicía, where the criminal efforts of the Liberals resulted in the shedding of the blood of innocents, an uprising of Indians could be repeated in El Quiché, particularly in Chichicastenango where Captain Ramirez had been stationed. (*El Imparcial*, November 2, 1944)

In the November 8, 1944, issue of the same newspaper is an article reporting a petition from Chichicastenango with one hundred signatures asking for the removal of Coronel Jesús Ramirez Mota. It concludes, "The citizens live in constant fear due to the hate that Colonal [*sic*] Ramirez sowed among the Indians against the ladinos."

Certainly the most stunning of all the events reported was the massacre in Patzicía. It is clearly not possible here to explore all the details that appeared in the press over a number of days following that event, but the following reports will provide a sample.[3] On October 21 at the instigation of individuals influenced by the Ponce arguments concerning the accessibility to land, some Indians of Patzicía attacked a number of ladino families. It was a bloody affair, in which children as well as women and men were slaughtered. News of the event was reported immediately to the departmental and national capitals, and to neighboring towns. Armed ladinos came from nearby Zaragoza, the Guardia Civil arrived from Guatemala, and a further blood bath was launched, the results of which were summarized by stating that the event "resulted in fourteen dead of the ladino race, and uncountable Indian cadavers, numerous wounded of both races, and a deep fear in the hearts of Guatemalans, unaccustomed to the unjustified reprisals of the Indians against the creoles—the terrible harvest of the absurd regime of the 108 days . . ."—that is, the period of Ponce's rule (El Imparcial, November 18, 1944).

Later it was noted that 254 people had submitted requests for aid for being damaged by the event, and 120 for recovery of material damages (El Imparcial, November 30, 1944). It was also reported that the Boy Scouts of Antigua, Guatemala, had provided economic assistance to fourteen wounded people and the families of the fifteen people killed at Patzicía— which, presumably, included no Indians (El Imparcial, December 5, 1944). What this tells of ladino behavior is most revealing in the almost total absence of concern about what happened to the Indians. The latter are merely an "uncountable number of cadavers," whereas details on the number of ladinos killed and the number given succor are carefully recorded.

The readiness of ladinos to turn to shooting was not solely reported from Patzicía. In Quezaltenango, Sunday, October 15, just after 6 PM, shooting began near the market plaza full of Sunday crowds and started a terrified stampede of people trying to avoid being killed. The shooting was attributed to the police and the army. One boy was killed. The events are attributed to efforts by agents of Ponce and by the then governor, Ernesto Ramirez (who was removed by the new jefe político Alfonso Arís on October 22nd). It was then further observed that "in the final fifteen days of the regime of General Federico Ponce V., government spies multiplied at an alarming rate, men and women with unfamiliar faces were everywhere, and it is said that many of them added to the terror by shooting at defenseless individuals, the majority of whom were wounded in the back" (Nuestro Diario, October 25, 1944).

In Guatemala City, these events appeared somewhat marginal to the revolution of October 20th, in which the forces of Ponce and the Ubiquistas were defeated. This relatively bloody military action saw more than three hundred wounded people treated in the General Hospital (Nuestro Diario, October 26, 1944; Handy 1984:105). A Junta Revolucionaria was formed under the leadership of Col. Jacobo Arbenz, Col. Francisco J. Arana, and the civilian, Jorge Toriello. This all but assured the election of Arévalo, as most of his competitors withdrew in his favor. There is no question that Arévalo enjoyed a broad basis of middle-class support. But the Patzicía massacre, and the wide-ranging reports of insurgent Indians that preceded it, reflected a serious doubt on the part of the indigenous population that their interests would be recognized. The massacre also unquestionably increased the level of mutual fear on the part of ladinos and Indians.

Indian and Ladino Stereotypes in Editorials

While much of the editorial writing reflects various aspects of ladino behavior, a broad analysis of such material is not possible here. Rather, I want merely to illustrate some of the stereotypes that appear, specifically those that contrast ladino character and behavior with that of the Indians.

One perspective is summed up in an editorial by Ovidio Rodas Corzo. After decrying the indigenista fervor in Mexico, he writes, "If I may be forgiven by Mexican indianists, all that is good in Mexico, the dynamic and the promising, is Latin" (*La Hora*, February 20, 1945).

A three-part series by Luis Cardoza y Aragón takes the position,

The nation is Indian. This is the truth which first manifests itself with its enormous, subjugating, presence. And yet we know that in Guatemala, as in the rest of America, it is Mestizo who has the leadership throughout the society. The Mestizo: the middle class. The revolution of Guatemala is a revolution of the middle class . . .

And what an inferiority complex the Guatemalan suffers for his Indian blood, for the indigenous character of his nation! . . . The Guatemalan does not want to be Indian, and wishes his nation were not. (*El Imparcial*, January 10, 1945)

Rufino Guerra Cortave, in an editorial concerning Indians, writes:

The events of Patzicía are too recent to have been forgotten, the crimes at the top of the Santa Maria volcano in 1917 can still be remembered with horror, and we could relate many others, secure in the judgment that the perpetrators, those originally guilty, were not really the Indians, but, rather were shameless ladinos. (*El Imparcial*, December 19, 1944)

The dangerous and menacing behavior of Indians was well portrayed in the news articles of the time and was considered common knowledge of the dominant society. The Chichicastenango parish priest remarked in the 1930s that "if organized and a bit educated the Indians might some night massacre all of the ladinos."[4]   Jorge Schlesinger's work on the Salvadorean *matanza* observed that "the communist revolution of El Salvador teaches us to what lengths a people oppressed by hunger and stimulated by promises of immediate social vindication can go; and history repeats itself . . ." (Handy 1989).

Yet, in spite of the news articles proclaiming the massacre of ladinos and reprisals on Indians in Patzicía, of the threatening conduct reported from Chichicastenango, San Juan Ostuncalco and elsewhere, the editorials essentially ignore these events.   Instead of delving into the significance of these alleged occurrences, they revert to a genre that emerged at the end of the nineteenth century, an indigenista rhetoric that seeks to deplore, but rationalize, the condition of the Indians as being something that can be corrected without fundamentally endangering the liberal approach.   Characteristic are the following:

1.   *Indians are low, lazy and despicable.*

Luis Cardoza y Aragón summarizes well how the Indians were generally treated: "almost always with depreciation, pejoratively.   He is represented as being guilty of everything" (*El Imparcial*, January 1, 1945).   Indeed, the editorials are relentless in this respect, as the following examples indicate.   It should be remembered, however, that these are not so much direct assertions as they are representative of the common attitudes of the time.

> We generally recognize that we are opposed to these compatriots, ignorant, filthy, lazy, sick, licentious, without consciousness. We have often felt ourselves rebel against their evilness. We have also found ourselves in agreement with those who would favor their gradual disappearance by whatever means that would progressively diminish their ranks.
>
> In addition: when we have witnessed row upon row of these robust but moronic beings bending low to kiss the bloody hand of their own unholy executioners, without the most minimal revulsion, we have wished that the earth would swallow them up, never to reappear. (Guerra Cortave, *El Imparcial*, December 19, 1944)

> Four centuries of oppression, cruelty and systematic brutalization of the native has made him so indolent and apathetic that he is resigned to his lot. . . . When it is said that the Indian is lazy, a cheat, a liar, ill adapted to work, one who needs to be constantly oppressed because he is an irresponsible subject who does not respect the obligations he has contracted, one forgets that this is due to his lack of education and inadaptability and that in reality he

is the pillar of the national economy which is based mainly on agriculture. (Schlesinger, *La Hora*, November 26, 1944)

Our Indian—we are assured—is by nature lazy, stubbornly opposed to work, and as soon as he has a few cents in his pocket to cover his basic needs he no longer wants to work. (Editorial, *El Imparcial*, February 12, 1945)

2. *Indians are incapable of self-direction.*
Clearly evident in the editorials is the fear that rises up in the ladino population at the suggestion of Indian self-determination and potential power.

The government is obliged to be vigilant in order to improve the conditions of the Indian, that he may be useful to the fatherland, and not become that amorphous mass that allows itself to be used, unconsciously, to support the iniquities of political parties which to date have left bloody tracks throughout the country. (*El Imparcial*, February 12, 1945)

In the provinces,

The countryman, the illiterate, the laborer, Indian or ladino, continues in his ignorance and consequently continues to be a danger, to be manipulated by the perverse maneuvering of the enemy. These beings, because of their lack of consciousness, are a cloud in our sky of democratic liberties. (Guerra Cortave, *La Hora*, November 8, 1944)

It pains us that these peaceful inhabitants would be contaminated with the poison of a misguided political policy—sights set on criminality, removing them from their fields of labor and forming them into an assault force willing to serve the perverse interests of a party that had set itself against—better said in a war to the death with—public opinion. (Valle, *Nuestro Diario*, October 25, 1944)

The threat of indigenous insurgency was totally attributed to the political agitation of the Poncistas. No credibility was given to the possibility that the Indians may have had long and serious legitimate complaints with the system.
3. *Indians are essential to the national economy and security.*
The importance of Indians to the national economy is given some attention. Since the advent of the Liberal reforms of the 1870s, Indians

had been required by law to labor for ladino agrarian enterprises. It was extremely likely that these laws would disappear under the incoming new government. The editorials, therefore, reflected a real fear of what might happen to the economy were control over Indian labor to be lost.

> In reality he is the true pillar of the economy of the country, which is based principally on agriculture. The government has the obligation to be vigilant in bettering the conditions of the Indian, so that he may be useful to the fatherland. (Schlesinger, *La Hora*, November 26, 1944)

> The Indian is the substantial and dynamic being of our country. . . The treasure—as we hear so often from certain people—of our country is not the unexploited mines, nor the virgin forests nor many other things, the treasure is the human element. (Arandi Pinot, *El Liberador*, December 27, 1944)

> The salary increase for the worker in the fields should be studied more in depth, because the surplus he has he will spend on alcohol which gradually poisons him. (Schlesinger, *La Hora*, November 26, 1944)

4. *Indians must be regenerated.*
Since Indians were obviously so low and despicable, but were also central to the welfare of the state, changes in their lot should be accomplished without upsetting the system. They should also be introduced slowly and gradually. A long essay in *La Hora* entitled "El Indio" argues that to "regenerate the Indian" it is not adequate to focus on literacy, which often merely places Indians in the position to be fooled by members of the "superior race." Fundamentally, it must start with the physical well-being of the Indian, and this can begin with getting rid of lice; then on to other parasites, worms, filaria, and so on (*La Hora*, November 9, 13, 15, 1944).
Jorge Schlesinger writes,

> The problem of incorporating the Indian into civilization is difficult, it requires arduous and persistent labor. Are we capable of it? Yes, but we need the cooperation and good will of all the men who make up the country. (*La Hora*, November 26, 1944)

> To those beings whose lack of consciousness are a cloud in our sky of democratic liberties, we must take the light, we must take reason to them, we must infuse the ABC's of a citizenry's civiliza-

tion which leads to a clear policy in the defense and benefit of the interests of the nation above any other interests, and to not submit nor adhere to the arbitrariness of despotic authorities who operate outside the law. (Guerra Cortave, *El Imparcial*, November 8, 1944)

The Indian and the ladino who never learned more than, perhaps, to spell out block letters, is not guilty if he cannot discern good from evil, and it is the duty of the rest of the Guatemalans of conscience, to show them the road to their own best interest, if they are to be part of this society. It is necessary to unify the national conscience and this can be done with patience and with only reason and patriotic honesty as guides. (Guerra Cortave, *La Hora*, November 18, 1944)

Let us consider that it is much better to accomplish the effective democratization of the Indian by education, slow but sure, and not by the giant leap typical of the brusque change from oppressed to oppressors, and the evil intentions of those individuals of bad faith who would guide them or push them along troubled paths that lead only to the provocation of crime. (*El Libertador*, November 9, 1944)

The Indian has to be better fed and has to be given medicines. He should be given food in accord with the number of calories which are consumed by a normal man working in the fields. A well nourished man, healthy and happy, produces more efficient work, increases his production, is more ambitious, raises his standard of living, and is anxious to improve himself every day. (*La Hora*, November 26, 1944)

Finally, in some contrast to these go-slow recommendations is the editorial entitled "Indianismo y latinismo" by Ovidio Rodas Corzo that argues:

For these reasons, to strengthen the Indian culture, is to condemn our country to eternal weakness, a perpetual cultural dualism, to be always a nation of irredeemable Indians without a continental personality. Because of this, our Indians must be westernized or destroyed; but we should not keep them in their entrenched static state because we will then be only a country for tourism; of curiosities; a kind of zoo for the entertainment of tourists; but never a nation. (*La Hora*, February 19–20, 1945)

What is impressive about the indigenista approach that so dominates these editorials is that the writers knew that Indians were capable of violent reactions, but they professed a studied ignorance of why these violent reactions were so likely. The indigenismo of this period was a mestizo invention that reflected a recognition that Indians were mistreated but refused to allow for an examination of the causes that produced it.

Ethnicity and Politics

An "ethnic group" is a *self-reproducing social collectivity identified by myths of a common provenance and by identifying markers*.[5] The identification and definition of ethnicity can take place in two ways. An ethnic group may be *externally identified* by members of another group, whether or not the identification has any reality for the individuals so labeled; and/or may be *self-identified* by individuals who thereby constitute such a group, regardless of what outside obervers think. The sociological salience of an ethnic group emerges most importantly, however, when it is both self-identified and externally identified, when its existence is significant both to members and to outsiders. When the rewards or the work of a society are distributed on the basis of ethnic group membership, such groups become political entities.

The *índios* or *indígenas* of Guatemala were first externally identified as a separate ethnic group by the invading Spanish in the sixteenth century. The Spanish, not sure at first that the Indians were human, found their labor useful and soon asserted them to be a separate category of human beings, distinctive by both race and culture. Prior to Spanish contact, Mayan Indian chiefdoms were in competition with each other and conducted trade with the Aztecs to the north, so there already existed regional ethnic groups. In Guatemala these were readily identifiable by the Spanish on the basis of the various branches of the Mayan language family, the Quiché, Cakchikquel, Tzutuhil, and others. The nature of the colonial settlement policy, however, led the Spanish to break up these larger chiefdom identifications, and to congregate the Indians into settlements of Spanish design. By the turn of the twentieth century the most significant unit for self-identification among the indigenous peoples was the community or the *municipio* (Tax 1937:423–444). There was a pan-Indian self-identification that was known in Spanish usually as *natural*, or "native," but because the Liberal regimes from Barrios on dealt with the Indians on a community basis, the term lacked any organizing potential. The significant ethnic group for the Indians was the *municipio* or community, and Indian individuals would refer to themselves as, for example, *San Pedranos* (from San Pedro), or *Maxeños* (from Santo Tomás Chichicastenango), and so on. By the twentieth century, the Indians made little use of the linguistic categories derived from the old kingdoms. In my own experience in the early 1950s, for some Cakchiquel speakers the term *Cakchiquel* was not always known; people spoke not *Cakchiquel* but *lengua*.

Thus, when the 1944 newspapers reported Indian uprisings, it was in terms of the Indians of Patzicía, or of Chichicastenango, or of Ostuncalco, or of San Andrés Itzapa. These communities of Indians were the political entities about which the ladinos were so apprehensive. The notion of the potential for a larger Indian identity also existed in ladino thinking; usually realized as one where an Indian uprising in one town might trigger a chain reaction in other communities.

The ladinos, too, were an ethnic group by this time. The sixteenth into the nineteenth centuries saw the emergence of racially mixed populations in Guatemala. In the *oriente*, the area Lutz and Lovell (chap. 2) have referred to as the "colonial core," the Spanish and mixed populations tended to displace Indians and blur Indian identity, leaving a variety of racially mixed peoples who were not always easy to distinguish from Indians. The emergence of coffee as a major crop in the nineteenth-century western highlands stimulated an expansion of plantation holdings, and in some instances, brought about a specific predation on Indian-held lands. Coffee production also brought about a tremendous need for labor that led the coffee owners to encourage the relocation of *oriente* ladinos to highland Indian communities. Carol Smith (chap. 4) has argued that as these people increasingly acted as merchants and administrative intermediaries between the owners and the Indian labor in the western highlands, they began to emerge as a distinctive ethnic group vis-à-vis their Indian neighbors. Thus, the ladino-Indian ethnic contrast, so well reported in the anthropological literature of the 1940s to 1970s, came into being less than one hundred years ago.

Ladino Strategies of Control

By 1944, control of the Indian population had grown more complex. The controlling parties involved not only the coffee producers who needed the labor, but also the ladinos who acted as agents for the landholding class. Moreover, the government generally, but most explicitly with the victory of the Liberals in 1870, became overtly concerned that Indians be controlled in order to provide the labor necessary for the coffee export production. The ladino control of Indians must be seen in terms of two sets of strategies. There was the specific concern of individual ladinos, what we can call a *popular strategy*. And there was the more general concern of the state, explicitly expressed through the government, the land owners, and the intermediary ladinos, that constituted a *state strategy*.

The ladino popular strategy involved a number of components: (1) a constant depreciation of Indian society and culture, illustrated by the commentaries described in the earlier section on the portrayal of Indian behavior in the news; (2) a constant effort to best Indians in the market economy, manipulating state support by whatever means to reduce Indian control over land and share of the market; (3) using both legal and illegal devices to inhibit Indians from full political participation by keeping them from voting or holding local offices or taking on roles that would allow them to govern ladinos; (4) periodically exercising force to remind the Indians that they must accept political, economic, and cultural subordination; and (5) hiding the constant fear of Indian violence, treachery, and rebellion that enabled ladinos to work directly with Indians on farms, in labor gangs, in the kitchen, and so forth.

While these strategies were clearly successful over much of the central and western highlands, there were important areas of variation. What Carol Smith (1978) has referred to as the "modern" economic core identifies the region from Quezaltenango through Totonicapán as a particular development within the Indian western highlands. This core evaded much of the direct exploitation by the state control system, and both Indian communities and individual Indians were more successful in economic enterprises and in control over local affairs.

Ladino state strategies consisted not only of those activities that specifically benefited individuals or groups, but also the exercise of policies of control by the governing bodies. In the 1944–1954 era, these materials suggest the presence of two different policies: those of the Poncistas in their attempt to obtain a victory in the 1944 elections; and those of the Arévalo campaign and the governing regime, 1944–1951. While both were essentially "Liberal" philosophies, the former reflected the conservative position that control over Indian labor was still important, but equally that Indians were available as a popular support. It also saw Indians as essentially a separate order, complementary and necessary to the more productive ladino sector. The Arévalo Liberals manifested an "indigenista" philosophy and were oriented toward removing forced labor laws of all kinds. Indians should, they felt, be incorporated within the larger body politic through further education and health measures. The Indians, if they were a separate order, were one that could be enculturated into the ladino life to a degree that would make possible a single nation.

The immediate inheritors of the Ubico regime were Ponce and the "Progressive Liberals." They openly offered German finca land to the Indians in return for their political support in an effort, seen by many as cynical, to create a kind of unsolicited populism. But these actions also played on the fears, distrust, and hatred that the Indians and ladinos felt about each other. Comments in the news articles make it clear most of the media supported the Arévalo candidacy, and that they regarded the efforts to stir up Indian unrest by Ponce as evil and traitorous to the national (i.e., "ladino") interests.

The Guatemalan reform period of 1944–1954 has long been recognized as essentially a bourgeois revolution, and there is little question that the general position taken by the incoming Arévalo regime did not diverge much from the classic line of Liberal interests in nineteenth-century capitalistic expansion. While clearly the legitimate inheritors of the Ubico "Progressive Liberal" regime, the Poncistas' indigenous policies were superficially most akin to those of the nineteenth-century Conservatives. The Arevalistas may have been reformers, but they were a liberal bourgeoisie whose views generally reflected the indigenista view evident in the editorials.

Arévalo's administration did introduce many social reforms, but those directed at the countryside were more aimed at the rural labor on farms than at the Indians as semi-independent campesinos. The Law of Forced Rentals required that landholders rent their excess lands at reasonable rates, and this challenged the notion of totally private control over property. While there has been no study of this, it is my impression that it was more effective in the eastern part of the country among ladinos than among Indians in the western highlands. Indians did receive some notice through the establishment of the National Indian Institute, but the organization was funded solely to carry on research and had no action, advocacy, or development functions. Perhaps the most important change directly affecting Indian-ladino relations was the opening up of the electoral process and the formation of new political parties that cleared the way for Indians to hold local civic posts. The election of Indians as mayors of towns that had long been controlled by ladinos came as a real shock to that group.

The issues became clearer in February 1945, when the constitutional convention considered a special "Indian Statute" that contained articles providing protection for Indian individual and communal lands, promoting cooperatives, and favoring intensive training in the Spanish language. The convention, however, rejected it. Two major newspapers took different sides of the issue: La Hora was against the statutes, while El Imparcial favored them, and the editors of both periodicals were active as members of the convention.

La Hora argued that since the immense majority of the population is indígena, there was no reason to have a special section of the constitution dedicated to them. The bettering of the Indian population should be the direct task of the Ministerio de Educación Publica, and not a fiction of a statute (H. M. Vasquez, *La Hora*, February 27, 1945).

El Imparcial argued in an unsigned editorial that the great protestations about the Indians' importance, which were in evidence prior to the elections, were now being forgotten:

> It appears that at the hour of the debate, the principle prevailed that it was not wise to establish a racial discrimination, nor was there any reason to consider the Indians' legal position to be different from that of the Mestizo or White or population of any other color; that all should be equal before the law.
>
> In fact, however, it [the statute] did not deal with fixing racial discrimination, but rather to accept a reality unquestionable in our country; the Indians who compose an immense majority of the Guatemalan population, live permanently unconnected with other groups, and, in spite of their number, they ought to be considered as a social class and economically weak. The question is not whether the Indian is inferior or superior to others; what we should ask is: How long are we going to continue considering the Indian as an element foreign to our condition as a civilized people, and to become seriously preoccupied with helping him to escape his abandoned position and the virtual vassalage in which he has lived? (*El Imparcial*, February 26, 1945)

The incomplete presidential term of Jacobo Arbenz (1951–1954) introduced significant changes in the strategies of control, and moved in some important ways to the left of Arévalo's position. For Arbenz the strategy of control was more complicated since he attempted a realignment of the power of these groups and confronted direct landholder and military hostility.[6] He established the agrarian reform law, which distributed state and private land to landless campesinos. And he sought to neutralize the military by providing arms to campesinos, an effort that was blocked when discovered by the army. As is well known, his policies were ultimately brought to ground by the combined efforts of the internal opposition and the U.S. Central Intelligence Agency.

In the present context, however, it is important to note that, like Arévalo, Arbenz did not promote policies that identified Indians as a particularly problematic population. The emerging labor unions, campesino leagues, and political parties did not form along specifically ethnic lines. The law of forced rentals and the agrarian reform did not single out Indians, but rather treated campesinos as a class. It is perhaps ironic that the failure to target Indians meant that when Arbenz was thrown out and Castillo Armas took over in 1954, the new regime also did not take out its ire particularly on Indians; the favors provided by the reforms were withdrawn from whoever had received them, primarily campesinos of either ethnic group.

Indian Strategies of Control

The strategies available to the Indians were few, basically those commonly available to the weak: playing off one party against another; the occasional use of violence under limited circumstances; and retreat, avoidance, and humility. The last of these is the strategy of survival. In human terms it exacts a fearful toll in psychological and physical misery, but it allows the individuals or the population to survive, and, over the long run, the potential of action survives.

In hindsight, both of the other two strategies—manipulation by dividing superior powers, and occasional violence—were important. The first was, of course, originally promoted through the efforts of the Poncistas. Later it became a common tactic in the political and land struggles within and between municipios (see Handy, chap. 8). The second, the use of violence, occurred irregularly despite ladino fears. Both these strategies are more effective if they can be coordinated among Indians of different communities. What frightened the ladinos about Ponce's offer of land was that the resulting Indian uprisings were ultimately reported in communities scattered all the way from the Honduran to the Mexican border, and in independent communities as well as those on plantations. The Revolutionary Liberals attributed this apparent coordination to the prevalance and cleverness of the Ponce agents. They did not consider (or suppressed with the usual amnesia) the fact that the Indians were the ones that acted, no matter who did the agitation.

By 1944 the Indians were able to respond publicly, openly, and politically over much of the country. There is no evidence that they were coordinated beyond responding to the common stimulus of the Poncista overtures. In at least one basic way, this was probably similar to the response elicited by the guerrillas in the late 1970s that led to clandestine sympathy toward the insurgency on the part of perhaps as many as 500,000 Indians.[7] In both instances non-Indian agents (and Indian agents in the 1970s) systematically tried to organize the Indians into some coherent action. But it must again be noted that the Indians were clearly ready to act.

The full significance of Indian strategy, and of the 1944 events in ethnic relations, would not be evident for some decades. In 1944 the Indians who rebelled against ladino authority were community-based Indians. There was no suggestion of a nationwide Indian ethnicity.

However, the general suppression of campesinos and the fear that followed on the victory of Castillo Armas's "Liberation" forces certainly contributed to a broader awareness of potential Indian identification at the national level.

The ten-year revolutionary regime made serious efforts to recognize the interests of the rural poor. These policies offended both the landowners and the army; so with direct help from the CIA, the Arbenz government was overthrown in 1954. The government then continued under the more conservative forces, but by 1963, the military effectively took over. This began what must be seen as a new era of the military state, under which governments were to be variously controlled directly by military officers or by surrogate civilians whom they allowed to take power through elections with constricted electoral slates.

It must be recognized that many things happened in the 1950s and 1960s, and to attribute the nationalization of the Indian ethnicity only to the effects of a frustrated reform era, and particularly to one that itself gave little attention to Indians, is not convincing. However, there is also little question that this decade, especially the Arbenz phase, marked a sociological awakening that was not squelched by subsequent repressions, but that provided the groundwork for the revolutionary era that is with us today. An awareness of this potential change was evident to the present writer in the 1950s (Newbold 1957). A broader Indian identity became visible in the streets by the regionalization of Indian clothing in the 1960s, and clearly evident in the increasing number of Indian professionals and Indians involved in organizing and revolutionary activity in the 1970s and 1980s. All this constitutes the emergence of a national-level Indian identity. Through the emergence of educated, literate, Spanish-speaking Indians with a national and international perspective and of Indians with active experience in insurgency, both groups familiar with the history of ethnic relations in Guatemala and with comparable models available elsewhere in the world, Guatemalan Indians initiated the formation of a new Guatemalan indigenous ethnicity. However, just as the earlier community ethnic groups could also recognize a wider population of *naturales*, so those involved in the development of the national Indian ethnic group are equally aware of a broader identity with aboriginal peoples elsewhere in the world.

The real significance of the events of the 1944–1954 period lies in this: it was the period when Guatemala's indigenous peoples, because they were given access to new rights as campesinos by a reform government, began to recognize that social change was possible. The formation of that national Indian identity is not complete, and the history of its origins remains to be written.[8]

The Captive Strategists

We have thus far discussed the images and strategies of 1944 as if they were embedded in a kind of partisan dispute. This is not unreasonable since they contain the residue of an unfinished conquest. Indian-ladino ethnic relations did not derive from Indian immigrants who accepted a subordinate role within an established state structure—as did the Chinese, Germans, or Lebanese. Rather, they derived from the fact that, while the Indians were forcefully subordinated by conquest, they were never assimilated within the Spanish colonial or independent Guatemalan society. Moreover, the Spanish and their mestizo and ladino successors depended on Indians as the central source of labor for their own welfare and development. To the degree that the Spanish and ladinos displaced the Indians from their own bases of subsistence, an economic dependence of Indians on the ladino-controlled production system was created. They are, thus, locked in a fear-ridden embrace from which neither can easily escape, and hence are captives of each other.

Thus through the colonial era, but much enhanced by the nineteenth-century export coffee cultivation, there emerged what was at once an agrarian class-based exploitative system predicated on political and religious subordination, and an ethnic differentiation that sought its rationalizing myth in socially and biologically inherited differences between the two populations.

The situation that thus evolved was structurally unstable and, therefore, dynamic; it incorporated an active mechanism for the generation of its own destruction. The basis of this mechanism was the constant suppression of the Indian population and their intentional marginalization from political and economic success. Certainly, hatred of the Spaniard, the mestizo, the ladino, has for centuries been a recurrent Indian emotion (Burgos-Debray 1984). Since the ladino state and popular strategies both periodically resorted to violence to enforce their interests, fear has been a constant motivation in Indian behavior as well. Moreover, this fear has intentionally been cultivated by the Spanish and ladinos. The most recent manifestation of this is, of course, the massive holocaust, the scorched-earth policy that destroyed so much of the Indian population in the recent period.

Fear and hatred, logically strong motivating forces within the Indian population, are not found there alone. They equally motivate ladino behavior. The image of Indians as uncivilized and somewhat bestial carries with it the fear of the unknown and uncontrolled. Indians— following the indigenista argument—must be civilized because, if not, they are unpredictable and may run wild, committing all sorts of mayhem. The ladino fear of Indian rebellion is clearly present in the 1944 reports from Patzicía, Quezaltenango, San Andrés Itzapa, and San Juan Ostuncalco.

What the news reporting and the editorial writing in the 1944 accounts show is a powerful reluctance to speak openly of the anxiety and hostility that lie so close to the surface of the ladino consciousness. For years the clear and unquestioned manner to contain the implications of this emotion has been to refuse to deal with it. It is not to be spoken of in public. And equally so, Indian hatred was to be dismissed from Indian behavior and ladino thinking. They are not to be spoken of in public.

There is little discussion of fear and hatred in the news articles. These qualities that run so deep in the ladino-Indians' relational systems are all but ignored, and the only reason given for Indian hostile behavior is that they are being manipulated by the evil Poncistas and Liberals. Indians are portrayed as capable of no self-generated action, as only responding to evil ladino stimuli. Likewise, the editorials give little suggestion that killing and death are the central events. They reflect the idea that the "Indian problem" stems from the Indians' lack of civilization, and that its solution can only be sought in terms of changing the Indians' society. The fault and responsibility lie entirely with the Indians. Of all the editorials, only that by Luis Cardoza y Aragón seriously suggests that some change would be appropriate in ladino conduct.

No mention is made of the Indian need for land. Probably because Indian labor is essential to national (elite and ladino) welfare, to give Indians land would mean they would be less available to work for the ladinos and would increase the direct competition for land with the ladinos. While such expressions are not common, an extreme position is expressed in a guest editorial by J. M. Paniagua who specifically addresses the need to retain the vagrancy law to assure that work will be done:

> So long as there is no vagrancy law that accords with our needs, the suppression of the "work card" would deal agriculture a mortal blow. It is argued that it is a harsh law, but our Indian requires harshness as long as he cannot meet his own needs. Who would criticize a farmer for putting a laborer in the local jail because the laborer does not want his child to go to school? Harshness, they might say; but harshness necessary to lift this child from the ignorance in which his father has lived. (*El Imparcial*, December 2, 1945)

This, of course, reflects the classic Liberal indigenismo position as expressed by Antonio Batres Jáuregui in 1894, where he simultaneously argues that the Indian should be removed from his communal lands, but be required to work on private lands. However, Batres Jáuregui differs from the 1944 editorials, for he recognizes directly that

the system has been to take the lands away from the Indians, to obligate them to work like slaves under the forced labor laws, not pay them more than a pittance for their labor on the fincas of certain potentates, sell them corn beer and cheap liquor in plenty, maintain them in crassest stupidity; in a word, treat them worse than the severest 16th century conqueror or the barbarous *encomendero* torturer and hangman.

This difference between Batres Jáuregui and the 1944 material might suggest a significant change over the half-century that separates these works. The earlier work does not hesitate to point up some prime reasons why the Indian is in the condition he is in. One of the major characteristics of the 1944 (and present) ladino position is a reluctance to bring these matters up for discussion or, indeed, even to recognize them. Thus, when an event such as Patzicía and the surrounding cases of Indian "unrest" occurred in latter 1944, they were primarily used in the press for ideological purposes, to raise an alarm or to cause a militant reaction, and not for social analysis or sophisticated political response. Little attention is paid to the accumulated frustration of the Indian community that had experienced centuries of political-economic subordination and exploitation under the pressure of state power.

Indeed, the contrast between the editorial focus on indigenista solutions for "the Indian problem," and the news reports of Indian mayhem, reveals a national amnesia within the ladino population concerning Indian-ladino relations. There is never a clear sense that the problems can be submitted to reasonable or open analysis, debate, or discussion. To bring these things up for discussion is threatening; it elicits the fear. How can ladinos work directly with Indians on farms, live as neighbors, share community responsibilities with them, depend on them for crucial elements in their life support, and at the same time admit to a fundamental fear of them? The most obvious answer is to deny it; to create other myths, myths that keep things quiet.

The news reports and editorials tell us little about the Indian view of the matter. It is fairly obvious that the Indians would have feared the ladinos, but whether they spoke of it, whether they were willing to discuss it, is not considered by the ladino voices of the press. But the very silence suggests that, for the ladinos at least, the relationship is not open for discussion.

Today the Indian population is making itself heard on the national scene. It is still barely recognized by ladinos; they tend to treat Indian *diputados* in congress as a kind of a game, and simply pay little heed to the growing Indian middle class that is as ambivalent but perturbed by the suppression of Indian ethnicity as it is desirous of the capitalist "good life." In 1944, the only way Indian concerns reached public notice (i.e., ladino notice) was when they resorted to public demonstrations and brought some force to bear on the scene. Today, the continuing silence of the ladinos suggests that they are not yet ready to open another road.

Notes

1. This is part of a work in progress. The newspaper material was gathered by Lic. Oscar Adolfito Haeussler. Arturo Arias, Edelberto Torres Rivas, José Antonio Montes, Julio Vielman, and Betty H. Adams offered helpful observations, but are not responsible for the product.

2. Evidence for this is not direct, but is repeated in the many complaints leveled by the opponents; it is hoped that further research will clarify the nature of Ponce's action.

3. A study of the Patzicía case is currently under way.

4. Cited in Handy (1989) from Sol Tax, "Notes on Santo Tomás Chichicastenango," Microfilm Collection of Manuscripts on Middle American Cultural Anthropology, no. 16, 1947.

5. This is a working definition of "ethnic group" devised for this research.

6. The opposition to the landholders was intentional; Arbenz, however, did not seek military opposition, but found it as his ideological position moved to the left. See the forthcoming work on this subject by Piero Gleijeses. ·

7. An estimate made by a long-time nonparticipant resident of the central highlands.

8. Arturo Arias's chapter in this volume (chap. 11) is a significant contribution to this subject.

8. The Corporate Community, Campesino Organizations, and Agrarian Reform: 1950–1954

Jim Handy

Department of History, University of Saskatchewan

One of the themes that has most interested anthropologists and historians when discussing Guatemalan rural history has been the role of Indian communities in shaping that history. Since the 1950s, when Fernando Cámara (1952) differentiated between "centripetal" and "centrifugal" communities and Eric Wolf (1957) described the major characteristics of the "closed, corporate community," this interest has increasingly focused on the relationship between these communities and the national economy and society—the manner in which the ·community resisted both economic and cultural integration with the "nation." The result has been that in the last three decades an impressive scholarship has more completely analyzed (1) the relationship between these communities and national society; (2) the effect that relationship has had on the development of the community and class differentation within the community; and (3) the role these communities have played in determining "national" history.

There is significant debate concerning the reasons for, effects of, and reaction to government policy in rural areas during the period called the Guatemalan "revolution" from 1944 to 1954. This is especially evident in those works that attempt to analyze the interaction of Indian communities and national institutions during that period. The policies of the revolution, more appropriately termed the reform period, especially the agrarian reform law from 1952 to 1954, have often been depicted as an attempt to confront the economic and political power of large landowners to benefit the rural poor. On the other hand, Ralph Beals (1967) in the 1960s suggested that the reforms with their "forced introduction of a party system and destruction of the traditional office holding pattern brought disastrous and rapid destruction of many Indian communities, particularly under the Arbenz regime." Robert Wasserstrom (1975) in the 1970s argued that the reforms provoked a struggle between incipient classes in Indian communities that prompted significant unrest and eroded much of the support the revolution enjoyed in rural Guatemala.

In the 1980s, Carol Smith (1984a) and George Lovell (1988), basing much of their analysis on Wasserstrom, linked the two arguments suggesting that this conflict helped break down the defensive institutions associated with the corporate nature of the community and paved the way for the subsequent two decades of repression.

While aspects of these arguments are essentially correct, this chapter suggests that they do not provide an accurate assessment of the interaction between rural communities and the state in the reform period. Instead, it argues that while there was substantial pressure on the structures of the corporate community and frequent class struggle in rural Guatemala, it was also a period of intense community identification. New village organizations were developing that more effectively represented the interests of campesinos and rural workers in both local and national government. The agrarian reform law placed some pressure on municipally controlled land, but the expropriation of such land was most often the result of tension within the community or a disagreement over the limits of the community itself. The most important result of the law was a dramatic increase in the amount of land available to community members. In addition, the willingness of a substantial proportion of the population of highland communities to embrace national organizations during the reform period suggests certain questions about the nature of "closed, corporate communities." In order to make this argument, this chapter will briefly sketch the major characteristics of highland communities and their interaction with national society, will outline the rural policies of the reform period, especially those of the administration of Jacobo Arbenz Guzmán from 1951–1954, and will discuss the reaction to them in rural areas.

The Concept of the Nation and the Spread of Agrarian Capitalism

Eric Wolf's concept of the closed corporate community is too well known to need extensive discussion here. Briefly, Wolf (1957) suggested that the corporate community "emphasizes resistance to influences from without which might threaten its integrity" and "frowns on individual accumulation and display of wealth and strives to reduce the effects of such accumulation." Wolf argued that the corporate community developed during the colonial period in response to demands on land controlled by community members and in the face of the perceived rapaciousness of the encroaching colonial society.

Although Wolf's concept appears to fit Guatemalan highland communities well, it is apparent that at various periods in Guatemalan history communities "opened" and "closed" depending on their relations with the broader political and economic system and in response to the demands placed on the community from outside (Wolf 1967; MacLeod 1973:327; McCreery 1976:452; Collins 1980).

Since independence these demands have been linked with two complementary processes: the spread of agrarian capitalism and attempts to inculcate the concept of the nation. From the Liberal "revolution" of 1871 to the beginning of the "ten years of spring" in 1944, the nation's rulers and the institutions of the state, most important, the military, devoted most of their energy to facilitating the spread of coffee cultivation. In doing so they often ignored the interests of, and developed policies perceived to be an attack on, Indian villages. As a result, village residents often strengthened their defensive posture toward outside society and the state. This, in turn, was used to justify more forceful measures by the military to compel village society to embrace the concept of the state and to participate more fully in the national economy.

By the 1940s these policies had contributed to increasing Indian reliance on wage labor on coffee fincas fostered partially by their diminishing land base. By the time of the 1950 agricultural census, ladino farm operators averaged 35 *manzanas* (1 manzana equals 1.7 acres) each, while Indians averaged only 4.4 manzanas. Because most ladino holdings were outside the highlands in areas where average landholdings were larger, these figures overstate the difference slightly, but even in the highlands, ladinos were only 12 percent of the farm operators but controlled 66 percent of the land. While many *municipios* continued to enjoy access to community-controlled land, much of this land was limited in quantity and usually not fit for cultivation (DGE, 1954 3:118).[1]

Ethnic tension, caused partly by this land dispossession and heightened by government attempts to control village government, permeated all aspects of rural Guatemala. However, the most apparent conflict in communities in the 1940s was a constant struggle among neighboring municipios over land, and an equally pervasive conflict among various components of the municipio, most often between the *aldeas* (hamlets) and the *cabecera* (municipal capital). While Sacapulas may have been an extreme case, Lovell's description of the municipio, where "various social groups . . . were in almost constant collision as each . . . sought to gain control over as much land in the vicinity of the town site as possible," is at least in some ways applicable to many other municipios (1983b:225–226). The conflict was prevalent enough to suggest that the generally accepted view that the municipio comprised the "community" be questioned (Carmack 1981:320–328). With these ideas in mind, let us now look at the relation between these communities and the "revolution."

The Community and the Ideology of the Reform Period

The civic demonstrations that prompted Ubico's resignation in 1944 and the coup by young military officers and civilians that overthrew his successor, General Ponce Vaídes, brought to power a generation of young, urban, middle-class reformers. Most of them shared a desire for individual freedom, economic development, and a more equitable social and economic order. They professed a belief in the need to integrate Indian cultures and Indian communities into the nation, and followed policies aimed at fighting what they perceived as lingering "feudalism" in the countryside by championing economic growth and diversification. In short, most perceived their "revolution" as essentially capitalist.

Government legislation in the early years of the period reflected this interest. The government established agencies and expanded institutions that operated in rural areas, dramatically increasing its presence in Indian communities. Perhaps of most importance in these newly expanded agencies was the government's concentration on education in rural areas. The government placed much emphasis on rural education and had gone to some length to investigate educational practices that would be more relevant and more effective in Indian communities, enlisting the assistance of the newly created *Instituto Indigenista Nacional* in the project. This rural education was clearly designed to foster patriotism and nationalism. Even the director of the Instituto made it clear he saw its major task as inspiring Indians to embrace national culture more actively and suggested that "indigenismo is the manifestation, the symptom, of a certain social ill-health" (Marroquin 1972:302). The *misiones ambulantes de cultura* (traveling cultural missions) were a particularly clear expression of the government's desire to spread a national culture to rural areas. These misiones had diverse duties, but stress was placed on "bringing the doctrine of the revolution" to rural communities and they were also to "disperse to the farthest corners of the republic the cult of the patriotic symbols and historic values of the nation" (*Revista de la Guardia Civil* 2:230–231).[2]

The formation and spread of political parties in Indian communities in rural Guatemala was an important aspect of the revolution. Nationally, political parties appeared, disappeared, and reappeared in a dizzying fashion between 1944 and 1951 as the political neophytes jockeyed for position. But by 1946, there was at least one slate linked to a national political party contesting for power in every municipio scheduled for election that year. By 1948, most municipios had more than one vigorous political party with national connections competing in elections. Their function as the embodiment of national political culture would ensure that they were important agents of nationalism in the community.

There was, however, an ambivalence to national policy in rural areas during the early years of the revolution. The 1945 constitution was an expression of the vigorous new political climate the young reformers envisioned. But, after intense, often bitter debate, the constitution spoke of respecting the existing Indian cultures while following "an integral policy for the economic, social and cultural advances of the indigenous groups" (Article 137, par. 15; reproduced in Silvert 1954:227). And the government committed itself to the provisions of the *Instituto Indigenista Interamericano,* which called for the government to "conserve and fortify the social discipline existing in the Indian community and coordinate the common aspirations of the group with the national aspirations of each country" (Girón Cerna 1946:60–111).[3]

The Municipal Law, decree 226, passed in April 1946, gave significant power and substantial autonomy to municipal government. Before the 1948 municipal elections, the only political party represented in most communities was the Popular Liberation Front, the most moderate of the "revolutionary" parties. By 1948, it was challenged in most municipios by the more radical Revolutionary Action Party. It more often represented poorer Indian campesinos, who used the elections to challenge the position of the local ladino elite, or occasionally the traditional Indian hierarchy, more often organized into the Popular Liberation Front. In community after community, the two battled for predominance in often bloody struggles. The local affiliates bent the national parties to their will in local contests, and the parties were used as weapons in what were essentially local contests for power. It is hard, in this early period, to see them as effective agents of the nation or as destructive to the "corporate community." Indeed, by 1948, Indians had used the new political opportunities provided by the reform government to elect Indian alcaldes in twenty-two of forty-five predominantly Indian communities in the highlands, indicating that this political opening was a major instrument for reinforcing community strength.[4]

The most important law affecting Indian communities during the early years of the reform period was the abolition of the vagrancy law that had been used as the principal means for forcing labor for the coffee harvest since 1934. Its abolition was greeted warmly in many communities. While it may be seen as a necessary step in the extension of the capitalist relations in the countryside, removing the major instrument of noneconomic coercion in the provision of the coffee labor force, it is hard to see this as an important tool in either the extension of the state or the destruction of the corporate community. In addition, while the military intervened frequently in rural areas, responding violently to any hint of rural unrest, its major tool for coercion and the major force for national integration via the military, the rural militia, had been disbanded in 1944 (Handy 1989).

Thus, it is hard to see any evidence of increased pressure on the corporate community during Arévalo's administration. While the young reformers believed in policies of vigorous national integration, their efforts in the countryside had been minimal. The most "repressive" or "negative" of the state apparatuses had been replaced by "positive educative" instruments that were not particularly determined in their pursuit of national integration. Some, like the school system and misiones, were strangled by inadequate funding and interest, while others, like the political parties, were made to conform to local conditions to win adherents. The constitution gave increased independence to municipal governments and pledged the government to protect the distinct cultural and organizational features of Indian communities.

Land Reform and Campesino Organization

During Arévalo's administration (1944–1951), the state trod rather gently in rural areas. However, Jacobo Arbenz Guzmán (1951–1954) initiated policies that had wide-ranging and dramatic effects in rural communities. The most important of these policies was the Agrarian Reform Law, decree 900, and the rural worker and campesino organizations that accompanied it.

At a May Day parade in 1952, with thousands of their members behind them giving support, representatives of the campesino league and workers' federation presented President Arbenz with a petition. The petition expressed their concern with the long and frustrating delay they had experienced in getting an agrarian reform law passed. It read in part, "For many years the Agrarian Reform has not been more than a promise and an inspiration. The workers and campesinos demand that the government quickly pass an Agrarian Reform." Less than two weeks later Arbenz sent a proposed law to congress, and after more than a month of debate, congress approved a revised law, at 1:10 in the morning of June 17, 1952 (*Octubre*, May 15, 1952).

I have described the Guatemalan Agrarian Reform Law, decree 900, at length elsewhere (Handy 1988). For the purposes of this paper, it should be noted that the law was designed to be the cornerstone of Arbenz's national economic program. It was meant to attack "feudalism" in the countryside, inspire more productive and more equitable agricultural production, and "develop the capitalist rural economy and the capitalist agricultural economy in general." The law was designed primarily to expropriate, with compensation, unused or underused land from large estates and to give that land either in outright ownership or in lifelong usufruct to individual campesinos or rural workers. Beneficiaries of the law would be assisted to use the land effectively through agricultural extension services and agricultural credit provided through a new National Agrarian Bank. Two other features of the law are especially important in our discussion here. Expropriations and parceling out of land were to result from local initiative. Campesinos and rural workers needed to "denounce" land to local agrarian officials before action would be taken under the law. And a minor provision of the law allowed that in cases of conflict between a municipio and a legally recognized *comunidad indigena* or *comunidad campesina* over municipally controlled land, the land was to be divided among members of the comunidad (Decreto 900, 1952).

The application of the Agrarian Reform Law prompted a major upheaval in rural Guatemala. As Arbenz expressed it, not only was the reform "the most precious fruit of the revolution and the fundamental base of the destiny of the nation as a new country," but it also caused "an earthquake in the consciousness" of the Guatemalan people (Arbenz 1953:6, 11). The epicenter of that earthquake was located in the rural communities.

Two aspects of the application of decree 900 concern us most here: the spur the law gave to campesino organization and the effect this organization had on local politics, and the application of the law to municipally controlled land. The necessity for agrarian reform in Guatemala was apparent to most of the young politicians involved in the Arbenz administration. The 1950 agricultural census indicated that 72 percent of the agricultural land in the country was controlled by slightly more than 2 percent of the farming units. Twenty-two fincas controlled 13 percent of the agricultural land in the country, while 88 percent of the farming units controlled only 14 percent of the land. This meant that almost half the farming units, 165,850 families, had fewer than two manzanas of land. This, of course, did not include the rural workers who controlled no land at all (DGE 1954, I:17–34). Moreover, surveys prepared by the Ministry of Agriculture in 1947 indicated that of the 3,803,974 manzanas in private hands in the country, only 449,103 manzanas were cultivated (*El Imparcial*, May 9, 1947).

Decree 900 proved to be remarkably successful in its central concern; land was rapidly taken from the hands of large landowners and turned over to the rural poor. It was successful primarily because of the willingness of campesinos and rural workers to organize and confront the violent opposition of the landowners. Less than a month after the passage of decree 900, the campesino league announced that four hundred Local Agrarian Councils, necessary to implement the law, had been formed. By October 1952, it was reported that there were more than three thousand. These local councils began quickly to rule on the flood of denunciations of land under the law that flowed into agrarian officers. By August 1952, the National Agrarian Department reported that they had received almost five thousand of them (*El Imparcial*, July 15 and August 1, 1952).[5] In total, by the time of the overthrow of the Arbenz regime in June 1954, 745,233 manzanas of land had been taken from almost 800 private fincas. Preliminary rulings had been made on close to 200,000 manzanas more. Over 70,000 plots of land were given to beneficiaries from private land. In addition, there were more than 22,000 beneficiaries on the 110 National Fincas, either given plots of land or integrated into cooperatives. Approximately 100,000 families received land in some form under the reform, benefiting perhaps as many as 500,000 people in a population of close to 3,000,000.[6]

The law, and a violent reaction by landlords, inspired a dramatic surge in campesino and rural worker organization. After its first national congress in 1951 attracted only 275 delegates, the campesino league claimed to represent 215,000 members in 1,600 local affiliates by October 1952. In 1954, the communist newspaper claimed there were 2,500 locals. While some of these claims have been disputed, it is clear that by 1954 there was a functioning campesino union in every major village and in many smaller aldeas in Guatemala. It was the largest organization in the country. The rural affiliates of the Guatemalan Labor Federation made it the second largest in the country. In 1951, it had over 200 affiliated rural unions. While the campesino league sapped some of its vigor in rural areas, it, too, grew dramatically after the passage of the agrarian reform law.[7]

The growth of the campesino league and the rural workers' union effectively shifted the focus of political action in Guatemala. A series of splits and mergers in the government-aligned political parties had, by the time of the passage of the agrarian reform law, ensured that three government-aligned, "revolutionary" parties (the Revolutionary Action Party, the Party of the Guatemalan Revolution, and National Renovation) fought for votes in rural communities along with any number of opposition parties or civic committees. In addition, the campesino league and workers' federation competed with each other for the affection of the rural poor. This complex competition ensured that for the first time in national history the rural poor had a number of powerful national institutions prepared to champion their cause (Handy 1985:117–126).

The secretary general of the campesino league, Leonardo Castillo Flores, other members of the peasant league executive, and Manuel Gutiérrez and Carlos Manuel Pellecer of the workers' federation, worked diligently trying to extend national services to rural affiliates, attempting to ensure that reform legislation was implemented in their communities, and protecting members from the violent attack of landlords, military representatives, and local government officials.   They also responded to individual pleas no matter how humble the petitioner. They attempted to get pregnant women and new mothers out of prison, sought scholarships for promising rural students, initiated action against teachers who belittled Indian students, searched for accommodation for needy campesinos and encouraged local organizers.[8]

Increasingly, the national political parties needed to take their demands into consideration when deciding on party policy and candidates for both local and national positions.   One example of the way the various affiliations worked to put pressure on the national executive of the parties occurred when the Party of the Guatemalan Revolution informed members of their local in Chichicastenango that they wanted them to support José Silva Falla for election as deputy of the department. The members of the party, mostly members of the campesino union, turned to the leader of the campesino league for assistance. They asked him to convince the party to "retire" Silva Falla because he was a traitor to their group, "all the Quiché Indians hate him" and "already consider him a political cadaver." They went on to suggest an Indian from San Juan Chajul as an alternative.[9]

As a result of the growing strength of rural workers and campesinos, the revolutionary parties that best reflected their desires dominated national and local politics after 1950. The Revolutionary Action Party was the strongest party in both municipal elections and congress. But even the party executive had to admit that in some areas, especially in the Oriente, the party was not an effective voice for the rural poor and "represented the reaction." Thus, in those areas the bulk of the rural poor supported the Party of the Guatemalan Revolution, and it easily won most municipios in elections there during the 1950s.[10]

The national political parties and local campesino unions made a concerted effort to win control over local government because by dominating these positions they could ensure that reform legislation was implemented in local areas. The way in which rural activists, linked to the campesino league and/or one of the revolutionary parties, were able to win local positions of power without first having met the traditional requirements of the civil/religious hierarchy caused resentment and conflict in many communities. In Alotenango, Juan Paxel, a local organizer for both the campesino league and the Revolutionary Action Party, was able to use organizing around the agrarian reform law to win the post of *alcalde* (mayor) for one of his followers. Almost immediately, conflict developed over control of municipal land and other elements of the corporate community. The conflict continued even after the traditional hierarchy, in alliance with local ladinos and another "revolutionary" party, won back control over local government in 1953 (A. Moore 1966).

There was occasionally a class component to this struggle, as Wasserstrom suggested. In Chinautla, 90 percent of the population was Indian but only 30 percent had enough land for subsistence. This group dominated the local government structure, both through the traditional hierarchy and, after 1945, through a local affiliate of the Popular Liberation Front. A campesino union affiliated with the Party of the Guatemalan Revolution was organized by a *mujer brava* (fierce woman) from the city. Incorporating both poor ladinos and Indians in its membership, it began organizing around the agrarian reform law and won local elections. After its members invaded a neighboring finca, the union's illegal activities sufficiently frightened the village elite that they formed an opposition political party not linked to the government and began to oppose violently both the local and national government (Reina 1957:575–587).

In two predominantly Indian communities in Jutiapa the local government was reported to be in the hands of wealthy farmers who opposed both the organization of a campesino union and revolutionary political parties. In Jutiapa proper, the 248 small landowners of the *comunidad indigena* petitioned to have the "agitation" caused by an organizer for the campesino league stopped. In a letter to *El Imparcial*, they asserted that "as owners and workers of our own property . . . we don't need *sindicatos*, we don't need anyone to organize against, nor do we want or need agitators or directors . . . We wish to dedicate ourselves to honourable work." The 248 petitioners represented only about 10 percent of the Indians in the community who owned land, however. In the neighboring municipio of Yupilitepéque a similar conflict developed. The campesino league representative complained that the local government was controlled by rich Indians who were making common cause with the local priest who was opposed to the campesino union and revolutionary parties.[11]

Still given the fact that Indian landholding, according to the 1950 agricultural census, was markedly inequitable, what is striking is how little of the conflict that appears in the records of this era was class-based conflict between rich and poor campesinos within a community. Most often the class base was buried in conflict between the cabecera and outlying aldeas or in ethnic tension. The situation of Santiago Chimaltenango and San Pedro Necta in the department of Huehuetenango was interesting in this regard. Chimaltenango had previously been an independent municipio and, with the coming of elections, Chimaltecos saw an opportunity to regain that status. Both presidential candidates in 1944, Juan José Arévalo and Adrian Recinos, visited the community, with Arévalo making promises to the Chimaltecos. The result was that, according to Juan de Dios Rosales (1950), the Chimaltecos were all staunch supporters of Arévalo, while the inhabitants of San Pedro Necta proper were predominantly *recinista*. Tension between the aldeas and the cabecera of Esquipulas Palo Gordo, in San Marcos, grew so intense in 1953 that two different Revolutionary Action Party slates were presented in the municipal elections, representing the aldeas and the cabecera, respectively.

Much of this conflict was ethnic in nature. During the early years of the reform period, the national press and the local ladino elite had sounded shrill alarms at the organization of Indians in rural areas, either in political parties or unions, claiming to see impending Indian massacres at every turn (Handy 1989). In San Luis Jilotepeque, Indians constituted about two-thirds of the 10,000 people in the municipio. While there were some ladino campesinos, the average ladino landholding was ten times that of the average Indian. Indians, who were the majority in the outlying aldeas, used their organization into a revolutionary party to have their candidate, a ladino, elected to the position of alcalde in 1948 and to take a majority of the positions in the municipal council for the first time that year. Later, when a campesino union was formed primarily with Indians from the outlying aldeas and began to pressure for a change in land tenure in the community, the ladino alcalde turned against the organized campesinos and the municipal government began to organize attacks on the union, including the killing of at least one Indian leader in 1954 (Gillin 1958:205–206).[12]

The spread of campesino organizations and the increasing importance of political parties in local elections may well have placed some pressure on the corporate institutions of highland communities. But this did not indicate a "forced introduction of the party system" as Beals has suggested, nor did it lead to the "destruction" of Indian communities. It was forced only in the sense that large groups within municipios, whether defined in class, geographic, or ethnic terms, used these political parties and revolutionary organizations to represent more adequately their interests in both local and national politics. The most important interest to be protected was control over land as the agrarian reform law began to be applied.

Decree 900 and the Corporate Community

The application of decree 900 prompted increased tension throughout rural Guatemala as numerous actors competed for the most important local asset: land. The most prevalent type of conflict was that expected by the government and rural activists: an intense, violent confrontation between large landowners and their agents on one side, and rural activists, revolutionary party adherents, and organized campesinos on the other. For two years this brutal conflict dominated politics in Guatemala and did much to inspire the military mutiny that ended the reform period in 1954. But other struggles were fought through the medium of the agrarian reform law as well.

The agrarian reform law gave resident workers on estates first priority for settlement on land expropriated under the law. This provision was deeply resented by neighboring campesinos. In many areas the amount of land expropriated from fincas was so limited that none was left for distribution after resident workers received their plots. As finca land had often been community-controlled land in the past and resident workers were often newcomers to the area, neighboring campesinos felt that many decisions by the agrarian department were grossly unfair. For example, in September 1953, the *Tribuna Popular* (September 11, 1953:2) ran a story on San Miguel Milpas Duenas's attempts to reclaim land taken from the community in 1722. The case was last ruled on in 1936 when Ubico found in favor of the finca owner, Salvador Falla Santos. The finca had been denounced under decree 900, and twelve caballerías and fifty-three manzanas were taken. As the newspaper pointed out, however, the land was only divided among those people who had been renting land on the finca. The 417 campesinos of the comunidad of San Miguel were no better off. They petitioned Arbenz to reverse the decision, pleading, "We have documents that prove our ancestral right over these lands and therefore we are asking President Arbenz, in order to do justice, to return these lands, finally, to our power." As in this case, the continuing corporate nature of land disputes was amply demonstrated as community after community petitioned the National Agrarian Department with long histories meant to illustrate their right to the land.

One of the most resented aspects of decree 900 was the provision affecting community-controlled land. There were 721,613 manzanas of municipally controlled land in Guatemala in 1950, and 56,000 *comuneros* had access to the land in some form of rental arrangement. In addition, there were 420,654 manzanas of land controlled by communities not constituted as municipios. The surveys done of rural communities by the Instituto Indigensita indicated that there was significant variation from community to community over the amount of community land available, its use within the community, and the importance it held for the local economy. Most municipally controlled land was used as common woodlot and occasionally pasture land and was not under cultivation. But a number of municipios had sufficient land to ensure that any who wanted could rent land from the municipio at a nominal sum (DGE 1951, 1954).

It is not clear from the available sources how "democratic" use of community-controlled land was, nor to what extent the municipio was seen as the legitimate "lord" of the land. In some communities the village elite used their domination of local government to ensure their privileged access to this land. Most often the elite lived in the municipal cabecera, and their control over municipal land was also a reflection of the privileged position of the cabecera in relation to the outlying aldeas. As the amount of land controlled by communities not constituted as municipios indicated, it would be distorting to presume that the municipio was the center of the "community" for many people, at least as regards community land.

The agrarian reform law did not "create" conflict between communities over land; rather, it was used as a weapon in a struggle that had gone on for years among "communities" variously defined. One example occurred in San Pedro Solomá, Huehuetenango, in 1947. The municipio had slightly over 8,000 inhabitants, 90 percent of them Indian (DGE 1957:100–111). Almost half the land was controlled by 129 ladino landowners. In addition, the municipal cabecera, with a population of 900, 60 percent of which was ladino, dominated municipal government and controlled the 15 caballerías of municipal land (DGE 1954 3:137). Indians in the aldeas had successfully regained title to the land in 1901 but had lost it to the town again in 1942. On August 24, 1947, "hundreds" of Indians marched to town to petition once again for the land to be returned to them. When they were met by a crowd of armed ladinos who tried to prevent them from entering, they attacked them and forced their way into the municipal building where they tried to find the deeds to the property. The *Guardia Civil* was called in and the Indians were forced from the building, with many injured in the process (*El Imparcial* August 26, 28, 1947).

It was partly these continuing conflicts over municipal land and the government's realization that much of this land was illegitimately held, that prompted the government to include a provision, article 33, under which municipal land could be expropriated in favor of a legally recognized comunidad in the case of conflict between the two. The law did not advocate the expropriation of all community land. Nonetheless, substantial municipal land was denounced during the revolution and 297,460 manzanas were taken. Most of this land was given out in usufruct to those who had denounced it or was kept as a forest reserve in the hands of the state.[13]

In many instances the decisions of the National Agrarian Council resulted in little change in land tenure in the community. People who rented reasonable amounts of land from the municipio before the denunciations were always given first priority in land given out under decree 900. They were now given official recognition of their right to do so, and rent, at 4 percent of the harvest, was still paid to the municipio.[14]

In a number of cases the agrarian reform was used to pry land out of the grip of the larger landowners who had monopolized municipal land. In Granados, Baja Verapaz, the campesino union of Llano Granados denounced community land called Las Balas in August 1952. Its members complained that "in the course of years, various people emerged who have appropriated grand extensions of this land. For this reason, as well as reducing our possessions to infinitely small quantities, we have had to rent from these people." A thorough search through land titles and numerous testimonies from campesinos in the community convinced the Departmental Agrarian Commission that the owners had abused their positions of authority as military commissioners and policemen under previous regimes to confiscate community land. The petitioners, all "legitimate sons of the pueblo, burdened with great numbers of dependents and excessively poor," received fifty-eight caballerías of land in the distribution.[15]

In some communities, the struggle for community land involved an attempt by one group or another within the community to use the agrarian reform law unfairly to control land to which many in the municipio enjoyed access. In San Miguel Petapa, the almost 4 1/2 caballerías of municipal land had been denounced under decree 900 by a workers' union representing sixty people. An organizer for the campesino league complained that this application of the law was grossly unfair, and at a public meeting the residents of the village argued that the decision endangered the whole economy of the community. They declared in a letter to the Agrarian Department, "What we want is ... that the four caballerías, twenty-five manzanas be exploited by all the people, without attending to any sectarianism of any type."[16]

One of the most violent confrontations occurred in San Juan la Ermita, Chiquimula. When the Local Agrarian Council along with two squads of Guardia Civil from neighboring communities arrived to give out expropriated municipal land in May 1954, they were met by four hundred armed men from the community, and a bitter battle raged. The Guardia Civil were forced to retreat and the land was never distributed (*Tribuna Popular*, May 5, 6, 1954).

Most of the denunciations of municipal land were, however, a reflection of the continuing conflict between municipios or between aldeas within a municipio over land. In December 1952, land controlled by the municipio of Salcajá, Quezaltenango, was denounced by the campesino union of the Canton Estancia of neighboring Cantel. Salcajá opposed the expropriation, saying that it would effectively transfer title to the municipio of Cantel, which already had land, and that taking the land from them "would profoundly damage the economy of the entire village." The campesino union on the other hand argued that the land had traditionally belonged to Cantel and had been ceded to Salcajá during the administration of Justo Rufino Barrios in 1874 because Salcajá had fought on the side of Barrios in 1870 and continued to supply soldiers to the Liberal armies after that. Agrarian officials investigated the case for over a year before deciding in favor of the campesino union in 1953.[17] Conflict between the municipios of San Pedro Pinula and Jalapa, between Zaragoza and San Andrés Itzapa, between San Luis Tuijmuj and Comitancillo, and between San Martín Jilotepeque and Yepocapa raged through 1953 and 1954 as groups from one community or the other claimed municipally controlled land through the agrarian reform law.[18]

There was just as much conflict between aldeas and between aldeas and the cabecera in numerous municipios. In San Jerónimo, Baja Verapaz, eighty campesinos of the aldea Santa Cruz used decree 900 to take control of the municipal land they had been renting from the municipio, for which they claimed they had been forced to pay exorbitant rent. In Patzicía, members of outlying aldeas attempted to take control of municipal land controlled by the cabecera, complaining that the alcalde was charging them unfair rent for the land. All of the communication was expressed in terms of a conflict between the cabecera and the aldeas. Throughout much of 1952 organized campesinos in the aldea Santa Bárbera fought with the municipio of Chuarancho in the department of Guatemala for the return of land they claimed had been taken from the aldea under Ubico.[19] The municipio of Aguacatán, Huehuetenango was torn apart in conflict over land between aldeas after the passage of the agrarian reform law (*Tribuna Popular*, September 6, 1954:2, 4).

While it is beyond the scope of this chapter to discuss at length the various ways these conflicts in rural Guatemala contributed to the overthrow of the government of Jacobo Arbenz and the end of the ten years of spring, this account would not be complete without some mention of it. By 1954, the government of Jacobo Arbenz was under intense pressure from many directions. The U.S. State Department had for four years attempted to isolate Guatemala diplomatically. The CIA had planned, organized, and in June 1954 launched an attack of exiles from Honduras. The Arbenz administration had also been opposed by various sectors within Guatemala. Landowners and opposition politicians opposed the agrarian reform law and other policies of the government. Many were concerned about the increasing influence they perceived communists to be exercising over the government and the president. Ultimately, the most serious opposition came from the military.

The military was concerned not only about external pressure, government policy, and communist influence. The agrarian reform law had ensured that organizations representing the rural poor would begin to displace the army as the dominant "national" organization active in rural areas. This displacement occurred at a time when the agrarian reform law was prompting increased levels of unrest in rural Guatemala, much of it created by the pressures felt by communities in their continuing struggle for land. A mutiny by the leading commanders in the army forced Arbenz's resignation on June 27, 1954. They acted because of a complex and complementary series of concerns, most of them intimately connected to their traditional role in rural Guatemala and the changes that the agrarian reform law was effecting in the interaction of rural communities with the state and national society. With the end of the decade of reform, a new period of interaction between highland communities and the state began. An obvious expression of the nature of this relationship was the return to former owners of close to 90 percent of the land taken under the agrarian reform law (Handy 1985:396–415, 1986:383–408).

Conclusion

The reform era, especially the final years after the passage of the agrarian reform law, was a period of intense conflict in rural Guatemala. Much of this conflict has been seen as pressure on the corporate institutions of the community, as suggested by Beals, and/or as conflict between wealthy and poor campesinos, representing "incipient classes," as argued by Wasserstrom. But a closer look at rural unrest during this period suggests a different interpretation of that conflict, an interpretation that leads to questions about the nature of "community" in rural Guatemala.

The extension of party politics to rural communities caused significant unrest. By the end of this era, most local governments were controlled by party slates aligned with one of the two dominant "revolutionary" parties. In many cases these were opposed by the traditional hierarchy or were composed of young men who had not gained prestige through the dual ladders of the civil/religious hierarchy. Nevertheless, it is important to balance this challenge with the benefits gained by this affiliation. Before 1945, local politics had often been dominated by the ladino elite, usually located in the municipal capital. Supplanting this local elite with parties linked to and in many ways answerable to campesino- and rural-worker-based organizations was a positive step forward, both in strengthening Indian and campesino control over community government and in giving Indian communities a more powerful voice in national politics.

The most serious challenge came with the expropriation of municipally controlled land under the Agrarian Reform Law. Partisan decisions by agrarian officials both hurt the economic base of a number of communities and angered many residents. Even well-meaning decisions meant to distribute municipal land more equitably occasionally threatened community control over land that had at times been jealously guarded for a century or more.

But few communities had enough municipal land to make a significant difference in the economy of the community or its members. Even in those communities where substantial community land was taken under the law, it is difficult to see this representing a challenge to the community itself. Land given to members of the community was in most cases not alienated from the community; the recipients could not sell or divest themselves of the land, and they continued to pay 4 percent of the harvest to the municipio.

More important, the majority of the expropriations of municipal land represented a factional conflict of some sort or another, often between Indians and ladinos, within the community itself or between communities. In many cases the decisions of the agrarian department marked only one more turning point in a long struggle between various municipios or between parts of municipios over land. Often this represented a disagreement over what constituted the community itself.

The reaction to the spread of revolutionary organizations linked to the national government and to the agrarian reform law can provide us with certain insights into the nature of community in Guatemala. Significant sectors of Indian communities readily, even eagerly, sought affiliation with such national institutions as the campesino league and revolutionary parties. They often did so with limited, local goals in mind: getting rid of a repressive alcalde or insuring the expropriation and proper distribution of a neighboring finca. But the broader goal can be seen as taking a step toward more completely perfecting that creation we call the community, obtaining control of more land, not less, choosing more responsive local government, and flexing more muscle in relations with departmental and national governments. Indians, and ladino campesinos, adopted national institutions during the revolution because they were logical adaptations to changing circumstances and because they could be used to better local conditions.

Many aspects of government policy during the reform era were designed to extend the influence of and allegiance to the national government. If adopted, they would lessen the isolation and autonomy of the corporate community. But would they necessarily have lessened the viability of community cultures and institutions? I think not. Community members were adapting national institutions at the same times as they were adopting them, just as they had done numerous times in the past. They were adopting them because they had proven effective in dealing with a national government with new priorities and new institutions. Communities were becoming less closed because they perceived the demands of the national government to be less rapacious than the Liberal governments that preceded the reform period. While there was no substantial evidence that politicians in power nationally demonstrated a willingness to value Indian cultures in a newly defined nationalism, the increased power and involvement of Indian communities and community organizations in their dealings with the national government may well have helped develop that sensibility.

The agrarian reform law was, as it stated, designed to extend capitalist relations of production in the countryside and provide credit for investment in small-scale agriculture. But it is not clear it would have had that effect, certainly not in the short term. The law was applied in such a way as to strengthen the hold of campesinos on land, to increase the number of small producers, and, it was hoped, to provide them with assistance in making their production more profitable. Over the long run, this might have contributed to easing people off the land and to a gradual increase in the size of small-scale agricultural holdings in Guatemala. But it is not clear that this would have been necessarily harmful, nor that this would have been the long-term result. The very feature of the law most criticized, that much land was given in usufruct rather than ownership, if maintained, would have been an important inhibiting factor in the spread of capitalist relations. At least in the short term, the agrarian reform law would have functioned to slow a process already apparent in Guatemala in the 1950s, the gradual proletarianization of the campesinos. As such, the agrarian reform law and the campesino organizations that accompanied it strengthened the viability of the community in Guatemala. They did not weaken it.

Notes

1. The best source for the importance of community-controlled land and its distribution is the study conducted by the Instituto Indigenista of close to one hundred communities, carried out between 1946 and 1957 and collectively titled "Sintesis socio-económico de una comunidad indígena," and located in the Archivo de Materiales Culturales, Instituto Indigenista, Guatemala City.

2. See also articles in *Diario de centroamérica* (November 13, 15, 1947); and Juan José Arévalo's "Al asumir la presidencia" (1948:16–17).

3. See *Diario de sesiones: asamblea constituyente de 1945* (1951, 503–519) for the debate on this issue.

4. The "Ley de municipalidades, decreto numero 226" is reprinted in *Revista de la Guardia Civil* (beginning June 16, 1946, and continuing until August 15, 1946). For a fuller discussion of the struggle between political parties in communities, see Handy (1985:231–243). The Indian Institute was cited in Kalman Silvert (1954:71).

5. See also the letter from C. Torres Moss, campesino league representative on the National Agrarian Council, to the secretary general of the campesino union in San Vicente Pacaya, Escuintla, October 14, 1952, in the Guatemala Documents located in the Manuscript Division of the Library of Congress (Guat. Doc.), reel 50.

6. This total comes from the Carátulas para expedientes, Records of the National Agrarian Department, private Fincas, located in the Archivos generales del Instituto nacional de transformación agraria (DAN, INTA). Information on beneficiaries comes from J. Arbenz, *Informe al congreso... 1954*, 11–13; *Tribuna Popular*, May 1, 1952, p. 10, and June 19, 1954, p. 5.

7. See also the correspondence of R. Schoefeld, American ambassador to Guatemala, to Dept. of State, August 21, 1951, in the General Records of the Department of State, decimal series 814; the public letter from C. Torres Moss, October 9, 1952, in Guat. Doc. reel 50. For skepticism concerning the number of unions, see B. Murphy, "The Stunted Growth of Campesino Organizations," in Adams (1970:418) and Neale Pearson (1964:41).

8. For examples of these activities by the two leaders, see Castillo Flores to Minister of Public Works, June 9, 1953, Guat. Doc. box 10; Castillo F. to Minister of Health, January 5, 1952, Guat. Doc. reel 50; Castillo to Minister of Agriculture, February 1, 1954, Guat. Doc. box 10; Castillo to chief of the Agrarian Department, June 10, 1954, Guat. Doc. box 10; Gutiérrez to subdirector of the Guardia Civil, July 31, 1952, Guat. Doc. reel 3.

9. Secretary general of the local PRG, Chichicastenango to Castillo Flores, May 27, 1954. Castillo forwarded the complaint to the PRG, June 6, 1954; both in Guat. Doc. box 10.

10. "Report of the Meeting of the National Democratic Front," May 16, 1954, Guat. Doc. box 6.

11. See the DGE 1954, tomo 1, 34; tomo 3, 141; DGE 1957, p. 104; Otilio Marroquin, local organizer for the peasant league, to the secretary of the organization, June 16, 1952, Guat. Doc. reel 51.

12. Also see secretary general of the peasant union in San Luis to Castillo Flores, March 30, 1951, Guat. Doc. reel 51; *Octubre*, February 19, 1953.

13. This total is taken from summarizing the Carátulas para expedientes, Municipal Lands, DAN INTA.

14. See, for example, the proceedings to divide the municipal lands of San Luis Jilotepeque, Jalapa, in Municipal Lands, Jalapa, INTA.

15. Municipal Lands, Baja Verapaz, INTA. Quotes come from the denunciation of the peasant union, August 28, 1952, and testimony before the Departmental Agrarian Commission, June 9, 1952.

16. Oscar Bautista González to the inspector general for National Agrarian Department, June 18, 1953, Guat. Doc. reel 50.

17. Municipal Lands, Quezaltenango, INTA. Quote comes from a letter to

Arbenz from the vecinos of Salcajá, January 15, 1953.

18. See a telegram from Gustavo Adolfo Solares, governor of Chimaltenango, to the secretary general of the workers' federation, May 26, 1954, Guat. Doc. reel 16; Max Salazar to governor of Chimaltenango, May 18, June 1, 1954, Guat. Doc. reel 37; *Diario de centroamérica*, August 28, 1953.

19. On San Jerónimo see Municipal Lands, Baja Verapaz, INTA. On Patzicía see Peasant League to governor of Chimaltenango, January 5, 1951, Guat. Doc. reel 52. On Chuarancho see *Octubre*, April 3, 1952.

9. Enduring Yet Ineffable Community in the Western Periphery of Guatemala

John M. Watanabe
Department of Anthropology, Dartmouth College

Introduction

Mesoamericanists commonly subject the Mayan communities of Guatemala's western highlands to either a diacritical or a situational reductionism. The first approach, which might best be characterized as "cultural essentialism," assumes that "community" for the Maya abides in distinctive patterns of local dress, speech, custom, and worldview, which are taken to be given and determinant (cf. Redfield 1934; Tax 1937, 1941). Conversely, the situational approach entails a "historical contextualism" that derives Mayan communities and their cultural distinctiveness from the past and present hegemony of the rest of Guatemalan society (cf. Stavenhagen 1968; Martínez Peláez 1971; Hawkins 1984). A central concept in Mesoamerican studies, Eric Wolf's model of the closed corporate peasant community (1957, 1986), partakes of both approaches, which perhaps explains its heuristic durability. Wolf argues that particular institutional features such as communal land tenure and ritually sanctioned "levelling mechanisms" typify these communities and developed locally "to equalize the life chances and life risks of [community] members" while also globally subordinating a "native peasantry" to a "dominant entrepreneurial sector" (Wolf 1957:8, 12). Unfortunately, the closed corporate model has come to be taken more as a substantive index of "community" rather than as the Weberian ideal type that Wolf intended: as Mayan communities vary empirically from the archetype of "shared poverty," insular localism, and cultural conformity, so their "community-ness" in general supposedly erodes, ultimately "swept aside" by the wider market-dominated, class-stratified society (cf. Tax 1941:42; Wolf 1957:13–14). Despite Wolf's concern with social processes, the "closed corporate community" has largely crystallized in the established wisdom as either a refuge of Mayan traditionalism or a refraction of Hispanic hegemony.

Recent work, however, by both historians and anthropologists, belies such static formulations. Historically, Mayan communities in Yucatán,

Chiapas, and highland Guatemala demonstrate a metamorphic yet enduring presence that obviates simple interpretations of them as either primordial Mayan survivals or instruments of enduring colonial oppression (cf. Carmack 1981; Wasserstrom 1983; MacLeod 1983b; Farriss 1984; Lovell 1985). Similarly, recent ethnographies reveal that Mayan communities can undergo apparently sweeping cultural changes yet retain an intense ethnic localism that, while no longer "closed" or "corporate," still makes them unquestionably communities (cf. W. Smith 1977; Warren 1978; Brintnall 1979b; Watanabe 1984; Burgos-Debray 1984). Furthermore, Carol Smith (1984a; 1987a) has championed the dynamic rather than passive role that this fact of community has played in the formation of Guatemalan society and economy, arguing that in this wider context "community" represents the locus of Mayan resistance to proletarianization by the state (1987a:214). Ironically, however, this emerging understanding of the relative, strategic nature of Mayan community often neglects the question of what, if anything, makes "community" so basic to Mayan peoples' ethnic identity or political struggle in the first place. The dilemma remains how to plumb this enduring yet ineffable "community" without succumbing to the static essentialism or sterile contextualism of the past.

This chapter suggests that the intrinsic nature of "community" in the Mayan highlands of western Guatemala begins with two irreducible realities: first, "place" as a physical locale with a given populace and resources; and second, "premises" as the conventional strategies for surviving in that place. Such a minimal conceptualization makes "community" largely a matter of empirical concern, but with several entailments. First, "place" posits no a priori constellation of local institutions or cultural practices that exclusively defines community. Instead, it draws attention to the ongoing existential concerns and "ecological" parameters that motivate "community," whatever its form. Rather than simply an artifact of its extrinsic consequences, "community" becomes a problematic social nexus that must also be explained in its own terms. Second, while "premises" largely serve actors' immediate ends of "getting along in the world," they also entail some minimal "consensus of tradition." That is, premises remain historically—not just pragmatically—motivated, forged out of prior places and premises, then tempered by contemporary circumstances and sensibilities. Such "constitutive constraints" (Watanabe 1984: 15–16) engender shared concerns, motivations, and aspirations—but not necessarily absolute conformity, institutional immutability, or total cultural consistency. Finally, the juncture of place and premise articulates the dialectical relation between local and global realities: just as global situations encompass local communities, so the immediacies of place and premise contextualize for local peoples these global forces. That is, people actively engage "the world" through local realities that are as tangible and "objective" as the larger natural and political ecology of which they are a part—realities by no means unilaterally determined by global hegemony.

For most Maya, then, "community" means relating to the world not only in particularly Mayan ways but from particular Mayan places as well. I use these two facts to examine the recent history of a single Mam town on Guatemala's western periphery. In particular, I hope to demonstrate how the local realities of place and premise have precipitated, as well as altered, this Mayan community during the last fifty years. I begin with the physical and existential parameters of the community, then discuss how the cultural premises embedded in these realities have affected local responses to changing national institutions and objectives, especially those of the Guatemalan state and the Catholic church since about 1950. I do so not because I see these external powers as absolutely, or even ultimately, determinant, but because each has impinged on this town in contrasting ways that highlight how "community" here can both accede to global hegemony and yet also constitute a significant determinant of that hegemony.

The Place

The Mam town of Santiago Chimaltenango lies at nearly 7,400 feet (2,242 meters) on the southern slopes of the Cuchumatán Highlands in the department of Huehuetenango, Guatemala. Although typical of *tierra fría* with a climate once described as "cold and healthy" (Recinos 1954:315), the rugged terrain of township lands varies from sheltered valley-bottoms where oranges and coffee flourish to more intemperate, intractable mountain peaks where corn and potatoes barely grow. Charles Wagley first carried out research in the town in 1937 (Wagley 1941, 1949), and I did so from 1978 to 1980, with brief return trips in 1981 and 1988 (Watanabe 1981, 1984).

Chimbal, as local residents call the town, confounds preconceptions about Mayan communities. First, it is economically stratified but remains ethnically homogeneous. Wagley reports that by 1937, Chimaltecos had already long forsaken communal land tenure, and clear wealth differences divided the community (Wagley 1941:61–62, 72–75; cf. Watanabe 1984:165–176). It bears noting that such internal stratification goes back to colonial times: as *corregidor* of Huehuetenango in the 1670s, the Guatemalan chronicler Francisco Antonio de Fuentes y Guzmán noted several "noble" Chimaltecos, one wealthy enough to pay the tribute of his destitute neighbors and to leave five hundred pesos to the church for masses to be said for his soul when he died (cf. Watanabe 1984:53–54). Nonetheless, the richest, most powerful individuals in the town have always been Chimaltecos, not ladinos. Indeed, few ladinos have ever lived permanently in Chimbal, and none in this century appears to have dominated it either economically or politically (cf. Watanabe 1984:168n).

Another apparent anomaly lies in Chimbal's socially insular but culturally opportunistic nature. Socially, the town constitutes a sizable, close-knit, "natural" community that largely coincides with the "political" boundaries of the municipio itself. Over two-thirds of the municipio's approximately 3,500 inhabitants live in the nucleated town center, with most other Chimaltecos residing in the two largest outlying hamlets. Although many families migrate seasonally to work on the coffee and cotton plantations of Guatemala's Pacific coast, the daily routines of local life, especially for women and children, seldom stray beyond the town and its surrounding fields. In testament to this, until 1982, the poor road into the town kept Chimbal one of the few municipios in Huehuetenango still lacking regular bus service to the provincial capital.

Despite such insularity, Chimaltecos have long had a reputation for adaptability: as early as the seventeenth century, Fuentes y Guzmán found them "so rational and intelligent that they are known generally as the *políticos* of Chimaltenango" (1972:24). Two centuries later, the 1880 Guatemalan census affirmed that "there is nothing remarkable about this town except that its inhabitants differ from others in the department in their affinity for progress, and many of them know how to read and write" (cited in Gall 1980:687). Since 1937, the town has changed dramatically: most Chimalteco men have forsaken their distinctive local dress; they have supplemented subsistence maize agriculture and migratory wage labor with traditional ladino occupations in trade, transport, cash-cropping, and labor recruitment. And much of the town's traditional "folk" Catholicism, including ritual obligations in the local civil-religious hierarchy and consultation of local shaman-diviners, has virtually disappeared.

Nonetheless, Chimaltecos have retained their language, their lands, and a resolute self-identity that continues to distinguish them from their ladino and Mayan neighbors alike. Although most men and many women in Chimbal speak adequate Spanish, Chimaltecos adhere to Mam as the language of hearth and haunts, and proper Mam speech represents the most ubiquitous index of being a *xjaal*, a morally correct person, as opposed to a *moos*—what Mam-speakers call ladino strangers or outsiders. Embedded in such propriety lies a deeper sense in which Chimaltecos consider themselves a "people apart," possessed of a distinctive—and superior—*naabl*, loosely translatable here as "manner" or "way of being" (cf. Watanabe 1989). This "way of being" involves abiding attachments to the place first settled by local ancestors and the immediate "condition" of one's blood and its effect on how one behaves. Through this association with the blood, *naabl* conventionally internalizes in each individual collective bonds of common ancestry, connectedness to ancestral places, and the propriety of ancestral precedents. Local identity thus represents a subtle interplay of premises about innate parentage and emergent behavior grounded in the immediacies of an enduring place. The resulting "community" would appear to integrate differences rather than homogenize deviancies, appropriate change rather than shrink from it. Perhaps this helps to explain Chimbal's seemingly opportunistic yet distinctive resiliency over the years.

Premises of Survival

Regardless of recent changes, three constants continue to shape Chimalteco life and livelihood: subsistence maize agriculture, inexorable population growth, and increasing involvement in Guatemala's cash economy. To live in Chimbal as a Chimalteco means to provision a household with enough corn to eat from one harvest to the next. Ever more mouths to feed constantly pressure Chimaltecos to intensify such efforts—then to improvise where they no longer can. Unfortunately, relative inaccessibility to markets, the resulting high cost of goods and transport, and finite local demand keep Chimaltecos from engaging wholly in petty trade or manufacturing free of farming, and indeed, only those with an already-secure subsistence base can afford to risk what capital they have in such secondary enterprises. When most Chimaltecos leave their fields to seek additional livelihood, they do so largely as unskilled agricultural workers.

At first glance, Chimbal fulfills Carol Smith's (1978) characterization of the "peasant periphery" of Guatemala's western highlands as market-restricted and labor-dependent. In the past, Chimaltecos relied on bush-fallow hoe cultivation to produce enough corn for sustenance plus a surplus to sell for needed commodities and a few luxuries (Wagley 1941). As early as 1937, however, unequal land distribution kept many Chimaltecos from such self-sufficiency, and fully three-quarters of the families in Chimbal had to supplement subsistence corn farming with wage labor (Wagley 1941:72–75). A doubling of the population between 1937 and 1964 only exacerbated problems of land scarcity, overuse, and declining productivity (cf. Wagley 1949:11; Gall 1980:687). Given their unchanging hoe technology and Wagley's 1937 calculations of production needs, by 1964, less than one household of every ten in Chimbal owned enough land to support itself without income from wage labor (cf. Wagley

1941:55; DGE 1968). The subsequent need to buy corn pushed local prices as high as U.S. $25 a quintal (1 quintal = 100 lbs.). Most Chimaltecos met these deficits in land and corn through migratory work on lowland plantations.

During the late 1960s, however, agricultural programs largely sponsored by Catholic Maryknoll fathers introduced chemical fertilizers into Chimbal. By the mid-1970s, land productivity had nearly tripled, and Chimaltecos were planting anywhere from a half to a third of the milpa that they had planted in Wagley's time (cf. Watanabe 1981:23–25). Smaller fields enabled land-poor Chimaltecos to remain self-supporting or to rent land from others without incurring prohibitive debts in money or labor. As of 1979, only four households in Chimbal (.6 percent) reported having no land at all (DGE 1982:42). Just over one-third (36 percent) of Chimalteco households remained economically self-sufficient in land, while another third had land, but not enough to support themselves. The remaining third possessed adequate land if given the fertilizer to make their fields sufficiently productive. Consequently, in 1978, about two-thirds of the households in the town sent at least one member to the plantations, but usually for only two months or less (Watanabe 1981).

Although still heavily dependent on plantation wage labor, many Chimaltecos now migrate for cash to buy fertilizer, not necessarily for lack of land or corn. With at least a marginally viable land-base in Chimbal, migrants rationalize such wage labor as an extension of their own economic interests rather than as complete alienation from the local subsistence economy (Watanabe 1981:32–33). The complementary labor demands of the corn and coffee cycles in Guatemala reinforce this perception: since most milpa work falls between April and August, and the heaviest demands of the coffee harvest come between August and December, Chimaltecos can migrate without unduly neglecting their own fields (cf. Wagley 1941:82–83). Also, improved roads and transport facilitate travel between town and plantation, allowing migrants to intersperse shorter stints on the coast with visits home rather than suffer the estrangement of prolonged absences (Watanabe 1981:31). Nonetheless, fertilizers have clearly locked local subsistence irrevocably into the need for cash, making Chimaltecos even more dependent on external sources of income.

In addition to this intensification of existing economic patterns, during the early 1960s Chimaltecos also began to diversify into cash-cropping in coffee. The construction of the Pan American Highway in the late 1950s eased access to markets, and the boom in coffee prices during the 1970s spurred Chimalteco production. By the end of the

1970s, coffee groves totaled nearly 9 percent of all landholdings, and over one-third (36 percent) of all Chimalteco households produced at least some coffee. Despite this scope, the scale of production remained small: in 1979, the average coffeeholding in Chimbal stood at less than half (.42) a hectare, average production at about 6 1/2 (6.38) quintals (cf. DGE 1982, 1983). By 1987, the local coffee cooperative had grown to 380 members, representing perhaps half the households in the town, and production had risen to over 4,500 quintals of dried coffee, valued at U.S. $360,000. Some of these proceeds went to growers who harvest one hundred quintals or more each year, but most co-op members still produce fewer than ten quintals of coffee annually. Even such modest profits, however, go far to ease household dependency on migratory labor—if not on volatile commodities markets.

Not all Chimaltecos, of course, own coffee, but local demands for labor have risen along with increases in coffee production. Despite steady or falling prices on the international market, devaluation of Guatemala's national currency during the 1980s has more than doubled the local value of Chimalteco coffee. This, plus competition for labor between Chimalteco growers and the coastal plantations, has kept daily wages in Chimbal about even with inflation, doubling between 1979 and 1987. Local wages, however, remain lower than on the plantations as Chimaltecos balance the benefits of work close to home against the dangers and disruptions of migration. Unfortunately, I presently have no information on the extent to which local employers have absorbed local demands for wage labor, but many Chimaltecos still clearly depend on plantation work. Despite this, when I returned to Chimbal in early 1988, even Chimaltecos without coffee felt that higher wages combined with continued subsistence farming left them "doing better" than they had been at the end of the 1970s. Unquestionably, more cash now changes hands in the town than did before, and not simply due to the inflation of recent years, which in any event has been less in the countryside than in the cities.

Economic stratification has obviously grown in Chimbal, but it has yet to ossify into a permanent class structure. In 1937, Wagley noted that despite clear wealth differences, most Chimalteco men acquired their fortunes during their own lifetimes due to the fragmentation of land through equal inheritance (1941:76). A generation later, this perhaps still holds true: at least some of the now-prosperous coffee growers in Chimbal began as poor men who migrated to the plantations in the late 1950s and 1960s, then used their earnings to buy land in Chimbal that they later planted in coffee. Once coffee became a viable proposition, however, skyrocketing land prices kept most latecomers from matching their predecessors' success, and today land suitable for coffee can no longer be had at any price in Chimbal. Aspiring Chimalteco growers have bought coffee land in the neighboring municipio of La Democracia, but they incur the added cost of "migrating" periodically to their own mini-*fincas* or of leaving Chimbal altogether, which some have done. Whether historical advantage leads to permanent class stratification will depend on the ability of Chimalteco coffee families to reproduce their wealth in the next generation. Equal inheritance may make this difficult, if not impossible, to do, while the value of even small plots of coffee makes any major accumulation of marginal coffee holdings by a few rich individuals equally unlikely.

Also, despite their relative wealth, even the richest Chimaltecos recognize their vulnerability. All coffee growers, even the largest, still plant enough milpa each year to provision their families in case the harvest should fail or the market turn down. Retrenchment remains an ever-present contingency in Chimalteco planning, even in the best of times. One enterprising Chimalteco perhaps put it best: faced in 1981 with inflation, falling coffee prices, and increasing political violence, he said to me that Chimaltecos were used to getting by with less than ladinos, that they could do without radios or fancy watches, that all they really needed to buy was sugar and salt, and beyond that a cup of coffee and a few tortillas would suffice.

Such retrenchment, however, also depends on the goodwill of one's neighbors when hard times hit. Today's hired worker may become tomorrow's companion in adversity. Thus, one Chimalteco who has prospered greatly in recent years has grown from perhaps an overly profit-minded opportunist to a civic-minded leader, twice town *regidor* (alderman) in the last five years and an active member of the local town improvement committee; although he still makes a tidy profit from the markup of goods in his store, he also sells to Chimaltecos on credit and charges no interest. Another man, one of Chimbal's larger coffee growers and a former catechist, invokes the Bible when speaking of the need not to exploit his workers with unreasonable quotas or stingy rations. Yet another Chimalteco avers, as others around him nod, that although they may be poor, they help each other where they can. And finally, a young man who has already spent long years on the plantations says that life there is nothing but work and orders, and no one cares; yet in Chimbal, family and neighbors sustain one another: "We don't just let each other die here." While hardly saintly rustics who readily share with anyone and everyone, Chimaltecos all realize that their own well-being still lies as much in people as it does in property, and this holds true for rich as well as poor.

Encountering the State

Chimalteco embeddedness in their particular place and absorption with their own premises of proper existence neither imply nor ensure their local autonomy. Instead, place and premise engender an existential sovereignty on which state authority constantly—and seemingly arbitrarily—impinges. As Carol Smith (1987a) has argued for Mayan communities in general, this sense of sovereignty finds expression primarily through changing Chimalteco adaptations to the exigencies of state fiat. During the last fifty years in particular, their responses to the shifting aims of the Guatemalan state have moved from appeal to state power to attempted appropriation of it, a process in which Chimaltecos have sought recognition increasingly on the state's terms rather than on their own. This reflects more the changing means of Chimalteco sovereignty rather than an ebbing of its essential ends. Not surprisingly, the focus of this ongoing encounter with the state has been land—both as the root of Chimalteco livelihood and as the touchstone of Chimalteco "place."

Up until the 1950s, local Chimalteco sovereignty lay vested largely in a hierarchy of rotating civil and religious offices, or *cargos*, that both delimited community boundaries through individual participation and concentrated authority in the hands of older men who could best afford the massive ritual expenditures demanded of the higher positions. Cargo rituals served to substantiate community legitimacy and to sanctify individual officeholders through appeal to local mountain deities and the Catholic saints whose images resided in the local church (cf. Watanabe 1984:155–164). Beginning in the late nineteenth century, however, questions of state sovereignty became increasingly relevant to local political life.

Two encounters brought home to Chimaltecos the seemingly arbitrary, but undeniable, power of the "modern" Guatemalan state. First, a rapidly growing population, as well as the land and labor policies of Guatemala's late nineteenth-century Liberals, prompted Chimaltecos to petition for a municipal land title in 1879. Conflicting claims from neighboring communities immediately embroiled Chimbal in litigation, leading to a survey of municipal boundaries in June 1880. When finally granted in 1891, however, the resulting title omitted nearly half of the public lands that Chimbal had originally claimed. This loss of land to the neighboring communities of San Pedro and San Juan decisively demonstrated the precedence of state dominion over local conventions of ancestral or ritually sanctioned claims. Eminent domain left Chimalteco elders with little recourse but historically mute protest and resentment (Watanabe 1984:166–168).

Worse still, forty years later a second encounter with the state dispossessed Chimbal of its lands entirely: on December 11, 1935, the government reduced the town to the status of an *aldea* (hamlet) of the neighboring municipio of San Pedro Necta (Gall 1980:686). Already sensitized to the power of state authority, Chimaltecos chose not to riot over this "loss" of their land but instead sent a commission to the capital to petition for the return of their sovereignty. Headed not by town elders but by a young Chimalteco who spoke Spanish and "was not afraid of ladinos," the Chimaltecos won back their land title, their Guatemalan flag, and their picture of the president—but they remained administratively beholden to ladino officials in San Pedro (Wagley 1949:8–9). Chimaltecos chafed under San Pedro "rule" until the elections of 1944, when they campaigned for Juan Arévalo in return for his promise to restore their municipal independence if he won (Dios Rosales, in Wagley 1949:124, 131, 133–134). Following Arévalo's victory, Chimbal became a municipio again on February 2, 1948 (Gall 1980:686); older Chimaltecos still recall that the provincial governor came for the celebration, and everyone got very drunk.

In addition to encroachments from without, growing pressures from within further eroded the old status quo. As traditional leaders repeatedly proved ineffectual in the face of state fiat, townspeople came to look increasingly to younger men whose fluency in Spanish and familiarity with bureaucratic ladino ways could better "defend" Chimbal. At least two of these new *políticos* also tended to shun formal cargo service, instead devoting themselves to entrepreneurial pursuits, especially as muleteers hauling coffee from nearby plantations to Huehuetenango (cf. Wagley 1941:46, 79; 1949:9, 97–98, 129, 131, 134). More generally, Chimaltecos, who had been buying and selling land within the municipio since early in the century, began in the 1920s to title their property with the municipal government secretary rather than trust entirely to the local alcalde (mayor) to validate individual claims to land. Far from intentional subversion of local authority, such action constituted a culturally motivated—if at first not entirely socially acceptable—form of "life insurance" in a place where in 1937 Wagley could conclude, "The desire for land permeates the society" (1941:83). Whether intentional or not, by the 1930s and 1940s, the alcalde's power to adjudicate local disputes depended increasingly on a fragile consensus between the litigants themselves to accept his judgment as final. If disgruntled parties chose to appeal local decisions to higher ladino authorities, the alcalde was powerless to stop any reversal of his rulings. Pressured from both within and without, local cargo officials gradually became less the sovereign givers of Chimalteco law and more the civil servants of ladino laws.

On the other hand, growing state hegemony did not simply sweep the community aside, nor did creeping anomie fatally vitiate it. Internally, mounting population pressure in fact intensified local consensus—and thus competition—over land and livelihood, but on the level of household sufficiency, not town sovereignty. Externally, however, abiding mistrust of ladino authorities still tempered contending local interests: despite the obvious power of legal titles, Chimaltecos also feared government taxation or confiscation if they registered their land (cf. Wagley 1941:77). In the end, many waited to obtain land titles until they could do so at their own town hall after Chimbal regained "independence" in 1948. Equally significant, these deeds most often simply acknowledged socially established facts of ownership rather than formalized any abstract notion of "property": documents rarely specified plot size or boundaries, but they always named owners of adjacent plots who corroborated the titleholder's claim. Despite its increasingly litigious nature, proof of ownership still remained largely a matter of "public recognition, not documents" (Wagley 1941:64; Watanabe 1984:171–173).

Regardless of the pressures, the old Chimalteco cargo system survived relatively intact until the 1944–1954 reform period. With no large landholdings near at hand to denounce or defend, Chimbal perhaps escaped some of the upheavals of political reform experienced by other Mayan communities (cf. Adams 1957), and Chimaltecos evidently inherited no lasting passion for land reform or political activism (cf. Wagley 1957:xxiii). Instead, the most enduring impact of the 1944–1954 reforms on Chimbal involved the advent of party politics and popular elections. By the mid-1950s, elections had effectively superseded the ritual obligations and strict age-grading of the old cargo system. The hierarchy of ranked offices would survive, but the elected officials at the top no longer felt obliged to perform the expensive rituals formerly required of them or sought the approval of town elders by always first serving lower cargos in the hierarchy. The transformation was indeed dramatic: one elderly Chimalteco proudly recounted to me how he had capped his cargo career by spending over U.S. $200 as First Regidor in 1952, but by the time his son served as regidor in 1960, the only expense required of him was a ceremonial meal at the beginning and end of his term (cf. Wagley 1957:xxiii–xxiv).

In one sense, party politics in Chimbal simply formalized already-waning associations between age and authority, and the ritual practices that had legitimated both. Younger, more "worldly" men became local party coordinators, preempting formal institutional control of local politics from their elders whose old ways could no longer cope with local concerns, especially over land. A fundamental transformation did occur

from a politics of ritually sanctioned consensus to one of institutionalized contention, but this coup neither represented the absolute triumph
of intrusive "foreign" ideologies and affiliations, nor did it simply
unleash the latent anomie of nastiness and self-interest supposedly
innate in all pragmatic, post-Redfieldian "peasants" (cf. Foster 1965).
The course of Chimalteco politics since the 1950s clearly demonstrates
that, while local relations with the state have changed, they continue to
reflect the place and premises of the community.

On one hand, the unresponsive, brutal state apparatus that has dominated Guatemala since 1954 has done little to inspire popular participation in national life. At the same time, more direct and formal ties to
national political institutions have tended to marginalize Chimalteco
politicians from their own community. Local políticos have come to
occupy an uncomfortable, if not impossible, position between a self-
absorbed ladino government and a suspicious Chimalteco constituency:
the more effective that town officials try to be with ladino bureaucrats
and functionaries, the more Chimaltecos fear that they will somehow
betray the community. Conversely, the constraints of place alone
suffice to distance—literally as well as ideologically—even the most
astute, committed Chimalteco leader from the centers of power. Simply
given their constituency and interests, local politicians play at best a
minor role in an already compromised national political process. Deliv-
ering the vote in a small "Indian" municipio means relatively little on
the national level, giving local party coordinators and their candidates
scant leverage with ladino politicians and officials. Add to this the
barriers of language, culture, and ethnic discrimination, and Chimalteco
politicians suffer even more the frustrations of an opaque, intractable
bureaucracy. Such futility in turn reinforces the skepticism, if not
outright mistrust, of their Chimalteco constituents, whose own frustrated expectations leave them all the more politically impassive.

Thus, far from splitting the community ideologically, Chimalteco
politicians must prove their worth by continually attempting to appropriate state resources—if not legitimacy—to local advantage. They woo
supporters on pragmatic issues, usually public works projects like
getting roads built and schools improved. The most relevant political
opposition still falls not between the parties or candidates themselves,
but between the community and the government, with the party in
power playing a highly circumscribed mediating role. Little separates
the different parties in Chimbal, and campaigns for alcalde generally
consist of the incumbents' defense of their record and charges by the
opposition of their sloth and negligence—the measure being how effective the incumbents have been in soliciting government assistance for
community needs.

Thus, although seen by both the state and the community at large as part of the state bureaucracy, local officials still attempt to represent the interests of a "sovereign" community before the state. When it suits them, they appropriate their bureaucratic status to express Chimbal's presumed ethnic sovereignty: in one perhaps trivial but graphic case, the head of a local road-improvement committee donned the traditional Chimalteco dress that he had given up in everyday life so that officials in Guatemala City would know that he came representing his community. What has changed during the last fifty years is not so much the loss of Chimaltecos' political will as Chimaltecos, but rather the ever-greater immediacy of state presence—most graphically demonstrated in the recent counterinsurgency campaigns of the Guatemalan army. Despite its ubiquity, however, state authority remains intrinsically foreign to Chimaltecos, at once inscrutable yet undeniable, mystifying yet final. The state's obvious power may prompt opportunistic Chimalteco appeals to it for local assistance, yet at the same time the very arbitrariness of this power only heightens Chimalteco mistrust of the ladino authorities who wield it. Regardless of motives or outcomes, the relationship between Chimbal and the Guatemalan state continues to sustain a dialectic of wary Chimalteco pragmatism rooted in premises of a politically motivated—not just ecologically delimited—place.

Redeeming the Soul

Chimalteco encounters with the Catholic church in recent years have similarly transformed as well as affirmed their sense of community. Until the mid-twentieth century, however, Chimbal and many Mayan communities like it remained outside the purview of a Catholic church largely vitiated by the anticlericalism of Guatemala's nineteenth-century Liberals. Removed from priestly scrutiny, Chimaltecos continued to nurture a two-fold "folk" Catholicism: a "cult of community" administered by cargo officials who cared for the local church and its saints; and a "cult of the soul" in which individual shaman-diviners outside the church attended to Chimaltecos' personal concerns with crops, health, misfortune, and individual destiny (cf. Wagley 1949:68–75; Watanabe 1984: 190). Only after the counterrevolution of 1954 did the Guatemalan church bestir itself against such traditionalism, in part because both state and ecclesiastical authorities saw the church as an important agent of less-radical, if not explicitly anticommunist, social change (Calder 1970:49, 73–74).

In 1943, two Maryknoll missioners arrived in Huehuetenango (Calder 1970:52), replacing the Mercedarian Order that had ministered to the region since colonial times. By 1950, a Maryknoll missioner based in the nearby Mam town of Ixtahuacán was making regular visits to Chimbal, although Chimaltecos had had contact with him as early as 1946. From the very beginning, due to their lack of personnel as well as their desire to establish strong local congregations, the Maryknolls concentrated their efforts on training small groups of native catechists to minister to their own communities (cf. Calder 1970:88–89; Watanabe 1984:204–205). Maryknoll fathers took up residence in the parish seat of San Pedro Necta in 1953, but except for the late 1960s, when a Maryknoll missioner carried out mainly linguistic work in the community, Chimbal itself has never had a resident priest. Consequently, local catechists have played a powerful role in shaping the "reformed" Chimalteco church.

The early Chimalteco catechists immediately declared a holy war against the drinking and idolatry of the traditional religion: by the late 1950s, they had succeeded in burning the *caja real*, the sacred chest traditionally cared for by cargo officials (cf. Oakes 1951:66–67), and had also denied the local shaman-diviners access to the church (cf. Wagley 1957:xxv). At the same time, they undertook extensive renovation of the church building itself, including a new roof and bell towers and removal of the balcony at the back of the church where drunken marimba musicians had formerly played during fiestas. Although they received strong support from the Maryknoll fathers in San Pedro, the Chimalteco catechists evidently carried out these reforms largely on their own. Even in the late 1970s, when a subsequent Maryknoll father suggested a reconciliation with certain traditions such as processions for the saints, most of the catechists still balked at this apparent backsliding.

The rapid success of the catechists' holy war appears to have derived largely from factors endogenous to the community rather than from external sanctions. First, as early as 1937, well before religious orthodoxy had begun to make itself felt, many Chimalteco men expressed embarrassment about performing rituals in public "like an oldster" (Wagley 1949:73–74, 112). Although they still professed faith in the practices themselves, Chimaltecos already clearly possessed a latitude in their religiosity that subsequent changes may have informed but by no means wholly engendered (cf. Wagley 1949:20n). Such pragmatism undoubtedly abetted the institutional triumph of orthodox Christianity in Chimbal, yet by the same token, it has also prompted many Chimaltecos today to live *sin religión* (without religion), as neither active traditionalists nor formally baptized Catholics or evangelicals. Perhaps to the chagrin of orthodox Catholic and evangelical alike, however, many if not most of these unreconstructed Chimaltecos still profess a first loyalty to the Catholic church, much as their ancestors before them considered themselves *buen católicos* (good Catholics), despite their obvious heterodoxy (cf. Wagley 1949:50). Presently, of the town's approximately 3,500 souls, perhaps 600 Chimaltecos have formally accepted Catholic baptism—of whom a goodly number backslide from time to time—with another 400–500 having joined the evangelical Central American Mission or one of several much smaller—apparently proliferating—sects in the town.

Second, unlike in many other highland Maya towns, Chimalteco catechists encountered relatively little organized opposition to their appropriation of the local church. Structurally, public religion in Chimbal had long centered on the church itself: care of the local saints lay with a handful of mayordomos attached to the church, not in elaborate *cofradías* (brotherhoods) with separate chapels and images (cf. Wagley 1949:83–84; Watanabe 1984:216–217). This relative dearth of institutionalized vested interests enabled the catechists to preempt the traditionalists largely by gaining control of the church building itself, and once they had, traditionalists had no other institutional grounds on which to oppose them. Also, despite their presumed religious authority, the old shaman-diviners lacked any collective organization of their own (Wagley 1941:68), and they too proved no match politically for the catechists. Even the most powerful of their number, who served as the ritual adviser to town elders and cargo officials, had already found his influence undercut by newly introduced party politics.

Third, the catechists also triumphed by identifying their reforms with already-existing holy places and practices. The first Maryknoll missioner perhaps initiated the strategy when he taught early converts the actual meaning of the Latin liturgy that had long been preserved but little understood by Chimalteco sacristans and cantors (cf. Wagley 1949:86; Watanabe 1984:204). Empowered by the newly revealed significance of long-accepted practices, the catechists could claim the legitimacy of an enduring local institution yet at the same time act as the radical redeemers of past iniquities—especially against the drunkenness and supposed deceit of the old shaman-diviners. Their authority derived not solely from the dictates of an intrusive Catholic orthodoxy but also from what was already there in the church of their ancestors. Physical renovation of the church itself concretely expressed this synergism of tradition and reform: on one hand, as a community project, it mobilized at least the tacit support of those who had yet to "accept" formal Catholicism but who nonetheless still considered themselves nominally Catholic. On the other hand, the resplendent new church substantiated the civic pride of Chimbal's recent emancipation from San Pedro rule, rendering catechist reforms an integral part of this restored identity. Renovations on the Chimbal church lasted throughout the 1950s, constituting a tangible, ongoing affirmation of local cooperation as well as independence.

Over the years, Chimalteco catechists have continued to foster the autonomy of the Chimalteco church. During the 1970s, they ceased attending sessions with the catechists in San Pedro and instead asked the priest to duplicate sessions with them in Chimbal. Since the counter-insurgency army occupation of the town in late 1982–1983, the church has gained renewed support from young and old alike. Youth groups have grown dramatically, and young men have formed several bands complete with guitars, trumpets, and electric bass and organ that play religious songs *ranchera*-style during church services. Similarly, in 1987, the church acquired a new ceiling with three skylights, a project organized by the catechists, built by volunteer labor, and financed by nearly U.S. $1,700 in donations from town residents, formal and "informal" Catholics alike. During the dedication of the new work, catechists' sermons drew repeated parallels between King David's building of the temple in Jerusalem, the sacrifices of Chimalteco ancestors to build the church in Chimbal, and the humble efforts of the living to embellish the accomplishments of their ancestors. Conflation of biblical king and Chimalteco ancestor, universal church, and ancestral church in Chimbal, powerfully expressed the rootedness—past iniquities and all—that even the most zealous catechists feel. The Catholic church in Chimbal remains a deeply Chimalteco one.

Unlike local politicians, whose legitimacy ultimately depends on affiliations or transactions outside of the community, the catechists have not become structurally marginalized from the community. This stems in part from the different powers that each represents: state sovereignty by definition intrudes and expropriates, incorporating local polities into its own exclusive order. Conversely, the church in Chimbal, at least in recent years, has relied more on the power of persuasion and inclusion, hoping to create a strong, locally based Christian community. Chimalteco catechists thus serve as true mediators between church and community: while they clearly draw their authority from the Maryknoll priest in San Pedro, they also represent the priest to the community at large. In fact, given the padre's relatively infrequent pastoral visits twice a month, and the turnover in Maryknoll personnel every six or seven years, the catechists themselves constitute the enduring core of the Catholic church in Chimbal. Consequently, they exercise power in both directions: to the community at large, their actions presumably reflect the wishes of the church hierarchy—whether they actually do or not; conversely, the priest in San Pedro cannot simply dictate doctrine to the catechists or challenge established policies without potentially jeopardizing his principal access to the community. Catechists know where their power lies: Maryknolls who express interest in learning to speak Mam often prompt frowns from some catechists at this perceived threat to their brokerage between priest and community.

Not surprisingly, catechist influence extends into local politics. During the 1970s, the local Christian Democracy Party (PDC) repeatedly won the Chimalteco town hall, despite the fact that the Army-controlled Institutional Democratic Party (PID) held the national presidency, effectively denying the alcalde any advantage of party connections in dealing with the government. The charismatic leader of the PDC in Chimbal largely engineered this, I believe, because his prominent position as a catechist enabled him to make the PDC appear a much more strongly "Chimalteco" party. At the same time, other catechists, as well as the bishop in Huehuetenango, disapproved of this mingling of church and state. Some catechists perhaps feared the taint of "foreign" politics on local church sovereignty, others that one of their number was becoming too influential. After this man served as provisional alcalde following the Rios Montt coup in 1982, the other catechists, in his words, "expelled" him from the church. He cites doctrinal differences as the "real" reason for his departure, but his political activism certainly contributed to the schism. He now heads his own "Church of the Pilgrims" in Chimbal and continues his committed involvement in community affairs.

Despite their power, Chimalteco catechists remain, like their political counterparts, creatures of their community. As a reformist rather than an evangelical church, they cannot simply dictate their own version of Catholic orthodoxy to the rest of the community but instead must tread the cautious line between doctrinal purity and local precedent. Precisely because they claim legitimacy as the revitalized yet still ancestral church of Chimbal, the catechists have a large nominal congregation of "informal" Catholics who have yet to *okslaal* (accept or believe) that they must accommodate or risk losing. This means at least forbearing, if not condoning, public church fiestas and saints' processions, even when this enables evangelicals in the town to excoriate all Catholics as drunkards and idolaters. Ironically, it may well be the established presence of the evangelical Central American Mission in Chimbal that makes the Chimalteco catechists as inclusive as they are: without the constant threat of evangelical defections, they might have long ago closed the doors of their own church to all but the most orthodox.

Even here, however, sectarianism has yet to sunder Chimbal irrevocably. As I heard one Chimalteco evangelical say to a Catholic neighbor, "There are many ways to God, but only one God. We all worship the same God." In a real sense, both churches toil under the realities of the larger community that they strive to "save." As time passes, the evangelical church will slowly attain generational legitimacy as a genuine part of the community. The Catholics, however, will perhaps always hold an advantage: regardless of their very real reforms, catechists can still rightly claim precedence as the church of the ancestors— and thus of all Chimbal. The premises of present convictions infused into the sacred place of ancestral works constitutes a compelling—and lasting—Chimalteco reality.

Conclusion

The community described in this chapter clearly contrasts with general characterizations of Guatemala's western periphery regarding both its relative wealth and cohesiveness. Whatever prosperity that Chimbal can claim obviously rests on local cash-cropping in coffee. This in turn derives ultimately from the accidents of local topography that despite the high altitude have enabled Chimaltecos to cultivate coffee on the sheltered slopes of the township's two major river valleys. Furthermore, only the globally marginal yet locally profitable value of this land has allowed Chimaltecos to grow any coffee here at all: unlike the higher, more rugged terrain of neighboring San Juan Atitán, suitable land for coffee exists in Chimbal—but not enough to have attracted ladino growers as did the lower, more fertile lands in the other neighboring town of San Pedro Necta.

At the same time, fortuitous circumstance by no means implies that Chimbal is unique among Mayan communities on the periphery in its efforts to diversify economically. Although here I can appeal only to anecdotal information, Chimaltecos today speak of men from Soloma who have returned from work in the United States with "bags full of money" to start bus and truck lines into northern Huehuetenango. In absolute contrast to ten years ago, Chimaltecos now almost invariably ask about work and wages in the United States and about the journey there and back. Similarly, a day's visit to the municipio of La Democracia where Chimaltecos now own coffee land near the Mexican border reveals pervasive smallholding in coffee, much of it apparently in Mayan hands. Even in the market town of Huehuetenango, more stores now sell accoutrements of small-scale coffee processing such as hand-cranked berry hullers and fumigators, and at least one of these ladino merchants has learned enough Mam to deal with his increasingly Mayan clientele in their own language. While suggestive, none of this, of course, obviates the fact that most Maya on Guatemala's western periphery remain locked into wage labor dependency, either locally or on lowland ladino plantations. But small-scale cash-cropping especially in coffee clearly constitutes an alternative to petty commodity production, trade, or transport that has made at least parts of the periphery somewhat less peripheral—and not simply on the state's terms.

Regarding its cohesiveness, Chimbal perhaps also appears exceptional, even by the standards of Mayan ethnography. That this cohesiveness is real, however, is nowhere more apparent than in Chimbal's survival of the counterinsurgency war and army occupation of 1982–1983. Scores, if not hundreds, of people died or disappeared in every community around Chimbal, butchered by the army on the most tenuous suspicions of "subversion." At most, five Chimaltecos were killed. When asked why Chimbal was so spared, Chimaltecos answered, "Because we are honorable people here," perhaps meaning that they had rejected the violence and destruction on both sides, but more to the point, that they had not denounced each other to the army out of self-aggrandizement, rancor against old rivals, or simply out of fear, as clearly happened in other towns. Others said it was because the night before the soldiers left, Chimbal's patron saint Santiago had ridden through town on his white horse, visiting on the army a warning to leave. More prosaically, Chimaltecos also simply had no local oppressors to subvert even if they had been moved to do so—no police station to bomb, no local *finqueros* to execute, and even the town hall, which ironically guerrillas from San Pedro burned down, stood more for Chimbal's own local sovereignty than for the state's. Similarly, Chimaltecos were pressed into the civil patrols, but unlike in other towns, they remained unarmed, and respected men in the community, not self-seeking military commissioners, served as patrol coordinators. More so than elsewhere, Chimbal's highly nucleated, largely face-to-face town life may have mitigated real or potential "defections." Perhaps Chimalteco *naabl*, their distinctive "way of being," did indeed save them after all.

I have tried to demonstrate in this chapter that such cohesiveness reflects the immediacies of a local but far from isolated or insular place endowed with cultural premises arising from both the sociality of that place and the conditions of state hegemony. During this century, Chimbal has experienced the sweeping consequences of increasing economic differentiation, incipient class stratification, political engulfment by the state, and religious disenchantment of the everyday world of field, hearth, and health. Far from belittling or dismissing these changes, my purpose has been to treat the locus of such changes, that is, the community itself, as a dynamic rather than residual factor in the process of change. For too long, naive reification of Wolf's "closed corporate peasant community" has reduced Mayan communities to little more than intricate but fragile mosaics of "shared poverty," political insularity, and cultural inscrutability that then shatter irrevocably under the impact of global modernity. Such a view stems more from the Mayas' historical silence than from historical reality. On one hand, "traditional" Mayan communities never presumed some mythic harmony. By their very nature, these age-graded communities of rural cultivators have always been divided by tensions between old and young over household resources and political power (cf. Brintnall 1979b), by economic inequities of the extended family household cycle (cf. Bossen 1984), by the atomism of kinship, residence, and economic necessity (cf. Carmack 1979; Wasserstrom 1983; Farriss 1984; Lovell 1985:135–137). On the other hand, while giving overt institutional form to inherent structural strains and widening individual aspirations, the transformations of recent years have neither vitiated local struggles for community nor erased local community boundaries. If nothing else, the history of Chimbal exemplifies the adaptive, contingent persistence of a Mayan town no longer closed or corporate, but still nonetheless a community.

Despite its greater nucleation, ethnic homogeneity, and relative freedom from direct ladino domination, Chimbal differs in degree, not kind, from other Mayan communities on Guatemala's western periphery. Recent studies of different Mayan towns in the region suggest a consistent pattern of local—most often ethnic—sovereignty asserted against ladino hegemony. Some communities, like Chimbal, have managed to diversify their livelihoods and thus survive. In Aguacatán, a municipio in southeastern Huehuetenango, growing prosperity from cash-cropping in garlic has split the community along religious, political, and "class" lines, although factional boundaries cross-cut each other and shift constantly. Despite increasing internal differentiation, however, local "modernization" has apparently resulted in little if any "ladinoization" in Aguacatec eyes. On the contrary, "the major and unifying theme of the institutional innovations . . . is the [Aguacatecs'] struggle against ladino domination" (Brintnall 1979b:168). As in Chimbal, a sense of local sovereignty, if by no means absolute solidarity, informs the changes taking place in the town, despite its larger size, greater ethnic diversity, and more entrenched ladino presence.

Other, more prosperous, "modernizing" Mayan towns, of which San Pedro Sacatepequez in the department of San Marcos represents one of the few (W. Smith 1977), also fail to assimilate straightforwardly to ladino ways. Deeply involved in regional trade, transport, and manufacturing, San Pedranos have shed most of their Mayan dress, speech, livelihood, and customs, yet they still retain a strong, at times militant, sense of local identity, especially vis-à-vis the neighboring ladino town of San Marcos. Although cosmopolitan in outlook, education, and experience, San Pedranos still acknowledge their Mayan heritage and their local roots, preferring to identify themselves as mestizos or *civilizados* (civilized ones), rather than as ladinos (W. Smith 1977; cf. Hawkins 1984).

Many if not most Mayan communities in the western highlands, however, more closely resemble San Miguel Ixtahuacán, a town north of San Pedro trapped by its marginality and exhausted milpa lands into migratory wage labor dependency (W. Smith 1977). In San Miguel, increasing poverty, political strife, and religious schisms have eviscerated townwide allegiances, yet even here, Miguelenses still foster more immediate affinities through the religious observances of individual hamlets, and still view education not as an escape from their community but as a way of defending themselves more effectively from outsiders (W. Smith 1977:76, 143–144).

Conversely, Rigoberta Menchú (Burgos-Debray 1984), a young Mayan woman from Uspantán in northern Quiché, testifies in her autobiography to a more inclusive, revolutionary potential of Mayan "community." Predicated on the mutual respect and responsibility that bind self and community, her moral outrage bursts the narrow confines of ethnic boundaries to encompass the struggle of all oppressed Guatemalans. No ideologue, however, her commitment grows out of her family and community life, undiminished by long absences, by death and terror, by political exile. Pervading her revolutionary awareness, and deeply motivating it, runs a constant refrain to keep the secrets of her ancestors, to guard her people and her heritage—and in so doing preserve her very sense of who she is—even though she knows that the Guatemalan army has long since butchered her family and razed her community. Whatever finally incites Mayan retrenchment to revolution, the dialectic of place and premise abides in both.

Such enduring yet ineffable community neither erases nor denies the structural violence of broader economic, political, and military realities in western Guatemala, but it does cross-cut these patterns as something more than the dying vestige of inveterate cultural conservatism or mystical sentiments about land and livelihood. Instead, "community" among the Maya of western Guatemala abides actively in the ongoing realization that their greatest surety—if not always security—lies in the familiarity of particular local places. Such rootedness constitutes a fundamental existential sovereignty that at base comprises what Henry Glassie (1982) has called "neighborliness": the commitment not necessarily to agree or to conform with others but to engage those nearest at hand in the immediacies of life—and so turn mere existence into meaningful human experience. Although proximity may make neighbors the closest of competitors, the racism, the violence, the hostile indifference so often encountered in the outside ladino world makes Mayan neighbors all the more mindful of the assurance of ongoing associations and the security of inescapable local reputation—of knowing who can be trusted and how far. This embedded existential sovereignty literally and figuratively grounds the changing economic, political, and cultural opportunism of Mayan communities. Short of wholesale destruction, "community" endures. That the Guatemalan state presently constitutes an imminent threat of just such destruction (cf. Manz 1988) makes it imperative for the Maya that their communities in fact endure—just as the limits of state power allow that some of these communities may yet, for a time, prevail.

10. Class Position and Class Consciousness in an Indian Community: Totonicapán in the 1970s[1]

Carol A. Smith
Department of Anthropology, Duke University

Indians were mostly reluctant participants in the revolutionary struggle that took place in Guatemala between 1978 and 1982. Guatemalans of all political persuasions considered Indians the most oppressed group in Guatemala, in both economic and political terms. They also assumed Indian support for a revolutionary struggle, until Indian political passivity belied this assessment. Was the widespread assumption of Indian economic oppression without foundation? Did Indians have a different political agenda from the revolutionary leadership? Were cultural differences between Indians and non-Indians so powerful that Indians failed to appreciate their oppression in class terms—terms that would create political unity between Indians and non-Indians? Does ethnic consciousness invariably block class consciousness or is it based in a material reality that standard class analyses ignore? These questions dominate discussions of the failed Guatemalan revolution on both the left and right. What I will add to this is an assessment of class and class consciousness in one nonrevolutionary Indian community as I found it to exist during the period just preceding the violent political upheaval.

In the particular community I examine, Totonicapán, the local discourse on class appeared to contradict the material reality of class. That is, Indians believed they all shared the same class position, that of oppressed Indians, and that their class oppressors were ladinos (non-Indians). Yet most Indians in Totonicapán worked for wages for other Indians in Totonicapán, and as workers shared the same "objective" class position as most ladinos. On the basis of this case, then, one could argue that Guatemalan Indians were mystified about class relations in Guatemala. Yet a closer examination of the material conditions in the community shows that Indian *ideas* about class created the material conditions by which Indians preserved themselves as a distinct economic class from non-Indians. In other words, they prevented "real" as opposed to "formal" class divisions within the community and through that created a material difference between Indians and ladinos.

On the basis of this case I will argue that classes in Guatemala are as much a product of the local discourse on class as they are of apparent material conditions. An Indian "class" does not now exist nor has it ever existed in western Guatemala as defined by the "objective" measures produced by the western discourse on class. But both Indians and non-Indians in Guatemala *believe* that Indians are a class, whether they consider that class to be based on relations of production, racial discrimination, or the political interests of a community. This belief shapes material behavior and political interests and in doing so, *creates* a material basis for the class division between Indians and non-Indians.[2] The broader implications from this study, then, are that one cannot separate material and discursive realities when assessing class relations and class consciousness in particular historical contexts.

The "Objective" Class Position of Guatemalan Indians

No Guatemalan or student of Guatemala will be surprised by my assertion that Indians believe themselves to be oppressed as "a class" in Guatemala. But whether citizen or scholar, they do so under the mistaken impression that Indians *do* constitute a class in objective terms.[3] It would seem a simple enough task to investigate the actual class position or positions of Indians empirically. I hoped to shed some light on the issue by carrying out a regionwide field study of rural class relations in the mid-1970s.[4] While neither the issue nor the investigation was at all simple, I was able to establish that nothing resembling a peasantry exists in Guatemala at present and that only some rural Indians (far from a majority) could be considered a rural proletariat (see C. Smith 1984a, 1984b, 1989). Most married adult men engage in many different forms of production, but the occupations that predominate are those of petty production and commerce.

The most unusual phenomenon I uncovered was the degree of differentiation in the region *by*, rather than *within* communities on the matter of wage work on plantations.[5] The central highland communities (in the departments of Totonicapán, Quezaltenango, Chimaltenango, and southern Quiché) send relatively few people to work on plantations seasonally, whereas many communities in the peripheral areas (Huehuetenango, northern Quiché, and northern San Marcos) send large numbers of people for three to four months each year. This pattern of differentiation has no obvious explanation (but see C. Smith 1978), nor does it correspond directly to the areas of greatest rural upheaval in the present.[6] The labor-exporting areas are farther rather than closer to the plantations. Both areas are equally land-short—labor-exporting communities actually have more land on a household basis than artisanal communities. And a study of household budgets showed household dependence on purchased commodities to be equally high in both core and peripheral parts of the region (Smith 1989).

Table 1, based on my regionwide survey of rural occupations and covering approximately 5 percent of all rural Indian households in western Guatemala in 131 different rural communities, gives some indication of the major income sources in core and peripheral communities and also gives one measure of the significant degree to which Guatemalan Indians depend upon nonagricultural activities for income. Aggregation of the data, however, disguises the degree to which communities emphasize one form of production over another. It also hides the fact that virtually every household has members engaged in different forms of production. Most Indian households in the region own and farm some land, but very few households depend mainly on their land for income. Many households have some members who could be considered wage workers, other members (mainly the elderly) who could be considered farmers, and yet others who could be considered petty capitalists (employers of wage labor).

Empirical investigations of Latin American "peasants" in the present era have often turned up data of this sort. The interpretation usually given is that traditional peasantries are presently in transformation, old precapitalist relations of production slowly dissolving as capitalist relations of production are established. This interpretation may be correct in the long run, but it gives us little guidance on how to describe and analyze rural class relations in the present. It also assumes what must be demonstrated: that the rural economy is moving in a predictable and linear direction of transformation, replicating the transformation process of classic capitalism.[7]

The "objective" class position of Guatemala's Indians is clearly far from simple or uniform. This makes the insistence of specialists that Guatemalan Indians have a single objective class position all the more striking—especially given the abundance of careful and detailed ethnographic investigation in Guatemala.[8] It also makes the beliefs of Guatemalan Indians about their class position—that they are oppressed as Indians rather than as peasants or workers—more problematic. I will argue that students of Guatemala have accepted the notion that Indians constitute a single objective class because the Indians they have studied convinced them that it was true. Indians have been convincing on this point not only through their words but also through the way in which they conduct their economic and political lives. In the case study that follows, I will attempt to demonstrate what I mean by this.

Table 1. Distribution of Rural Occupations in Western Guatemala: Indian Males, All Primary Occupations
(based on stratified, random sample; listed by percentage)

	Communities		
	Core	Peripheral	All
No. of Individuals	*N*=1,341	*N*=1,556	*N*=4,150
Agriculture			
subsistence	9.4	10.7	13.0
local wage	7.8	13.0	11.4
plantation-wage	1.3	14.2	8.1
Subtotal	18.5%	37.9%	32.5%
Commerce	20.7	14.1	16.8
Manufacturing			
crafts	5.4	7.9	7.0
artisanry	25.1	15.7	18.8
crafts-wage	.7	.9	.9
artisanry-wage	22.6	11.1	14.4
Subtotal	53.8%	35.6%	41.1%
Construction			
building	4.1	8.8	6.1
building-wage	1.5	3.5	2.8
Other			
services	.5	.1	.5
government	.7	—	.3

Note: These data are based on my 1977–1978 survey of rural occupations in 131 representative hamlets in the western highlands of Guatemala.

The Economic Organization of Totonicapán

San Miguel Totonicapán is an especially interesting case for two reasons. First, it is far from a "traditional" Indian community in either cultural features or material conditions. For these reasons, some have considered it a "ladinoizing" community (Adams 1960), though Totonicapeños themselves are quite militantly Indian in self-identification. To the extent that Totonicapán retains a distinct conception of itself as Indian without any of the traditional (or obvious material) bases for such, the Totonicapán case helps illuminate the complex link between material conditions and cultural belief that creates an ethnic boundary in Guatemala. Second, while strongly Indian in self-identification and famous in Guatemala for confrontational political tactics and a history of serious rebellions against the state (Carmack 1979), Totonicapán played little active role in the most recent revolutionary struggle, which is so clearly identified with Indians. Since the evidence presented below suggests that Totonicapán Indians do not lack a sense of their oppression as Indians within Guatemala—that they may even hold this belief more strongly than most Indians do—the Totonicapán case helps illustrate the complex link between political belief and political action.

Totonicapán's economy is similar to those of other artisanal communities in western Guatemala, of which there are some twenty in a region holding about 120 predominantly Indian municipios. But Totonicapán has some unusual demographic characteristics, which make its self-definition as a "community" especially interesting. The municipio of Totonicapán is unusually large: more than fifty thousand Indians live dispersed in the forty-eight traditional, rural cantones (hamlets) of the municipio. It is especially urban: the town of Totonicapán (population about six thousand) heads the much larger territory of the department of Totonicapán. Because department capitals such as this one carry out most of the state's administrative work in the region, the town of Totonicapán houses a fair number of ladino bureaucrats and petty officials who lack roots in the area. Yet the municipio of Totonicapán has proportionately fewer ladinos in its territory than most Indian municipios, all rural people and a good majority of the urban people of Totonicapán being Indian. Unlike most Indian communities, however, Totonicapán is relatively wealthy. Few people have to work seasonally on the lowland plantations, and the incomes of many rural people in this municipio rival those of the professional, bureaucratic elites (mostly ladino) of the region. Totonicapán is also occupationally specialized to a high degree. Very few people earn their living exclusively from farming.

Totonicapán's wealth does not derive from plentiful resources. Most families eke out little more than three months of staples from their small plots of land. The wealth of Totonicapán, like that of several other centrally located municipios in the western highlands, derives from artisanal production and sale. All Indians in Totonicapán own some land, which they farm themselves. But no Indian is a major landowner, few Indians lack supplementary sources of income, and virtually all Indians, even those with very small or very large plots of land, work their own land as well as hire labor during peak agricultural seasons. The difference between large and small landowners in the community is vast on a relative scale (from ten acres to less than one-tenth of an acre), but small on an absolute scale. Income and class differentiation, to the extent that they exist in Totonicapán, rest upon position in nonagricultural activities, mainly artisanry and commerce.

Totonicapán holds no artisanal specialty exclusively, unless one counts the production of painted boxes, nor does it specialize heavily in any one product, though this was the tradition of the past. Its primary products today are tailored goods, woven cloth, simple furniture, leather goods, and pottery. Most of these goods are purchased by rural Indians of the western highlands or by the urban working class: tourists consume very little of Totonicapán's output. In 1978 nearly 42 percent of male heads-of-household in the municipio produced artisanal goods as their primary occupation (see table 2).[9] Most other households counted at least one artisan among their numbers. In addition, almost 25 percent of male heads-of-household were long-distance traders in the region, most of them sellers of Totonicapán specialties. This pattern of dependence on sources of income outside of farming was established in Totonicapán and several other Indian municipios long ago, observable in the first occupational census of the area, taken in 1880.[10]

Table 2. Occupational and Age Distribution of Male Household Heads, Rural Totonicapán—Primary Job Identification
(survey by C. A. Smith 1977; N=7,125)

Primary Job	Percentage	Average Age
Agriculture (24.4%)		
self-employed	10.4	56.8
wage labor	14.0	32.0
Artisanry (41.8%)		
self-employed[a]	27.4	43.5
wage labor	14.4	25.3
Simple crafts	4.8	44.4
Construction	5.0	28.3
Commerce	23.8	42.5
Other[b]	.4	34.6

[a] This figure includes 956 weavers, 442 carpenters, 354 tailors, 75 potters, 66 leather workers, and 59 others.
[b] Most males in this category are professionals such as teachers or lawyers.

Most of the artisans of Totonicapán produce goods for market sale in enterprises that utilize only family labor.[11] Less than 10 percent of the households (8.4 percent) hire artisanal labor on a regular basis, but since some artisans hire many workers, many more households have one or more individuals in them working for wages in enterprises that are not their own. The use of wage labor in artisanal production has existed in Totonicapán for at least four generations. Yet the status of wage worker is seen as an impermanent one, in that workers are expected to establish their own enterprises soon after marriage. And, in fact, wage workers are typically young men (very few young women) who have not established households of their own (86 percent). Their households of origin operate their own enterprises (often in different branches of production) with other family members.

Thus, if we ignore for the moment that handful of households that obtain the bulk of their incomes from local or plantation farm labor, we find very few households in Totonicapán that can be considered proletarian households. One could, of course, find individuals who fit the standard definition of a proletarian. But given that production is organized on a household basis in Totonicapán, and that propertyless individuals almost always belong to households with property, it distorts economic reality to talk of individual position in production.

On the other hand, we find a fair number of households that can be considered petty "capitalist," in that they hire wage labor regularly in order to produce commodities for sale in a market with the aim of enlarging their enterprises. In studying the budgets of several of the largest petty capitalists, however, I found that they extracted little in the way of surplus value from their workers (C. Smith 1984b). The wages of artisanal workers virtually match the profits earned by the enterprise owners. The enterprise, of course, earns far more than the individual worker. But the enterprise earnings invariably result from the labor of several family members, in addition to workers and apprentices; and if one divides the profit among all nonwage workers, it is about the same as the wage of a journeyman worker. The enterprise does extract surplus value from its apprentices: apprentices cost nothing more than a small food ration (and a certain amount of lost production time) but actually produce quite a lot of value after a short period of learning. Apprentices usually work for two to three years without pay and then typically continue working for pay for several years with the person under whom they apprenticed.

Since workers rarely head independent households, their wages become part of the total income of another family enterprise. Most households expect their wage earning members to save a large portion of their incomes for the purpose of setting up their own households and artisanal enterprises. Depending upon how heavily a family subsidizes them, workers can become independent in two to five years. Virtually all wage workers become enterprise owners after several years of work. And virtually all enterprise owners began their enterprises by earning wages with which they accumulated the capital needed to begin their own operations.[12]

Artisans need little capital to begin their own enterprises. An enterprise can be established with as little as U.S. $200 and no more than $500. This compares to an annual average wage for an artisanal worker of about $600. Thus, in the system of artisanal production in Totonicapán the taking on of apprentices almost always creates workers whose earning power is high enough that they can become competitive with their teachers in a few years—especially if subsidized by their households of origin, as almost all are.[13] Though most apprentices and some workers are technically exploited by this system, none that I talked to felt exploited by it. They often pointed out to me that they not only learned their skill when working without pay, but also learned the ropes of the business and made the contacts necessary for selling their products at a later stage of their careers.

Large enterprises, those with five or more workers and one or two apprentices, fail with astonishing regularity.[14] A large enterprise needs a large family workforce in addition to hired workers, it needs an active and astute enterprise director (usually the household head) to buy and sell, and it needs a very regular clientele in order to employ its workers continuously. Most of the large enterprises on which I have histories (some 250) did not disappear as such when they failed, but merely contracted to a family level, perhaps later to expand again. Large enterprises never lasted more than a single generation; a widow or widower sometimes maintained an operation, but the second generation did not. Disintegration of the enterprise came about for various reasons: sons and daughters inherit their parents' wealth equally, mortuary practices squander much of the accumulated capital, and business activities are usually interrupted for at least a year after the death of the head. These practices, in the face of intense competitive pressure, place serious limits on the accumulation process in petty commodity production. Thus, while most artisans hope to head a large operation some day, relatively few succeed. None who do succeed, moreover, create a business dynasty.

In sum, both historical and contemporary evidence suggests that while economic "classes" have existed in a technical or formal sense in artisanal production in Totonicapán for at least four generations, permanent class differentiation had not taken place in the 1970s. I have tried to explain this phenomenon elsewhere (C. Smith 1984b), arguing that the high level of artisanal wages and low level of capitalization maintains the steady circulation of apprentices and workers into the ranks of employers in each generation. In that essay, I tried to account for the high level of artisanal wages in regional, national, and international contexts. Here I ask a different question. Why do the petty capitalists in this community not try to obtain cheaper wage labor for their enterprises from other communities? In regional perspective, the wages of Totonicapán workers are quite high: about twice the amount that a plantation worker earns, the only generalized wage in the region, and a wage much higher than that prevailing in most Indian communities.[15] If the employers in Totonicapán hired cheaper labor, they might be able to capitalize their enterprises to the extent that workers could not easily establish the competitive enterprises that keep local wages high and local profits low. At the very least they would make larger profits, and there is no reason to expect that the petty capitalists of Totonicapán, who are engaged in a fully commoditized form of production, are disinterested in higher profit levels. Yet at no time had employers in Totonicapán taken on workers from other communities, whether Indian or ladino, whether from far or near, whether cheap or dear.

Lack of available outside labor cannot explain the phenomenon. Indians in Guatemala are not unwilling to leave their communities to find work. After all, nearly 10 percent of the adult males in the highlands seek seasonal work every year on the lowland plantations (more in bad years), and a significant number migrate permanently each year. Most Indians in the region, moreover, would prefer artisanal work in Totonicapán for the same if not lower wages than they could earn on plantations (since plantation work is especially arduous, unhealthy, and promises no future independence). Because artisans in Totonicapán frequently visit the more impoverished communities in the region to sell their products, they do not lack opportunity for finding cheap labor for their enterprises. Many merchant-artisans of Totonicapán, in fact, have very close ties to people in the communities they visit. Yet to my knowledge, no artisans in Totonicapán recruited workers from outside their own community.

Let me place this problem in a broader context. Economic activity in Totonicapán and other artisanal communities of the western highlands met all the conditions that Lenin thought would inevitably "enrich the few, while ruining the mass," that is, that would create permanent class differentiation among peasants. All means of production were commodities (land and capital equipment were freely bought and sold). Producers sold most of their goods and purchased most of their raw materials in an open market. Individuals were free to accumulate capital, and no direct communal or cultural barriers existed to prevent accumulation. The distribution of assets in artisanal communities, moreover, was quite unequal. In addition, rural artisans in western Guatemala faced powerful competitive pressure—they held no protected monopolies and had to compete in a perfectly open market. Most important, labor power in the region had become a commodity. No individuals in these artisanal communities were completely devoid of assets (every household owned some land and the tools needed for artisanal production), and thus no fully proletarianized households existed. But Lenin argued—and most agree with him—that the very conditions described above, a fully commoditized, competitive economy, would engender the processes that would create a mass proletariat, completely devoid of means of production. My study showed that these conditions had not done so over at least a one-hundred-year period (C. Smith 1984b).

Quite clearly, then, something other than economic conditions in the region acted as a brake on class differentiation within Indian communities, for the economic conditions were more than propitious. Cheap labor, "free" of property and "free" to move, not only existed in the region, but existed as a "real" proletariat for the plantation and urban economies. Indian employers in Totonicapán and elsewhere knew about this labor and also knew that high local wages ate up most of their profits. And Indian workers receiving relatively high wages had neither the economic nor the political leverage to prevent employers in their communities from bringing in cheaper competitors. Since these economic conditions had existed in the region for a fairly long period, why did they not have the expected effect? Tradition? Cultural inertia? This is what the data suggest as an answer. It is also the answer commonly given by those scholars who recognize the disparities between economic conditions and human responses. But this view, just like the view that insists that class differentiation is taking place in Indian communities of the western highlands because conditions call for it, opposes material forces to nonmaterial forces rather than seeking to explain their mutual interaction.[16] Let us seek a more dialectical explanation for the phenomenon and examine how Guatemalan Indians actively shaped the material circumstances given to them.

The Meaning of Community in Indian Guatemala

Changing economic conditions in the 1970s were not without material effect on Indian communities. Transformations wrought by the plantation economy—loss of Indian resources, commodification of the Indian economy, growing Indian dependence on cash income, and so forth—did foster "real" as opposed to "formal" class differentiation among Indians. But rather than stratifying *classes within communities*, these forces stratified *communities within the region.* Some communities, like Totonicapán, were made up of relatively undifferentiated artisans; others were made up of relatively undifferentiated farmers; and yet others were made up of relatively undifferentiated seasonal workers. Those Indians completely dispossessed of property (i.e., fully proletarianized) were simply lost to Indian communities through migration to non-Indian parts of the region. Thus, community ideology not only preserved relatively homogeneous Indian communities, but it also made the labor "freed" from those communities available to non-Indian employers. Moreover, the ideology about community held in Totonicapán did more than reflect its economic conditions and class structure. It actively maintained certain economic conditions (competition, small scale of production) and a particular class structure (relatively homogeneous) within that community.

The inescapable conclusion is that, while Indian communities could not transcend the economic pressures exerted by the plantation economy, they were not simple objects of those pressures. While they had to react to changing material circumstances, they could react in ways of their own choosing and in ways that included concerns for aspects of their lives that were not strictly material. And while subjected to rather simple and particular economic forces, they did not have to come up with any particular or simple response. The cultural conception of community remained a force in Indian economic choice, even though the retention of community had no apparent economic underpinnings. We must now ask what made this cultural conception so powerful—powerful enough to suppress individual economic interest. In other words, we must ask why preservation of community "tradition" was important to Indians in economic circumstances that can in no way be considered traditional.

Anthropologists have rarely raised this issue as a problem. Since tradition is assumed to be nothing more than historical residue, located in cultural conceptions, and since all social groups—whether communities, ethnic groups, or nations—are assumed to carry as part of their cultural baggage various cultural conceptions that no longer fit present "material" circumstances, "tradition" has been for many a convenient explanation for the contradictory features of any given society. Some scholars, in fact (e.g., Geertz 1973), have assumed that culture always changes more slowly than "social structure" (the latter defined as the material part of life) and that the disjunction between culture and social structure is the constant propellant of structural change. Intriguing as this proposition is, it begs several major questions. Which traditions are retained? How are they retained? Why are they retained? And, just as important, how are these "traditions" reinterpreted each generation so as to give meaning to a present lived reality? Thus, many scholars today find the issue of tradition problematic, something that cannot be used as an explanation until it is explained itself. In the case at hand, we must consider how cultural conceptions and traditions within Indian communities have shaped Indian response to certain material pressures. Let us begin with what people said.

When I asked artisans in Totonicapán why they did not recruit cheaper labor from other places, they did not give me very satisfactory answers. Or perhaps they did, but these answers require some interpretation. Their reply was the standard refrain heard by anthropologists: "we just do not do things that way here—it is not our custom." A typical (if slightly more elaborate) response was the following:

Well, they are different from us ("tienen otra costumbre"). And not having a family here, where would they live? How could they farm? Without kin, perhaps they would not behave properly. The kids here are intelligent, hardworking, respectful, they don't give us any trouble. (Pause) It's just that people from other parts are different from us, they have other customs.

To my surprise, no one said that in bringing outsiders to Totonicapán, artisans might lose some of their trade or craft secrets. Few artisans with whom I talked, in fact, ever discussed the problem of creating competitors through training workers. When prodded on that point, they would usually shrug and say, "You're right, but what can we do?" And when explaining why they did not recruit workers from other communities, few people mentioned any specific problem that might arise: that outside workers might marry their women, try to settle in the community, buy up some of their scarce land, take jobs away from their own youths. They only pointed to a "general" problem: that people from other communities, whether Indian or not, would not "fit" into the Totonicapán community—"tienen otras costumbres."

Real capitalists, of course, rarely worry about whether or not cheap workers will fit into a community. They may worry about whether or not outside workers will stir up trouble in the workplace, and they may not consider it worthwhile to bring in cheaper workers whose higher turnover rates would cost them production time. But these did not appear to be the worries of the employers I queried, who in other contexts would be quite articulate about worker problems (the high local turnover rate, the high wages, the lack of "diligence" among the youths of today). The problem they saw, and here I am only adducing from wide and fragmentary evidence of the sort I present below, was the destruction of their community as a unified political front against the outside world, this unity based on the specific ethnic identity of Indians in Totonicapán and their "costumbres."

The community of Totonicapán is not a "moral" community in the sense often depicted in the literature on peasants. Internal divisions and conflicts are as pervasive and powerful as a Samuel Popkin (1979) would expect. The size of the community (more than fifty thousand rural Indians), its internal territorial divisions (the forty-eight cantones), and the mediation of the marketplace in most material exchanges among community members all counter the density and multiplicity of personal ties that Craig Calhoun (1982) thinks essential to the making of a moral community. No antimarket or anticapitalist "counterhegemony" exists in this "peasant" tradition, contrary to James Scott's (1977) claim about "general" peasant traditions. For one thing, most Totonicapán Indians are market oriented rather than subsistence oriented, and have been so for many generations. And most people in Totonicapán hope to outrank other community members in wealth and power through successful expansion of their business enterprises. Everyone saw inequality of wealth and local position as part of the natural order of things. No employer felt morally compelled to pay a "just" wage—they paid only the prevailing rate, determined by the scarcity of local labor.

But while I reject the usual depiction of a peasant moral tradition as applicable to this case, I nonetheless want to argue that the sense of community in Totonicapán was strong enough in the 1970s to prevent individual employers in the community from maximizing their own economic interests. In that sense, then, the sense of community in Totonicapán reflected one kind of class consciousness.

I introduce the notion of class consciousness here, rather than some other term, in order to suggest that the unity of Totonicapán—in its opposition to outsiders—stemmed from its unity of opposition to an external structure of "class" domination. What I will describe is clearly a complex and contradictory form of class consciousness, but one based on certain objective features of the class structure in western Guatemala. That is, overriding the many divisions of the community based on rank, age, religion, and even materially based class was a very powerful concern to preserve a community that would struggle as a unity against the class differentiation that people in that community saw as most salient to their lives: between those on the inside (Indians of their community) and those on the outside with power (mostly ladinos). This concern was felt as much by the largest Indian employers of the community, who rivaled the ladino "elites" in wealth if not political power, as by the poorest worker in the community. Nor was this a "false" sense of classness, in my view, for such Indians were as vulnerable to the ladino structure of domination (what is, in fact, the Guatemalan state) as any one in the community.

My argument, in short, is that all of the Indians in Totonicapán shared a feeling of solidary classness against the external ladino world. And not only did they articulate consciousness of this classness, they also articulated the view that it rested upon their customs or singular cultural identity (their "costumbres"), something that would be destroyed if people from other communities (with different "costumbres") came to reside within it. Having stated my basic premise, I must now back up and attempt to define some of my terms, using insofar as possible the political discourse on class, community, and culture that existed in Totonicapán. In particular I will try to show how Indians of Totonicapán conceived the external "structure of domination"; what they saw as the essential elements in opposing that structure; and through this show why local community rather than a wider ethnicity was the vehicle of class struggle at the time of my study.

Culture and Politics in Western Guatemala

I use the term "ladino structure of domination," by which I mean the institutions and structure of the Guatemalan state, because the Indians of Totonicapán were quite careful to distinguish between personal and institutional features of domination. Rural Indians would often describe the few local ladinos as outsiders, as exploiters, as nasty and "uncivil" people. But they did not fear or define them as class enemies. Let me illustrate this contention with a conversation I had with a friend (a wealthy, Indian artisan in Totonicapán) about the local ladino mayor (alcalde), who destroyed the central park in Totonicapán in order to "modernize" it. (The local Indians who used the park frequently to rest, to meet friends and family, and for their children's recreation while marketing, were furious and clamored for the mayor's resignation; ultimately, he did resign, to be replaced by another ladino mayor.) In the course of our conversation, my friend made several important distinctions:

> Don Chepe [the mayor] is not really a bad sort [mala gente]; he is a fool, but then he doesn't understand our customs. He mistreats the poor Indians here, but not all of us. [So why did you elect him, I ask.] We elected him because we wanted our road fixed. If Don Chus had been elected [an Indian candidate for office], he couldn't have done it. [The assumption was that only a ladino could manipulate the state apparatus for the benefit of the community.] Besides, it really doesn't matter who is mayor. Everyone in politics is out for himself. [Here the speaker made a hand gesture indicating

a bribe.] And why not? Nothing changes. The political system can't help us here. [Why not, I ask.] Because it is only of/for the ladinos. It's like this everywhere in Guatemala . . . We Indians never wield real political power in Guatemala. We can protest, we can struggle, but we can't change things. [But you could get rid of Don Chepe, I suggest.] Yes, but Don Chepe is not the problem, we would have to put someone just like him in his place.

I had conversations of this sort with many Indians in Totonicapán and found that most people made the kind of distinctions this person did: that particular local ladinos were not the "bad guys" (mala gente); that only local ladinos could manipulate the state bureaucracy; that the political system worked to favor ladinos; and that this situation—ladino political domination—was general in Guatemala. In other words, most Indians believed that it was a whole structure of political domination that oppressed them, rather than a particular local clique of ladinos.

The economic ramifications of this structure were frequently pointed out to me in conversations about the problems faced by Indian traders. Almost every trader or artisan I talked to had at least one story about how he had lost some (or all) of his capital through extortions exacted by officials, police, or ladino merchants outside of Totonicapán. When this happened outside the community, the Indian trader/artisan felt quite helpless to do anything about it—rarely would one take such a case to court. When it happened within the community (and such episodes were uncommon), the victim was much more likely to find some form of redress. Several people observed that the system worked precisely in that way. ("Our" ladinos take from them, and "their" ladinos take from us.) In fact, however, the system worked that way only for rich Indians. The Totonicapán bureaucrats and police, recruited mainly from outside the municipio, "took" from anyone who was poor or politically vulnerable, and most such people were local Indians. But the local artisans, who felt completely vulnerable to economic extortion or dangerous political caprice outside their community, did feel a certain safety within it.

The feeling of safety within the community was not without foundation: in the years I lived in Totonicapán, they did get rid of the "bad" mayor, successfully resisted higher commercial taxes twice, and forced ladino officials to admit Indian girls wearing native dress into the local secondary school (after a fairly prolonged struggle that included violence). Totonicapán Indians recognized that their control even within the community was tenuous, limited, and required them to follow certain informal rules (like electing ladino officials). But at the same time, they recognized that solidary action within the community—on important occasions, anyway—could be effective. And thus they saw that solidarity of community was worth protecting.

I must admit that it is difficult to describe the basis upon which Indian solidarity rested in Totonicapán, other than a general sense of opposition. Indians would frequently refer to their special "customs," but few such customs were general. Not only was Totonicapán very large and tended toward hamlet rather than municipal endogamy (the hamlet endogamy rate was 74 percent), but major political and religious differences divided the community. The traditional political-religious *cargo* system that involved all important Indian males in annual municipio-wide offices had disintegrated in the 1920s, and with it went most shared religious belief.[17]

Dozens of competing Protestant sects operated in the municipio, involving nearly one-quarter of the Indian population. Catholics were divided among nonpracticing traditionalists, practicing traditionalists, and Acción Católica. These religious differences were strongly felt and often divided families. All Indians spoke the Mayan language, Quiché, but some were trying to teach only Spanish to their children (most adults also spoke Spanish). All adult Indian women wore traditional dress, but men had long given up Indian clothing and some young girls dressed like ladinos. More subtle uniformities may have existed in Totonicapán— how Indians addressed one another, how decisions were made in all-Indian groups, how Indian workers and owners related to each other (mostly like fictive kin, with the "elder" versus "junior" model of behavior). But my general impression was that while there were many things that *most* Totonicapán Indians did and believed, there were very few things that *all* Totonicapán Indians did and believed.

Whatever it was based upon, the content of Totonicapán Indian identity was not fixed in "tradition." It was something renewed in each generation and created dialectically in opposition to the ladino world. I believe that virtually all tradition could disappear in Totonicapán and yet the feeling or consciousness of local Indian identity would remain. Let me hasten to add that few Indians of Totonicapán would have agreed with me. They were convinced that their "costumbres" played a role in their protection against the outside world. And that belief created a reality of action when it came to recruiting outside workers. In other words, rich Totonicapán artisans did not employ cheaper outside workers, even though this directly contradicted their material interests, because they believed it would destroy the unity of their tradition. And they believed the unity of their tradition was worth protecting: they held an ideology about the bases needed for unified political struggle. One result of this practice, shaped by the local ideology of political struggle, was a real, material unity of local tradition and community—something that other material circumstances did not and could not create.

Let me try to give a fuller sense of the Totonicapán view of community from another conversation I had with a Totonicapán Indian. The particular conversation I report here took place in 1971 with an independent artisan from a rural hamlet bordering another municipio and far from the urban center (and marketplace) of Totonicapán. The part of the conversation I quote took place after a long discussion about the reasons for founding a new marketplace in the hamlet. I had just asked whether the hamlet might eventually petition to become an independent municipio, now that it had its own marketplace. (This was not an unusual sequence of events in western Guatemala, though in most cases hamlets petitioning for municipal status were trying to reconstitute a preexisting municipal entity.) His response was:

No, we still belong to Totonicapán, our political life resides in the cabildo [traditional assembly] of Totonicapán. [What political life, I ask.] Well, if something happens to one of us traders, we take it to the cabildo in Totonicapán; that is where we settle our political matters. (Why not create your own cabildo or take it to Santa Cruz [which was closer], I ask.) In Santa Cruz they have other issues; their elders (principales) do things differently, they couldn't protect us. And if we built our own cabildo, it would not have the strength of the cabildo in Totonicapán. Totonicapán is the home of Atanasio Tzul (a nineteenth-century Indian rebel leader, well known to virtually everyone in Totonicapán, but little known elsewhere); and in Totonicapán the ladinos do not bother us too much. Besides, we have the same customs as the others of Totonicapán. (It strikes me, I remark, that your customs are not all that different from the people in Santo Tomás [a neighboring hamlet of Santa Cruz].) That is not true. Those people are quite unlike us. It is true that they speak Quiché, but we Indians ("naturales") are not all the same. Each people ("raza") has its own traditions, its own way of doing things. In Santo Tomás, the people are more humble ("humilde") than we are, they do not have our sense of pride. The people of Santo Tomás are Indians too and also mistreated by ladinos. But they do not defend themselves the way we do. Not like Totonicapeños.

I cannot pretend that this conversation was a typical one. This person's view of the situation was unusually pointed, political, and eloquent, one of the reasons I wrote it down later that day. But in conversations around this same topic with Indians who were not so articulate, much the same thing was communicated: that Totonicapán identity was based on political unity; that other Indians shared similar political-economic circumstances, but faced them differently; that Totonicapán's ethnic identity or "culture" was rooted in a history of oppositional tactics and means rather than in particular visible traditions, such as language, ways of dressing, religious beliefs. Another way to put it is that within their community—a community historically forced upon them by outside political manipulation—Totonicapán Indians shared a language of political discourse that they had helped to shape through hundreds of years of struggle with state (ladino) authorities.

Bringing politics into the picture seems to solve the apparent contradiction between culture (community "tradition") and economic interest. It suggests that there was no basic contradiction because community solidarity had an economic payoff. All Indians of Totonicapán could expect a greater material return by defining themselves as relatively homogeneous campesinos pitted against the ladino structure of domination (rather than fragmenting along lines of individual interest) because the close link between economy and politics in Guatemala forced a collective and political response from Indians. Thus, Indians struggled through communities to preserve their long-term or common economic interests (as a "class") rather than short-term, individual interests (as incipient "classes").

The problem with this conclusion, however, is that it does not explain why Indians would struggle to preserve that which forms the basis of their oppression in Guatemala—the ethnic identity embedded in their community solidarity. (Remember that all Totonicapán Indians claimed that community solidarity rested upon retention of Indian "customs.") Had the Indians of Totonicapán chosen to pursue their individual interests (by, for example, hiring outside labor), thus dissolving community boundaries, internal homogeneity, and the very basis of Indian ethnicity, they would face little of the oppression as individuals that they suffered as a community of Indians.

To deal adequately with the various questions raised above, therefore, requires further deconstruction of the meaning of class and ethnicity in Guatemala. Ethnicity in Totonicapán and other highland communities involves more than the Indian-ladino distinction; it also encompasses cultural differences among Indian communities. And besides being implicated deep in political struggles in the western highlands, ethnicity plays a major role in subjective "class" identity and in local theories or ideologies of class. Embedded in the meaning of ethnicity, then, are most of the problematic concepts with which I am attempting to deal here: community, culture, class, and politics. Ethnicity defines concrete groups engaged in real material struggle today. Yet the definitional boundaries of ethnicity are based on myth and ideology, historically rooted but given new meaning by the everyday experiences of real people in each generation. It follows that we must understand the subjective meaning Guatemalans attach to ethnicity before we can understand any objective "facts" about Guatemala that involve ethnically defined groups.

The Relational Determination of Indian Consciousness

In interpreting the various materials presented above, I run into the two major contradictions that existed with respect to Indian "class" and "class consciousness" in the 1970s. On the one hand, there were two objective class positions held by all Guatemalan Indians: their position in relation to means of production (whether as worker, owner, or employer), in which all Indians were defined by themselves as workers, but a great many Indians were also owners and even employers; and their position in relation to political power and the state, in which all Indians were defined by the state as politically subordinate and without certain rights, regardless of their economic class position.

On the other hand, Indians defined only one of their two kinds of class positions in collective action of any sort, that of being politically subordinate or "Indian," and they did so only as members of a particular community. That is, Totonicapán Indians focused upon their Totonicapán Indian identity, rather than upon their general Indian identity or upon their general worker, owner, or employer identity. What is interesting about this selection of identity for political and economic action is that the condition of being Indian was not particular to Totonicapán, but a more general experience, whereas the condition of being an employer or worker was a specifically Totonicapán experience—because the community itself had so defined it.

In the 1970s no general sense of "ethnic" opposition—of all Indians versus all ladinos—existed in Guatemala. Each Indian community felt its sense of opposition in isolation from other Indian communities. The question, then, is why Indians selected one out of several potential class identities as the overriding one when it came to decisions about which political line or which political interest to follow. The materials given above suggest that it is necessary to go beyond a simple theory of material interests. We must deal with how beliefs have shaped perceptions of possible political action—that is, we must deal with the realm of culture and tradition. Yet in order to understand why class consciousness was community-specific for most Indians in the 1970s but could change in some places so that some non-Indians could be included in the category of oppressed in the 1980s, it is necessary to look beyond any one "given" or "traditional" construction of political action and meaning. Finally, we will never explain how Indians determine which of their contradictory class positions to emphasize as long as we consider Indians alone. We can understand class identity only in a relational sense, and thus we must understand who Indians defined themselves against, why, and how that might have led to an emphasis on community over general Indian identity.

Did Indians define themselves as communities against other similar communities? In other words, was the relevant opposition to them other Indian municipios? Various Guatemala specialists have suggested as much in arguing that the division of general Indian ethnicity into local community ethnicity, with each municipio claiming its own special identity, resulted from the competition of municipios with each other for scarce resources, especially for land. Intense competition between municipios existed, to be sure, but my work in Totonicapán showed that hamlet-level competition over resources, within the municipio, was even more intense than municipio competition, and yet this did not destroy the municipal basis of ethnic identity. Nor did Indians ever assert a hamlet identity over their municipal identity. Other scholars have argued that the municipio-wide political-religious cargo system provided the basis for community identity. They also predicted that with the demise of the cargo system, municipio-specific ethnic identity would disappear. But the evidence at hand seems to refute that view. Many municipios in western Guatemala have not had a cargo system for more than fifty years (e.g., Totonicapán), yet community identity remains strong. While community identity stems from political organization and struggle on a community basis, an argument I elaborate below, the cargo system was just one way of organizing for struggle, not the only way.

I do not have enough information to claim that most Indian municipios felt little sense of opposition to or competition with other Indian municipios. But in Totonicapán, which I can vouch for, the feeling about other municipios was much more complicated than that. The Indians of Totonicapán felt little kinship with other Indians, even neighboring groups or those sharing the same language, but they did not feel opposed to them. And while the Indians of Totonicapán had a strong sense of identification with their hamlet (where a basis for community solidarity obviously existed in kinship, close familial relationships, marriage, and even remnants of community property), their active social and political allegiance was to the municipio—an entity that created a sociological basis for community solidarity only through political struggle. Indians clearly defined themselves in opposition to ladinos and to a whole political apparatus of ladino domination. But Indians did not deal politically with ladinos or the state as a whole. Except for brief historical moments they had to face ladinos and the ladino state as communities. They had to do so because those were the terms of struggle given to them by the state.

The municipio, which is almost always the basis of Indian community, is not a "natural" or traditional entity. It had been created by the colonial state politically out of other more "natural" units as an apparatus for the state administration of Indians (C. Smith 1984a). Hamlets, if anything, were the natural units, often a single extended cognatic lineage, often holding communal property, often following rules of intermarriage. Such units were arbitrarily regrouped following the ravages of the conquest; often people of different language as well as custom were forced into the municipal unit (cf. Hill and Monaghan 1987). During the entire colonial period, state control of the Indians operated through the municipio and its state-appointed (ladino) and locally selected (Indian) administrators. Through this experience, in my view, the political meaning of Indian community was forged. And the relevant meaning was the municipio, the unit of political struggle.

This pattern of administration and control, which operated through municipios and involved the political opposition of Indian subjects and ladino power-holders, neutralized Indians as a unified political force in Guatemala. But it did not eliminate Indian struggle. At the time of my study, which ended in 1978, most Indians in western Guatemala perceived only one possible form of political action as a group or class: that of struggling as a community, which was almost always the municipio, against an outside structure of domination (which they saw as ladino) by which means they could ameliorate some of the oppression they experienced in their lives. Indians of Guatemala had, historically, been quite successful in this form of struggle (C. Smith 1984a). The Indians of Totonicapán had been especially so: they had led a major independence movement against the Spanish Crown in 1821 (under Atanasio Tzul)—which helped topple the Crown, even though it did not rid them of the state; they had always been in the forefront of breaking down imposed barriers to Indian participation in national economic life (obtaining elementary schools in the pre-1944 period, sending their sons and later their daughters to secondary schools in the 1960s, traveling and trading widely, learning artisanal skills once monopolized by ladinos, buying trucks, accumulating capital, and employing workers before most other Indians did). And they had more political clout within their community than did the vast majority of Indians in the western highlands. So even though their struggle was a defensive one, with no possible chance of becoming a struggle of liberation, it was a struggle in which limited victories were possible—as long as the community exerted strong and undivided pressure against the state authorities.

We must understand, therefore, that the kind of political conscious-ness that Indians have is determined not just by a general Indian experience, but by its specific manifestation in the kind of relations that Indians have had with their oppressors, the ladino state. And, histori-cally, the ladino state has dealt with Indians through the municipio. It has moved against Indians, as Indians, only twice. It did so right after independence, during a brief Liberal period, in which the ladino state tried to impose Guatemalan "citizenship" on all Indians (see chap. 4). It met with massive rebellion. And the rebellions for the first time in Guatemalan history involved Indians from many different communi-ties, organized in a unified resistance. The ladino state quickly desisted in its effort to bring civilization to the savages.

Indians were relatively passive in the following period when one would have expected much more resistance. As Barrios moved against Indian communities in the 1880s to create the coffee plantation econ-omy, alienating Indian land, labor, and many of their rights, he was very careful to move against them in traditional ways, allowing them to protest through their municipal councils and courts for redress (see McCreery 1976, chap. 5). Indians did resist, of course. But they did so in community-specific rather than unified ways. Out of this resistance, Indian culture and community on a municipio basis was strengthened even further, so that one finds the municipio-specific economic adapta-tions to the plantation economy I described above.

The second time the ladino state moved against Indians as a whole was in 1980, when the state perceived all Indians to be potentially subver-sive. Under the Lucas García regime, the government reacted brutally, arbitrarily, and totalistically against the potential threat of a united Indian resistance, and in doing so helped create it. The response of many Indians, once again, was to unify in struggle, with the development of an all-highland plantation union, with the growth of all-Indian political organizations, and with support for insurgent groups in the region. The Indians who joined these organizations were those who, because of state actions, saw no possibility of redress through local or community channels. The Indians who stayed out, like the people of Totonicapán, continued to believe in the effectiveness of local struggle. The people of Totonicapán were not so wrong—their situation today is much better than that of most Indians who engaged in armed struggle (see C. Smith 1988; Carmack 1988). It is true that this particular segment of an all-Indian "class" did not constitute itself as a "class for itself." But this does not mean that Totonicapeños failed to engage in class conflict and class alignments in daily life. It means only that the nature of objective conditions, subjective perceptions, and political experience in Totonicapán were such as to prevent their identifying with others in similar political-economic conditions.

But we should not despise these isolated forms of struggle. After all, this Indian culture that we romanticize would not exist in even its present defensive form had this form of struggle not taken place for more than 450 years. What this struggle created was pressure against internal class formation that would have led to Indian factions that were opposed to each other rather than indifferent to each other. And out of it arose a generalized sense of cultural oppression and class resentment that may later be tapped—communities capable of carrying out another, potentially more liberating, kind of struggle in the future. Most Amerindians lost in this phase of the struggle at some point over the last 450 years, but the Guatemalan Indians of the western highlands, no doubt because of their parochialism, continue to put up a resistance to cultural as well as economic and political oppression that is virtually unprecedented.

Notes

1. Parts of this paper have been excerpted from the Working Paper Series, no. 162, The Wilson Center, Smithsonian Institution, 1984. I am grateful to the Center for giving me the time to write up these materials.

2. Revolutions often point out how faulty our social analyses are, especially our understanding of class. Sidney Mintz (1974) shows that only after the Cuban revolution, when scholars began to discuss where, when, and why it happened, did it begin to dawn on them that the class in Cuba widely known as the "peasantry" did not exist. The same is true of Guatemala, except that many scholars have yet to come to this realization.

3. Most anthropologists who have worked in Guatemala have characterized Guatemala's Indians as peasants (e.g., Tumin 1952; Reina 1966; Colby and van den Berghe 1969; Warren 1978; Carmack 1979), though others have seen them as petty capitalists (Tax 1953) or petty commodity producers (C. Smith 1984a). Most nonanthropologists, seeing the broader economic system of which Indians are a part, consider Guatemala's Indians a disguised or semiproletariat (e.g., Torres-Rivas 1971; Stavenhagen 1975; Solórzano 1977; Williams 1986). Most agree, however, that Indians do form a single objective class.

4. Between 1976 and 1978 I spent approximately 2 1/2 years carrying out a systematic survey of occupation, production, and class relations in western Guatemala. I included 131 rural hamlets in my survey plus twelve urban barrios, selecting them to represent the diversity of economic strategies I had discovered in my earlier marketing work in the region. (For further details about this study, see C. Smith 1989.) My research was funded by NSF Grant BNS-78-21476, and I am grateful for that support.

5. Most Indians of western Guatemala farm small plots of privately held land, but since 1920 less than one-quarter of the Indians have gained the bulk of their incomes from farming. Most make up the difference between their own

production and their subsistence needs in one of two ways: they earn wages from seasonal work on plantations or they earn cash from producing and selling artisanal goods. Which strategy land-short Indians will pursue depends not only on plantation demand for labor, but also on the general state of the national economy. In 1970, when I carried out my first regional survey of rural Indian occupations, about 40 percent of Indian households sent one or more of their adult members to the plantations annually to earn additional income. In 1978, when I carried out another survey, only about 20 percent did so. The full-time farming population held steady in the later period (mainly through the increased use of chemical fertilizers) but the proportion of the Indian population earning additional income from artisanal production and sale shifted from about 40 percent to about 60 percent of the total. Since traders and artisans earn far more than seasonal plantation workers, this shift in occupation suggests that rural Indians benefited from expansion in the export economy during the 1960s and 1970s as much as other people in the region did. That the real wages of plantation workers increased in this period also supports this conclusion. Plantation demand for seasonal labor did not decrease during this period. If anything, it increased.

6. The areas of greatest violence in the recent upheaval were four: Chimaltenango and southern Quiché (part of the regional core or central area, where most Indians obtain incomes from local farming and petty commodity production and trade); and northern Quiché and northern Huehuetenango (part of the regional periphery, where most Indians are impoverished and many depend heavily on seasonal work on plantations).

7. Alain de Janvry (1982) describes this recent literature on rural class relations, paying special attention to Latin America. He also represents the view that the complexity of local class relations in the present results from the process of transformation from precapitalist to capitalist relations of production. I have critiqued this position in C. Smith (1984b).

8. See note 3.

9. In 1977 I carried out a complete occupational census for all Indian households in Totonicapán (rural and urban, although only the rural population is shown in table 2). I have analyzed this census in some detail elsewhere (C. Smith 1984b; 1989).

10. At the time of Guatemala's first national census in 1880, certain core-area Indian municipios such as Totonicapán already showed considerable specialization outside of agriculture. On these grounds and on the basis of travelers' accounts, I have surmised that petty commodity production began on a major scale in western Guatemala even before the imposition of the plantation economy (C. Smith 1984a). It was certainly well established throughout the region by 1920.

11. Merchants, whether local or urban, hold little economic power over Totonicapán artisans. Most artisans provide local merchants with goods on a consignment basis, bankrolling the merchant rather than vice versa. Other artisan families sell their own goods on a retail basis, one member of the family devoting most of his or her time to this; virtually no artisan uses credit to obtain either capital or raw materials.

12. I base these generalizations upon several hundred life histories and also upon the age distribution of apprentices, workers, independents, and employers of wage labor in Totonicapán. In weaving, the average age of these types of workers was, respectively, 17, 26, 33, and 37.

13. I should note in this context that Totonicapán apprentices seek a master artisan from whom they learn—they are not actively recruited by potential employers. A relatively small number of people apprentice in their original households—people frequently observe that it is difficult for a son to learn from his father—but many apprentice with distant or ritual kin (about 55 percent, counting all kinship categories). A large number of youths apprentice in hamlets other than their own (48 percent). In all cases, the apprentice or his parents have some knowledge of the person from whom they solicit training, but that knowledge may be fairly casual.

14. The dependency of the Totonicapán economy on the general health of the regional economy can be seen today when, as a result of the enormous economic dislocations of recent years, nearly half of Totonicapán's weavers have gone out of business (see C. Smith 1988).

15. It is important to note that no generalized wage level exists in western Guatemala. The wages set by the plantations for seasonal labor serve as a general barometer, to be sure. But each highland community establishes its own wage in relation to the plantation wage (in most cases for agricultural labor), and that "community wage" tends to regulate wage levels in all branches of production in the community. In Totonicapán, for example, agricultural workers (mostly the very young or the very old) earned in 1976 slightly less than artisanal workers, Q2.50 per day. Most artisans in all branches earned about Q3.50 per day. Yet in a neighboring township, workers at each level earned only one-half these wages.

16. Virtually all Guatemalan Marxists now insist that differentiation within Indian communities is at an advanced state, supporting this view with data on income and wealth differentials within communities. So far, however, no one has actually looked at the pattern of differentiation over time, nor have they measured the degree to which surplus value is extracted *within* Indian communities. Guatemalan Marxists should not be singled out, however. Dozens of articles in the *Journal of Peasant Studies* "prove" the existence of differentiation in peasant communities with data on wealth differentials. Few scholars object, since most assume that peasant differentiation is inevitable with the growth of a commodity economy.

17. The traditional cargo system disintegrated in most Indian municipios after 1950, when Guatemalan municipios could for the first time elect their own officials. It had fallen apart earlier in some municipios, such as Totonicapán, and still functions in others that are otherwise quite similar (Momostenango). No simple correlate, such as wealth, size commercialization, percentage of non-Indians, or the like, explains where the cargo system remains and where it does not. Whether it continues to function or not, however, it has increasingly taken a less important role in the political affairs of the municipio. Elected officials, who may or may not be Indians, now constitute the primary governing body of Indian municipios.

11. Changing Indian Identity: Guatemala's Violent Transition to Modernity

Arturo Arias

Institute of Latin American Studies, University of Texas

This chapter investigates the transformations in power and ethnic relations that Guatemala has experienced since the late 1960s. Articulating cultural phenomena with political phenomena, the Indian population was the principal protagonist in a profound social movement that eventually sought to take power by armed force and very nearly achieved that goal. And, as a reaction to that social movement, the army, with its virtual monopoly of state power, has attempted to reorganize the ideological-integrative structure of Guatemalan society in the 1980s. Recognizing the cultural and political forces generated by the Indian organizations and their real and symbolic power, the army has sought to destroy them in order to implant new institutions and symbols that operate with lesser degrees of contradiction to the dominant ideological and political direction of the nation.

My point of departure is the supposition that popular culture, however dispersed or ambiguous it may be, possesses features that are unique rather than simple deformations or imitations of the dominant culture. As in many dependent social formations where the dominant culture is not the expression of the locally dominant groups, particularly in its socioeconomic and political dimensions, but rather has imitated and adapted the cultural expressions of the world hegemonic centers, the situation is complex.

In these dependent social formations, diverse ethnic groups coexist with the dominant (if derived) local culture. These popular cultures, generally expressions of dominated precolonial groups, usually possess an even greater cultural cohesion than the dominant sectors of the same social formation. While they possess very distinct cultural features, dominated ethnic groups usually participate as "clients" of the dominant culture, even when they cannot participate as "authors" or "collaborators" of that culture (Martínez Peláez 1971:595–596). Where a dominated group maintains its own ethnic-cultural identity, that very identity easily becomes a force for the mobilization of that group. The defense of a specific ethnic identity reinforces those cultural-ideological norms that solidify the group, which makes destruction of old structures and transformation of the social system possible.

Many explanations have been put forth to account for the transformation of Indian consciousness in Guatemala, such as those that see it as the direct result of evangelical work carried out by Catholic missionaries, invited to the country after 1954 by the reactionary government put in power by means of the CIA-sponsored invasion (Melville and Melville 1970). However, Indian sectors were also linked to the national and international capitalist sector throughout the decade. Since the 1940s, most ladino social scientists have asserted that dependence on subsistence farming in Guatemalan agriculture, especially in the highlands where the majority of the Indian population lives, has historically constituted a major barrier to the development of specifically capitalist relations of production (Monteforte Toledo 1959). In fact, however, many Indians have been involved in a cash economy since the 1930s (cf Tax 1953; Bunzell 1952; C. Smith 1984a, 1984b). Thus, we must seek a deeper explanation for the remarkable change in worldview of so many Guatemalan Indians, forging the creation of an Indian movement that cut across previous lines of language and community. Let us examine the events of the 1970s as they affected Indian communities in many parts of the highlands, with evidence especially from the departments of Quiché, Quezaltenango, and Chimaltenango, for the antecedents to and evidence of this transformation.

Antecedents of Change: The 1960s

Two trends of the 1960s brought changes to Guatemalan society that had a strong impact on Indian communities. Following the 1954 coup that returned Guatemala to military rule, the army maintained its authority through fraudulent elections and death squads. In response, a small, urban guerrilla movement arose and sought its base among the hungry and landless ladino peasants of eastern Guatemala. The United States, through the newly established Alliance for Progress, offered military aid and training, thus enlarging and strengthening the counterinsurgency capacity of the army, and the guerrilla movement was quickly and brutally destroyed.

In this "safer" investment climate, national and international elites promoted the development and diversification of Guatemala's economy. The creation of the Central American Common Market, together with the Alliance for Progress and other development programs, fostered the introduction of new crops for export, introduced new levels of technology and modernization, and stimulated even greater production

in the traditional export crops. Foreign investments stimulated industrial production, particularly targeting the new Central American
Common Market. Multinational corporations and their Guatemalan
partners built modern hotels and promoted the formation of a tourist
industry and the development of artisan production and wage work tied
to tourism (Ja C'Amabal I'b 1986).

> These processes contributed to major social and economic diversifi-
> cation in the Guatemalan countryside, processes with particular
> impact on Indian communities. In the highlands, textile industries
> began to appear, finding markets outside the local and regional
> environment, making incursions to the capital city and even in the
> international market. The growth in demand for artisan products
> stimulated production on a large scale and commercialization on a
> national and international scale. (Ja C'Amabal I'b 1984:6)

For Indian communities, this unprecedented commercial growth
brought about the construction of new highways and an increase in
transportation services, and brought mass communications media to
many of these communities for the first time.

> In the large villages and their surrounding fields, and in areas which
> began to be penetrated by highways, sectors of the *campesino*
> population began to learn to speak Spanish, breaking the barrier of
> monolingualism. They began to learn to read and write, accepting
> ideas and knowledge from beyond the borders of their language and
> community. People could buy radios and radio stations sprang up
> which spoke to them of their problems and linked them to a larger
> world. (Ja C'Amabal I'b 1986:7)

These external processes acted on the internal economic, political, and
religious issues confronting Indian communities. The tension and
resolution of these issues began to change the perspective and worldview
of many Indians.

The traditional control of Indian communities was in the hands of a
group of men known as *principales* (elders) who achieved their position
by ascending through the ranks of the civil-religious hierarchy and who
often used their positions to gain control of land or Indian labor. From
their ranks came those known as *costumbristas*, the defenders of the
"customs," particularly the traditional Indian agricultural and religious
rituals.

As the agricultural land base in Indian communities decreased and as
the externally driven commercial activity increased, those Indians

involved in the commercial sector, such as the Medrano family of Santa Cruz del Quiché, the Guzmán family of Nebaj, or the Alvarado family of Cantel, began to consolidate their economic power by buying and selling outside of the markets controlled by the principales in their own communities. This allowed them to free themselves from the subjugation imposed by the latter through ceremonial services and religious rites, mechanisms that had impeded their accumulation of capital. They confronted the costumbristas' monopoly of religious rites and codes as well, and thereby placed themselves at the head of a movement rebelling against their communities' traditional beliefs. They found support in the Catholic organization Acción Católica (Falla 1978a:427).

The foreign Catholic clergy who arrived after 1954 were incorporated into groups organized by Acción Católica. Working with the catechists and Delegates of the Word of Acción Católica (and thus also members of the communities' commercial sectors), these clergy directed the task of breaking the costumbrista structure. In some communities this unleashed a long and bitter conflict, at times extremely harsh and not without violence. There were near-lynchings, confrontations with machetes, rocks, and knives among members of a community as they sought to control the local church and to command the loyalty of community members (Falla 1978a; Brintnall 1979a; Cabarrús 1979).

It was in this larger framework that the commercial sectors, now strongly linked by Acción Católica, won their struggle within the communities and began to implement previously unfamiliar methods of development. The cooperative emerged from this process as a new model of agricultural organization. Cooperatives introduced to their members, all of whom were members of the community, new avenues for credit and savings and the consumption of new products, especially chemical fertilizers. Cooperatives began to sponsor political, social, religious, and even sports activities and developed into autonomous local entities.

Despite their reformist character, the growth of the cooperatives brought about serious conflicts with the local powers, thus accelerating the radicalization of Acción Católica's members and their mentors:

A little later, in Santa Cruz del Quiché the difficulties between the governor during the time of Peralta [Col. Enrique Peralta Azurdia, Chief of State, 1963–1966] and the Quiché cooperative began due to the sale of fertilizer at a lower price. Quiché's wealthy ladino merchants felt threatened because the cooperative had lowered the price of fertilizer and could also compete with them with other products. They went to the governor who, by way of a threat from the government, informed the Nuncio that either the priest who had organized it must leave or all of the Sacred Heart of Jesus missionaries working in the Department would be expelled from the country. His [the priest's] superior exiled him from Guatemala. The cooperative, rather than being intimidated, doubled its membership in two years and the blow equally spurred on Acción Católica in Santa Cruz and those in neighboring municipalities who learned the facts. (Falla 1978a:455)

Due to these confrontations, Acción Católica organizers and their students began efforts in 1965 to organize a *Liga Campesina*, which would have as its general goal the defense of Indian rights from ladinos and the authorities. Short courses in leadership and group organizing were offered in the capital. From these efforts, the leadership of the Partido Democracia Cristiana de Guatemala (DCG) organized the Federación Guatemalteca de Campesinos, a mixed organization of rural Indians and ladinos, an autonomous entity of the party. Nevertheless, as the country's political situation became more unstable, the federation was seen as linked to the guerrilla movement and found its objectives impossible to achieve. Similarly, its members began to be labeled "communists," generating fear among both the members of Acción Católica and those priests who began to argue that they did not want to "get involved in politics." The federation's activities languished and ceased, frustrating and radicalizing all those who had placed their hopes in that new political alternative.

In spite of this, the apparent achievements in the level of agricultural production, particularly due to the use of fertilizers, created great expectations among Indian campesinos. Even though many were unable to take advantage of these improvements, the illusion that life was finally changing for all Indians was great (Ja C'Amabal I'b 1984:455).

The first qualitative alteration of worldview was realized in many Indians communities through the conflict between Acción Católica and costumbrista groups. The conflict itself had revolutionary implications. The reduction in the political power of the principales was equivalent to redefining the community in relation to its own history. The costumbristas embodied the link to the ancestors and the ancestral link was what justified the right to land the community considered within its domain.

From there, the claiming of identity passes through a whole series of groups of ancestors who have been established in a place and who are going to be defined as the communal identity. (Garcia Ruiz n.d.)

But as the community's land base eroded and residents sought other ways of making a living, the worldview of the agricultural past ceased to provide an adequate ideological framework for defining community relations. The costumbristas' displacement in the mid-1960s implies the gradual displacement of agriculture as the indigenous populations' modus vivendi.

The second transformation came from the Indians' growing dependency on fertilizer. Gustavo Porras (1978) points out that the extension of capital into the rural economy meant the *minifundio's* incorporation into the money economy through the production of agricultural commodities, which the growth of urban centers stimulates, as well as through the acquisition of consumable goods, especially fertilizers, which now constituted an indispensable technical base. The necessity for capital in order to produce constituted a radical transformation in the conditions of production in Guatemala, not only because of what that by itself signified, but also because of the dynamic it generated.

As capital, even though in very small quantities, became indispensable for the first time for the minifundista Indians, it changed their relationships, even that with corn. Corn changed from being a product for home consumption to a commodity to be sold in the marketplace. In addition, Indians reduced the size of the *milpa* (corn field) in order to allow space for more commercial crops such as wheat, which lacked the symbolic relationship they had with corn.

Thus, through consumption as well as production, the traditional isolation of the Indian farmers was broken, and they began to forge a wider vision of the social structure, which, in the final analysis, determined the conditions under which they could produce.

1970–1976: Developing Indian Consciousness

Development fever and rapid transformations were contagious, and, despite the contradictions, were promoted by the state as well. In 1970, the government supported development plans for the small agricultural sector within the framework of the Plan for National Development.[1] The essence of this plan was the control and concentration of agriculture credit by the state. Complementary institutions (banks, agrochemical companies) increased and speeded the internal marketing of products, particularly extending the use of chemical fertilizers and other consumable goods. To help necessary capital for "technification" reach local levels, cooperatives were converted into intermediaries between the small producer and the state credit system. In fact, this change served to neutralize and co-opt the cooperatives. They gradually lost their margin of autonomy and became instruments of official policy (Ja C'Amabal I'b 1984:9).

The developmentalist stage was not in vain. Through it the Indians reformulated their manner of dealing with departmental heads (i.e., with the local expression of the state). In facing that apparatus, the need and the conditions for an autonomous structure to defend Indian interests began to coalesce. More important, the initiative for this movement came from Indian communities, even though it had the missionaries' guidance and the institutional support of their respective orders and of the DCG. With the Plan for National Development, the state sought to generate new mechanisms for reassuming control and reorienting this important sector of civil society under its own ideological-integrative mechanisms. These were not the guidelines generated by the communities, but were mandated by the extraordinary growth of the agroexport sector of the economy during this decade, promoted and encouraged by the state, acting on behalf of Guatemalan and international elites (Williams 1986; Moors 1988). The whole of Guatemalan society—including the Indians—appeared to be in a process of abandoning its secular backwardness to begin the transition toward modernization that, without challenging class relationships or redistributing land, wealth, or income, would extend monetary relations and broaden the consumption of merchandise.

For the minifunidistas, these rapid transformations represented more than opting for commercial crops in order to have a little capital with which to buy transistor radios and fertilizer so that the earth could yield more. Beyond the consumer products and their associated indebtedness (directly to the state or with the cooperative as an intermediary), these transformations implied renouncing an ancestral form of thought and the elaboration of new ways of seeing the world by redefining Indian relations with the state and their links to the national economy and the international capitalist system. It was in this new space that a young generation of Indians began their work. These few hundred young people were the children of the first Acción Católica leaders, and they had been brought up on the experiences of the 1960s and prepared by the priests as community leaders for Acción Católica.

As part of the training process implemented by the Christian churches and institutions during the height of developmentalism, a small number of Indian leaders not only completed their secondary studies in their respective departmental capitals but were also given scholarships to continue university studies in the nation's capital. The arrival of Indians who did not intend to hide their ethnic identity and who energetically defended themselves from racism shook up the university environment during those years and opened another focus on the polemical debate among the urban intelligentsia about the Indian situation in the country.

This debate was never easy. In the critical self-evaluation by groups that survived the guerrilla debacle of the 1960s, the lack of capacity to mobilize the Indians massively was outlined as one of the principal causes of that defeat (Ramirez n.d.). Interest in the debate, however, was found not only among those on the left, but also in the most diverse sectors of Guatemalan society: the government, the army, business circles, the press, and in large sectors of public opinion. That interest was largely due to the Indian population's accelerated process of incorporation into the market economy, "in their decisive inscription into the network of capitalist relations" (Solórzano Foppa 1982:44–47).

The academic debate was, for the most part, polarized into two positions. The first, based on the analysis in *La Patria del criollo* by Severo Martínez Peláez, first published in 1971 by Editorial Universitaria de Guatemala, underestimated the Indian masses' political capacity and fell into a form of revolutionary paternalism: "to create the Revolution in order to save the Indian" (Chamix 1982:47–57). The other, contained in *Guatemala: una interpretación histórico-social*, by Carlos Guzmán Böckler and Jean-Louis Herbert (1970), idealized everything Indian to alarming levels. With respect to this second position, Mario Solórzano says the following:

It is possible to discover an unhealthy inclination in diverse authors to be enthusiastic about the growth of an Indian bourgeoisie. For them, the growth of this bourgeoisie would be a positive and hopeful step toward the Indian population's liberation, as if being exploited by an Indian *patrón* were better than being exploited by a ladino patrón. In light of the development of an Indian bourgeoisie, less attention is paid to being bourgeois than to being Indian. No care is taken whatsoever to analyze the development of this bourgeoisie. How did this group accumulate its capital? What labor force does it utilize and how is it compensated? How is the land of other less fortunate Indians appropriated? What relations does it maintain with the national power structure? Overall, Guatemalan researchers are not asking these questions, and, by exalting the Indian bourgeoisie, appear to prefer one form of exploitation over another, without even knowing if, in reality, it is different. (Solórzano Foppa 1982:45)

The problems raised by Solórzano remained sticking points throughout the decade.

Regardless of the external debate, Indian communities continued to search for new values to reestablish their commonality, their identity, and their place in the new environment. They sought a substitute for the ancient sacred bonds, now eroded by the rapid changes their communities had experienced, which could link self, neighbor, and place. The New Testament Christian patterns and values introduced by the missionaries and carried forward by Acción Católica, known as liberation theology, served as the point of departure for this search.

From these roots, a literacy campaign was begun in 1972 that lasted three or four years. The number of participants, both teachers and students, in this campaign was relatively small, probably not exceeding one thousand. The literacy program encompassed not only learning to read and write, but also the teaching of Spanish to Indians who did not speak it. The method of teaching departed from traditional methods of teaching literacy by focusing on the necessities and problems that Indian people were facing at the time, and was based on the methods developed by Paulo Freire (1970). Fertilizer provided one example:

> There were many problems associated with obtaining *abono* [fertilizer] for many of the peasants from Santa Cruz del Quiché. Throughout the Green Revolution, we were within five to six years of reaching its peak. Nevertheless, inflation and greater poverty, greater misery among the campesinos, made obtaining fertilizer more difficult. I spoke of fertilizer because, when we began the literacy campaign, one of the key words, a generator of discussion, was "abono." We used its composition: beginning with "a," continuing with "bo"; and then later with "ba," "be," "bi," "bo," "bu," common combinations. Then we would introduce "n." Furthermore, due to the sounds, the syllables, it is a word that lent itself to the Indian *compañeros* conjugating its syllables. (Ceto interview 1983)

Literacy workers began to "scratch at" many problems derived from the Indian campesinos' situation in this manner, as a form of progressively generating their awareness, of raising their consciousness, of forging a new identity.

The vast majority of literacy workers had previously participated in the catechization experiences launched by the Christian organizations, closely linked to Indian commercial sectors, which grew out of Acción Católica. Similarly, all were Indians from different parts of the department who had studied at the secondary school in Santa Cruz del Quiché, and as students had initiated their activism in the departmental capital as members of Juventud de Acción Católica Rural Obrero (JACRO). Subsequently, in 1970, the women's branch of the same organization, Juventud de Acción Católica Rural Obrera Femenina (JACROF), was formed.

Paralleling these organizations, other groups were also formed that reflected the ongoing redefinition of Indian identity. The Asociación Indígena Pro Cultura Maya-Quiché, later called Asociación Pro Cultura Maya-Quiché, was formed in 1971. This was an Indian association with conspicuously Indian claims that centered its action on undermining oppression and discrimination in the cultural sphere, thus accelerating the consciousness of Indian identity. It operated primarily in Santa Cruz del Quiché and Quezaltenango.

In 1973, it was this association that initiated the struggle to give the one-hundred-quetzal (the quetzal was the equivalent of the U.S. dollar at that time) prize awarded to the department's ladina queen to the Indian queen as well. Until then, the Indian queen had been given only twenty-five quetzales, based on the argument that she did not have to buy a white formal gown for the coronation ceremony. They also demanded equal titles and treatment (a carriage and a coronation ceremony) for both the young women.

About the same time, a group of students formed the Asociación de Forjadores de Ideales Quichelenses (AFOIQUI) to promote the formation of soccer and basketball teams and the teaching of chess. In 1973, they actively participated in the literacy campaign being promoted in the Santa Cruz del Quiché area.

Another organization appearing around this time was Pastoral Indígena, an informal association of Indian priests. In addition to its own literacy and evangelization campaigns, it made the promotion of consciousness of Indian values its goal. This was ananother step in Acción Católica's evolution toward greater commitments of a political nature. Differing from the previous groups, it had the advantage of operating at the national level, with important centers in the national capital and Quezaltenango, the country's second largest city where many of the Indian bourgeoisie were located, as well as in Quiché, Totonicapán, and the Verapaces. Through the Pastoral Indígena, Indians of different language groups (not just of different municipios, but people who were beginning to think of themselves as Ixiles, Quichés, Cakchiqueles, and so forth) became acquainted with one another, discussed common problems and solutions, and expanded their own vision beyond the conspicuous problems of their immediate area and community. As a result, in 1974 this group gathered momentum and maintained a high level of activity until the 1976 earthquake shifted their attention to relief efforts.

Another program with national characteristics appearing at this time was that of the Seminarios Indígenas, which began in 1972. It promoted a series of meetings bringing Indian leaders together to discuss among themselves what they considered their people's most pressing issues. As simple as this was, such gatherings had never taken place before, and they were valued highly by those who participated in them.

These were great enough events, with sufficient characteristics to call them national in that there was a level of representation of ethnic groups, villages, not in that it was a large, transcendental movement for the popular organizations of those times. Those seminars were propelled by Indians who were professionals in some manner—teachers, university students, or former teachers. They were sufficiently radicalized and believed that, in order to develop an Indian struggle and to resolve the country's situation, it was necessary to form Indian organizations. (Ceto interview 1983)

The first seminar was held in the city of Quezaltenango, and drew representatives from many Indian zones. According to the participants, the seminar was of high quality in the sense that there was a good level of discussion, frankness, and the possibility to discuss sensitive issues. It gave birth to the vision of a more developed Indian struggle than that which had previously been considered.

Among those who initiated the Indian seminars were several members of the Indian bourgeoisie, formed essentially from the commercial sector, and their intentions were directed at formulating a worldview that did not question their position as a class. Although divergent directions arose from these meetings, they did not appear to disrupt the enthusiasm for the program.

In the seminars, the Indians' social, cultural, economic, and political situation was dealt with, from which came several diverse paths because one of their characteristics was not a totally developed homogeneity of thought, but rather the fervor of Indian consciousness translated into efforts, into initiatives, into an overall search. (Ceto interview 1983)

In late 1973, the Central American Common Market, recently shaken by the "soccer" war between El Salvador and Honduras in 1969, was overwhelmed by a monetary crisis as a result of the oil embargo and the appearance of inflation in Guatemala. As a consequence, markets were closed and the effects of an economic recession were felt in the country's interior. This undercut many of the development processes, thus closing off possibilities and expectations that had been generating since the early 1960s. The country once more began to polarize socially and politically.

This situation had special effects in the highlands. Small and medium agricultural production fundamentally based on the use of fertilizers was cut short when the price of fertilizers, derived from petroleum, rose from Q2.85 to Q18.00 per hundred pounds. This resulted in bankruptcy for thousands of campesinos. Most of the time, the cooperatives became indebted to the banks or the United States development agencies, with their lands mortgaged and their expectations frustrated. At the same time that cultivation of such crops ceased to be affordable, the crisis also reduced the national and Central American market for fruits and vegetables coming from the Guatemalan highlands. Thousands upon thousands of campesinos were forced to migrate to the plantations and to the capital. (Ja C'Amabal I'b 1984:443)

As a result, the Indian campesinos experienced sudden, unexpected misery. This contributed to accentuating class differences in the communities, according to some of the Indians who lived through these events.[2] In many cases, marginal Indian farmers were forced to sell their lands and become wage earners on land that had been theirs, or they had to rent or sharecrop that land. The land's new owners were often the Indian bourgeoisie who sought to concentrate greater amounts of land in their hands and to control the market of consumable items. This created very difficult and tense situations, with outbreaks of rebellion in some areas. In the Ixil region, the Gurriarán brothers, both Catholic priests, reported disturbances but lacked the leadership to transform them into a campaign of greater scale.

Those confrontations also complicated the search for a new worldview that could encompass the dizzying rate of change. As class differences within the communities increased, the crisis of values became deeper and more pronounced. The traditional structure of authority was basically undermined. Capitalism made its presence known at the economic level but was absent at the level of ideological production, resulting in a crisis of community authority, tradition, and symbolic structure.

The literacy workers who participated in the Indian seminars, sensitive to the conditions being experienced, understood that it was time to proceed to another level of work. Their restlessness went beyond seeking solutions to the problems of poverty by simply teaching the poor to speak, read, and write Spanish. Study groups, with topics such as peasant rights and the rights of all Guatemalan citizens, were formed. They studied the country's constitution in order to know what it said and to contrast what was written with reality. This, in turn, raised the issue of human rights and the discussions became more explicitly political.

At the same time that this work was proceeding in the departmental capitals of Santa Cruz del Quiché and Quezaltenango, the small rural villages and towns were reducing their dependence on the departmental

capitals where the exploiting circles—outfitters, distillers of aguardiente, moneylenders, merchants, and municipal offices, the arm of the
central political power—were located. A real rupture in the existing
power arrangements appeared when in rural centers and communities
members of Acción Católica founded schools and carried out education
and consciousness-raising of the young people, developing a new, or-
ganic, young leadership core. The work going on in remote communities
and that taking place in those departmental capitals with Indian majori-
ties remained divorced from one another. For the rural communities, the
departmental capitals were the very symbol of exploitation. And for the
restless Indian students in those capitals, the answer to their restlessness
came more from the programs being developed in those cities and from
the Indian professionals there.

This division also acquired class characteristics. In fact, the Indian
bourgeoisie concentrated itself in the departmental capitals where the
search for political power was pursued through more traditional channels. Many members of the Indian bourgeoisie were also members of the
DCG, and were mobilized by General Efraín Ríos Montt as that party's
presidential candidate in the 1974 elections. In those elections, various
members of the Indian bourgeoisie presented themselves as candidates
in their respective departments. The majority did so through the DCG,
but some also appeared even on the rolls of the Partido Revolucionario
(PR), which, in spite of its name, was politically to the right of the DCG
and had been in power from 1966–1970. These candidacies were, however, not individual efforts, but rather responded to the interests of
specific Indian groups. Thus, Professor Fernando Tetzahuic Tohón was
said to be the candidate of the Indian group, Patinamit (meaning "in or
near the city Iximché"), even though he presented himself as a PR
candidate (Falla 1978b:438–461).

In fact, in the 1974 elections, Tetzahuic Tohón, native of Tecpán, was
elected a deputy from the department of Sololá, and Don Pedro Verona
Cúmez, DCG, native of Comalapa, was elected from the department of
Chimaltenango. This was the first time in Guatemalan history that
Indians were elected as national deputies who continued to identify
themselves as Indians at that level and who derived their power from
Indian bases. This victory generated expectations of access to power at
the national as well as the local level for sectors of the Indian bourgeoisie.

Nevertheless, for the rural communities, those elections—won by the
DCG but denied by means of fraud to which not only the candidate but
also the DCG party acquiesced—implied that all possibilities of electoral political participation were closed. The fraud's magnitude gave
evidence as never before that Guatemalan Indians would never be
permitted to exercise power won by the ballot.

That was the situation in general terms until the end of 1975. The class breach between Indian bourgeoisie and rural cultivators appeared to be opening more and more, permanently breaking the Indian communities' historic cohesion. It was necessary to go through the excruciating experience of the earthquake for both sectors to come together again.

1976–1979: The Search for Roads to Change

On February 4, 1976, the entire Guatemalan highlands was jarred by a massive earthquake. More than one million people were made homeless in less than forty-five seconds. The strongest effects of the earthquake were felt in the departments of Guatemala, Sacatepequez, Chimaltenango, and the southern part of Quiché. The areas of northern Sololá, central Quiché, Totonicapán, and northern Quezaltenango were less affected. The majority of the victims were Indians.

The earthquake provided a true trial by fire for the local leadership in the affected rural communities. Overnight, they were effectively forced to exercise all political and social responsibilities, with minimal resources and no communication with either the departmental or national capitals. In order to solve the immense necessities generated by the earthquake, the young leaders responded, working tirelessly to cope with the immediate crisis. The critical situation lasted for several days, and in the most severely affected areas, several weeks. Thus, when their communities needed them the most, these young leaders' efforts exceeded their communities' expectations.

On the other hand, the central government, overpowered by the magnitude of the event, was practically incapacitated from responding to the emergency and the need for national reconstruction. It therefore tolerated the fact that the communities took the initiative and virtually conducted themselves as local *poderes populares*, local assemblies that negotiated directly for aid with international agencies.

The earthquake also provided visible evidence of the country's terrible inequalities. National and international news reports showed that the houses destroyed were those with the weakest construction, and that the poorest Guatemalans, the Indians, were the ones who suffered the highest losses.

As the government recovered from the shock, the army tried to monopolize all international aid in order to funnel it through their own channels, reselling that aid for profit. This was witnessed by observers such as Catholic priests and foreign relief workers operating in the area and by the Indians who were to have been the recipients of that aid. Those who could not pay the prices, arbitrarily set by army officers and their merchant colleagues, starved or froze to death. All of this opened the population's eyes.

From that moment, the literacy work, the work of the Christian communities, the work of political discussion, began truly to be transformed into organizational work with certain political perspectives. Knowledge of the reality in which they lived was now a fact for vast sectors of the Indian population. The crisis of values, the lack of coherence of a new worldview, persisted. But the response to both began to achieve an explicit interest in supporting activities and groups that could lead to "something" that would help change the existing situation.

The young leaders talked in general about the need to "organize." But, practically speaking, none of the "organizers" had any meaningful experience that would allow them to decide what type of organization they sought or needed. Then, after wide-ranging discussions in which all (or at least all men) equally participated, and basing their decisions on the old values of communal decisions by consensus, these organizers began an open discussion to carry forward the collective search for a structure more adequate to their needs. First they studied the Acción Católica model for organizing, detecting its limits for the tasks ahead. Not all of its members had reached the same degree of consciousness about how to confront exploitation, oppression, and discrimination. And, in the political nature of the struggle, "a Christian organization cannot necessarily raise those issues" (Ceto interview 1983).

They also studied the Ligas Campesinas, implemented during the height of developmentalism, but found them limited by a legal framework that had become extremely suspect after the 1974 fraud. Even fewer possibilities were offered by the traditional political parties.

There sometimes existed certain situations of deceit. People were transported in trucks and they would give them a quetzal or fifty centavos so they would support or vote for one candidate or another. This was the manner of convincing the people. I myself was a Christian Democratic delegate in 1972 during the municipal elections in Canillá, San Andrés Sacabajá. Political parties could not be the answer, as it had been attempted two, three, four times. They were not the answer. (Ceto interview 1983)

The Indian bourgeoisie, however, reached different conclusions. Their attitude sprang from those events that led Tetzahuic Tohón to leave the PR in mid-1976. When the PR demanded that Tetzahuic resign from a leadership position in Congress, he refused, citing the decision of his support group, Patinamit, in opposition to that resolution. At the same time, Tetzahuic began to propose publicly an Indian seat in Congress. Though impractical, that idea mobilized the political ambitions of many members of the Indian bourgeoisie. At a July support meeting held in the capital, Patinamit put forth the slogan, "It does not matter what party a deputy belongs to so long as he is Indian and knows how to represent our interests." In analyzing these events, Ricardo Falla confirmed Joaquín Noval's suggestion that "what is truly important is that the Indians and ladinos who exercise any power at any level of articulation within the national power structure are oriented toward conserving and increasing it" (Falla 1978b:443).

The image of numerous politically active Indians headed by Tetzahuic had a strong impact on public opinion. Allusions were made to the movement's "Marxist" nature. In reality, Tetzahuic, who had received an evangelical education, belonged to Patinamit's most conservative wing and had sought alliances with the extreme right. Nonetheless, the prospect of an Indian political party began to grow:

> The following meeting of Patinamit took place in San Francisco el Alto, Totonicapán, on September 25 . . . There were two purposes. The apparent one was to honor Professor Don Adrián Chávez . . . and the second, underlying, was to deal with aspects of national political life and to establish alternatives for participation in the 1978 general elections. It was thus a meeting with national political goals . . . The lines for entering the nation's electoral political struggle were now being drawn. (Falla 1978b:443)

As Falla points out, the homage paid at that time to Don Adrián Chávez made clear the profound symbolic meaning that Indian culture had to the Indian bourgeoisie; this meaning was born of the need to reelaborate the symbolic codes of the older traditions in order to form a new worldview that would make entrance into modernity possible without adding to the contradictions and internal disintegration threatening the Indian community. Don Adrián Chávez fulfilled that function perfectly. Teacher and professor, founder of the Academia de la Lengua Quiché in Quezaltenango, translator of the *Popul Vuh*, creator of an alphabet for the Quiché language and an internationally known personality, he was the ideal man to personify that need. He embodied the rescue of Indian identity "whose crisis has been especially felt by Indians who have reached diverse degrees of scholarship and have been separated from rural labor" (Falla 1978b). By exalting Don Adrián Chávez, the Indian bourgeoisie was "exalting and appraising their own lives, as they suffered a crisis of identity and had broken the barrier that condemned them either to be campesinos or cease to be Indians by means of study and other duties undertaken outside their community of origin" (Falla 1978b:445). In the following elections, Don Adrián Chávez was named the third candidate for Quezaltenango to Congress by a dissident group of the PR (PRA) within the DCG.

On November 20, 1976, Patinamit met in Chimaltenango to initiate the formation of an Indian political party:

> In these moments the Indigenous Party of Guatemala was put forward. It was intended to have "representatives of the Kekchí, Quiché, Cakchiquel, Mam, Kanjobal, Tzutujil, Pocomam, Chortí, Ixil and other indigenous ethnic groups." Only those ladinos who "conformed to Indian guidelines" would be allowed to participate. (Falla 1978b:447)

The press and congress attacked that idea vigorously, citing it as unconstitutional because it was "racist and fomented class struggle." Thus, on December 11, the members of Patinamit met again, with around two hundred delegates present, to form a party called Frente de Integración Nacional (FIN). The change in name was a response to public criticism. As Tetzahuic explained in a press conference, the new name meant that the party "intended to unite ladinos and non-ladinos and not to discriminate based on race or poverty" (Falla 1978b:448). Nevertheless, all members of the directive committee were Indians.

FIN submitted documents to register itself as a pre-party committee on April 19, 1977. Its activities throughout that year turned to forming alliances with both the DCG and the right-wing alliance supporting General Lucas García for president, in exchange for the promise of committee memberships. The FIN's meteoric jumps from one party to another in an effort to obtain candidates and the fever among its members to be candidates contributed to a rapid loss of prestige. The major force behind electoral politics in the end was the army, with which FIN began to forge an alliance—an alliance sealed by the support given to General Lucas García in February 1978 in exchange for the promise that his government would support FIN as a political party. Nevertheless, the tremendous electoral fraud by which the army imposed General Lucas García's presidency not only took all legitimacy away from the electoral process at the national level, but also caused FIN and its leaders to lose prestige. As if this were not enough, with all the expectations of a seat in Congress, not one single Indian deputy was elected and only two became stand-in deputies.

Among the base communities, radicalized since the 1973–1974 period, the Indian bourgeoisie's failed attempts confirmed that a struggle based on the legality of those who exploited, repressed, and discriminated was not possible:

We wanted an organization that was of all the campesinos. We
wanted an organization that was of all Indians, but not only of the
Indians nor only of the ladinos, but rather of all tillers of the earth,
that there all would join together, an organization that would be
capable of struggling for the needs, for the rights of rural people, but
would not fall for the political parties' deceit. (Ceto interview 1983)

Organizing required a high degree of secrecy, because repression had
already begun to appear in El Quiché; an open, public organization would
have been immediately destroyed.

Among the Ixil Indians of northern Quiché, the Christian Base Communities were successful in their organizational and *conscientización*
activities due to the more backward material conditions, the great
distance from the departmental capital, and the nearness of the Ixcán
jungle where the clandestine Ejército Guerrillero de los Pobres (EGP) had
operated since early 1972.

The Indian bourgeoisie of Nebaj perceived these activities as very
dangerous. They had accumulated capital through contracting cheap
labor for jobs required by the local ladino landowners and by the large
coffee, sugar, and cotton plantations along the country's southern coast.
Their circle of power also included commerce (ownership of stores,
trucks, and the town's only mechanical corn grinder) and finance
(making loans). In January 1973, Sebastián Guzmán, principal of the
principales of Nebaj and First Confrère of the Cofradia de Santa María,
the most important in the village, and eleven other members signed a
letter addressed to General Carlos Arana Osorio, the president of Guatemala. In it, they asked for his direct intervention, because "there is
now among us a bad seed, the communists, who are fighting against us
with cooperatives and other idiocies" (Gurriarán n.d.). Indians had been
called many things but this was the first time that the accusation of
communism had been leveled against a group of Indians by other
Indians—members of the Indian bourgeoisie.

In November 1975, the same call was reiterated. This time the request
was sent to the army commander of the Santa Cruz del Quiché zone "to
come and finish off the village's guerrillas" because "they are pure
Cubans." In January 1976, in Sebastián Guzmán's home, the Indian
principales drew up the first black lists. The following month, only a few
weeks after the earthquake, a group of them traveled to Santa Cruz del
Quiché to meet with representatives of the army's intelligence service
(G-2) in the military zone. There, they turned in the blacklists with
names, personal data, characteristics, and photos. On March 1 of that
same year, the army occupied Nebaj for the first time. On March 19,

1976, the repression began with the assassination or kidnapping of Christians, leaders of cooperatives, directors of development committees, and popular organizations.

With this experience in mind, veteran organizers like Vicente Menchú from Acción Católica, from the Christian Base Communities, and from the Ixil area decided that great precautions should be taken. They extended the underground organizing meetings until 1977 and maintained secrecy as long as possible, until the young organization, later to become the Committee for Campesino Unity (CUC), was strong enough to resist the reactionary onslaught.

The earthquake relief efforts, sponsored by progressive Catholic groups and by urban labor unions such as the National Workers' Central (CNT), brought Indians of different communities together with activist ladinos. At the same time, consciousness-raising and organizing efforts began to develop on the southern coast. Out of these, larger meetings of catechists, cooperativists, and members of some agrarian unions were held. Connections developed between Indians in the Chimaltenango and southern Quiché zones in the highlands, and rural workers on the southern coast of the country, thus slowly weaving a relationship between Indians and poor ladinos. These, however, proceeded with difficulty, because of the racism that even poor ladinos displayed toward Indians, and the Indians' mistrust of ladinos of whatever class.

On May 1, 1977, many Indians descended from the highlands and saw a public demonstration for the first time in their lives. They did not participate in the real sense of the word, but rather studied what the people were shouting, how they were organized, what the signs they carried said, what the speakers said. They later evaluated whether or not they had understood the events. That allowed the nascent organization to study for nearly two months what demonstrations were, what purpose they served, and whether or not they were a form of struggle that would serve them.

On October 20 of that same year, a large number of Indians participated at a demonstration commemorating the democratic revolution of 1944, but even then without identifying themselves with any organization. Once more, this allowed them to evaluate what it felt like to be in a demonstration and to draw lessons from that experience.

One month later, in November, a transcendental event took place that qualitatively contributed to the definition of an Indian identity, the Ixtahuacán miners march. The miners—ladinos and Mam Indians—who worked in the antimony and tungsten mines in the northwest highland municipality of Ixtahuacán, Huehuetenango, initiated a 351-kilometer march to the nation's capital, demanding improved working conditions. They followed the Pan American highway, which crossed the entire Indian zone of the western highlands: Quezaltenango, southern Totonicapán, northern Sololá, southern Quiché, and all of Chimaltenango and Sacatepequez. After nine days, they entered the capital accompanied by 150,000 people, including students, settlers, government employees, workers, and campesinos. It was undoubtedly the largest demonstration seen in the country since 1954. That great march, along with one by the workers of the Pantaleón sugar plantation located on the southern coast, which took place at the same time, created a growing feeling of euphoria in the mass organizations.

The miners' march forced the Indians to take another organizing step. There were, at that time, various groups in Santa Cruz del Quiché, in Chimaltenango, and on the southern coast. They had arisen from different efforts, the Ligas Campesinas on the southern coast and the Christian base communities in the highlands. Until the miners' march, those groups had only maintained slight coordination, but in order to give the miners the support they needed it became necessary to coordinate on a broader scale, so everyone would go out to the highway:

> To give them *atol de plátano, atol de maiz, chuchitos, tamales,* to give them sodas, *aguas* . . . And all of this implied the work of a very large organization. It was to organize the groups so they would organize their support. Not only to greet and walk with the miners . . . but also to organize cultural acts in every place they passed through. For example, they would arrive at a crossroads and there would be a large number of campesinos offering them food and drink, and at the same time holding a large meeting in both the Indian language and Spanish during which the miners and the people who met them would speak. (Ceto interview 1983)

By coordinating efforts, these groups were able to provide support and accompany the miners from Quezaltenango to San Lucas Sacatepéquez, a distance of almost 275 kilometers.

Based on the success of this experience, the organizers decided to push forward with the organization. They began preparations in February 1978, with the goal of participating in the May 1 demonstrations. In March, all grass-roots groups received invitations to an April meeting in one of three regions (southern Quiché, Chimaltenango, and the southern coast). At those meetings they decided to participate as an organization in the May 1 demonstration and established themselves as the Comité de Unidad Campesina (CUC). Their idea was to struggle aggressively (though not as armed combatants) for the interests and rights of rural people, a struggle not based just on legalities.

Just prior to May 1, the slogans most deeply felt by the grass-roots groups were endorsed. They included: "No more forced recruitment by the Army," "Lack of land," "No to repression," "No to discrimination," "No to the high cost of living." In turn, CUC's manifesto was based on those slogans.

On May 1, four times the number of people expected had gathered, and the CUC contingent formed an impressive procession several blocks long. They marched in four rows, carrying as megaphones the speakers from their village churches, lowered from their habitual places for that day. A Quiché Indian, later murdered by the army in 1981, and a poor ladino from the coast were designated as CUC's speakers.

The May 1 demonstration was transcendental for the country's political life. The presence of Indians in the street, with their typical clothes and their tump lines, with slogans painted on sleeping mats instead of sheets, immediately aroused great applause and "*vivas*" from the observers. Ladino workers were heard shouting "¡Vivan los campesinos! ¡Vivan los indígenas!" The Indian contingent was led by a row of torches and by Indians carrying machetes and hoes as symbols of Indian rural work.

The murder of one hundred fifty Kekchí Indians took place in the northeastern village of Panzós only twenty-nine days after this event, shaking "the highlands, indicating to what point the regime would go in response to the legal claims and demands of the campesinos" (Ja C'Amabal I'b 1984). As a result of the massacre, all popular and democratic organizations called for a demonstration on June 8. Now, for the first time, CUC appeared as one of the organizers of a popular mobilization. They broadcast announcements on the regional radio stations in the Quiché, Cakchiquel, and Kekchí languages.

The presence of the Indian contingent in that demonstration was both large and of great consequence. Sympathy for CUC began to be generally felt. The organization grew and found a favorable reception in the heart of the democratic and popular movement. In September 1978, CUC made inroads in the Verapaces, initiating work in the Rio Negro community, Rabinal. By then, the CUC's positions were being defined more and more in class terms:

CUC is the CLEAR HEAD with which to analyze the situation of our class brothers and our friends who join in struggle, and to know our enemies in order to combat them. CUC is the HEART IN SOLIDARITY that was born in order to bring all workers of the countryside together and to unite with organizations conducting the same struggle. It is an important step in the campesino-worker alliance, because that unity is the heart and the motor of the revolution. CUC is the COMBATIVE CLENCHED FIST because we have learned that we, the exploited, conquer our rights with the force of the action we undertake, not by humiliating ourselves before the promises, laws, and deceits of the rich. (Ceto, Calel, and Tipaz 1982:17)

The organization's structure was formed on the basis of assemblies and commissions on the local, regional, and national levels. When the organization was still small, all the members of an area would come together in the local assemblies. By early 1980, growing numbers of members and increased repression impeded those assemblies, forcing meetings to be held by three to five local *responsables*. In the regional assemblies, delegates from different areas participated in order to discuss local problems and to carry out political analysis. The national assembly was the organization's highest level, where the directives governing CUC were discussed and where its political features and activities were elaborated. Corresponding to these assemblies, permanent coordinating commissions existed at each level. La Comisión Nacional de Coordinación (CONACO) gathered CUC's highest leadership, who, for security reasons, were never publicly revealed. Regional and local coordinating commissions (CORECO and COLACO) were also established.

In the mid-1960s, the struggle within Indian communities had been between the "costumbristas" and the commercial sector linked with Acción Católica. By the mid-1970s the community was found divided among three groups: the costumbristas, the commercial sector now clearly delineated as the Indian bourgeoisie, and the radicalized Indian campesinos who no longer recognized either of the two previous groups as their natural leaders. By then, class differences began to prevail. While "traditionalists," like Sebastián Guzmán of Nebaj, or bourgeois Indians, like Fernando Tetzahuic of Tecpán, searched for political power within the regime's narrow legal limits and joined with right- and extreme-right-wing groups for the sake of their quotas of personal power, the radicalized Indian campesinos leaned to the left, seeking convergence with poor ladinos, organizing a mass movement that was situated outside the prevailing limits of legality.

Ethnic identity had been transformed in the search for political force. Now, identity was a tangible, verbalized, phenomenon, around which the articulation of political practices was sought. But the symbolic practices, the worldview, and the unconscious codes had been discarded without the formation of new ones to substitute for them. Thus, in concrete practice, just as identity was being talked about more openly, it was experiencing its deepest crisis. The rapidity of the changes taking place during this decade broke down the traditional values and ties that held Indian communities together. Acción Católica had become the substitute for traditional organizational mechanisms in the 1960s and early 1970s, but as the class struggle sharpened within those indigenous communities, this model was discarded. The Indian bourgeoisie leaned more toward the traditional political party structure. The radicalized Indian campesinos leaned more toward revolutionary mass organizations. The tensions between these models, when added to the "transitional crisis" of Guatemalan society (Porras 1978) produced the open conflagration at the end of that decade.

1979–1982: The Incorporation of Indians in the People's War

In 1978, the state initiated a counterinsurgency plan to strike at the popular, democratic movement in order to separate it from the more explicitly revolutionary movement: the political-military organizations, which, by means of guerrilla columns, had initiated their armed activity in 1975 and whose operations grew immensely, especially in 1979. Until late 1978, indigenous ethnic groups had favored mass organizations over armed struggle, but in early 1979, the army's active presence began to be felt throughout the highlands, and this began to generate changes in that judgment.[3]

The CUC, embodying the claims most deeply felt by significant sectors of the Indian campesinos, grew enormously and became radicalized as it grew. In 1979, it changed its methods of struggle, and began implementing actions such as sabotage, propaganda bombs, blocking highways, and barricades. Those activities now constituted support for armed struggle.

In the Ixil area, the zone most affected by repression since 1975, the Indians began to consider the option of joining the guerrillas. Many now knew from personal experience that these guerrilla organizations supplied a structure for the survival of the community in light of the collapse of local cooperatives, schools, health clinics, and other institutions inherited from the developmentalist phase.[4] They also constituted an alternative for the youth to avoid forced military service and a new mechanism for resolving the crisis of ethnic identity by seeking structural changes in the socioeconomic formation by means of armed struggle. The clearest demonstration of the Indians' incorporation into armed struggle came on Sunday, January 21, 1979, when the Guerrilla Army of the Poor (EGP) occupied the village of Nebaj, the most important town in the Ixil triangle.[5]

Throughout 1979, various indigenous groups also appeared, periodically holding meetings in the city of Quezaltenango. These groups grew out of the Indian seminars and were associated primarily with the Indian bourgeoisie of that area. They adopted a variety of names: Chilam

Balam, Federación de Indígenas de Guatemala, Tojiles, Nuestro Movimiento, Cabracán, and so forth.   Distinguished figures of the Indian bourgeoisie such as Don Adrián Chávez, Miguel Alvarado from Cantel, and Father José Serech were among their spokesmen.   Their position stressed the cultural aspects of ethnic problems and excluded class struggle:

> The reactionary positions of *indigenismo* and the lack of concrete
> alternatives . . . produced in some Guatemalan Indian petit bour-
> geois sectors, those who had become professionals (principally
> teachers and lawyers) in the city and who therefore were separated
> from their villages, an attitude favorable to the position—very
> widespread throughout South America—that Indian struggle should
> have an exclusively Indian character and that, even more impor-
> tantly, should be against the ladinos who were the inheritors of
> colonial power.   For them, everything proposed by the ladinos
> disguised manipulation and was to be viewed with suspicion.   All
> elements of western culture were to be combatted because the only
> authentic culture was Indian. (Ocampo de la Paz n.d.)

They stated that the territories invaded by the Spaniards and ladinos should be recovered, that Indian culture and power should be recuperated at all costs, and that their history, interrupted in the sixteenth century, should be resumed.   The segregationist and separatist ideas of Indian struggle, along with an overestimation and idealization of their culture, achieved the mobilization of some sectors, but that mobilization was based on hatred of ladinos and was a racist response by the Indians to the system's racism.[6]

It was against this background that the events leading up to the burning of the Spanish Embassy occurred, an act of barbarity without equal, which signaled a new and important turn in the incorporation of Indians into the guerrilla movements.   In the fall of 1979, a commission of Indians representing CUC traveled to the capital to ask the president, General Lucas García, to stop the repression in the Ixil area where three thousand army troops were stationed.   The president refused to receive them, and, faced with this dilemma, the commission went to a session of congress to present their demands, where they were also rebuffed. Desperate due to the seeming futility of their efforts, the group peacefully occupied the Spanish Embassy on January 31, 1980, with the hope of thus finding international recognition and relief for their situation. The Guatemalan government's response was to massacre the entire group by burning them alive inside the embassy.

The burning of the embassy was the definitive watershed for most

Indians. For them, there were now no options left other than to join the popular war being waged against the reactionary regime. And, from that date on, a latent state of massive insurrection against the state began in both the central highlands and the northwest.

There were two immediate Indian responses. The first was a strike by sugarcane workers on the South Coast:

> That combative strike of 70,000 workers, was the first time in rural Guatemalan history that solidarity was manifested between migratory workers [Indians from the highlands] and agricultural workers [ladinos]. This was the most important mobilization in the history of workers on the South Coast. (Ja C'Amabal I'b 1984:15)

The other response was the February 14 meeting of Indian leaders at the Iximché ruins, near Tecpán, capital of the Cakchiquel nation until 1524, called by the CUC leadership. There, after a day of discussion, they produced a document titled "Los pueblos indígenas de Guatemala ante el mundo," which immediately became popularly known as the "Declaración de Iximché." The document, expounding Indian claims, was virtually a declaration of war against the regime.[7] It ended with a quotation from the *Popol Vuh* that became a slogan for the popular movement:

> That all arise, that all be called. That there be neither one nor two groups among us who remain behind the rest!

From that moment forward, and throughout the year, thousands of Indians joined the guerrilla organizations. The majority of the Indians, most of the CUC members, and Indian members of Acción Católica joined the EGP, the largest of the guerrilla organizations, which operated in the capital and the departments of Sacatepequez, Chimaltenango, Quiché, Huehuetenango, and the Verapaces. A smaller number of Indians joined ORPA (Revolutionary Organization of People in Arms), which operated in San Marcos, Quezaltenango, Sololá, and Chimaltenango. Very few Indians joined the FAR (Rebel Armed Forces) and even fewer the PGT (Guatemalan Workers Party). Their motivation was expressed in their declaration of intention:

> In light of this situation, we lamentably must resort to defending ourselves with the same arms the army utilizes. We, the Guatemalan people, all the campesinos, all Indians as they say, the natives, those here by birthright, have the right to defend ourselves. The

only road left for us is with the same arms the army utilizes against us. (Ixmata n.d.)

Between 250,00 and 500,000 highland Indian people participated in the war in one form or another. Generally, paramilitary organizations, forms of self-defense, were organized to provide food and clothing for the permanent guerrilla units whose members were mostly Indians with relatives in the various villages. Indians also began to collaborate in large military operations. When the EGP guerrillas occupied the villages of Chichicastenango and Sololá, local Indians cut telegraph lines and blockaded the highways with nails, barricades, fallen trees, and other objects for several kilometers in both directions to prevent the army from reacting in time.

The high point of revolutionary effervescence was reached in 1981, and the entire country was touched by acts of resistance and rebellion. No one perceived then that the counterinsurgency was slowly taking the initiative against the popular and urban movements. The triumphalism of the moment caused the vast majority of CUC militants to join the guerrilla organizations, thus, in fact, dissolving that organization. Similarly, in several highland zones, people organized spontaneously without any type of ideological guidelines. One of the negative consequences was that regional leaders sought to capitalize on the phenomenon and to utilize that effervescence for their own ends. Similarly, by imposing a military plan over the political one, regional leaders overnight became "directors of guerrilla fronts," evidently without having even minimal training for that position.

As a part of that revolutionary tide's ascent, the indigenista groups also greatly increased their activity. The idea of fusing all organizations into one was discussed, but did not crystalize because great tension existed between the orthodox indigenistas, whose frontrunner was Manuel Alvarado, and the "Marxists," a word used derogatorily by the former to refer to Indian campesinos who resented both ethnic-cultural and class oppression.

For the Guatemalan army, the time had come to cut that movement to ribbons. They correctly saw danger not in the guerrillas' military capacity, but rather in the enormous mobilization of the Indians in the highlands. This was why a campaign of genocide was initiated against the insurgent Indian population in November 1981.

As Gustavo Porras (1978) has already pointed out, we must note that the revolutionary crisis resulted from the modernization efforts initiated by the state. The state simultaneously fulfilled the role of agent for development and repressor of the population in order to keep the modernizing features introduced from bringing about changes in the power structure. Those attempts at modernization, nevertheless, generated expectations in the rural population and unsettled traditional order by generating rapid changes in society's class composition, especially among Indian cultivators and rural middle sectors.

These structural changes crashed into the centuries-old traditional culture and dictated changes in the superstructure, one that previously had been resistant to modification. But then, the worldview that legitimated an existing precapitalistic order no longer made sense of the new, more explicitly capitalistic relations of production, and material expectations (improvement in the living standard, access to a world previously forbidden, and so forth). All congruence between traditional ideology and people's daily lives, and identity, so intimately and sensitively tied to that ideology, ruptured, thus precipitating the revolutionary crisis.

Notes

1. This was a program put forth by President Gen. Carlos Arana Osorio as he took power. Arana was president from 1970–1974.

2. Domingo Hernández Ixcoy, a subsistence Indian from the rural area of El Quiché, and Francisca Alvarez, a member of the Indian bourgeoisie in Santa Cruz, have both attested to this phenomenon.

3. "We had no indication of any cooperation, but we heard that various people we knew had met the guerrillas and knew what routes they took through the mountains. The general attitude was that the guerrillas could help change things for the better, but none of our acquaintances were inclined to either join or actively cooperate with them.

"In the beginning, people gave passive support to the ORPA. They felt no urgency to join them. In one of their talks, the guerrillas told the people to 'passively resist' the military. As the violence increased, nevertheless, there were rumors that people from the village were joining them. Now, fifteen people from the area belong to the ORPA." (Testimony taken from "Los indígenas y el movimiento guerrillero," in *Polémica*, no. 9, San José, 1983, p. 52.)

4. Many Indians joined the guerrillas for a short time, and later returned to their land or went to the southern coast as wage laborers.

5. "At 6 a.m., about one hundred guerrillas, the majority Indians in olive-drab uniforms, came running into the village from various points. While some guarded the village's exits, others occupied strategic points. The Hacienda Police surrendered immediately. The National Police resisted about two hours before surrendering. The only death during the occupation was that of Enrique Brol, one of the principal landowners and the link with the army in the area. The meeting was held in the central market at 8:15 a.m. with about three thousand spectators. All of the speakers were Ixil Indians who spoke in their own language. Two of the four were women. In the market, which is central to all of the Ixil

zone, were Ixil, Quiché, Aguacateca, and Mam merchants, who later spread news of their experience throughout the highlands" (*Polémica*, no. 3, 1982).

6. In the early 1980s, the United States security apparatus took advantage of this experience when they tried to assemble an Indian alternative to that offered by guerrilla movements by seeking links between Guatemalan indigenistas and Miskito counterrevolutionaries in Nicaragua. Regarding this, please see the direct testimony of the Guatemalan Indian leader, Rigoberta Menchú (Burgos-Debray 1984). For more information, see Arias (1984).

7. Among others, the document gathers the following themes:

To end with all of these evils the invaders' descendants and their government, we must struggle allied with the workers, peasants, students, settlers and other democratic and popular sectors. We must strengthen the unity and solidarity between Indians and Ladinos, now that the popular movement's solidarity with the Indian struggle has been sealed with their lives in the Spanish Embassy. The sacrifice of those lives brings us closer, now more than ever, to a new society, to the dawn of the Indian.

That the blood of our Indian brothers and their example of firm and valiant struggle strengthen all Indians to continue forward and conquer a life of justice.

For a society based upon equality and respect; that our Indian people, as such, be able to develop their culture, broken by the criminal invaders; for a just economy in which no one exploits others; that land be communal as our ancestors had it; for a people without discrimination, that all repression, torture, kidnapping, murder and massacres cease; that forced recruitment by the army cease, that we all have the same right to work, that we not continue being utilized as objects of tourism; for the just distribution and utilization of riches as in the times during which the life and culture of our ancestors flourished. (From "Los pueblos indígenas de Guatemala ante el mundo," in *Cuicuilco*, no. 1, Mexico, July 1980, p. 5)

12. Conclusion: History and Revolution in Guatemala[1]

Carol A. Smith
Department of Anthropology, Duke University

The current meaning of revolution has been given to us by the theories and ideologies spawned in the nineteenth century by the French Revolution and developed in the twentieth century by the successful practice of revolution throughout the Third World. The French Revolution was unique, not just because it was one of the first unleashed by the forces of early capitalism, but because intellectual treatments of it made "revolution" a novel social and discursive phenomenon.[2] Later, the Russian Revolution of 1917, based on the theory and practice that resulted from the French Revolution, defined the terms of all subsequent revolutions. No social transformation that took place before the Russian Revolution, no matter how radical, can be considered a revolution in the same terms. Once Marxists came to dominate world discourse about the bases and practice of revolution, the very meaning of the term *revolution* changed. As Antonio Gramsci observes, "the events of 1917 ... marked a decisive turning-point in the [world] history of the art and science of politics."[3] This obvious point has been neglected in most theoretical discussions of twentieth-century revolutions, which have been couched in the analytic categories of Barrington Moore (1966) rather than of Marx—even as twentieth-century revolutionaries have been dominated by the rhetoric of Lenin.[4]

The fact that the very meaning of the phenomenon under investigation, such as revolution, changes over world-historical time places certain limits on historical comparison.[5] We cannot compare the attempted Guatemalan revolution of the 1980s with the Carrera movement or with colonial revolts, for example, without taking into account the possibilities given to each of these epochs by both material and discursive circumstances. It is not that the political struggles before the twentieth century were necessarily of limited scale and ambition compared to the attempted revolutions of the 1960s and 1980s, though most of them were. The Carrera movement had a much larger popular following than the guerrilla insurgency of the 1960s (discussed below) and was of equivalent if not greater social consequence. Yet revolution-ary transformation was not a popular demand in the nineteenth century, and the only blueprints of what a revolutionary transformation would be were those held by the elite liberal reformers of that era (chap. 3).

On the other hand, we can learn a great deal about the forces causing social transformations in general by careful examination of a particular historical case and locating that case in world history. And our under-standing of world-historical transformation is enriched by considering how local histories help change the meaning and goals of social transfor-mation, including revolutionary change. The historical pattern of political struggle in Guatemala bears on the most current attempt at revolution insofar as it helps define the powers, interests, and histori-cally changing relationship between the main social actors in Guate-mala, Indian communities and the state. Through this it may be possible to understand not only why many Indians supported armed struggle in the 1980s, but why that armed struggle failed; it may also be possible to foresee how the positions of the main actors in the conflict were transformed by the attempt, in ways that will color all future political struggles in Guatemala. This brief review of political struggle in Guatemala is designed, therefore, to illuminate how the terms of political action were affected by both local and world-historical events.

Premodern Political Struggles

Let us begin by considering the different ways in which Indians resisted the colonial state. Two patterns emerge, depending on whether we consider only violent oppositional movements or include in the analysis the nonviolent "weapons of the weak" (Scott 1986). Severo Martínez Peláez (1973) has examined forty cases of Indian revolts indexed in the colonial archives. From this we find that more than half of the revolts occurred after the Bourbon reforms (between 1780 and 1821), fifteen of them after 1815, when the state attempted to reimpose the Indian tributes that had been suspended in 1812. In the years between 1600 and 1750 there were only six major revolts. From the timing of Indian revolts it becomes clear that oppressive social conditions are far from sufficient to bring on violent reaction on the part of the oppressed. The iniquities of Spanish rule were as fully realized between 1600 and 1750 as they were after that period; the Bourbon reformers were if anything less oppressive, though they attempted to change the mechanisms of surplus extraction (chaps. 2, 3).

Why, then, did so many rebellions occur in the last few years of the colonial period? If we look at the particular grievances behind the revolts, we find that the rebellious Indians were angered by what they considered to be unjustified abuse of traditional authority—whether by priests, local elders, or state officials.[6]   Indians did not question the authority of the state, per se, but rather looked to the state for redress. From this we may conclude with Moore (1978) that popular rebellions are fueled by a locally formed rather than universal sense of injustice. Or we may conclude with Theda Skocpol (1982) that, while peasants are always potentially rebellious, they will take action only when the state instruments of control have been weakened, as appeared to be the case in the Bourbon reform period. We may also note that the gradual secularization of the clergy weakened state control over the native population, following van Oss's observation (1986) that the missionary church played a role for the colonial state that the military was to play in the postcolonial period. We must amend van Oss's argument by observing that church legitimacy was established by ideological as well as coercive means (chap. 1). These three interpretations are not mutually exclusive, but they do not reveal the real issues at stake in Guatemala between the two main actors, Indian communities and the state. For this we must consider nonviolent forms of resistance and how they shaped state response.

Throughout the Spanish Empire, the Crown had reached an accommodation between its own interests (revenue) and those of its subjects, both Creoles (who wanted local control) and Indians (who wanted relative autonomy). By granting considerable local power to the Creoles while exercising some restraint, mainly through the church, over their behavior with respect to Indian resources, the Crown was able to maximize its revenue at minimum expense. As many scholars, including those in this volume, have documented, this policy led to Indian communities taking a particular form—corporate and relatively autonomous—which also provided them certain weapons for resisting a deeper level of state penetration. Maintenance of local cultural traditions was one of those weapons, which is not to deny that it was a weapon forged by colonial oppression. Once this weapon was forged, however, the Crown had a very difficult time increasing its demands on Indian communities to meet its needs, created by external pressures, for increased revenue. Hence the numerous revolts of the late colonial period and the consequent inability of the state to maintain order. Were we to argue with Skocpol that the Bourbon state was therefore weaker than its predecessors, we would merely be stating a tautology. The Bourbon state was if anything the stronger colonial state, in the sense of having greater infrastructural power (a better organized and rationalized control apparatus). But it lost *legitimacy* and, through that, control throughout the empire among both Indians and Creoles, because it changed the rules of governance without developing a legitimating ideology for popular consumption (chaps. 3, 4).

Daniel Contreras (1951) has argued that the Indian revolt of 1820 in several municipios in the department of Totonicapán was the first step in Guatemala's independence movement. Given that the independence movement was an empirewide phenomenon, one has reason to agree with Contreras's critics that he overstates the case. Yet the foregoing analysis gives us reason to believe that the Totonicapán revolt was indeed Guatemala's local manifestation of rebellion, illustrating and exacerbating the declining powers and legitimacy of the Spanish Crown in the Americas. Of course the Indians did not win (though they did not again pay the now illegitimate tribute, the reimposition of which was the immediate cause of the revolt); the revolt was brutally repressed by the state, and Guatemala's Creole elite subsequently took charge of the Guatemalan state. On the other hand, the states that subsequently formed in nineteenth-century Guatemala had little more success than the Bourbon state in their attempts to eradicate the weapons of political struggle that Indian communities had created for themselves in the colonial period.

Let us now consider state development in Guatemala as a phenomenon affected as much by local resistance as by world-historical forces. Guatemala's first coherent postcolonial regime was that of Mariano Gálvez (1831–1839), whose notions about state governance and social justice were strongly colored by the United States and France. As Woodward, Smith, and McCreery (chaps. 3–5) show, these notions did not take hold in the very different social context of nineteenth-century Guatemala. Gálvez was forced to resign in the face of a major popular uprising headed by Rafael Carrera, whose social platform was conservative rather than revolutionary. What this popular movement and its institutionalization through Carrera represented in Guatemalan political history (a return to the conservative institutions of the colonial period, a last-ditch attempt by the church to retain power, the ascendancy of ladinos over white Creoles in national politics, or an attempt to stave off capitalist forms of development) is still a matter of debate in Guatemalan historiography. But with respect to the issues under consideration here, the Carrera revolt can be seen as another, even more powerful, form of popular resistance to a state attempting to take greater control over local communities. Carrera's conservative policies, in turn, played a significant role with respect to preserving Indian means to resist state intrusion, bringing "to full fruition," in McCreery's words, the indigenous development of the institutions and organization of the corporate Indian community.

Given that the liberal goals of the Creole elite for the state and economy, albeit significantly changed, were eventually realized during the Barrios period, when a coffee-export economy directly intruded upon the traditional way of life of Indian communities, can we still argue that local forms of organization shaped the political and economic outcome in Guatemala? McCreery and Carmack (chaps. 5 and 6) show that we can, as long as in doing so we do not ignore the impact of world-historical forces. In response to those forces, the Barrios reforms established a more intrusive export economy and a more coercive state than had ever existed before in Guatemala, changes that in some respects resembled those taking place in the rest of the isthmus. But as C. F. S. Cardoso (1975) shows comparatively, and McCreery (chap. 5) shows through the particulars of Guatemalan history, certain characteristics of the Guatemalan state and economy were given to it by local social relations: plantations were larger, coercive means to obtain labor more frequently used, Indian land and communities less disrupted, and the state held a greater monopoly over violence than anywhere else in the isthmus.

McCreery provides strong evidence that the consequences for Guatemala's rural communities, though hardly benign, were not nearly as drastic in transforming the bases of Indian resistance as previous scholars have argued. At the same time, McCreery shows how the nature of political struggle in Guatemala was decisively changed by the state's development of greater and deeper coercive powers—new communications systems, a professionalized army, and greater control over public and local officials in the local communities—paid for by coffee-generated revenues. Violent local revolts against the authorities, which reached a peak in the 1860s, virtually disappeared by the 1890s, as Indians increasingly took their grievances to the courts. Thus, while the state and plantation economy had to reach a certain accommodation with Indian communities that allowed those communities to preserve certain traditions and institutions, they also transformed those communities in significant ways (on this, see Carmack, chap. 6). Most important, political initiative was now largely in the hands of the state.

What is most notable about the political struggles of the nineteenth century is that state attempts to tamper with local political autonomy in an effort to create a modern nation-state met greater popular resistance (the Carrera movement) than did state attempts to transform the national economy in ways that directly impinged on Indian livelihood (the Barrios reform period). Creating a mass of semiproletarianized Indians on the one hand, and a land-based semicapitalist oligarchy on the other hand, did not lead to the social conflagration predicted by such scholars as Jeffrey Paige (1975). Because the process did not directly impinge on local *political* autonomy, the most momentous economic transformation in Guatemala's history occurred during a period of relative peace. We can understand this paradox only by understanding how the earlier failed attempts at socioeconomic transformation (the Bourbon and Gálvez reforms) transformed both the methods and the goals of the state (chap. 4).

Modern Political Struggles

The kind of state and economy introduced by Barrios in 1871 remained little changed until 1944, at which point world-historical events and ideologies began to play a much more significant role in Guatemalan history. World War II shook up the simple balance of forces described above, as it did throughout Latin America. With foreign investors taken up with the war effort, Guatemalans began expanding their own investments in industry and other forms of agriculture (cotton, sugar, cattle). Frustrated by the scarcity of labor (tied up in semicontractual relations with the coffee oligarchy), and by their exclusion from political power (monopolized by the coffee oligarchy), many of the "new rich" in Guatemala supported a change in government. Other urban Guatemalans, especially students and professionals, influenced by the world rhetoric of "democracy versus tyranny" that characterized the war period, organized protests against the dictatorship of Jorge Ubico. In 1944 the last of Guatemala's old-fashioned dictators resigned, eventually to be replaced by Guatemala's first democratically elected governments. The period 1944–1954, sometimes called Guatemala's ten years of spring, introduced many important social and economic reforms, though few of them were to survive the following period of military rule.

Most scholars assume that Indians were pawns rather than players in the changes wrought by the 1944–1954 period. But, according to Adams and Handy (chaps. 7, 8), this is not entirely accurate. Handy shows that Indians were especially active in taking advantage of the reforms affecting land, labor, and local governance. Freed in 1945 from the last coercive mechanism by which the coffee oligarchy obtained seasonal labor, the passbook system, Indians became more active in their own economic enterprises. With the land reform decree of 1952, they began to petition for land. And though many Indian communities resented the intrusion of the state in local governance with the decree that forced local elections, which more often than not transformed indigenous political forms such as the cargo system (see Adams 1957), most Indian communities began to define electoral politics in accordance with their own interests.

The implications of this historical revision of Guatemalan history are two: first, Indians continued to use any openings given to them to retain what they could in the way of local political and economic autonomy; and, second, the changes wrought by external forces on the organization of Indian communities were greater in form than in substance (chaps. 9, 10). At the same time it is also clear that in failing to create a strong popular constituency among the Indians by appealing to their interests as Indians rather than as campesinos, Arbenz's reform government had little ability to resist a weakly organized counterinsurgency force.

James Dunkerley asserts that the U.S.-assisted military coup of 1954, which ended the reform period, instituted a "long wave" of national history ". . . upheld thereafter by a series of governments that in effect constituted a single regime despite significant variations in style and method" (1988:427). The new regime, he continues, ". . . positively *reversed* [Guatemalan] history" (1988:429). Perhaps its most important effect in this hemisphere was that a generation of Latin American radicals lost faith in peaceful, legal, and reformist methods of social change and began to accept the necessity of armed struggle. Michael McClintock agrees that Guatemala's modern state originated in the 1954 coup, but points out that "in 1954 there was neither an apparatus, nor a counter-insurgency orientation encouraging wholesale murder along modern lines" (1985:30). This was to emerge in the 1960s with the assistance of the United States, which helped set up a modernized army and intelligence system. The excuse for the military buildup was a Cuba-inspired insurgency movement (see Gott 1972), whose combatants never numbered more than five hundred. The poor, rural ladinos of eastern Guatemala were selected as the support base for this first "modern" insurgency.

Like the 1944–1954 reformers, Guatemala's guerrilla leaders in the 1960s considered Guatemala's Indians to be marginal to political and economic life. Their position on the "Indian question" is summed up in an early statement by Guatemala's Communist party (the PGT) as follows:

> Indian peasants in some areas of Guatemala . . . have the worst
> standard of living in the country; but their cultural backwardness,
> the downtrodden state in which they have been living since the
> times of Spanish colonial rule, their relative isolation from the
> economic and political life of the country . . . have resulted in a
> situation in which these people are, by and large, politically inac-
> tive. . . . Nor . . . will they be the main support of the democratic
> national liberation revolution maturing in the country. . . . The
> main forces of the revolution, and the most active, are concentrated
> in the south and eastern areas of the country and in those areas of
> the highlands where political and economic development are at a
> higher level. (Cited in Dunkerley 1988:508)

As it turned out, the political and economic development of Guatemala's poor rural ladinos was not "at a higher level," and the guerrilla-led insurgency, led by disaffected members of Guatemala's army, did not have strong popular support anywhere (ibid.:454).

But while the threat posed by the 1960s guerrilla movement was small (mainly for lack of a popular base), the state response to it was massive. Forces at both local and world levels (i.e., both the guerrilla movement in eastern Guatemala and the "cold war") converged in the creation of Guatemala's military state.[7] New instruments of state control included a vast intelligence network, the use of rural military *comisionados* charged with supervising public order, the development of a mobile military police—who were legally charged to "lend assistance . . . to the owners or administrators of estates, haciendas . . . and all rural properties . . . and repress through licit means any disorder that should occur [among the peasant masses]" (McClintock 1985:64)—paramilitary death squads, sophisticated physical and psychological torture techniques, a subservient sensationalist press, the circulation and publication of death lists that included virtually any opponent or presumed opponent of the new social order, and the actual killing or "disappearance" of such individuals. Economic institutionalization of the military also took place over the following two decades, the army acquiring its own bank, credit institutions, and publishing house, as well as the means to take control of productive resources (Aguilera Peralta 1980). All of these elements of military coercion and control existed by the late 1960s, but the state was not fully militarized until the 1980s.

Most modern political struggles in Guatemala are marked by the apparent absence of Indian involvement. In retrospect it becomes obvious why these attempts at social transformation had little appeal to Indians. Indeed, had these attempts at reform and revolution been successful in their own terms, the consequences for Guatemala's Indian majority might well have been worse than they were in the late 1970s, when the most massive attempt at armed revolution took place in western Guatemala, the Indian heartland.

Ideological Struggle in the 1980s

The attempts made by Indians in the 1970s to create a new role for themselves vis-à-vis the Guatemalan state, documented by Arias (chap. 11), were reformist rather than revolutionary. The attempts were fueled in part by Guatemala's booming economy, which helped create a wealthier and better educated group of Indians, and in part by the "liberal" legacy of 1944–1954. But in the eyes of the Guatemalan state,

Indian attempts at reform carried a revolutionary threat, not only because they *did* challenge the traditional social order, but because new revolutionary groups forming in Guatemala were making strenuous efforts to draw disaffected Indians into their cause. To the state it was not inconsequential that survivors of the 1960s guerrilla-led insurgency, who had explicit revolutionary goals based in Marxist theory, were now operating in parts of the Indian highlands (Payeras 1983).

Relatively little information exists to date on the relationships that developed between the guerrilla leadership, mostly university-trained ladinos, and its new social base, the Indians.[8] But we can see in the documents produced by the different armed groups some of the difficulties they faced in addressing the specific needs of Indians qua Indians and their Marxist convictions about the centrality of class to a modern revolutionary struggle.

The PGT statement on the Indian question in 1982 moves very little from its 1964 position cited above. Among other things, it denies the present reality of minority or "national" status to Indians in Guatemala. Thus:

> The large Indian mass is constituted by various small minorities, whose particular most distinctive feature consists of a multitude of languages. . . . so fragmented that we cannot identify [them] as a nation. . . .They were neither unified nor communal in the past, much less so after the ravages of conquest . . . they can only be unified effectively into Guatemalan society through the revolution. (PGT 1982)

Apparently aiming to differentiate its position from those staked out in 1982 by the EGP and ORPA (see below), the PGT continued to deny the specificity of ethnic oppression, though it dropped much of the rhetoric about the fact that Indian culture is little more than the deformation wrought by colonialism, namely:

> Not only do some ladinos exploit some indians, but some indians exploit some ladinos. Thus we cannot supplant the centrality of class struggle with an assumption about an ethnic contradiction between indians and ladinos. In fact, indians are more likely than ladinos to own property. [But as their property resources shrink], it is breaking the old and absurd separation between indians and ladinos imposed by the dominant classes through the forced isolation of indian communities. While we must pay attention to the particularity of indian oppression, it is the basic view of our party that WE SHOULD SIMPLY INCORPORATE INDIAN COMMUNI-

TIES INTO THE REVOLUTIONARY PROCESS THROUGH
THEIR SITUATION AS AN EXPLOITED CLASS, keeping in mind
the particular ways in which their consciousness of oppression is
expressed. (PGT 1982, emphasis in original)

The two guerrilla groups who worked mostly with Indians in the
western highlands, the EGP (the Guerrilla Army of the Poor) and ORPA
(Organization of the Revolutionary People in Arms), made a far greater
attempt to deal with specific forms of Indian oppression. Their abstract
discussions of the issues, however, did not make clear how Indians were
to be mobilized and for what—whether the issue of greatest importance
to Indians was land, markets, political power, or racism. Rather than
attempting to determine through study and analysis what Indians might
want in a new social order, in order to draw them into the struggle, the
EGP and ORPA tried any and all strategies (Black 1984; Dunkerley 1988).
Thus, some groups emphasized the issue of land, some emphasized the
issue of working conditions on the plantations, others emphasized
ladino control of local trade and markets. In this way, both groups
incorporated some Indians into the revolutionary effort, but in limited
numbers. With Indian incorporation, however, the definition of the
Indian problem in Guatemala began to change from an emphasis on the
material conditions oppressing Indians to an emphasis on cultural and
racial oppression.
The clearest statement on these issues was that developed by ORPA
in 1978. Reportedly the most "Indian" of the revolutionary groups and
the group most concerned with the Indian question, ORPA rejected the
anthropological view that discrimination in Guatemala rests on ethnic
(cultural) rather than racial criteria, arguing instead as follows:

When we considered ideological issues [such as racism] before, we
spoke about false consciousness. Now we would state that the false
consciousness in Guatemalan society has been to ignore racism. . . .
While we can insist that racism is a mechanism of *class* exploitation, we also have to see it as an independent mechanism of oppression. . . . The virulence of racism among the popular and intermediate classes in society [can be explained] by the identification of
those sectors with the dominant groups in society. . . .The racist
will never have an identity or culture of his own . . . he must go to
the native society to find some of his own culture, [for] what is
valid in Guatemalan culture is the recognition of its native base.
Guatemalan culture without this recognition is empty and negative. . . . For a revolution to take place we must have the assistance
of the native people. The destiny of [all] the exploited is thus indis-

solubly linked to the destiny of the [racially] oppressed. Since the racism of the exploited racist is essentially superficial, it is reversible. But we cannot expect it to disappear overnight, by a simple decree or economic transformation. For this reason the struggle must continue on the ideological terrain, as well as on the political and military terrain. (ORPA 1978; reprinted 1982)

This statement on the "Indian question," like that of the EGP, cited below, appears very different from that of the PGT. But the main difference is that ORPA and the EGP recognized the reality of racism to the oppressed (which the PGT did not deny), from which they concluded that it was not a form of false consciousness, nor could one expect cultural-racial oppression to disappear without struggle on the specific ideological level. On the main point, however, all groups appeared to agree: racism/or the cultural oppression of Indians/or the mere perception of overriding differences not based on class had somehow to be eradicated in order to promote the necessary revolutionary unity. The difference, then, was more tactical than substantive.

Making a good-faith effort to deal with the demands of their Indian cadre, the United Revolutionary Front of Guatemala (URNG), which represented all groups in the revolutionary struggle, gave official sanction to both sets of concerns (race and class) in a January 1982 policy statement, in which one of their five revolutionary goals was the following: "The Revolution will guarantee equality between Indians and Ladinos, and will end cultural oppression and discrimination" (URNG 1982). The URNG elaborated this position only slightly, essentially to affirm that the cause of Indian oppression was rooted in Guatemala's class structure and to suggest that cultural oppression would be eradicated with the political participation of Indians in the revolutionary struggle.

By addressing the issue of cultural oppression, the URNG did not, however, resolve the questions concerning the present real basis of the material oppression of Indians. Nor, in the absence of a theory of the relation between cultural and material oppression, did it even address the cultural issues clearly. Finally, it did not address how a socialist project could be based on the present needs of Guatemala's Indians, whether material or cultural. In fact, as the issue came to be discussed more fully after 1982, the goals of Indian cultural autonomy and of socialist (i.e., national) development were seen to involve a certain amount of contradiction.

The clearest statement of the contradictions perceived by those in the armed struggle was voiced in the EGP's 1982 statement on the Indian question, possibly the most searching discussion of the issues published.

Their statement continued to affirm the view that Indian culture is based in colonial distortions, but argued that the proletarianization process is currently central in determining the nature of Indian social relations. In this way they recognized the diversity of economic and social forms the proletarianization process had produced:

> Many of the indigenous cultural expressions which survive today are the result of forms of economic organization, legal relations and political and ideological mechanisms stemming from the Spanish cultural influence, although shot through with the world vision inherited from the Maya-quiché. . . . In those parts of the country- side most strongly integrated into the capitalist economy the strati- fication of the [Indian] peasantry gives rise to rural middle sectors . . . even an indian bourgeoisie . . ., who in spite of their class condi- tion do not escape ethnic-cultural oppression and discrimination. (EGP 1982:20)

The EGP statement went on to warn that Indian nationalists, "in the absence of revolutionary theory," were liable to take their "more refined sense of ethnic identity" in the direction of "racist and indigenist ideas." In short, the ethnic question could not be divorced for the class/agrarian question. Thus, it became the "ethnic-national *contradiction*":

> The colonialists' need to preserve the basic Indian economic and social organization in order to facilitate the exploitation of a rural labor force is one of the key factors which explains why the Indian culture, revolving around precapitalist agriculture based on maize and the corresponding level of social organization could survive in the new colonial society; but it also explains why this culture could not develop . . . [and why] THE ETHNIC NATIONAL CONTRA- DICTION IS ONE OF THE FUNDAMENTAL FACTORS IN ALL POSSIBLE REVOLUTIONARY CHANGE. (EGP 1982:21–22, emphasis in original)

Having identified the Indian problem and having made it central to their revolutionary program, however, the EGP went on to argue that the class question was, in the last instance, the most important revolution- ary question:

> The class contradiction in our country is complemented by the ethnic-national contradiction, [but] the latter cannot be resolved except in terms of the resolution of the former. . . . The Indians as such are not part of the motive force of the revolution [except] as

poor peasants, as semi-proletarians, as agricultural and industrial workers . . . [Hence] the task of revolutionaries consists of strengthening national-ethnic consciousness, recognizing its specificity and intrinsic revolutionary value, but at the same time reforming, complementing, [and] investing this awareness with revolutionary class politics. Otherwise, the revolutionary process runs the risk of becoming distorted, turning into a four-centuries late liberation struggle which today can have no revolutionary content. THE MAIN DANGER IS THAT THE NATIONAL-ETHNIC FACTORS WILL BURST FORTH IN DETRIMENT OF CLASS FACTORS. (EGP 1982:25, emphasis in original)

An EGP leader, Comandante Benedicto, elaborating the implications of this position in a 1982 interview (CENSA 1983), observed that with material development, those aspects of Indian culture based on precapitalist forms of production could not survive, nor could it be a socialist goal to preserve precapitalist forms of production.

At approximately the same time that Benedicto articulated his views on the national question, a different interpretation of cultural oppression was voiced by several indigenous groups and individuals within the EGP, who later broke with the EGP over the national question. Their position was essentially separatist.[9] Attacking all unilinear evolutionary theories, Marxist and non-Marxist alike, they argued that cultural differences do not reduce to material or class differences and that cultural oppression will not be eliminated by granting official "political and economic equality" to Indians. They demanded full self-determination, whether or not that interfered with other socialist goals such as general material progress of the national economy. Essentially, they argued like Benedicto that Indians could maintain the political autonomy of their communities and their cultural distinctiveness only if they retained the small family-based properties on which their way of life was based. Because the new society Indians envisioned could not rest upon fully socialized (developed) forces of production, it seemed that Indian goals and socialist goals were distinctly incompatible.

With these breaks in philosophy on the national question, Guatemala's revolutionary "unity" ended in 1982, even before the URNG was militarily defeated in 1983. An Indian perspective on the Indian question had finally emerged by 1982, but it challenged the basic socialist goal of development. Thus, it seemed to vindicate the earlier orthodox Marxist position about Indian marginality to the socialist revolutionary project. The accommodationist solution proposed by the URNG did not directly face the issue embedded in the question of cultural oppression. As can be seen by the careful wording about the primacy of economic over cultural divisions in the EGP formulation, the revolutionary groups assumed that assimilation would be the long-run solution to the Indian question, a solution to be achieved through economic development and material equality. To date, these issues have not been resolved by Guatemala's revolutionary leadership, though it is obvious that considerable progress was made.[10]

Guatemalan revolutionaries began with a traditional (Western) socialist vision of economic oppression and social transformation, and to the extent that they clung to that vision they had relatively little success in incorporating the Indian masses into the struggle. When the vision changed from one of economic oppression to political oppression, Guatemalans of many different ethnic groups and classes could unite behind the cause. At first reductionist, insofar as class was seen to determine culture, the rhetoric changed to give recognition to the political and historical bases of cultural identity. At first essentialist, in that most held to a single meaning for Indian and ladino and believed that any change threatened or challenged cultural authenticity, most groups came to appreciate that culture was as protean a social force as socialist rhetoric. Finally, all began to see the political potential of cultural traditions and to recognize that a "revolutionary culture" was the product of politics rather than of simple economic relations.

What few people realized at the time these debates were taking place is that the very discussion was changing the nature of the struggle and, equally important, changes in the struggle were changing the terms of the debate. But, while people were gradually choosing to struggle to change the conditions of their existence, they could not choose the conditions under which they would struggle. That Indians were increasingly being drawn into a modern socialist vision of struggle (and through that changing the socialist vision) was a most frightening prospect for the other major actor in Guatemala's political system, the state. And the state now had the means and will to crush a slowly developing social movement.

Attempts to Create a "Strong" State

The 1980s counterinsurgency campaign provided the military with the chance to deepen its control over both state and civil institutions in Guatemala, especially in the western highlands, where state presence had previously been weak. Beginning selectively in 1975 in response to guerrilla actions and moving toward the indiscriminate use of violence against anyone in their way in 1980—after the successful farmworkers strike led by the Committee for Campesino Unity (CUC)—the Guatemalan military determined to eradicate subversion by attacking those

Indian settlements in which any form of popular mobilization had developed (*Cultural Survival Quarterly* 1983; Carmack 1988). The period of rural terror, roughly 1980 through 1983, involved village massacres, selective torture and assassination of rural leaders, burning of houses and crops in wide swaths, and displacement of nearly half the Indian population of the highlands. No one knows the exact numbers, but human rights agencies commonly report that at least fifty thousand people were killed, three to five times that number were forced into permanent exile, while up to a million people (half the rural Indians dwelling in the western highlands) were physically displaced for some period of time.[11]

After the destruction, a new phase of militarization was begun as the military state faced the human and economic wreckage it had created in three years of burning, looting, and murdering highland Indians; this new phase involved the reorganization of civil society along military lines (cf. C. Smith n.d.). The first step was instituting a military presence throughout the countryside. Whereas before, the army had been concentrated in four urban bases, today it has major bases in each of Guatemala's twenty-two departments and garrisons in virtually every town having more than ten thousand people. Smaller military camps or squadrons remain permanent fixtures in the rural areas of highland municipios where insurgent groups made (and continue to make) their presence known. Taking in some seven to eight thousand new recruits each year, mainly from rural areas by coercive means, the army incorporates between 10 and 20 percent of the rural male population between the ages of eighteen and twenty-four for two-year hitches.[12] Once released from direct military service, many recruits become military commissioners in their local areas, paid to assist in further recruitment and to gather local military intelligence. Military commissioners often helped the army organize "voluntary" civil patrols in their communities.[13]

The civil patrol system became the cornerstone of military control over Indian communities, insofar as it organized (and continues to organize) Indian communities into paramilitary forces under direct military command. The system was established in virtually every municipio of the western highlands between 1982 and 1983, after the military had replaced elected officials with appointed ones. But it remains in place as the main local-level political weapon of the military, even now that local officials have been reelected. As of 1984 the system incorporated nearly one million men and included virtually all male Indians in the western highlands between the ages of sixteen and sixty. Men conscripted into the patrols are required to undertake unpaid service in their local area for eight to twenty-four hours every four to fifteen days, depending on the size of their local community and the strictness with which local population movement needed to be controlled (Krueger and Enge 1985). As of 1988 these militias remain on active duty in about half the area previously covered—mainly in the areas where insurgency/counterinsurgency efforts were strongest (WOLA 1988). But they remain everywhere a means of registering and keeping tabs on the whereabouts of all rural Guatemalan civilians.

The other major means by which the military established its power in the western highlands have been economic. It had become obvious to the military (if not to the oligarchy) that the rural Indian highlands could not be secured in military terms as long as it was subject to intense economic exploitation. Thus, one of the first army development plans called for an "improvement in the standard of living of the [rural] population in order to diminish existing contradictions" (Ejército de Guatemala 1984:1). The same publication also places emphasis on the issue of national integration, emphasizing the particular importance of "establishing a nationalist spirit . . . incorporating our different ethnic groups" and stimulating within civil society "a new way of thinking, developmentalist, reformist, and nationalist."

Most economic measures taken by the military have been strictly coercive. Thus, between 1982 and 1983 the army herded those Indians remaining in the areas of greatest rural unrest (especially in the departments of El Quiché and Alta Verapaz) into several dozen "model villages" along the major strategic roads they built in the area (Guatemalan Church in Exile 1984; Richards 1985). By refusing to allow the resettled population to farm their distant plots of land or seek employment outside the area, the army effectively made some 10–15 percent of the highland Indians totally dependent for basic economic survival on handouts from state or military-controlled relief agencies.

But other military economic programs have been more subtle. Thus, by making some model villages into development poles (sites of military-directed economic programs), the army planned to reorganize the highland economy in ways that would tie most of the rest of the Indians in the region, formerly independent farmers and artisans, directly to the major agroexport businesses—as producers rather than workers. The basic strategy here was to secure the area by eliminating independent (artisanal) forms of production, giving former "peasants" and seasonal plantation workers a stake in national development plans.[14] Along with the construction of model villages and development poles, the military briefly (1982–1986) took over the direction of all development efforts in the western highlands, public and private, by way of a program known as the "Inter-Institutional Coordination System." A Guatemalan army publication (1984) argued that military coordination of development efforts in the western highlands would ensure the rapid and efficient development of the highlands along lines that would also ensure the "security" of the area.

The Guatemalan army seemed fully prepared to take on all of the functions of the state plus a number of functions usually exercised by civil society in 1982; but by 1985 it had found the cost of doing so (i.e., maintaining a state form that was considered illegitimate not only to locals but to virtually all international powers and agencies) too high. Guatemala's economy, like those of other Central American countries (Inforpress 1987), was in a period of negative growth; and Guatemala, unlike most other Central American countries, received much less external aid, economic as well as military. Thus, in order to change its world status as a pariah state, the military allowed general elections to take place in 1985 in which all political parties that had no direct ties to the armed opposition were allowed to compete.

In September 1985, 68 percent of Guatemala's voters chose the most moderate candidate (a Christian Democrat) and the second civilian in thirty-three years to have headed the Guatemalan government. In contrast to the electoral pattern during the previous thirty years, the 1985 elections were relatively honest and most Guatemalans were pleased by the outcome. Since the elections, however, pessimism has set in largely because of the inability of the new president, Vinicio Cerezo, to transform the major institutional structures of Guatemala, specifically the powers held by the military and by the owners of the major agroexport industries. As Nairn and Simon put it, Guatemala's "first chief of state in twenty years who would not order the killing of an unarmed civilian . . . has stated publicly that he will not plan social reforms because the army would oppose it" (1986:13–14). Coup attempts and threats throughout Cerezo's term in office (the most publicized occurring in May 1988 and May 1989) have kept Cerezo closely in line with military policy (G/NIB 1988:23:1).[15]

The elections, paradoxically, have strengthened the military vis-à-vis other groups competing to control the Guatemalan state. Military "security and development" programs, once they became "democratic" programs, now receive far greater support, both internally and externally, than they ever did before, underwriting the army's attempt to substitute economic for coercive means of control at the local level. Equally important, the democratic facade allowed the army to challenge the political power of the oligarchy for the first time in modern history. Convinced that the rapaciousness of the oligarchy was responsible for the strong guerrilla challenge to the state in the early 1980s, the army now seeks to bring the oligarchy as well as the general populace under state control.[16] What they want from the oligarchy is what they want from everyone else: loyalty (e.g., local rather than external investment), revenue (e.g., a more fairly distributed tax burden), and submission to state-determined policy (e.g., that state rather than private organizations, such as the hired guns of the oligarchy, determine which "subversives" should be eliminated). It is too early to say that the military High Command now constitutes Guatemala's new ruling class. But it is clear that the military is now much more than the coercive arm of the oligarchy.

Most contemporary analyses of the current Guatemalan state (e.g., Anderson and Simon 1987; AVANCSO 1989) emphasize its political sophistication in using the electoral process and a rhetoric of democracy to disguise the dominant role of the military and its continued use of violence to maintain order. But in the long run of history, what distinguishes the current state from prior regimes is the relative independence of state policy from oligarchic interests and the penetration of the state apparatus down into Indian communities. On this latter point, the interests of the military and the oligarchy are distinctly at odds, especially should the state provide the means whereby Indians could become economically independent of the plantation labor system.

Yet despite opposition from the oligarchy, the state now concerns itself more than ever before with the development of economic and social service infrastructure in Indian communities.[17] Not only has it built roads, schools, and clinics throughout the rural areas, but it has increased aid to a wide variety of development projects; it has also firmly established a bilingual educational program in Indian areas—not with the aim of maintaining Indian culture, but with the aim of drawing more Indians into school and through that into state institutions and into an integrated "nationalist" project. In addition to augmenting its own development projects, the Cerezo government has strenuously sought to bring foreign development projects into Indian communities, which aim to increase the economic self-sufficiency of Indian communities (Annis 1988; AVANCSO 1989). Finally, the current regime directs much more attention than previous regimes to political organization and electoral politics in Indian communities, with the objective of involving more Indians in national-level politics. The point of all these efforts is to end, once and for all, the resistance of Indian communities to Guatemalan state policy—that is, to integrate Indians, economically and politically, into a single Guatemalan nation.

A New Historical Epoch?

Scholars concerned with development in the Third World are in broad agreement about the critical role of the state in fashioning a path to economic growth (e.g., Burawoy 1985) and the centrality of economic

development to Third World nationalist ideology (e.g., A. Smith 1986).
Until recently, however, most analysts plausibly argued that the state
and military apparatuses in Third World states were essentially instruments of local and external capitalist classes, who preferred a relatively
"weak" state, one that was cheap to operate and that gave business
interests maximum room for economic maneuver. "The colonial state
was indeed an interventionist, although not necessarily a strong, state
whose 'function' was to establish the supremacy of the capitalist mode
of production" (Burawoy 1985:214). As capitalist growth in the early
postwar period increased the poverty of the masses and fueled nationalist sentiments among the middle sectors, Third World states frequently
found it necessary to maintain what was still a traditional social order
by force of arms. Hence the development of strong militaries in much
of the Third World. Most scholars consider the rise of strongly repressive
state apparatuses to be a symptom of the continuing weakness of Third
World states—with respect to creating a national consensus and an
integrated national development project (see, e.g., A. Smith 1986; Migdal
1988).

Until recently, Guatemala certainly represented such a case.
Guatemala's military was assisted to power in 1954 by large national and
international capitalists in order to end a period of major social reform
that had begun to threaten their interests (cf. Immerman 1982). Those
who came to power merely attempted to maintain the existing social
order through repressive means without challenging the goals or the
methods favored by the oligarchy. They certainly had no ambitions
about restructuring civil society in Guatemala. Today, however,
Guatemala's military appears to have much broader goals, goals that
could transform the nature of class, ethnic, and political struggle in
Guatemala. In seeking to curb the oligarchy, to diversify the economy,
and to create a wide national consensus (by actively seeking to assimilate Indians economically as well as culturally, for example), the Guatemalan military is also attempting to create a "strong" state (see chap. 1),
one whose instruments of control are not only vastly expanded but are
also operative at the local level—that is, *within* the Indian communities
of the western highlands (C. Smith n.d.).

What gives the military state greater potential to penetrate Indian
communities than other forms of the Guatemalan state is the fact that
the military knows them better than any other state-level institution.
The lower level of the military command structure is made up of Indians
who know the local languages; military intelligence is concerned with
local (indigenous) issues and has many local Indians in its pay; in
addition, the military seems much more willing than any other state-
level institution to acknowledge its ties to the Guatemalan *pueblo*

including the *pueblos de indios*. In terms of personnel as well as ideology, the military encompasses all layers of Guatemalan society (Aguilera Peralta 1980)—one reason the military is more comfortably nationalistic than previous state regimes dominated by the white oligarchy. Under military leadership the possibility for the Guatemalan state to obliterate traditional divisions of civil society, realigning them along new lines, is greater than in any time in history. Should the military's nationalist vision prevail, Guatemala's state will be stronger than ever before, its strength residing not simply in force and the skillful exercise of terror, but in knowledge of how to exercise power and use terror at all levels of society, even within Indian communities.

Such a development would be one logical way to resolve the major political contradictions in Guatemala, the response of Guatemala's army to the failure of other state forms to develop Guatemala's economy, control general social unrest, and "capture" what has until now remained relatively autonomous Indian communities. Should the army succeed, it would certainly be a new historic pattern for Guatemala.

But to develop in this direction, the Guatemalan state would not only have to eradicate its main historical enemy, the politically autonomous Indian community. It would also have to suppress a historically new form of resistance that is being generated today throughout the Third World—the antistate discourse that erupted in the late 1980s. This new political discourse, which scholars have yet to treat in any detail (see Laclau and Mouffe 1982), rejects top-down development strategies led by strong centralized states (whether socialist, as in Eastern Europe and China; or capitalist, as in Korea and Mexico) and asserts a different political agenda stressing democracy, local autonomy, multiculturalism, and individual human rights. One effect of this antistate discourse is that people throughout Latin America increasingly reject armed struggle and the standard socialist agenda as the path to social transformation (see Winn 1989). Supporters of this new political and ideological position presently exist in Guatemala, though they appear to be weakly organized in contrast to the supporters of the "strong" military state.[18]

On the other hand, every attempt previously made by the Guatemalan state to resolve the existing political contradictions (usually by coercive means) has always generated new contradictions as well as new forms of Indian resistance. Rarely, in fact, has it even eradicated traditional forms of Indian protest, a most striking example of which occurred in the municipio of Cantel during the height of military oppression.[19] In 1983 military officers from a nearby base tried to organize "voluntary" civil patrols in Cantel (formed virtually everywhere else at this time) by calling all adult men to a meeting in the town center. As the army officers began describing the task, the men of Cantel turned their backs and started whistling. (A local source, who noted that this was the period when almost anyone in Guatemala would be killed by the military on the slightest provocation, suggested that the Cantel reaction was entirely spontaneous.) After this went on for some minutes, the military men left. The army made a second attempt to organize the patrols one week later and met the same local response. Some weeks later, according to Cantel sources, men from the secret G-2 (the military intelligence group) came to Cantel at night and dragged out about twenty men from the town known to be local leaders of some sort. These people were never seen again. Ultimately, however, civil patrols were never organized in Cantel.

This chilling example of Indian defiance of state authority resembles in some respects the 1820 Totonicapán rebellion, whose leaders were shot or jailed but whose followers never again paid tribute. But at this point in history the possibilities given by passive resistance are greatly reduced. As the power of Guatemala's state penetrates down to the community level, often dividing groups within the community against each other, it is much less possible for Indian communities to struggle as communities against the state. If Indian culture is to survive the present attempts by the state to eradicate it, it will have to survive in a different form.

There are clear signs that the tragic events of the early 1980s have created conditions that may allow this to happen. One notable effect of the recent violence is that many fewer ladinos now live in the western highlands; local Indians now fill their vacated positions of power, both political and economic.[20] One might expect that the formation of an Indian elite would destroy the unity and autonomy of the traditional Indian community. But the history of Indian communities shown in the preceding chapters indicates that vast transformations can occur within and around Indian communities without destroying their unity vis-à-vis the Guatemalan state (see, in particular, chaps. 9, 10). So far it seems that community sentiment not only remains strong, but that this sentiment exercises a powerful restraint on the newly wealthy or professional Indians, few of whom feel any loyalty to the state.[21] Certainly that very element that allowed the Guatemalan state to penetrate down to the community level (i.e., a vastly expanded military apparatus, which visited untold brutality on Indian communities) has also vastly increased Indian distrust of the state.

Another significant effect of the violence is a certain receptivity to the new "democratic, multicultural" political currents of the late 1980s among Guatemalan Indians. A small group of Indian intellectuals, who maintain contact with the Indian base (still located within local communities), are attempting to forge broader networks and associations of

Indians within and across language areas in Guatemala and are tentatively reaching out to other Indian associations in the hemisphere. A glimpse into the aspirations of such groups can be found in a recent statement on the politics of development by COCADI (1989), one of several Indian development-cultural institutes that have cropped up in the highlands over the past five years. Clearly separate in aims from the remaining elements of the armed struggle, these groups neither are recognized by nor seek recognition by the state. One of their goals is to achieve local development on local terms with local leadership, retaining autonomy from the state by dealing directly with nongovernmental development agencies. But the primary goal appears to be the creation of a new and stronger *general* Mayan identity, one that maintains the values of the past while dealing with development issues in the present—a goal they recognize to be highly charged in political terms (see Cojtí Cuxil 1989). Other more directly political Indian groups are forming, such as the associations of Indian Christian Democrat mayors in Huehuetenango and El Quiché, who are attempting to develop an Indian political agenda in the electoral arena.

One can see in these new political developments, on the part of both the state and various Indian groups, certain major shifts together with a certain continuity in the basic struggle between Indians and the state. The state is attempting once again to eradicate Indian cultural identity by attempting to draw Indians into the larger Guatemalan nation. But now the state is trying to do so by establishing its presence and programs *within* Indian communities and by using means that are economic as well as coercive. And Indian leaders are once again attempting to maintain Indian identity and local autonomy within a multicultural nation. But this time Indian leaders are attempting to develop a unified political and economic agenda for Indians—as well as forge a new pan-Indian identity. Whatever the outcome of these new developments, it appears that Guatemala may be entering a new historical epoch.

Conclusions

The first conclusion we reach by looking at the historical pattern of political struggle in Guatemala is that there have been two main groups of actors: the rural populace, mostly Indian, who have lacked political representation in the state from the conquest to the present; and a small white elite, who controlled the state for all but a brief pause in Guatemalan history. Because of the oppositional way in which these groups have defined themselves (in terms of race and culture as well as class), the issues of contention have included not only those of political and economic justice, but those of individual and group identity. The struggles between Indians and the state have generated various other divisions in Guatemala: that between Indians and ladinos, that between different Indian communities, and that between different economic sectors and regions in the country. While these secondary divisions have generated a good deal of conflict on their own, they have rarely done so without bringing into play the primary contradiction in Guatemala, that between Indians and the state.

There are two anomalous cases in this regard, real but unrealized attempts at social transformation in which Indians failed to play a leading role: the 1944–1954 reform period and the 1960s insurgent movement in eastern Guatemala. Identifying these movements as historically anomalous helps to explain why both efforts failed to institutionalize change in Guatemala. Both were movements brought on by economic forces and ideological currents based outside of Guatemala proper. And both failed to provide new solutions to the central political issue in Guatemala, the place of Indians within what was to be a new social order. By assuming that the only solution to the "Indian" problem in Guatemala was assimilation, a solution strongly rejected by Indians themselves, these movements were unable to find the mass support needed to obtain their objectives.

The occurrence and failure of these non-Indian social movements, together with the failure of the 1980s revolutionary attempt, allow us to reach a second conclusion: that the new worldwide discourse about social justice and "revolution" that came out of the earthshaking events of 1917 reached Guatemala as it reached most of the world in the twentieth century, but did not meet the social conditions that would allow a radical transformation of Guatemalan society. Essentially, the promise of justice provided by a world ideology, which had no concept or strategy for multicultural states, came up short against a particular local history. Guatemala's social circumstances were such that radical social movements led by splinter groups from the white ruling class were doomed to failure as long as they did not draw upon the Indian majority of Guatemala. The successive failures at popular mobilization in the twentieth century, however, played a major role in transforming the revolutionary strategy of the 1980s—which *did* attempt to mobilize Indians and which *did* develop a new analysis of the Indian question, if only belatedly. Had this transformed strategy been fully realized in the most recent revolutionary attempt (i.e., had the cultural and political autonomy of an Indian nation become a central revolutionary goal), it would have increased the chances of a successful revolution in Guatemala; and had a revolutionary society been constructed whose agenda was the creation of a multicultural socialism, it would have affected the world-historical meaning of revolution as well.

The third conclusion we reach by looking at the pattern of political struggles in Guatemala, is that the state has historically been the main adversary of Indian communities. Coercive rather than economic or ideological mechanisms, together with certain traditions established in the colonial period, have been the primary means by which the Indian population has been controlled. This is not to say that a powerful landed oligarchy has been absent in Guatemala, nor to deny that the state was frequently a tool of the oligarchy. The point here is that the economic power of the oligarchy was insufficient to control Indian labor without use of the coercive mechanisms exercised by a state apparatus. We cannot conclude from this that Indians would consider any exercise of state power illegitimate—they did recognize a proper realm for the colonial state and indeed held a certain reverence for the Crown and, in the postcolonial period, the personage of the president. But the boundary for the proper exercise of state power, established by a long colonial tradition, was the boundary of the corporate Indian community. That boundary was partially breached by the state with the creation of a plantation economy, but only by the careful and, McCreery asserts, "subtle" use of coercive power. Various forms of economic coercion then moved into the breach, marking an important turning point in the nature, if not the institutions and traditions, of the Indian community (Carmack, chap. 6). Though the community and tradition survived, the community was much less corporate than before.

Yet it is important to recognize that state coercion was still needed to deliver a labor force to the plantation oligarchy as late as 1945, meaning on the one hand that the Indian labor force remained incompletely proletarianized, and on the other hand that agrarian capitalism was not fully realized after more than a century of attempts by the Creole elite to create it. The coffee oligarchy used the state to deliver what it needed (mainly labor), but it also required the state as its instrument of control.

What the state created by its changing but continuous use of coercion against them were the strongest institutions of civil society in Guatemala: the corporate Indian communities. Thus, our fourth conclusion is that corporate Indian communities formed not in response to economic exploitation per se, but in response to state attempts to eliminate local political autonomy. We cannot pinpoint the precise historical moment in which corporate Indian communities were formed, because different events played critical roles in different places. Nor can we argue that from a certain point forward (say, the late colonial period or the early plantation period), corporate Indian communities formed that continue to exist today. The corporate Indian community (together with a powerful socially formed sense of Indian identity) is not a historical survival, it is constantly formed and reformed political response to real existing conditions, mostly political but also cultural and ideological. Finally, we cannot argue that to remain corporate the Indian community had to remain closed to events and processes occurring outside of it. Guatemala may have the strongest corporate "peasant" communities in the world, but they have rarely, if ever, been closed.

A fifth conclusion is suggested by the recent militarization of Guatemala's state and, increasingly, of civil society, around the logic of permanent counterinsurgency. This step-up in coercive means of popular control reveals the essential weakness of civil institutions in Guatemala, apart from those of the corporate Indian communities. To use Gramsci's terms, "the State [is] everything, civil society [remains] primordial and gelatinous" in Guatemala, whereas in the West "the State is only an outer ditch, behind which there [is] a powerful system of [hegemonic] fortresses and earthworks."[22] We can attribute the under-developed state of civil society in Guatemala to the fact that its "national question" has never been solved—that a modern Guatemalan nation remains a hope rather than a reality. The persistence of Indian culture in the face of the most recent and brutal attack on it by the state (Manz 1988; Lovell 1988; Carmack 1988) suggests that resistance against the state exists even now, possibly in a stronger form than before. Thus, while the state itself has grown stronger, in the sense of achieving greater infrastructural and despotic powers over time, it remains decidedly weak with respect to ideological (hegemonic) control. Since such states are inherently more vulnerable to and more likely to generate popular resistance, the possibility for violent revolution remains high in Guatemala.

Our final conclusion is that the dialectic of violence that forced changes in Guatemala's now militarized state will force changes in the forms of Indian resistance. As state power penetrates to the local level, breaking the solidarity of traditional Indian communities, new forms of cultural resistance will have to be invented. One possible form would be the development of a pan-Indian identity that would unite Indians as a whole (rather than as separate communities) into a distinct multicultural nation within Guatemala, with its own political agenda.[23] A more likely form, given the historical pattern of Indian resistance, would be the further fragmentation of Indian cultural communities, over which the state would have little ability to maintain control and surveillance. Throughout history, Indian communities have maintained themselves through diversity, which has prevented them from forming a united Indian nation that could proclaim its own national sovereignty. But this "weakness" has also been the source of Indian cultural "strength," since no centralized power in Guatemala has ever found a single cultural source or symbol to destroy through which Indian culture *in general* would be eradicated. Whatever new forms of cultural struggle develop will, like past forms, determine Guatemala's political destiny. We can only hope that new political currents in the world will prevent another round of violent confrontation between the culturally renewed Indian communities and the militarily reinforced state.

Notes

1. Parts of this essay are based on two talks I have delivered a number of times: "History and Revolution in Guatemala" and "The National Question: A Revolutionary Debate in Guatemala." The number of people who made useful comments on them is too great to list here, but I would like to express my appreciation to them in general. In addition, I would like to thank Marcie Mersky, Rachel Garsky, Paula Warby, Howie Machtinger, Charlie Hale, and two anonymous reviewers for specific comments on this paper.

2. As Frederick Crews has recently noted, "If we ask which theory, since the time of the French Revolution, has proved most consequential for the reshaping of human existence, only one answer is conceivable: it is Marxism" (Crews 1985:449). Crews deals primarily with the intellectual impact of Marxism on Western thought. But the point is even more relevant with respect to revolutionary transformations in the Third World.

3. This quote is taken from Perry Anderson (1977), who cites the critical edition edited by Valentino Gerratana: Antonio Gramsci, *Quaderni del Carcere*, vol. 3. Turin: 1975, pp. 1614–1616.

4. Here I refer to the recent theories of revolution developed by Wolf (1969), Migdal (1974), Scott (1976), Paige (1975), Skocpol (1979), and Tutino (1986). Gerard Challiand (1978), in contrast, provides strong evidence that Third World revolutions have been inspired and shaped by the rhetoric of Lenin.

5. Raymond Williams (1983) makes the general case for this point in his book, *Keywords*, as does Michel Foucault (1980) in slightly different terms. While the point is well taken, neither influential thinker has suggested how one might then go about making historical comparisons. It seems evident that one must proceed along the lines indicated here.

6. I should note that Martínez Peláez believed his study to show that economic grievances were at the root of most colonial revolts. Yet it is clear from his own evidence, provided as an appendix to the article, that while many revolts concerned the tribute exacted by the Crown, they almost always involved what appeared to the Indian community to be an unjustified change in them, whether by the Crown or by a dishonest local official.

7. In particular, the successful Cuban Revolution changed U.S. policy with respect to Latin America, and under the Alliance for Progress an effort was made to create the military capacity to fight local rebellions such as that which developed in eastern Guatemala in the 1960s.

8. The best sources on this, apart from the documentation and discussion provided by Arias (chap. 11), include Burgos-Debray (1984), Frank and Wheaton (1984), Manz (1987), Davis (1988), and Stoll (1988).

9. My information on the Indian separatists once located within the EGP is based on personal interviews conducted in 1983 in Mexico City.

10. In 1987–1988 two new statements on the "ethnic-national question" surfaced from different groups within the armed struggle. One statement, entitled "La cuestión étnico-nacional en Guatemala," is reputedly by FAR (Rebel Armed Forces), who had made no previous declaration on the issue. The statement merely acknowledges the centrality of the "ethnic-national question" to the armed struggle in Guatemala, scolds other groups for taking a "culturalist" position (which aligns them with the dominant sectors in Guatemala), and reiterates the centrality of imperialism and class in the creation of Guatemala's ethnic-national problem. The statement does, however, make clear that FAR's revolutionary goals include the right to Indian self-determination—in the cultural arena. The second document, published as "Tesis sobre la cuestión étnico-nacional" in a Mexican journal *Opinion Politica* (no. 11, September 1987), is unsigned but reputedly a statement by a new faction of the EGP. In this statement, for the first time, an argument is made for the necessity of the revolutionary state to recognize the national (territorial) autonomy of Guatemala's Indians and their right to self-determination in the social, political, and economic, as well as cultural, arenas.

11. In April 1982, before the heaviest army sweeps undertaken during the Rios Montt regime, the Guatemalan Bishops Conference estimated that more than one million Guatemalans, or one-seventh of Guatemala's total population (mostly located in the western highlands where the Mayan Indian population is concentrated), were displaced (Krueger and Enge 1985). Nobody has been able to determine exactly what proportion of these people was killed as opposed to displaced within or outside of Guatemala, though most people recognize that the actual loss of life was very high—at least fifty thousand since the beginning of the counterinsurgency campaigns. The official Guatemalan censuses report a 22.9 percent loss of population between 1973 and 1981 in the three Ixil municipios of Nebaj, Chajul, and Cotzal (Richards 1985). Yet military sweeps and killing continued in these municipios well beyond 1981. For a fuller depiction of the first phase of counterinsurgency in Guatemala see Americas Watch (1982), Amnesty International (1981), Davis and Hodson (1982), *Cultural Survival Quarterly* (1983) and *Cultural Survival Report* (1983), and Manz (1988).

12. My estimate of the number of rural men drafted into the army is based on local accounts of the number of men annually drafted. It fits McClintock's (1985) assessment that the number of enlisted men in the Guatemalan army after 1980 varied from fifteen thousand to eighteen thousand. For further information on the organization and ideology of the military, see Sereseres (1985).

13. The fullest accounts of the organization of the civil patrol system in Guatemala can be found in Krueger and Enge (1985) Richards (1985), and McClintock (1985). Information on the origins and organization of the military commissioner system can be found in McClintock (1985).

14. The development-pole strategy currently seems to be on hold, possibly because other institutions (such as USAID) are carrying out programs much like those planned by the military (for further documentation on this, see C. Smith n.d.).

15. The thesis of the "permanent counterinsurgency state" in Guatemala is asserted by Anderson and Simon (1987), who argue for the continuation and strengthening of the pattern under Cerezo. They quote a zone commander in Cobán to that effect, who observed, "The same Army strategy that guided Rios Montt also guided, in his turn, Mejía Victores. . . . 'But don't think,' added the Cobán colonel, 'that Cerezo is any different. He is just a continuation of everything that's gone on before'" (p. 35).

16. The military put its cards on the table in a public meeting with the oligarchy in August 1987, arguing that Guatemala's elite owed both a social and a security debt to the "family of Guatemala" (Anderson and Simon 1987:10). They demanded both a tax reform and support for the Arias peace plan, indicating that they, rather than the oligarchy, would determine the nature of foreign policy in Guatemala (see AVANCSO 1989).

17. Among the more effective methods of drawing Indians into national Guatemalan politics is the policy of providing 8 percent of government revenues to municipios (the lowest level of state administration), in a way that favors the least developed and most politically marginal areas (i.e., the Indian highlands). This policy was not Cerezo's or that of his party, the Christian Democrats; redistribution of government revenue was made into law by the 1985 constitution, written when the military was still fully in control of state policy.

18. For evidence of this, one need only scan recent Guatemalan newspapers. More formal documentation can be found in the various publications of three Guatemalan research institutes, Inforpress, AVANCSO, and FLACSO.

19. While Cantel is a relatively traditional Indian community in some respects (Nash 1967), the presence in it of a large industrial textile factory that employs a considerable number of local Indians has made the town more experienced in organized (union) resistance and less vulnerable to economic reprisal by the military.

20. Many ladinos fled the highlands during the period of violence, but the most notable case is that of northern Huehuetenango, where ladinos controlled most important businesses as well as local political office. Today in municipios such as Soloma and San Miguel Acatán, where few ladinos now reside, Indians own most of the bus lines and wholesale and retail businesses, and are increasingly filling professional positions. The transformation in the public transportation system is notable everywhere. Whereas more than 50 percent of the bus lines were owned by ladinos in the early 1970s, more than 80 percent of a much expanded system is now owned by Indians.

21. Those Indians who have been most exposed to circumstances which in the past would have led them to desert their communities are today precisely those leading or organizing pro-Maya cultural and development organizations, such as those discussed below.

22. These quotes are again taken from P. Anderson (1977), from volume 2 of the *Quaderni del Carcere*, pp. 236–238 (see note 3).

23. Anna Blume pointed out to me that this particular outcome is most unlikely on the strength of the very arguments made in this book.

Bibliography

Actas de la Asamblea (Guatemala). 1839.

Adams, Richard N. 1956a. "Cultural Components of Central America." *American Anthropologist* 58:881–907.

———. 1956b. *Encuesta sobre la cultura de los ladinos de Guatemala.* Translated by Joaquín Noval. Seminario de Integración Social Guatemalteca, Publication no. 2. Guatemala: Editorial del Ministerio de Educación Pública.

———, ed. 1957. *Political Changes in Rural Guatemalan Communities: A Symposium.* Middle American Research Institute, Pub. 4. New Orleans: Tulane University.

———. 1960. "Explotación de la madera en el muncipio de Totonicapán." *Boletín del Instituto Indigenista Nacional* 2:7–31.

———. 1970. *Crucifixion by Power: Essays on Guatemalan National Social Structure, 1944–1966.* Austin: University of Texas Press.

Adams, Tani. n.d. "San Martín Jilotepeque: Aspects of the Political and Socioeconomic Structure of a Guatemalan Peasant Community." Unpublished manuscript.

AEG. Archivo Eclesiástico de Guatemala (also called Archivo de la Curia), Guatemala.

AGCA. Archivo General de Centroamérica, Guatemala. Documents cited by division (*asignatura*), bundle (*legajo*), document (*expediente*), and year.

AGCA MG. Archivo General de Centroamérica, Ministerio de Gobernación.

AGCA-ST. Archivo General de Centroamérica, Sección de Tierras.

AGI. Archivo General de Indias, Seville. Documents cited by division (*ramo*) and bundle (*legajo*).

Aguilera Peralta, Gabriel. 1980. "Terror and Violence as Weapons of Counterinsurgency in Guatemala." *Latin American Perspectives* 25:91–113.

Americas Watch. 1982. *Human Rights in Guatemala: No Neutrals Allowed.* New York: Americas Watch Committee.

Amnesty International. 1981. *Guatemala: A Government Program of Political Murder.* London: Amnesty International Publications.

Anderson, Benedict. 1980. *Imagined Communities: Reflections on the Origin and Spread of Nationalism.* London: New Left Books.

Anderson, Ken, and Jean-Marie Simon. 1987. "Permanent Counterinsurgency in Guatemala." *Telos* 73:9–46.

Anderson, Perry. 1977. "The Antinomies of Antonio Gramsci." *New Left Review* 100:3–77.

Annis, Sheldon. 1987. *God and Production in a Guatemalan Town.* Austin: University of Texas Press.

———. 1988. "Can the World Bank Be a Grassroots Funder in Rural Guatemala?" Unpublished manuscript.

Arbenz Guzmán, Jacobo. 1953. *Informe al congreso . . . 1953.* Guatemala City: Tipografía Nacional.

Arévalo, Juan José. 1948. *Discursos en la presidencia, 1945–1948.* Guatemala City: Tipografía Nacional.

Arias, Arturo. 1984. "El movimiento indígena en Guatemala, 1970–1982." In *Movimientos populares en América Central 1970–1982,* compiled by Rafael Menjivar. San José: EDUCA.

Arriola, Jorge Luis. 1961. *Gálvez en la encrucijada: Ensayo crítico en torno al humanismo político de un gobernante.* México: Costa-Amic.

Asamblea Constituyente. 1839a. *Dictamen de la comisión de negocios eclesiásticos de la Asamblea Constituyente, sobre el reestablecimiento de las Ordenes Regulares.* Guatemala: Imprenta del Gobierno.

———. 1839b. "Dictamen á la comisión de organización provisional sobre establecer un régimen de protección y fomento en favor de los indios." *El Tiempo* 1(21) August 2, 1839:81. The decree of August 16 is in no. 27, August 30, 1839:106–107.

AVANCSO (Asociación para al Avance de las Ciencias Sociales en Guatemala). 1988. *La politica de desarrollo del estado Guatemalteco, 1986–1987.* Cuaderno 2. Guatemala: Inforpress Centroamericana.

———. 1989. *Politica exterior y estabilidad estatal.* Cuaderno 5. Guatemala: Inforpress Centroamericana.

Baloyra, Enrique A. 1983. "Reactionary Despotism in Central America." *Journal of Latin American Studies* 15:295–319.

Barth, Frederick, ed. 1969. *Ethnic Groups and Boundaries: The Social Organization of Cultural Difference.* Boston: Little, Brown.

Batres Jáuregui, Antonio. 1894. *Los indios: Su historia y su civilización.* Guatemala: Tipografía La Unión.

Beals, Ralph. 1967. "Acculturation." In *Social Anthropology,* edited by Manning Nash. Vol. 6 *Handbook of Middle American Indians.* Austin: University of Texas Press, 449–468.

Beltranena Sinibaldi, Luis. 1971. *Fundación de la república de Guatemala.* Guatemala: Tipografía Nacional, Ediciones del Sesquicentenario de la Independencia.

Black, George. 1984. *Garrison Guatemala.* New York: Monthly Review Press.

Bloch, Maurice. 1983. *Marxism and Anthropology: The History of a Relationship.* Oxford: Oxford University Press.

Boletín del Archivo General del Gobierno. 1937. "Año de 1763 Autos formados sobre la Real Cédula para que esta Real Audiencia con la brevedad y recerva [*sic*] posible, remita una relación individual de los Correimientos y Alcadias Mayores de este Reyno." *Boletín del Archivo General del Gobierno.*

Guatemala.

Borah, Woodrow. 1983. *Justice by Insurance: The General Indian Court of Colonial Mexico and the Legal Aides of the Half-Real*. Berkeley: University of California Press.

Bossen, Laurel Herbenar. 1984. *The Redivision of Labor: Women and Economic Choice in Four Guatemalan Communities*. Albany: State University New York Press.

Braiterman, Jared I. 1986. "A Conflict between Modernity and Peasant Society in 1830's Guatemala: The Galvez Reforms and the Carrera Uprising." Honors' thesis, Harvard College.

Brigham, William T. 1887 (1965). *Guatemala: The Land of the Quetzal*. Gainesville: University of Florida Press.

Brintnall, Douglas E. 1979a. "Race Relations in the Southeastern Highlands of Mesoamerica." *American Ethnologist* 6:638–652.

———. 1979b. *Revolt against the Dead: The Modernization of a Mayan Community in the Highlands of Guatemala*. New York: Gordon and Breach.

Browning, David. 1971. *El Salvador: Landscape and Society*. Oxford: Clarendon Press.

Bunzel, Ruth Leah. 1952. *Chichicastenango: A Guatemalan Village*. American Ethnological Publication 22. Locust Valley, N.Y.: J. J. Augustin.

Burawoy, Michael. 1985. *The Politics of Production*. London: New Left Books.

Burgos-Debray, Elisabeth, ed. 1984. *I . . . Rigoberta Menchú: An Indian Woman in Guatemala*. New York: Monthly Review Press.

Burns, E. Bradford. 1980. *The Poverty of Progress: Latin America in the Nineteenth Century*. Berkeley: University of California Press.

———. 1986. *Eadweard Muybridge in Guatemala, 1875: The Photographer as Social Recorder*. Berkeley: University of California Press.

Cabarrús, Carlos Rafael. 1979. *La cosmovisión k'ekchi' en proceso de cambio*. San Salvador: UCA Editores.

Calder, Bruce J. 1970. *Crecimiento y cambio de la iglesia católica Guatemalteca, 1944–1966*. Estudios Centroamericanos del Seminario de Integración Social Guatemalteca, no. 6. Guatemala: José de Pineda Ibarra.

Calhoun, Craig Jackson. 1982. *The Question of Class Struggle*. Chicago: University of Chicago Press.

Cámara, Fernando. 1952. "Religious and Political Organization." In *Heritage of Conquest*, edited by Sol Tax. Glencoe, Ill.: Free Press, 142–164.

Cambranes, Julio C. 1985. *Coffee and Peasants in Guatemala*. Stockholm: Institute for Latin American Studies.

Cancian, Frank. 1967. "Political and religious organizations." In *Social Anthropology*, edited by Manning Nash. Vol. 6 of *Handbook of Middle American Indians*. Austin: University of Texas Press.

Cardoso, Ciro F. S. 1975. "Historia económica del café en Centroamérica." *Estudios Sociales Centroamericanos* 10:3–57. Cardoso, Ciro F. S., and Héctor Pérez Brignoli. 1977. *Centro América y la economía occidental (1520–1930)*. San José: Editorial Universitaria de Costa Rica.

Cardoso, F. H. 1977. "The Consumption of Dependency Theory in the United

States." *Latin American Research Review* 12:7–24.

Carmack, Robert M. 1972. "Barrios y los indígenas: el caso de Santiago Momostenango." *Estudios Sociales* 6:52–73.

———. 1973. *Quichean Civilization: The Ethnographic, Ethnohistoric, and Archaeological Sources.* Berkeley: University of California Press.

———. 1979. *Historia social de los Quichés.* Seminario de Integración Social Guatemalteca, no. 38. Guatemala: Editorial José de Pineda Ibarra.

———. 1981. *The Quiché Mayas of Utatlán: The Evolution of a Highland Guatemalan Kingdom.* Norman: University of Oklahoma Press.

———. 1983. "Spanish-Indian Relations in Highland Guatemala, 1800–1944." In *Spaniards and Indians in Southeastern Mesoamerica,* edited by M. MacLeod and R. Wasserstrom. Lincoln: University of Nebraska Press, 215–252.

———. n.d.a. "Aproximación a una historia de los indígenas de Guatemala en el siglo XIX." In *Historia general de Guatemala,* edited by Jorge Luján Muñoz. Forthcoming.

———. n.d.b. "Peasant Rebels of Tecpanaco: The Political Ethnohistory of a Guatemalan Indian Community." Manuscript in preparation.

———, ed. 1988. *Harvest of Violence: The Mayan Indians and the Guatemalan Crisis.* Norman: University of Oklahoma Press.

Carmack, Robert M., John D. Early, and Christopher H. Lutz, eds. 1982. *The Historical Demography of Highland Guatemala.* Institute for Mesoamerican Studies, Publication No. 6. Albany: State University of New York.

Carnoy, Martin. 1984. *The State and Political Theory.* Princeton: Princeton University Press.

Carrera, Rafael. 1839a. "Felicitación del General de Brigada Rafael Carrera a la Asamblea Constituyente del Estado," Archivo General de Centro América, B, leg. 1411, exp. 32977; also in *El Tiempo* 1(11) June 14, 1839:41. This message was read to the assembly on June 13. *Actas de la Asamblea* 1(5) October 19, 1839:23.

———. 1839b. "Rafael Carrera, General de Brigada de las armas del Estado, a los pueblos que componen." *El Tiempo* 1(16) July 18, 1839:62.

Castellanos Cambranes, Julio. 1985. *Café y campesinos en Guatemala, 1853–1897.* Guatemala: Editorial Universitaria.

CENSA. 1983. *Listen, Compañero: Conversations with Central American Revolutionary Leaders.* San Francisco: Center for the Study of the Americas and Solidarity Publications.

Ceto, Pablo. 1983. Interview by Arturo Arias. Unpublished.

Ceto, Pablo, Antonio Calel, and Magdalena Tipaz. 1982. "CUC: Los hombres de maiz escriben su historia." *Boletín Internacional* (FP-13, Mexico) 5:17.

Challiand, Gerard. 1978. *Revolution in the Third World.* New York: Penguin.

Chamix, Pedro. 1982. "La importancia revolucionaria de conocer los movimientos indígenas." *Polémica* 3:47–57.

Chandler, David. 1988. *Juan José de Aycinena, idealista conservador de la Guatemala del siglo XIX.* Guatemala: Centro de Investigaciones Regionales de Mesoamérica.

———. 1989. "Peace through Disunion: Father Juan José Aycinena and the Fall of the Central American Federation. *The Americas* (October 1989).

Clegern, Wayne M. 1979. "Transition from Conservatism to Liberalism in Guatemala, 1865–1871." In *Hispanic-American Essays in Honor of Max Leon Moorhead*, edited by W. Coker. Pensacola, Fla.: Perdido Bay Press.

COCADI (Coordinadora Cakchiquel de Desarrollo Integral). 1989. *Cultural maya y políticas de desarrollo*. Chimaltenango, Guatemala: Ediciones COCADI.

Cojtí Cuxil, Demetrio. 1989. "Problemas de 'la identidad nacional' guatemalteca." In *Cultural maya y políticas de desarrollo*, edited by COCADI. Chimaltenango, Guatemala: Ediciones COCADI, 139–162.

Colby, Benjamin N., and Pierre L. van den Berghe. 1969. *Ixil Country: A Plural Society in Highland Guatemala*. Berkeley: University of California Press.

Collins, Anne C. 1980. "Colonial Jacaltenango, Guatemala: The Formation of a Corporate Community." PhD diss., Tulane University.

Contreras R., J. Daniel. 1951. *Una rebelión indígena en el partido de Totonicapán en 1820: el indio y la independencia*. Guatemala: Imprenta Universitaria.

Cook, Sherburne F., and Woodrow Borah. 1971–1979. *Essays in Population History*. 3 vols. Berkeley: University of California Press.

Cortes y Larraz, Pedro. 1958. *Descripción geográfico-moral de la diócesis de Goathemala*. Guatemala: Sociedad de Geografía e Historia.

Crews, Frederick. 1985. "Dialectical Immaterialism." *American Scholar* 54:449–465.

Crosby, Alfred W., Jr. 1972. *The Columbian Exchange: Biological and Cultural Consequences of 1492*. Contributions in American Studies, no. 2. Westport, Conn.: Greenwood Press.

Cuicuilco. 1980. "Los pueblos indígenas de Guatemala ante el mundo." Mexico, *Cuicuilco* 1:5, July 1980.

Cultural Survival Quarterly. 1983. *Death and Disorder in Guatemala*. Cambridge, Mass.: Cultural Survival, Inc.

Cultural Survival Report. 1983. *Voices of the Survivors*. Report no. 10. Cambridge, Mass.: Cultural Survival, Inc.

Davis, Shelton H. 1970. "Land of Our Ancestors: A study of Land Tenure and Inheritance in the Highlands of Guatemala." PhD diss., Harvard University.

———. 1988. "Introduction: Sowing the Seeds of Violence." In *Harvest of Violence: The Mayan Indians and the Guatemalan Crisis*, edited by Robert M. Carmack. Norman: University of Oklahoma Press, 3–38.

Davis, Shelton, and Julie Hodson. 1982. *Witness to Political Violence in Guatemala: The Suppression of a Rural Development Movement*. Boston: Oxfam America, Impact Audit no. 2.

de Janvry, Alain. 1982. *The Agrarian Question and Reformism in Latin America*. Baltimore: Johns Hopkins University Press.

Demarest, William J., and Benjamin D. Paul. 1981. "Mayan Migrants in Guatemala City." *Anthropology UCLA* 11:43–73.

de Solano, Francisco. 1977. *Tierra y sociedad en el reino de Guatemala*. Guatemala: Editorial Universitaria.

de Vos, Jan. 1980. *La paz de Dios y del rey*. Mexico: Editorial y Litografía Regina de Los Angeles.
DGE (Dirección General de Estadística, Guatemala). 1951. *Mensaje Quincenal* 28 (December 1951).
———. 1952. *Mensaje Quincenal* 30 (February 1952).
———. 1954. *Censo agropecuario de 1950*, tomo I–III. Guatemala: Ministerio de Economía.
———. 1957. *VI Censo de población, 1950*. Guatemala: Ministerio de Economía.
———. 1968. *II censo agropecuario de 1964*, tomo I. Guatemala: Ministerio de Economía.
———. 1982. *III censo nacional agropecuario 1979*, vol. 1, tomo I. Guatemala: Ministerio de Economía.
———. 1983. *III censo nacional agropecuario 1979*, vol. 2, tomo I. Guatemala: Ministerio de Economía.
Diario de centroamérica. 1947, 1951.
Diario de sesiones: Asamblea constituyente de 1945. 1951. Guatemala.
Dios Rosales, Juan de. 1949. "Notes on San Pedro la Laguna." Microfilm Collections of Manuscripts on Middle American Cultural Anthropology (MACA), University of Chicago, 25.
———. 1950. "Notes on Santiago Chimaltenango." Microfilm Collections of Manuscripts on Middle American Cultural Anthropology (MACA), University of Chicago, 30.
Dunkerley, James. 1988. *Power in the Isthmus: A Political History of Modern Central America*. New York: Verso.
Dunlop, Robert G. 1847. *Travels in Central America*. London: Longman, Brown, Green and Longman.
Early, John D. 1975. "Changing Proportion of Maya Indians and Ladino in Guatemala, 1945–1969." *American Ethnologist* 2:261–269.
———. 1982. *The Structure and Evolution of a Peasant System: The Guatemalan Case*. Gainesville: University of Florida Press.
Ebel, Roland H. 1969. *Political Modernization in Three Guatemalan Indian Communities*. Middle American Research Institute, publication 24. New Orleans: Tulane University.
EGP (Ejército Guerrillero de los Pobres). 1982. "The Indian Peoples and the Guatemalan Revolution." *Compañero* 5:17–26.
Ejército de Guatemala (Guatemalan Army). 1984. *Polos de desarrollo*. Guatemala: Editorial de Ejército.
Evans, Peter, Dietrich Rueschemeyer, and Theda Skocpol, eds. 1985. *Bringing the State Back In*. London: Cambridge University Press.
Falla, Ricardo. 1971. "Actitud de los indígenas de Guatemala en le época de la independencia 1800–1850." *Estudios Centroamericanos* 278:701–718.
———. 1978a. *Quiché rebelde: Estudio de un movimiento de conversión religiosa, rebelde a las creencias tradicionales en San Antonio Ilotenango*. Colección "Realidad Nuestra," vol. 7. Guatemala: Editorial Universitaria de Guatemala.
———. 1978b. "El movimiento indígena." *ECA* 353:438–461.

Farriss, Nancy M. 1978. "Nucleation versus Dispersal: The Dynamics of Population Movement in Colonial Yucatán." *Hispanic American Historical Review* 58:187–216.

———. 1983. "Indians in Colonial Yucatan: Three Perspectives." In *Spaniards and Indians in Southeastern Mesoamerica: Essays on the History of Ethnic Relations*, edited by Murdo J. MacLeod and Robert Wasserstrom. Lincoln: University of Nebraska Press.

———. 1984. *Maya Society under Colonial Rule: The Collective Enterprise of Survival*. Princeton, N.J.: Princeton University Press.

Feldman, Lawrence H. 1985. *A Tumpline Economy: Production and Distribution Systems in Sixteenth Century Eastern Guatemala*. Culver City, Calif.: Labyrinthos.

Fiehrer, Thomas M. 1977. "The Baron de Carondelet as an Agent of Bourbon Reform: A Study of Spanish Colonial Administration in the Years of the French Revolution." PhD diss., Tulane University, New Orleans.

Flemion, Philip. 1973. "States' Rights and Partisan Politics: Manuel José Arce and the Struggle for Central American Union." *Hispanic American Historical Review* 53:600–618.

Flores Alvarado, Humberto. 1971. *La proletarizacion del campesino de Guatemala*. Quezaltenango, Guatemala: Editorial Rumbos Nuevos.

Foster, George M. 1960. *Culture and Conquest: America's Spanish Heritage*. Viking Fund Publications in Anthropology, no. 27. New York: Wenner Gren Foundation for Anthropological Research.

———. 1965. "Peasant Society and the Image of Limited Good." *American Anthropologist* 67(2):293–315.

Foucault, Michel. 1980. *Power/Knowledge: Selected Interviews and Other Writings, 1972–1977*. Translated by Colin Gordon. New York: Pantheon Books.

Fowler, William R., Jr. 1987. "Cacao, Indigo and Coffee: Cash Crops in the History of El Salvador." *Research in Economic Anthropology* 8:139–167.

Fox, Richard, ed. n.d. *Nationalist Ideologies and the Production of National Cultures*. New York: Cambridge University Press. Forthcoming (1990).

Frank, Luisa, and Philip Wheaton. 1984. *Indian Guatemala: The Path to Liberation*. Washington, D.C.: EPICA Taskforce.

Freire, Paulo. 1970. *Pedagogy of the Oppressed*. New York: Seabury Press.

Fry, Nathaniel G. 1980. "Liberal Land Reform in Guatemala and Peasant Reaction in the Montaña, 1821–1838." MA thesis, Tulane University.

Fuentes, Carlos. 1985. *Latin America: At War with the Past*. Toronto: CBC Enterprises.

Fuentes y Guzmán, Francisco A. 1969–1972. *Obras históricas de don Francisco Antonio de Fuentes y Guzmán, Recordación florida* [1690]. Madrid: Ediciones Atlas.

G/NIB (Guatemala/News in Brief). 1988. Developments between May 11 and July 1988. New York: Americas Watch Committee.

Gaceta de Guatemala. 1847–1871. Guatemala.

Gaceta extraordinaria. August 14, 1841. Guatemala.

Gaceta oficial. 1842–1846. Guatemala.

Gall, Francis. 1980. *Diccionario geográfico de Guatemala*, tomo III. Guatemala: Instituto Geográfico Nacional.

Gallardo, Ricardo. 1958. *Las constituciones de la República Federal de Centro-América*. 2 vols. Madrid: Instituto de Estudios Políticos.

Garcia Laguardia, José Maria. 1971. *La génesis del constitucionalismo guatemalteco*. Guatemala: Editorial Universidad de Guatemala.

Garcia Ruiz, Jesús. n.d. "Lenguaje y cultura: elementos de reflexión." Unpublished paper.

Gasco, Janine. 1987. "Cacao and the Economic Integration of Indigenous Society in Colonial Soconusco, New Spain." PhD diss., University of California, Santa Barbara.

Geertz, Clifford. 1973. *The Interpretation of Cultures: Selected Essays*. New York: Basic Books.

Gellner, Ernest. 1983. *Nations and Nationalism*. Oxford: Basil Blackwell.

Gibson, Charles. 1974. "Review of *Spanish Central America: A Socioeconomic History, 1520–1720*, by Murdo J. MacLeod. *Hispanic American Historical Review* 54:505–507.

Gillin, John. 1945. "Parallel Cultures and the Inhibitions to Acculturation in a Guatemalan Town." *Social Forces* 24:1–14.

———. 1948. "Race Relations without Conflict, a Guatemalan Town." *American Journal of Sociology* 53:337–343.

———. 1958. *San Luis Jilotepeque*. Seminario de Integración Social Guatemalteca, no. 7. Guatemala: Editorial del Ministerio de Educación Pública.

Girón Cerna, Carlos. 1946. "La nueva paz del indio." *Universidad de San Carlos* 4:60–111.

Glassie, Henry. 1982. *Passing the Time in Ballymenone: Culture and History of an Ulster Community*. Philadelphia: University of Pennsylvania Press.

Gleijeses, Piero. n.d. *The 1944–1954 Guatemalan Revolution* (working title). Princeton: Princeton University Press. Forthcoming.

Godelier, Maurice. 1978. "The Concept of the 'Asiatic Mode of Production' and Marxist Models of Social Evolution." In *Relations of Production*, edited by D. Seddon, 209–257. London: Frank Cass.

Gonzáles Casanova, P. 1965. "Internal Colonialism and National Development." *Studies in Comparative International Development* 1:27–37.

Gott, Richard. 1972. *Guerrilla Movements in Latin America*. Garden City, N.Y.: Doubleday.

Gramsci, Antonio. 1971. *Selections from the Prison Notebooks*. New York: International Publishers.

———. 1975. *Quaderni de Cacere*. Vol. 3. Edited by Valentino Gerratana. Turin: n.p., 1614–1616.

Grieshaber, Edwin. 1979. "Hacienda-Indian Community Relations and Indian Acculturation." *Latin American Research Review* 14:119.

Guatemala Documents (Guat. Doc.). Washington, D.C.: Manuscript Division, Library of Congress. Documents listed by reel or box number.

Guatemalan Church in Exile. 1984. *Guatemala, a New Way of Life: The Development Poles*. Special ed. 4 (5):1–28.

Gurriarán, Xavier. n.d. "Sebastián Guzmán, principal de principales." Mimeo-

graph.
Guzmán Böckler, Carlos, and Jean-Louis Herbert. 1970. *Guatemala: una interpretación histórico-social*. Mexico City: Siglo Veintiuno.
Handy, Jim. 1984. *Gift of the Devil: A History of Guatemala*. Toronto: Between the Lines Press.
———. 1985. "Revolution and Reaction: National Policy and Rural Politics in Guatemala, 1944–1954." PhD diss., University of Toronto.
———. 1988. "The Most Precious Fruit of the Revolution: The Guatemalan Agrarian Reform, 1952–1954." *Hispanic American Historical Review* 68:675-705.
———. 1989. "'A Sea of Indians': Ethnic Conflict and the Guatemalan Revolution, 1944–1952." *The Americas: A Quarterly Review of Inter-American History* (October).
Hawkins, John. 1984. *Inverse Images: The Meaning of Culture, Ethnicity, and Family in Postcolonial Guatemala*. Albuquerque: University of New Mexico Press.
Herrarte, Alberto. 1963. *La unión de Centroamérica (tragedia y esperanza)*. 2d ed. Guatemala: Ministerio de Educación Pública.
Hill, Robert M., II, and John Monaghan. 1987. *Continuities in Highland Maya Social Organization: Ethnohistory in Sacapulas, Guatemala*. Philadelphia: University of Pennsylvania Press.
Holleran, Mary P. 1949. *Church and State in Guatemala*. New York: Columbia University Press.
La Hora. 1944–1945. Guatemala.
Hunt, Eva, and June Nash. 1967. "Local and Territorial Units." In *Handbook of Middle American Indians*, vol. 6, edited by Manning Nash. Austin: University of Texas Press, 253-282.
Immerman, Richard H. 1982. *The CIA in Guatemala: The Foreign Policy of Intervention*. Austin: University of Texas Press.
El Imparcial. 1943–1945, 1947–1952. Guatemala.
Inforpress. 1987. *Guatemala 1986: The Year of Promises*. Guatemala City: Inforpress Centroamericana.
Ingersoll, Hazel. 1972. "The War of the Mountain: A Study of Reactionary Peasant Insurgency in Guatemala, 1837–1873." PhD diss., George Washington University.
Ixmata, Gabriel. n.d. "El pueblo de Guatemala: su vida, su cultura y su revolución." Mimeograph.
Ja C'Amabal I'b. 1984. "La primera gran confrontación: El movimiento campesino indígena del altiplano guatemalteca." Paper presented to the United Nations Subcommission on Ethnic Minorities, Geneva, August 1984.
———. 1986. "Algunos elementos de aproximación a la situación de la población india guatemalteca." Paper presented at the First Conference on Human Rights and Autonomy, Managua, July 1986.
Jonas, Susanne, and David Tobis, eds. 1974. *Guatemala*. New York: NACLA (North American Congress on Latin America).
Jones, Chester Lloyd. 1940. *Guatemala, Past and Present*. Minneapolis:

University of Minnesota Press.

Jones, Grant D. 1983. "The Last Maya Frontiers of Colonial Yucatán." In *Spaniards and Indians in Southeastern Mesoamerica: Essays on the History of Ethnic Relations*, edited by Murdo J. MacLeod and Robert Wasserstrom. Lincoln: University of Nebraska Press, 64-91.

Jones-Borg, Barbara E. 1986. "Ethnohistory of the Sacatepéquez Cakchiquel Maya." PhD diss., University of Missouri, Columbia.

Kincaid, A. Douglas. 1987. "Peasants into Rebels: Community and Class in Rural El Salvador." *Comparative Studies in Society and History* 29:466–494.

King, Arden R. 1974. *Coban and the Verapaz: History and Cultural Process in Northern Guatemala*. Middle American Research Institute, Publication 37. New Orleans: Tulane University.

Kitchen, James D. 1955. "Municipal Government in Guatemala." PhD diss., University of California, Los Angeles.

Kramer, Wendy J. 1990. "The Politics of Encomienda Distribution in Early Spanish Guatemala: 1524–1544." MP thesis, University of Warwick.

Krueger, Chris, and Kjell Enge. 1985. *Security and Development Conditions in the Guatemalan Highlands*. Washington, D.C.: WOLA (Washington Office on Latin America).

Laclau, Ernesto, and Chantal Mouffe. 1982. "Recasting Marxism: Hegemony and New Political Movements." *Socialist Review* 12:91–113.

LaFarge, Oliver. 1940. "Maya Ethnology: The Sequence of Cultures." In *The Maya and Their Neighbors*, edited by Clarence L. Hay et al. New York: D. Appleton Century, 282–291.

LaFarge, Oliver, and Douglas Byers. 1931. *The Year Bearer's People*. Middle American Research Institute, Publication no. 3. New Orleans: Tulane University.

El Liberador 1944–1945. Guatemala.

Lovell, W. George. 1983a. "Settlement Change in Spanish America: The Dynamics of *Congregación* in the Cuchumatán Highlands of Guatemala." *Canadian Geographer* 27:163–174.

———. 1983b. "Landholding in Spanish Central America." *Transactions of the Institute of British Geographers* 8:214–230.

———. 1985. *Conquest and Survival in Colonial Guatemala: A Historical Geography of the Cuchumatán Highlands, 1500–1821*. Kingston and Montreal: McGill-Queen's University Press.

———. 1988. "Surviving Conquest: The Maya of Guatemala in Historical Perspective." *Latin American Research Review* 23:25–57.

Lovell, W. George, Christopher H. Lutz, and William R. Swezey. 1984. "The Indian Population of Southern Guatemala, 1549–1551: An Analysis on López de Cerrato's *Tasaciones de Tributos*." *The Americas* 40:459–477.

Lovell, W. George, and William R. Swezey. 1982. "The Population of Southern Guatemala at Spanish Contact." *Canadian Journal of Anthropology* 3:71–84.

———. 1990. "Indian Migration and Community Formation: An Analysis of Congregación in Colonial Guatemala." In *Migration in Colonial Latin America*, edited by D. J. Robinson. Cambridge: Cambridge University Press.

Luján Muñoz, Jorge. 1976. "Fundación de villas de ladinos en Guatemala en el último tercio del siglo XVIII." *Revista de Indias* 36:51–81.

———. 1988. "Agricultura, mercado y sociedad en el Corregimiento del Valle de Guatemala, 1670–1680." *Cuadernos de Investigación*, no. 2. Dirección General de Investigaciones. Guatemala: Universidad de San Carlos.

Lutz, Christopher H. 1981. "Population Change in the Quinizilapa Valley, Guatemala, 1530–1770." In *Studies in Spanish American Population History*, edited by David J. Robinson. Dellplain Latin American Studies, no. 6. Boulder: Westview Press, 175–194.

———. 1982. *Historia sociodemográfica de Santiago de Guatemala, 1541–1773.* Serie Monográfica, no. 2. Antigua, Guatemala: CIRMA.

———. 1988. "Guatemala's Non-Spanish and Non-Indian Population: Its Spread and Demographic Evolution, 1700–1821." Unpublished manuscript.

———. n.d.a. "Introducción histórica a las memorias nahuatl de varios pueblos guatemaltecos." In *Memorias nahuatl de Guatemala del siglo XVI* (provisional title), edited by Karen Dakin and Christopher H. Lutz. Mexico: Instituto de Investigaciones Filologicas/UNAM. Forthcoming.

———. n.d.b. "Evolución demográfica de la población no indígena, 1524–1700." In *Historia General de Guatemala* II, edited by Jorge Luján Muñoz. Forthcoming.

———. n.d.c. "La población no española y no indígena: sus divisiones y evolución demográfica, 1700–1821." In *Historia General de Guatemala* III, edited by Jorge Luján Muñoz. Forthcoming.

Lyons, Grant. 1974. "Louisiana and the Livingston Criminal Codes." *Louisiana History* 15:243–272.

McClintock, Michael. 1985. *The American Connection: State Terror and Popular Resistance in Guatemala.* London: Zed Press.

McCreery, David. 1976. "Coffee and Class: The Structure of Development in Liberal Guatemala." *Hispanic American Historical Review* 56:438–460.

———. 1983a. "Debt Servitude in Rural Guatemala, 1876–1936." *Hispanic American Historical Review* 63:735–759.

———. 1983b. *Development and the State in Reforma Guatemala, 1871–1885.* Papers in International Studies, Athens: Ohio University Center for International Studies.

———. 1986. "'An Odious Feudalism': Mandamiento and Commercial Agriculture in Guatemala, 1858–1920." *Latin American Perspectives* 13:99–118.

———. 1988. "Land, Labor and Violence in Highland Guatemala: San Juan Ixcoy, Huehuetenango, 1893–1945." *The Americas* (October) 237–249.

McFarlane, Anthony. 1982. "Riot and Rebellion in Colonial Spanish America." *Latin American Research Review* 17:212–221.

MacLeod, Murdo J. 1970. "Las Casas, Guatemala, and the Sad but Inevitable Case of Antonio de Remesal." *Topic: A Journal of the Liberal Arts* 20:53–64.

———. 1973. *Spanish Central America: A Socioeconomic History, 1520–1720.* Berkeley: University of California Press.

———. 1983a. "Ethnic Relations and Indian Society in the Province of Guatemala, ca. 1620–ca. 1800." In *Spaniards and Indians in Southeastern Mesoamerica: Essays on the History of Ethnic Relations*, edited by Murdo

J. MacLeod and Robert Wasserstrom. Lincoln: University of Nebraska Press, 189–214.

———. 1983b. "Papel social y económico de las cofradías indígenas de la colonia en Chiapas." *Mesoamérica* 4(5):64–86.

———. 1985. "Los indígenas de Guatemala en los siglos xvi y xvii: tamaño de la población, recursos y organización de la mano de obra." In *Población y mano de obra en América Latina*, edited by Nicolas Sánchez-Albornoz. Madrid: Alianza Editorial.

MacLeod, Murdo J., and Robert Wasserstrom, eds. 1983. *Spaniards and Indians in Southeastern Guatemala: Essays on the History of Ethnic Relations.* Lincoln: University of Nebraska Press.

Madigan, Douglas. 1976. "Santiago Atitlán, a Socio-Economic and Demographic History." PhD diss., University of Pittsburgh.

Mallon, Florencia. 1983. *The Defense of Community in Peru's Central Highlands.* Princeton: Princeton University Press.

Mann, Michael. 1986. *The Sources of Social Power*, vol. 1. London: Cambridge University Press.

Manz, Beatriz. 1988. *Refugees of a Hidden War: The Aftermath of Counterinsurgency in Guatemala.* Albany: State University of New York Press.

Marcus, George E., and Michael M. J. Fischer. 1986. *Anthropology as Culture Critique.* Chicago: University of Chicago Press.

Markman, Sidney David. 1966. *Colonial Architecture of Antigua, Guatemala.* Philadelphia: American Philosophical Society.

Marroquin, A. 1972. "Panorama de indigenismo en Guatemala." *América Indígena* 32:291–317.

Martínez Peláez, Severo. 1971. *La patria del criollo: Ensayo de interpretación de la realidad colonial guatemalteca.* Guatemala City: Editorial Universitaria.

———. 1973. Los motines de Indios en el periodo colonial guatemalteco." *Estudios Sociales Guatemaltecos* 5:201–228.

Marure, Alejandro. 1895. *Efemérides de los hechos notables acaecidos en la República de Centro-América desde el año de 1821 hasta el de 1842.* 2d ed. Guatemala: El Progreso Nacional.

Marx, Karl. 1976a. *Capital.* Vol. 1, translated by Ben Fowkes and David Fernbach. London: Penguin and New Left Books.

———. 1976b. "Results of the Immediate Process of Production." In the appendix to *Capital*, vol. 1. New York: Viking Press.

Maudsley, Anne C. M. 1979 (reprint). *A Glimpse of Guatemala and Some Notes on Ancient Monuments of Central America.* New York: Blaine Ethridge.

Melville, Thomas, and Marjorie Melville. 1970. *Whose Heaven, Whose Earth?* New York: Knopf.

———. 1971. *Guatemala: The Politics of Land Ownership.* New York: Free Press.

Memoria del Ministerio de Fomento, 1924. 1924. Guatemala.

Memoria del Ministerio de Gobernación–1891. 1891. Guatemala.

Mendelson, E. Michael. 1967. "Ritual and Mythology." In *Social Anthropology*, edited by Manning Nash. Vol. 6 of *Handbook of Middle American*

Indians. Austin: University of Texas Press, 392–415.

Mendez Montenegro, J. C. 1960. "444 años de legislación agraria, 1520–1957." *Revista de la Facultad de Ciencias Juridicas y Sociales de Guatemala,* Epoca VI.

Menéndez, Isidro, comp. 1956. *Recopilación de las leyes del Salvador en Centro América.* 2 vols. 2d ed. San Salvador: Imprenta Nacional.

Meneray, Wilbur E. 1975. "The Kingdom of Guatemala during the Reign of Charles III, 1759–1788." PhD diss., University of North Carolina, Chapel Hill.

Miceli, Keith. 1974. "Rafael Carrera: Defender and Promoter of Peasant Interests in Guatemala, 1837–1848." *The Americas* 31:72–95.

Migdal, Joel. 1974. *Peasants, Politics and Revolution.* Princeton, N.J.: Princeton University Press.

———. 1988. *Strong Societies and Weak States.* Princeton, N.J.: Princeton University Press.

Mintz, Sidney. 1974. "The Rural Proletariat and the Problem of Rural Proletarian Consciousness." *Journal of Peasant Studies* 1:291–325.

Monteforte Toledo, Mario. 1959. *Guatemala: Monografía sociológica.* Mexico: Instituto de Investigaciones Sociales, UNAM.

Montúfar, Lorenzo. 1878–1887. *Reseña histórica de Centro América,* 7 vols. Guatemala: Tipografía de "El Progreso."

Moore, Alexander G. 1966. "Social and Ritual Change in a Guatemalan Town." PhD diss., Columbia University.

Moore, Barrington, Jr. 1966. *The Social Origins of Dictatorship and Democracy: Lord and Peasant in the Making of the Modern World.* Boston: Beacon Press.

———. 1978. *Injustice: The Social Bases of Obedience and Revolt.* White Plains, N.Y.: Sharpe.

Moors, Marilyn M. 1988. "Indian Labor and the Guatemalan Crisis: Evidence from History and Anthropology." In *Central America: Historical Perspectives on the Contemporary Crises,* edited by Ralph Lee Woodward, Jr. New York: Greenwood Press, 67–83.

Mörner, Magnus. 1967. *Race Mixture in the History of Latin America.* Boston: Little, Brown.

———. 1985. *Adventurers and Proletarians.* Pittsburgh: University of Pittsburgh Press.

Mosk, Sanford A. 1955. "The Coffee Economy of Guatemala, 1850–1918." *Inter-American Economic Affairs* 9:6–55.

Murphy, B. 1970. "The Stunted Growth of Campesino Organizations." In *Crucifixion by Power,* edited by R. N. Adams. Austin: University of Texas Press.

Nairn, Allan, and Jean-Marie Simon. 1986. "Bureaucracy of Death." *New Republic,* June 30, 194:13–17.

Nairn, Tom. 1977. *The Break-up of Britain.* London: New Left Books.

Nash, Manning. 1967. *Machine Age Maya: Industrialization of a Guatemalan Community.* Chicago: University of Chicago Press.

Naylor, Robert A. 1967. "Guatemala: Indian Attitudes toward Land Tenure." *Journal of Inter-American Studies* 9:619–639.

Newbold, Stokes [Richard N. Adams]. 1957. "Receptivity to Communist Fomented Agitation in Rural Guatemala." *Economic Development and Cultural Change* 5:338–360.

Newson, Linda A. 1985. "La población indígena de Honduras bajo el régimen colonial." *Mesoamérica* 9:1–44.

————. 1986. *The Cost of Conquest: Indian Decline in Honduras under Spanish Rule.* Boulder, Colo.: Westview Press.

————. 1987. *Indian Survival in Colonial Nicaragua.* Norman: University of Oklahoma Press.

El Noticioso. 1862. Guatemala.

Nuestro Diario 1944–1945. Guatemala.

Oakes, Maud. 1951. *The Two Crosses of Todos Santos: Survivals of Mayan Religious Ritual.* Princeton: Princeton University Press.

Ocampo de la Paz, Manuela. n.d. "Etnia y clase en la revolución guatemalteca." Manuscript.

Octubre. 1952, 1953. Guatemala.

Orellana, Sandra L. 1976. "Ethnic Identity and the Tzutujil Maya: A Socio-Political Analysis, 1250–1815." PhD diss., University of California, Los Angeles.

————. 1984. *The Tzutujil Mayas: Continuity and Change, 1250–1630.* Norman: University of Oklahoma Press.

ORPA (Organización del Pueblo en Armas). 1982. "Del racismo." *Polémica* 3:65–70.

Paige, Jeffrey M. 1975. *Agrarian Revolution: Social Movements and Export Agriculture in the Underdeveloped World.* New York: Free Press.

Painter, James. 1987. *Guatemala: False Hope, False Freedom.* London: Latin American Bureau.

Palma Murga, Gustavo. 1986. "Nucleos de poder local y relaciones familiares en la ciudad de Guatemala a finales del siglo XVIII." *Mesoamérica* 12:241–308.

Pansini, Joseph J. 1977. "'El Pilar,' a Plantation Microcosm of Guatemalan Ethnicity. PhD diss., University of Rochester.

Parker, Franklin D. 1970. *Travels in Central America, 1821–1846.* Gainesville: University of Florida Press.

Pavón, Manuel F. 1840. "Informe del Consulado sobre las monedas del Sur en circulación, Guatemala, 20 de junio de 1840." *El Tiempo* 1(108) June 28:430–431 and 1(148) December 5:592.

Payeras, Mario. 1983. *Days of the Jungle.* New York: Monthly Review Press.

Pearson, Neale. 1964. "Confederación nacional campesina de Guatemala and Peasant Unionism in Guatemala." MA thesis, Georgetown University.

Percheron, Nicole. n.d. "Producción agrícola y comercio de la Verapaz en la época colonial." *Mesoamérica.* Forthcoming.

PGT (Partido Guatemalteco de Trabajo). 1982. "Sobre la cuestión étnico-nacional." *Polémica* 3:65–70.

Piel, Jean. 1989. *Sajcabajá: Muerte y resurrección de un pueblo de Guatemala, 1500–1970.* Guatemala: Seminario de Integración Social.

Pineda de Mont, Manuel, comp. 1869–1872. *Recopilación de las leyes de Guatemala,* 3 vols. Guatemala: Imprenta de la Paz.

Pinto Soria, Julio C. 1981. *Estructura agraria y asentamiento en la Capitanía General de Guatemala (algunos apuntes históricos)*. Guatemala: CEUR.
———. 1983. *Raíces históricas del estado en Centroamérica*. 2d ed. Guatemala: Editorial Universitaria.
———. 1986. *Centroamérica, de la colonia al estado nacional (1800–1840)*. Guatemala: Editorial Universitaria.
———. 1987. "El valle central de Guatemala: un análisis acerca del origen histórico-económico del regionalismo en Centroamérica, 1524–1821." *Cuadernos de Investigación* no. 7. Dirección General de Investigación. Guatemala: Universidad de San Carlos.
Polémica. 1982–1983. San José.
Popkin, Samuel. 1979. *The Rational Peasant: The Political Economy of Rural Society in Vietnam*. Berkeley: University of California Press.
Porras, Gustavo. 1978. "Guatemala: la profundización de las relaciones capitalistas." *ECA* 353:374–406.
Ramirez, Ricardo. n.d. "Documento de marzo de 1967." Mimeograph.
Recinos, Adrian. 1954. *Monografía del departamento de Huehuetenango*. 2d ed., expanded. Guatemala: Ministerio de Educación Pública.
Redfield, Robert. 1934. "Folk Ways and City Ways." In *Human Nature and the Study of Society: The Papers of Robert Redfield*, vol. 1, edited by M. P. Redfield, 172–182. Chicago: University of Chicago Press.
———. 1956a. *Peasant Society and Culture*. Chicago: University of Chicago Press.
———. 1956b. "The Relations between Indians and Ladinos in Agua Escondida, Guatemala." *América Indígena* 16:253–276.
Reina, Ruben E. 1957. "Chinautla: A Guatemalan Indian Community." PhD diss., University of North Carolina.
———. 1966. *The Law of the Saints: A Pokomam Community Culture*. New York: Bobbs-Merrill.
Revista de la Guardia Civil. November 30, 1946. Guatemala.
Reyes Illescas, Miguel Angel. 1985. "Guatemala: en el camino del indio nuevo." *Boletín de Antropológia Americana* 11:51–73.
Richards, Michael. 1985. "Cosmopolitan World-view and Counterinsurgency in Guatemala." *Anthropological Quarterly* 3:90–107.
Rivera Paz, Mariano. 1839. *Memoria que presentó a la Asamblea Constituyente, en su primera sesión, el Consejero Gefe del Estado de Guatemala, por medio del Secretario del Despacho de Relaciones*. Guatemala: Imprenta del Gobierno del Estado.
Rodríguez, Mario. 1955. "The Livingston Codes in the Guatemalan Crisis of 1837–1838." In *Applied Enlightenment: Nineteenth Century Liberalism, 1830–1839*, Middle American Research Institute, Publication 23:1–32. New Orleans: Tulane University.
———. 1978. *The Cádiz Experiment in Central America, 1808–1826*. Berkeley: University of California Press.
Rosada, Héctor. 1987. *Indios y ladinos: un estudio antropológico-sociológico*. Guatemala: Editorial Universitaria.
Rubio Sánchez, Manuel. 1982. *Los jueces reformadores de milpas en Cen-*

troamérica. Publicación especial, no. 23. Guatemala: Academia de Geografía e Historia de Guatemala.

Ruz, Marío Humberto. 1984. "Fray Juan Ramírez, los indios y la Guatemala del siglo XVII." *Estudios de Cultura Maya* 25:177–205.

Said, Edward. 1978. *Orientalism.* New York: Pantheon.

Sanchiz Ochoa, Pilar. 1976. *Los hidalgos de Guatemala: realidad y apariencia en un sistema de valores.* Publicaciones del Seminario de Antropología Americana. Sevilla: Universidad de Sevilla.

Sapper, Karl. 1985. *The Verapaz in the Sixteenth and Seventeenth Centuries: A Contribution to the Historical Geography and Ethnology of Northeastern Guatemala.* Translated by Theodore E. Gutman. Los Angeles: Institute of Archaeology, University of California.

Schmit, Patricia Brady. 1978. "Guatemalan Political Parties: Development of Interest Groups, 1820–1822." PhD diss., Tulane University, New Orleans.

Scott, James C. 1976. *The Moral Economy of the Peasant.* New Haven: Yale University Press.

———. 1977. "Hegemony and the Peasantry." *Politics and Society* 7:267–296.

———. 1986. *Weapons of the Weak.* New Haven: Yale University Press.

Sereseres, C. 1985. "The Guatemalan Legacy: Radical Challengers and Military Politics." In *Report on Guatemala,* edited by School of Advanced International Studies, Johns Hopkins University, Boulder, Colo.: Westview Press, 17–50.

Shanin, Teodor, ed. 1971. *Peasants and Peasant Societies.* London: Penguin Press.

Sherman, William L. 1968. "Abusos contra los Indios de Guatemala (1602–1605): Relaciones del Obispo." *Cahiers du monde Hispanique et Luso-Brésilien: Caravelle* 11:5–28.

———. 1979. *Forced Native Labor in Sixteenth Century Central America.* Lincoln: University of Nebraska Press.

Siegel, Morris. 1941. "Resistance to Culture Change in Western Guatemala." *Sociology and Social Research* 25:414–430.

Silvert, Kalman. 1954. *A Study in Government: Guatemala.* Middle America Research Institute, Report 21. New Orleans: Tulane University.

Simon, Jean-Marie. 1987. *Guatemala: Eternal Spring, Eternal Tyranny.* New York: Norton.

Simpson, Lesley Byrd. 1952. "Exploitation of Land in Central Mexico in the Sixteenth Century." *Ibero-Americana* 36. Berkeley: University of California Press.

Skocpol, Theda. 1979. *States and Social Revolutions.* Cambridge: Cambridge University Press.

———. 1982. "What Makes Peasants Revolutionary?" *Comparative Politics* 14:351–375.

Smith, Anthony D. 1983. *State and Nation in the Third World: The Western State and African Nationalism.* New York: St. Martin's Press.

———. 1986. "State-making and Nation-building." In *States in History,* edited by John A. Hall. Oxford: Basil Blackwell.

Smith, Carol A. 1978. "Beyond Dependency Theory: National and Regional

Patterns of Underdevelopment in Guatemala." *American Ethnologist* 5(3):574–617.

———. 1984a. "Local History in Global Context: Social and Economic Transitions in Western Guatemala." *Comparative Studies in Society and History* 26(2):193–228.

———. 1984b. "Does a Commodity Economy Enrich the Few While Ruining the Masses?" *Journal of Peasant Studies* 11:60–95.

———. 1985. "El desarrollo de la primacía urbana en Guatemala." *Mesoamérica* 8:195–278.

———. 1987a. "Culture and Community: The Language of Class in Guatemala." In *The Year Left: An American Socialist Yearbook*, edited by M. Davis et al. London: Verso, 197–217.

———. 1987b. "Regional Analysis in World-System Perspective: A Critique of Three Structural Theories of Development." *Review* 10:597–648.

———. 1987c. "Ideologías de la historia social." *Mesoamérica* 14:355–366.

———. 1988. "Destruction of the Material Bases for Indian Culture." In *Harvest of Violence: The Mayan Indians and the Guatemalan Crisis*, edited by R. Carmack. Norman: University of Oklahoma Press.

———. 1989 "Survival Strategies among Petty Commodity Producers." *International Labour Review* 128:791–813.

———. n.d. "The Militarization of Civil Society in Guatemala: Economic Restructuring as a Consequence of War." *Latin American Perspectives.* Forthcoming (1990).

Smith, Carol A., and Jefferson Boyer. 1987. "Central America since 1979, part I." *Annual Reviews in Anthropology* 16:197–221.

Smith, Carol A., Jefferson Boyer, and Martin Diskin. 1988. "Central America since 1979, part II." *Annual Reviews in Anthropology* 17:331–364.

Smith, Gavin. 1989. *Livelihood and Resistance: A Study of Peasants and the Politics of Land in Peru.* Berkeley: University of California Press.

Smith, Robert S. 1963. "Financing the Central American Federation, 1821–1838." *Hispanic American Historical Review* 43:483–510.

Smith, Waldemar R. 1975. "Beyond the Plural Society: Economics and Ethnicity in Middle American Towns." *Ethnology* 14:225–243.

———. 1977. *The Fiesta System and Economic Change.* New York: Columbia University Press.

Solís, Ignacio. 1979. *Memorias de la Casa de Moneda de Guatemala y del desarrollo económico del pais.* Guatemala: Ministerio de Finanzas de Guatemala.

Solórzano, Juan Carlos. 1985. "Las comunidades indígenas en Guatemala, Chiapas y El Salvador (Siglo XVIII)." *Anuario de Estudios Centroamericanos* 11:93–130.

———. 1987. "Rafael Carrera: Reacción conservadora o revolución campesina? Guatemala 1837–1873." *Anuario de Estudios Centroamericanos (Universidad de Costa Rica)* 13:5–35.

Solórzano, Valentín. 1977. *Evolución económica de Guatemala.* Guatemala: Editorial Universitaria.

Solórzano Foppa, Mario. 1982. "El nacionalismo indígena: una ideología burguesa." *Polémica* 3:44–46.

Spalding, Karen. 1984. *Huarochirí: An Andean Society under Inca and Spanish Rule.* Stanford: Stanford University Press.

Stavenhagen, Rodolfo. 1968. "Classes, Colonialism, and Acculturation." In *Comparative Perspectives on Stratification: Mexico, Great Britain, Japan,* edited by J. A. Kahl. Boston: Little, Brown.

———. 1975. *Social Classes in Agrarian Societies.* Garden City, N.Y.: Doubleday.

Stephens, John L. 1841 (1969). *Incidents of Travel in Central America, Chiapas and Yucatan.* New York: Dover.

Stern, Steve J. 1982. *Peru's Indian Peoples and the Challenge of Spanish Conquest.* Madison: University of Wisconsin Press.

⌐ Stolcke, Varena. 1984. "Women's Labours: The Naturalisation of Social Inequality and Women's Subordination." In *Of Marriage and the Market,* edited by K. Young, C. Wolkowitz, and R. McCullagh. London: Routledge & Kegan Paul.

Stoll, David. 1988. "Evangelicals, Guerrillas, and the Army: The Ixil Triangle under Rios Montt." In *Harvest of Violence: The Mayan Indians and the Guatemalan Crisis,* edited by Robert M. Carmack. Norman: University of Oklahoma Press.

Szwed. John F. 1975. "Race and the Embodiment of Culture." *Ethnicity* 2:19–33.

Taussig, Michael. 1987. *Shamanism, Colonialism and the Wild Man: A Study in Terror and Healing.* Chicago: University of Chicago Press.

Tax, Sol. 1937. "The Municipios of the Midwestern Highlands of Guatemala." *American Anthropologist* 39(3):423–444.

———. 1941. "World View and Social Relations in Guatemala." *American Anthropologist* 43(1):27–42.

———. 1942. "Ethnic Relations in Guatemala." *América Indígena* 2:43–47.

———, ed. 1952. *Heritage of Conquest: The Ethnology of Middle America.* New York: Macmillan.

———. 1953. *Penny Capitalism: A Guatemalan Indian Economy.* Washington, D.C.: Smithsonian Instititute of Social Anthropology.

Taylor, William B. 1979. *Drinking, Homicide and Rebellion in Colonial Mexican Villages.* Stanford: Stanford University Press.

Tedlock, Barbara. 1982. *Time and the Highland Maya.* Albuquerque: University of New Mexico Press.

Thompson, E. P. 1963. *The Making of the English Working Class.* New York: Vintage.

El Tiempo 1839–1841. Guatemala.

Tilly, Charles. 1975. *The Formation of National States in Western Europe.* Princeton: Princeton University Press.

Tobar Cruz, Pedro. 1959. *Los montañeses.* 2d ed. Biblioteca Guatemalteca de Cultura Popular, vol. 30. Guatemala: Ministerio de Educación Pública.

Torres-Rivas, Edelberto. 1971. *Interpretación del desarrollo centroamericano.* San José, Costa Rica: EDUCA.

———. 1981. *Crisis del poder en Centroamérica.* San José, Costa Rica: Editorial

Universitaria.

Tribuna Popular. 1952, 1953, 1954.

Tumin, Melvin. 1952. *Caste in a Peasant Society: A Case Study in the Dynamics of Caste.* Princeton, N.J.: Princeton University Press.

Tutino, John. 1986. *From Insurrection to Revolution in Mexico.* Princeton, N.J.: Princeton University Press.

URNG (Unidad Revolucionaria Nacional de Guatemala). 1982. "Proclamation of Unity." Pamphlet, January 1982.

van den Berghe, Pierre. 1968. "Ethnic Membership and Cultural Change in Guatemala." *Social Forces* 46:514–522.

van Oss, Adriaan C. 1986. *Catholic Colonialism: A Parish History of Guatemala, 1524–1821.* London: Cambridge University Press.

Van Young, Eric. 1984. "Conflict and Solidarity in Indian Village Life: The Guadalajara Region in the Late Colonial Period." *Hispanic American Historical Review* 64:55–79.

Veblen, Thomas T. 1975. "The Ecological, Cultural and Historical Bases of Forest Preservation in Totonicapán, Guatemala." PhD diss., University of California, Berkeley.

Wagley, Charles. 1941. *Economics of a Guatemalan Village.* Memoirs of the American Anthropological Association, no. 58. Menasha, Wisc.: American Anthropological Association.

———. 1949. *The Social and Religious Life of a Guatemalan Village.* Memoirs of the American Anthropological Association, no. 71. Menasha, Wisc.: American Anthropological Association.

———. 1957. *Santiago Chimaltenango: estudio antropológico-social de una comunidad indígena de Huehuetenango.* Translated by Joaquín Noval. Seminario de Integración Social Guatemalteca, Publication 4. Guatemala: Tipografía Nacional.

Warman, Arturo. 1981. *We Come to Object: The Peasants of Morelos and the National State.* Baltimore: Johns Hopkins University Press.

Warren, Kay B. 1978. *The Symbolism of Subordination: Indian Identity in a Guatemalan Town.* Austin: University of Texas Press.

Wasserstrom, Robert. 1975. "Revolution in Guatemala: Peasants and Politics under the Arbenz Government." *Comparative Studies in Society and History* 17:443–478.

———. 1983. *Class and Society in Central Chiapas.* Berkeley: University of California Press.

Watanabe, John M. 1981. "Cambios económicos en Santiago Chimaltenango, Guatemala." *Mesoamérica* 2(2):20–41.

———. 1984. "'We Who Are Here'": The Cultural Conventions of Ethnic Identity in a Guatemalan Indian Village, 1937–1980." PhD diss., Harvard University. Ann Arbor: University Microfilms.

———. 1989. "Elusive Essences: Souls and Social Identity in Two Highland Maya Communities." *Ethnographic Encounters in Southern Mesoamerica: Essays in Honor of Evon Zartman Vogt, Jr.,* edited by Victoria R. Bricker and Gary H. Gossen. Albany: Institute for Mesoamerican Studies, State University of New York, 263–274.

Webre, Stephen A. 1980. "The Social and Economic Bases of Cabildo Membership in Seventeenth Century Santiago de Guatemala." PhD diss., Tulane University.

———. 1981. "El cabildo de Santiago de Guatemala en el siglo XVII: una oligarquia criollo cerrada y hereditaria?" *Mesoamérica* 2:1–18.

Williams, Raymond. 1983. *Keywords: A Vocabulary of Culture and Society*, rev. ed. London: Fontana Books.

Williams, Robert. 1986. *Export Agriculture and the Crisis in Central America*. Chapel Hill: University of North Carolina Press.

Winn, Peter. 1989. "The Southern Cone: Socialism Fades Out of Fashion." *The Nation* 248:882–886.

WOLA (Washington Office on Latin America). 1988. *Who Pays the Price? The Cost of War in the Guatemalan Highlands*. Washington, D.C.: Washington Office on Latin America.

Wolf, Eric R. 1957. "Closed Corporate Peasant Communities in Mesoamerica and Central Java." *Southwestern Journal of Anthropology* 13(1):1–18.

——— 1959. *Sons of the Shaking Earth*. Chicago: University of Chicago Press.

———. 1966. *Peasants*. Englewood Cliffs, N.J.: Prentice-Hall.

———. 1967. "Types of Latin American Peasantry." In *Tribal and Peasant Economies: Readings in Economic Anthropology*, edited by George Dalton. Austin: University of Texas Press, 501–523.

———. 1969. *Peasant Wars of the Twentieth Century*. New York: Harper & Row.

———. 1982. *Europe and the People without History*. Berkeley: University of California Press.

———. 1986. "The Vicissitudes of the Closed Corporate Community." *American Ethnologist* 13:325–329.

Wolf, Eric R., and Edward Hansen. 1967. "Caudillo Politics: A Structural Analysis." *Comparative Studies in Society and History* 9:168–179.

Woodward, Ralph Lee, Jr. 1965. "Economic and Social Origins of the Guatemalan Political Parties (1773–1823)." *Hispanic American Historical Review* 45 (1965):544–566.

———. 1966. *Class Privilege and Economic Development: The* Consulado de Comercio *of Guatemala, 1793–1871*. Chapel Hill: University of North Carolina Press.

———. 1971. "Social Revolution in Guatemala: The Carrera Revolt." In *Applied Enlightenment: Nineteenth Century Liberalism, 1830–1839,* Middle American Research Institute Publication 23, 43–70. New Orleans: Tulane University.

———. 1976. *Central America: A Nation Divided*. New York: Oxford University Press.

———. 1979. "Liberalism, Conservatism, and the Response of the Peasants of La Montaña to the Government of Guatemala, 1821–1850." *Plantation Society in the Americas* 1:109–129.

———. 1983. "Population and Development in Guatemala, 1840–1870." *SECOLAS Annals, Journal of the Southeastern Council on Latin American Studies* 14:5–18.

———. 1985a. *Central America: A Nation Divided.* 2d ed. New York: Oxford University Press.

———. 1985b. "Central America from Independence to *c.* 1870." In *The Cambridge History of Latin America,* vol. 3., *From Independence to c. 1870,* edited by Leslie Bethell. Cambridge: Cambridge University Press, 471–506.

———. 1985c. "The Economy of Central America at the Close of the Colonial Period." In *Estudios del Reino de Guatemala: homenaje al profesor S. D. Markman,* edited by Duncan Kinkead. Sevilla: Escuela de Estudios Hispano-Americanos, 117–134.

Wortman, Miles L. 1982. *Government and Society in Central America, 1680–1840.* New York: Columbia University Press.

Zamora Acosta, Elías. 1983. "Conquista y crisis demográfica: la población indígena del occidente de Guatemala en el siglo XVI." *Mesoamérica* 6:291–328.

———. 1985. *Los mayas de las tierras altas en el siglo XVI: tradición y cambio en Guatemala.* Sevilla: Diputación Provincial de Sevilla.

Zilbermann de Luján, Cristina. 1987. *Aspectos socioeconómicos del traslado de la Ciudad de Guatemala (1773–1783).* Publicación Especial no. 31. Guatemala: Academia de Geografía e Historia de Guatemala.

Index

hegemonic power, 14